Praise for
The Freelancer's Survival Guide

Kris's guide is the most succinct and comprehensive guide I have seen for anyone who is in business for themselves. This book is not just for writers, but for entrepreneurs of all kinds. When people come to me for business advice, this is my number one referral in the area of business books.

—Beth Plutchak,
Beth Plutchak Consulting LLC

Of all the motivational, business, and creative books I've read, *The Freelancer's Survival Guide* is easily the most useful. Accessible, thorough, well written, and exceedingly practical, this is a book guaranteed to make you re-examine every facet of your business—and come out better for it.

—J. Daniel Sawyer
Audio Producer, Freelancer Writer, and
President of ArtisticWhispers Productions

Rusch does an excellent job of breaking down and summing up all of the pitfalls and pleasures of freelancing. If you're thinking about freelancing, invest in this book and save yourself a bundle.

—Matt Forbeck, freelance author and game designer

People often ask me for tips on how to make it as a freelancer. Now there's a book I believe in that I can recommend.

—Kelly Cairo, owner, Cairo Communications

Kris Rusch is an old pro and she knows her subject backwards and forwards. There is a wealth of valuable information here for anyone trying to go it on their own down the freelance road. Worth the cost and then some.

—Steve Perry,
New York Times Bestselling Author

Essential reading for anyone considering a career outside the domain of corporate America. Along with decades of experience as a freelancer herself, Kris Rusch brings unique and vital insight to the question of how to succeed as a small business owner.

—Steven Mohan, Jr., writer

Kristine Kathryn Rusch's *Freelancer's Guide* is indispensable for anyone currently freelancing or even contemplating a career change. Rusch's advice, based on 30 years of personal experience, is more than a guide to a freelancing career; it's a guide to handling any aspect of life through turbulent waters.

—Michael A. Burstein,
award-winning author of *I Remember the Future*

Kristine Kathryn Rusch's *Freelancer's Guide* is both deep and broad in terms of the content and value it offers to independent business owners of all types. Indispensable.

—Mark Terry,
freelance writer, editor, and novelist

Without a doubt the best, most essential book for writers who are contemplating quitting their day jobs and doing the writing thing full time. I wish it had been around when I went freelance for the first time back in 1980; I have friends who have absolutely relied on Rusch's advice and it never leads them astray.

—Orson Scott Card
New York Times bestselling author

Not many people understand the publishing business as well as the author business—Kris Rusch is one of them. Her *Freelancer's Survival Guide* is balanced, ambitious, and packed with information that all writers, editors, and publishers should read.

—Kevin J. Anderson,
New York Times bestselling author

The Freelancer's Guide is a wonderful source for what you need to know when you need to know it in your writing career.

—Ray Vukcevich, writer

I wish *The Freelancer's Survival Guide* had existed when I was first starting out, but better late than never. Kristine Kathryn Rusch still knows twice what I do about writing and publishing. Good thing she's put all her wisdom down in a book so I can start stealing some of it.

—Steve Hockensmith,
New York Times bestselling author

Even though I've freelanced for 30 years publishing non-fiction books, newspaper articles, and magazine articles, I still learned from this book and it will be invaluable to my fiction career. It's much more than a "how-to" book. It's a "how-come" book. Every time I thought to ask why, the book already had an answer for me.

—Maggie Lynch,
Distance Education Guru

The Freelancer's Guide has been incredibly helpful. I have learned a lot of vital information that has given me the courage to move forward with my writing career.

—Rebecca Shelley,
author of *Heroin Guns*

Kristine Kathryn Rusch's *Freelancer's Guide* saved my life. My life as a writer. Her advice can be hard, but it packs a wallop, kind of like tough love. *The Guide*'s advice is the most concentrated and purest product you'll find anywhere on this topic. Taken as recommended, it will cure what ails the (freelance) writer in you.

—Bob Sojka
retired scientist and emerging fiction writer

An indispensable guide for freelance writers...or freelancers of any kind. It doesn't matter if you're an experienced professional or just starting out, Kris Rusch has offered the kind of information and guidance virtually everyone should have.

—Russell Davis,
bestselling author and editor

Clear. Exhaustive but not exhausting. Full of information for anyone who works for themselves.

—GraceAnne DeCandido,
writer, editor, teacher, freelancer

As a fledgling freelancer, *The Freelancer's Guide* not only answers questions I have, but the questions I didn't know how to ask yet.

—Steven Saus, author

Before I started reading *The Freelancer's Survival Guide*, I doubted I'd ever be able to freelance. I'm still not sure when, or even if, I can do it, but now I know what I'll have to do if I'm going to be successful.

—Dave Hendrickson, writer

The Freelancer's Survival Guide is invaluable to anyone considering working for themselves. Whether you're a dabbler or diving in with both feet, a newbie or an old hand, Rusch peppers this volume with gems of wisdom and perspective that can spell the difference between joy and pain.

—Michael D. Britton, professional writer

This is a bible for freelancing, a how-to, a checklist that anyone considering freelancing or wondering about the next step or what's wrong with their business picture must read. Don't go out into the real world without it!

—Thea Hutchinson,
Event Planner, Dana Cain Events

Every freelancer needs this book close at hand for continuous reference. Enlightening, supportive and constantly helpful.

—Brenda Carre, writer

Filled with helpful information for the beginning freelancer.

—Laura Ware, writer

The sage advice in *The Freelancer's Guide* is invaluable. Nowhere else will you find in one place such a treasure trove of experience-wrought wisdom for anyone interested in working as a writer or any kind of freelancer regardless of the field. This is a must read.

—Joshua Graham,
author of *Beyond Justice*

Reading *The Freelancer's Survival Guide* armed me with a range of tools and knowledge I'll certainly need when I make the jump to freelancing, without sugarcoating or sentimentalizing the tough, always scrambling life of a person who is his or her own boss. Reading it also made me really, really appreciate my current day job.

—Michael Jasper,
novelist and technical writer

This highly entertaining book gives you the easiest opportunity to learn everything you need to know before you go in business for yourself.

—Mary Jo Rabe, librarian

The information contained in this *Guide* is invaluable for those already in business or looking to start a business of any kind, writing or otherwise. In fact, anyone who's ever dreamed of being an entrepreneur should have this reference guide on their shelf. Forewarned is forearmed and this *Guide* is the best way to arm yourself for being self-employed that I've ever seen!

—Louisa Swann,
Swann Gardens, Inc.

I have been freelancing as a consultant for twelve years and I still found Kris's *Guide* enlightening and informative. Kris's insights will help prepare anyone considering "going it alone." Thank you, Kris!

—Karen Abrahamson, consultant

Up close, I've watched two freelance businesses fail and one succeed. Had they followed even half of what Kris has gathered here, the other two would probably still be around.

—Matt Buchman
Business Process Project Manager
Lean Process Specialist

Kris Rusch writes the best advice in the business for freelancers. Her columns are a graduate degree in making it as a freelancer.

—Denise Little
agent, writer, book packager, freelancer

Both immensely practical and inspirational, *The Freelancer's Survival Guide* covers the day-to-day business details necessary to succeed as a freelancer as well as address the psychological and emotional factors that can make or break a career.

—Susan J. Kroupa, freelance writer

Do you know how to freelance? Me neither. That's why I read this book and its warnings about financial, mental, and organizational pitfalls on the road to freelancing success and freedom.

—Melissa Yuan-Innes, M.D. and writer

Crucial for anyone contemplating the leap to full-time freelancing, and essential for the part-time freelancer as well.

—Dayle A. Dermatis, author

As someone who has worked freelance in the advertising business between full-time jobs over 25 years, I found that Kris hit upon every major point that a freelancer needs to know in an insightful and productive manner. Her information should be useful to anyone who is or is considering freelance work in any field.

—Stuart C. Hellinger,
Advertising Executive

THE FREELANCER'S SURVIVAL GUIDE

Kristine Kathryn Rusch

The Freelancer's Survival Guide

Third Edition

Copyright © 2013 Kristine Kathryn Rusch

All rights reserved

Published 2013 by WMG Publishing
www.wmgpublishing.com
First published in a slightly different version at kristinekathrynrusch.
com on the blogs "The Freelancer's Survival Guide" from April 2009 to
August 2010 and "The Business Rusch" in November 2012.
Book and cover design copyright © 2013 WMG Publishing
ISBN-13: 978-0-615-75629-5
ISBN-10: 0-615-75629-8

WMG Publishing
www.wmgpublishing.com

Table of Contents

Introduction

When I initially came up with the idea for *The Freelancer's Survival Guide* more than ten years ago now, I never imagined what it would become. I thought I would write a short book about the various things a freelancer needs to know to survive in the modern business world. I still have my initial outline and looking at it, I have a hunch that had I written it, the book would have been one-third the length of this one.

It isn't that I have learned so much more in the past ten years; it's just that I hadn't realized how much people wanted to know.

I started my writing career in non-fiction. I saw non-fiction as a way to make money to support my fiction-writing career. At least, that's what I tell people. If you actually look at my writing history, you'll see that I have always written fiction and non-fiction simultaneously—beginning with the newspaper I "published" for my neighborhood at the age of ten and sold for a nickel per copy.

I worked as a journalist, mostly in radio, and published articles on business from college onward. My non-fiction style has always been colloquial—while I like imparting information, I prefer to do so in a personal way. I have published a lot of fiction books, from collections to novels, but *The Freelancer's Survival Guide* is my first non-fiction book.

Honestly, it would not exist if it weren't for my blog. Although I thought of writing this book for years, I always had other projects that took my time and interest. Articles are relatively easy to write, and they take little time. A non-fiction book, on the other hand, takes as much time as a novel. I started the book twice, believing I could just putter at it, and never finished it. I knew I did not want to make the concentrated effort—losing months, maybe a year, of my writing time—to write the *Guide*.

Particularly when I knew what would happen to it. If I sold it—a big if, non-fiction editors told me, because the book wasn't geared toward one kind of freelancer (writers, for example) but because I geared it to all different kinds of people who want to work for themselves—the book would go to the back of the bookstore, and disappear along the shelves. It would have a month-long active publication life, and from then on, it would have to accompany me to conferences and book fairs if I wanted to keep the *Guide* in print.

I did want to keep it in print, but not because I wanted to earn a fortune at it and because I wanted it to be a bestseller. Writing a book like this is not the best way to become a household name.

I honestly had no interest in writing the *Guide* for me. I wanted to write it for all the freelancers I've met, all the people who are struggling through start-ups, all the people who are struggling to survive. I also wanted it for the people whose businesses were succeeding, but who had no idea what to do with that success. I wanted a book I could hand out to my students, yes, but also a book that someone else could find, someone in a small town who didn't go to conventions or book fairs or conferences, someone who needed a friend who had gone through the hardships of running her own business and could give some advice.

When the Great Recession started, I realized I had missed my publishing window. I should have *finished* the *Guide* in 2005 or 2006, so that I could have found a publisher who would have had the book on the stands by late 2008, when people—having lost their jobs—decided they might as well work for themselves. I even saw the book as being useful to people who weren't planning on starting their own businesses, people who just needed help organizing their time and their finances while they searched for a new job. Looking for a job in a down economy is, in essence, working for yourself.

I moped for a few months, thinking I had missed an opportunity, and then I realized that changes in technology had given me another option. I could write the book a chapter per week, and upload that chapter on my website. If the experiment didn't work—if no one came to read the blog—then I would have some chapters and my outline, and I could approach publishers.

Frankly, that's what I expected would happen.

Instead, I went through a personal revolution. I got readers and donations to keep me writing from my very first post. The readership grew. Over the seventy weeks it took me to finish the *Guide*, I received enough donations to equal a nice non-fiction advance from a New York publisher. I did not expect that at all. I also got a larger readership than I would have if the *Guide* had been published as I mentioned above. In fact, the readership is still growing. I got e-mail just this morning from a woman who discovered the *Guide* a week ago, and is slowly reading her way through the blog posts.

After I finished three chapters, I did send a proposal to my agent, so that he could market the book to major publishers. He wasn't enthusiastic about the project (for the reasons I mentioned above), although he did have a few ideas about marketing it. By the time he got those ideas to me, I was growing more and more reluctant to publish the book conventionally. It was the middle of the summer—not a good time to mail out a book—and we agreed to put it on hold.

I never went back. By the fall, I realized I wanted to publish this book myself. I wanted small distribution and more importantly to me, I wanted to be able to keep the book in print. I decided to do an electronic edition that I would give to anyone who had donated to keep me working, as well as a print edition.

It wasn't that farfetched for me to publish the book. As you'll discover when you read this, I used to co-own a publishing company with my husband Dean Wesley Smith. I know what it takes to publish a book, and how hard you have to work to market it. I also knew that I would need to do some organization work and trimming to make the *Guide* work in book form. My only concern was editing. Although I had won awards for my editing, editing yourself is a dicey proposition. Eventually I decided to hire an editor to make sure the manuscript was in order.

Fast-forward another year. I finished the blog version *Guide* a few weeks ago. I have just finished organizing all of the posts. Some combined into a single post; a few got cannibalized into other posts. I had to make some decisions as I did this, decisions that will affect what you read.

I decided to keep the conversational tone. The chapters were originally blog posts. Many times, the posts would not have existed without reader feedback. Indeed, the *Guide* is as large as it is because of reader comments, e-mails, and suggestions. So rather than try to artificially adopt that "expert" tone, I decided to leave the chapters as close to the blog posts as they can be. Sometimes, I've included a date—especially when an event or a news story inspired my post. Sometimes I haven't.

I did divide this *Guide* into sections, which makes it very different from the blog. The sections cover large topics, such as Money Management. I did this so that you can skip around as you need to.

As I set up those sections, I realized that they could also stand alone as short books. I have carved the *Guide* into nine short books, covering everything from *Goals and Dreams* to *How to Negotiate Anything*. All of the material in the short books is in the *Guide*, but not all of the material in the *Guide* is in the short books. However, if you have a friend who needs advice on only one subject—say, *Time Management*—then you can buy him that short book without giving him this entire tome.

Like the *Guide*, the short books are available in print and electronically. This is another benefit of doing the *Guide* myself. I know that many people buy how-to books for only one section. I have how-to books that I've dog-eared in the middle, but haven't touched the beginning. By doing the *Guide* myself, I unwittingly gave myself the ability to be flexible.

I am continuing a business blog on my website, called *The Business Rusch*, and as I learn more about the topics contained herein, I will update the sections. I'll probably update this book once a year or so. Just check on my blog, click the *Freelancer's Survival Guide* tab, and see if I've added updates at the bottom of the table of contents. You can find all of the original blog posts and the excellent comments from readers at kristinekathrynrusch.com.

I owe a great debt of gratitude to the online readers of *The Freelancer's Survival Guide*. Without you people, I never would have finished this book. It would have existed as an outline and half-finished chapter in my computer for decades. I also owe a lot to Michael J. Totten, who discussed the practicalities of running a blog on a website (you can find his spectacular blog on foreign affairs at michaeltotten.com). Michael is the one who suggested the donate button, and I did it, although I was skeptical. That—and the willingness of readers to support my endeavor—changed everything.

So did novelist Scott William Carter. He was at the initial meeting on e-publishing with Michael, Dean, and me. Scott's the one who helped me design the website, held my hand when I had a crisis (too often to imagine), and had some truly spectacular ideas of his own.

If you have comments or questions about the *Freelancer's Survival Guide*, feel free to contact me through my website. As I mentioned, this is an ongoing project—and there will probably be supplements down the road.

I have had a surprising amount of fun putting this book together. What I initially saw as unrewarding work has turned into a life-changing event.

Which—if you think about it—is the essence of freelancing. It's fun and it's life-changing. It's also a lot of work, although if you do it right, that work is not at all unrewarding. It is, in my opinion, the best kind of work possible—doing what you love, on your schedule, and on your own terms.

—Kristine Kathryn Rusch
Lincoln City, Oregon
September 3, 2010

Note on the Third Edition:

I'm keeping this short so that we won't add too many pages up front. Suffice it to say that after the death of a friend in 2011, I realized I had left an important section out of the *Freelancer's Guide*. I never mentioned how to keep a business alive after your death. I wrote a piece for my business blog. It's geared toward writers, but it does apply to all freelancers. Also, for the third edition, we have an index courtesy of Nanette Cardon. A big thanks to her for putting in all of the time. Thanks also to WMG Publishing's Allyson Longueira who figured out a way to make the third edition easier than it should have been. And thanks to all of you for the letters, e-mails, comments, and continuing support of my nonfiction blog. I hope you enjoy the book.

—Kristine Kathryn Rusch
Lincoln City, Oregon
November 20, 2012

Section One:
Getting Started

Chapter One
Job Description

My title for this chapter of the Guide, Job Description, should be impossible to write about, given the task I assigned myself. I wanted to discuss various freelancing jobs, not just freelance writing. The jobs should be so different that I shouldn't be able to describe them in a single article.

But they're not.

Because at its core, all freelancing is the same.

When someone else hires you to work at their business, you do a specific job for them. The radio station I worked for years ago hired me to put out one half-hour newscast per weeknight, manage hourly news updates throughout the three-hour morning show, and make certain that someone anchored the noon to one talk show. I also had to do wall-to-wall political coverage on Election Day, and handle any emergency situation that came up. My duties included maintaining the newsroom, handling the volunteer staff, and training new reporters.

I also had to attend radio station staff meetings, have a monthly meeting with the program director, and justify my budget with the station's financial manager. I had a lot of skills—from anchoring to reporting to engineering—and I used them all, sometimes within the same day. I also did a lot of writing.

I had an assigned area (the news room), an assigned budget, and assigned timeslots for my various newscasts. I took my job very seriously. If I failed, we had half an hour of nothing (dead air in radio terminology) from 7:00 to 7:30 at night. I can't tell you how many times I scrambled to fill that half hour because someone failed to show up for work. More than once, I wrote and engineered the entire newscast myself. A few times, I wrote, anchored, and engineered it.

I worked hard. However, when the newscast ended at 7:30, I had half an hour of clean-up and prep for the morning show, then I could go home. The radio station continued broadcasting. Other people monitored the evening schedule. Someone else paid for the lights and the heat and the extreme cost of the transmitter. If the station got knocked off the air by lightning, someone else dealt with that emergency. I had no responsibilities from eight in the evening until five in the morning. If no one showed up by then for the morning shift, the daytime DJ called me, and I had to come in for the updates. But if I didn't get the call, I got to sleep in.

The structure of that job was so absolute, I can remember it twenty years later. I still dream about it—showing up at 5:00 a.m. to find the DJ gone, the transmitter off, and the station broadcasting dead air. In my dreams, I scramble to put together a newscast while sitting in the booth as the disk jockey, playing the music, and rebooting the station itself. (People who've worked in radio know that one person can't do all those things by herself—which is why these dreams are nightmares.)

Whenever you're an employee, someone else provides the structure. They give you an assigned area, people to work with, tasks to finish, and, in many cases, a budget. You work within those structures, and for your time, you receive a paycheck. If you're lucky, you also receive some benefits—health insurance and paid time off.

When you become a full-time freelancer, you lose all of this structure.

This is one of the areas where first-time freelancers struggle. When they quit their day jobs (or in the case of this economy, got forced out and decided to go it alone), they imagined spending all day every day doing exactly what they love.

Unfortunately, that's not how it works.

As Bob Cooper, who works as a freelance copyeditor and proofreader, wrote to me when I started this series, "Whatever someone chooses to do as a freelancer, a major component of that will be not doing the actual work that they enjoy, but rather the just-as-important work of keeping their business viable—which involves primarily self-marketing to keep the flow of new work coming in, but also the mundanities of timekeeping, bookkeeping, tax planning, etc. And if they're not good at any or all of those things, what to do? Spend money to hire someone to do it for you? Spend time (and maybe money) learning how to do it properly yourself? Ignore it all and hope it goes away?"

Other chapters of the *Guide* deal with a lot of the individual items he mentions from bookkeeping to marketing to hiring employees, but for the purposes of this chapter, his overall point is marvelous. A major component of the job will be things the freelancer never considered before she went full-time freelance.

Or as Lyn Worthen, who runs a technical communications consulting firm, Information Designs, says, "Too many aspiring freelancers forget that they have to wear ALL the hats in their business (at least until they get to the point where they can hire additional hat-wearers)."

And once you're at the point of hiring an additional hat-wearer, you may not want that person. Remember what you were like as an employee? Some days were good, some were bad; but the consequences of a mediocre performance were simple: if the boss didn't like it, you got fired.

Remember this whenever you think of hiring anyone. No one cares about your business as much as you do. No one will work as hard as you will. And no one will be as vigilant as you are about mistakes. So caution, caution, caution about hiring anyone to take the burden off of you—particularly the burden of managing your money.

What is your job description as a full-time freelancer? Jack of All Trades. The Boss and the Minion. You have become Da Man. And to throw in one more cliché, the buck really and truly does stop with you. The day job had an invisible structure as well. If you worked in a corporation or an organization with more than two employees, you probably saw only a handful of the things it took to run that business. You had no idea how, for example, to pay employees (payroll taxes are a nightmare), how much it cost just to keep the doors open every day, and what kind of volume had to be done every month to keep the business viable.

At the radio station, I got to know my newsroom, my reporters, my news sources, and the schedule. I only worried about the budget when our long-distance phone bill got too big, usually during some big national news cycle. I had no idea what it took to maintain the station's equipment or to monitor the seasonal ratings. I didn't have to worry about the pledge drives (we were listener-sponsored) or the occasional problems with the FCC.

As a full-time freelancer, I have become an expert at tax law as it pertains to my business. I loathe accounting and bookkeeping because I'm dyslexic and numbers truly vex me. But Quicken has made that part of my life easier. I keep my own books, handle my own finances, and act as my own financial advisor. Do I consult others? Daily. But the final decisions are always mine.

I remain current with the news, not just the industry news, but economic trends, national stories, and—because my work sells all over the world—international events. I constantly monitor the web. I try to scan at least three newspapers per day, listen to several news sources, and look through as many industry websites as possible.

I also monitor what everyone else in my industry does. Some folks would say I'm keeping up with the competition, but I know that writers don't compete with each other. However, I can learn from what books other writers are publishing, what deals they make, and the mistakes they make. I'm a fervent believer in learning from other people's mistakes. I already make too many of my own—I made a few doozies at the turn of the century that cost me dearly—and I simply don't want to reinvent every single wheel. It's too painful, time-consuming, and difficult.

In the mistakes area, I take a leaf from Elvis Presley's tough business manager, Colonel Tom Parker. Parker knew he would make mistakes, but he got angry when he made the same mistake *twice*. Parker had a lot of bad attitudes about business, but this is a good one: it acknowledges that you will make mistakes—a lot of them—but you should always make new mistakes, not keep repeating the old ones.

I market my own products, a task that sometimes takes hours per day. I do the design, packaging, and mailing. I try to keep up on new technology that makes these tasks easier, although I'm not quite as vigilant on that as I should be.

I maintain my own equipment—and I'm realistic about what I need. I need two computers—one for my internet work and one for my writing. The internet computer has to be able to process a lot of material rapidly. The writing computer can be little more than a glorified typewriter. I need a printer, a cell phone, and an internet connection. I need to see a lot of movies, read a lot of books, and watch a lot of television. I try to keep up with the recording, gaming, and comics industries as best I can. Why do I do this? Because I work in the entertainment industry, and I need to keep up on what's going on within it.

I know what my actual product is. That may sound silly, but many first-time business owners often don't realize what their business actually is. Writers, for example, are particularly bad about this. Many writers don't know what they sell (and sales are the heart of this business). Writers don't sell stories. They don't sell manuscripts. They sell (or more accurately license) portions of their copyright. Most people in the entertainment industry work that way. So I monitor legal sites, reading articles on copyright, and am constantly reading about court cases and lawsuits involving copyright.

People who sell things like jewelry gain other areas of expertise. They learn about gems (how to tell real from fake) or the differences between gold and gold leaf. At our casual lunch one Sunday, two jewelry makers discussed various beads (while I snoozed) because one type was cheaper and worked better than another.

You have to become an expert in your field. Not just in the production of the material, but in all aspects of the business.

I probably spend twelve hours of my day (conservatively) doing the things I need to do to run my business. Of those twelve hours, I actually spend four to six—one-third to one-half—doing what I love. What I love to do is put new words on the page. (Or, as my husband says, make things up.) The rest of the time is about money management, marketing, research, and continuing education.

If your idea of full-time freelancing means spending all your time doing exactly what you love, with a lot of time off and someone else to handle "the business" (whoever that someone else might be—from an accountant to a lawyer to an agent), then you should probably keep your day job.

Successful freelancers by necessity must understand how to run a business. They have to know how to manage money, time, and themselves. All of this can be learned, and most of us learned it while we freelanced—through a lot of trial and error.

However, if the very idea of handling everything from paying the light bill to shilling your own product gives you the willies, then don't become a full time freelancer. Do what you love part time and keep your day job. You'll be happier—much happier.

So how do I describe my job? I am my own boss—with all the ups and downs that entails. I am responsible for the good and the bad in my business, for the successes and the failures.

And, honestly, I wouldn't have it any other way.

Chapter Two
A Freelancer's Priorities

From the moment we're born, someone else imposes structure on our lives. First our parents set the agenda. Then our schools chime in. Finally, our employers tell us what to do and when to do it.

Most people set their own hours only on weekends or during vacation. One of the hardest things for a retiree to get used to is the abundance of free time. We receive training from the very first breath we draw in how to respond to other people's needs and demands. We don't know how to respond to our own.

Most people who start working for themselves get nothing done in the first six months. These are productive folk who used to work full time, deal with their families, and conduct their businesses on the side. Suddenly, faced with 24 hours with no schedule at all, their productivity vanishes. Many find their waking hours sucked up by television or video games, Facebook or family visits, or in my case the first time I tried to freelance, reading two to three novels per day.

First let me state that a decline in productivity is *normal* for anyone who quits her job to become a full-time freelancer. Without the structure, the freelancer doesn't know how to organize her time. It's a subtle thing, but a very real one.

And it's frightening.

In 1985, after quitting one of my many part-time jobs, I moved into a new one-bedroom apartment. I was going through a divorce, my best friend had moved out of the city, and I lived in a new neighborhood. My very first weekend in that apartment, I received no phone calls and talked to no one in the neighborhood.

I wondered if I existed at all.

I have had that feeling many times throughout the years. It means that I let myself get too isolated. Not only is work an economic necessity, it's also a social gathering point, one that doesn't seem valuable until it's gone.

The loneliness and the lack of structure often cause panic. Those two things, more than financial worries or lack of success, cause the freelancer to hurry back to the nine-to-five world.

Structure comes from establishing priorities. Once you know what's truly important, then you make sure that thing gets done first.

Here are the priorities that I believe all freelancers should have in their lives. I've put these priorities in order from most important to least important. Your list might look different. First, I'll give you the list. Then I'll explain each item and why I placed it where I did.

A Freelancer's Priorities

1. **Family**
2. **Health**
3. **Work**
4. **Leisure**

Seems simple enough, right? If I said the list aloud, most of you would nod, thinking that you understood. But there are elements in each category that I can guarantee most first-time freelancers have never considered.

Let's take them in order.

Family

By this, I don't necessarily mean your biological family. I mean the people that you live with and the people that you love. Family should always come first.

Think of it this way: When you have a day job, family and work compete. But your work has given you structure. You know you'll be home at, say, 5:00 p.m. From 5:00 p.m. until you go to bed, you have an opportunity to be with your family, an opportunity that most people use.

You schedule doctors' appointments during lunch, parent-teacher conferences after work, and occasionally ask for time off to attend your daughter's soccer game. But these are scheduled events, just like your children's bedtimes. You know where you need to be, when you need to be there, and how you have to work around your nine-to-five job.

Most successful full-time freelancers schedule family time around their work, just as they would if they have a nine-to-five job. Sometimes it takes training. Some good friends of mine consistently ask me out to dinner, which falls right in the middle of my workday. I'm a harsh boss and I only give myself an hour for dinner, including prep and clean-up time. Going out takes an hour and a half or two hours, which gets in the way of my work schedule. I have to repeatedly explain to these friends that I cannot come to dinner because I work during that time. I know they don't understand, but they're slowly learning. Now they only ask me out to dinner on very special occasions—the kind of occasion that would cause me to ask my real-world boss (if I had one) for the extra time off.

As you're learning to plan your schedule, figure out how much family time you normally have, how much more you need/want, and how to fit it in. Then divide the hours in your weekly schedule, placing the family time on the calendar first.

Health

Everyone plans to take care of their health but very few people do. It's extremely important for freelancers to monitor their health because if they get sick, they don't get paid. I've seen more than one career cut short by freelancers who put off basic health care because they didn't have the time or the money or the proper insurance to solve a minor problem that eventually became major.

First, limit snacking. First-time freelancers always gain weight because the refrigerator is only a few steps away. Do what it takes— whether that is scheduling your eating times or failing to buy your favorite snacks.

Drink a lot of water. Not fruit juice, not Red Bull, not alcohol. Water. There are two reasons for that. First, water cleanses the system, keeping toxins out and helping to fight fatigue. Second, water flows through you pretty quickly. Most freelancers are doing work they love, and don't move around much, which puts them at risk for repetitive injuries. A glass of water per hour equals one bathroom break per hour, which means getting up once per hour and walking around. Sometimes staying healthy is just that easy.

Get enough sleep. Most people need six to eight hours per night. A lot of creative people take a twenty-minute refresher nap in the afternoon. Sleep allows you to think clearly and perform at your best. It also staves off illness. However, don't sleep too much. Some first-time freelancers sleep ten to twelve hours per day. That's as unhealthy as sleeping too little. Get the recommended amount of rest, no more and no less.

Begin an exercise routine and/or maintain your exercise routine. Exercise improves mood—which is important, considering how much time freelancers spend alone (people who spend time alone are prone to depression). Exercise also improves blood flow, oxygen intake and nearly everything else. If you pay attention to studies of almost every disease and chronic condition, you'll learn that people who exercise do better than who don't exercise.

I'm a loner. I don't like exercising around other people. So I go for a run, a solitary bike ride, or a half hour on the elliptical machine six days per week. I prefer the run or the bike ride, simply because it gets me outside in the fresh air.

If you're not a loner, schedule a daily walk with a friend or join the local cycling club. Keep your gym membership and use it at least five times per week. Yes, exercise takes time from both family and work, but it is not a leisure activity. It's a necessity—especially now that you're not walking around the office, taking the stairs from the parking lot, or running errands all over town. Exercise improves health, reduces stress, and boosts creativity. Need I say more?

Get routine check-ups, even if you have to pay for them yourself. Do not let a high deductible get in the way of maintaining your health. That includes eye exams and dental exams. No fun, I know, but essential to a long-term freelancing career. If you catch a problem early, you have a better chance of recovery. You'll also lose less work time to illness. Get a flu shot, take your vitamins, and do all the other things that go into prevention. Freelancers don't get paid sick days, so it's better not to get sick.

Finally, socialize at least once per day. It sounds silly to say this, particularly in the health category, but freelancers are prone to loneliness, which is an extremely destructive emotion. My husband Dean (who also freelances) and I go out to lunch every day, often at the same restaurant. We see people, talk to friends, and touch base with the community. One of my freelancing friends swims with the masters (adult) swim team four times per week. Another friend takes an hour per day to run errands that he could easily get his wife to do. It gets him out of the house and seeing people, which is all we freelancers need.

Work

This is the actual thing you quit your day job to do. Give it at least as many hours per week as you gave that day job, preferably more. The harder you work, the more success you will have.

Schedule the same time for work every day and post that schedule on your fridge or on your family's bulletin board. Tell your friends not to interrupt you during that time, unless it's an emergency—just like you would expect them to do if you worked for someone else.

Know this, however. If you do not stick to your schedule, your friends and family won't either. If you think missing one day won't hurt, then the next week you'll miss two. Eventually, you'll go back to getting nothing done, and you'll become frustrated and angry with yourself.

It'll take time to set up this schedule. You'll have to find the best hours for your business and the best hours for you. I'm a night person, but I do most of my business with people who live in New York City. I live in Oregon. I make sure I'm available at noon my time (3:00 p.m. New York time) just in case I need to return a phone call or answer important e-mails. That's a compromise between my schedule (I'd prefer to start work mid-to-late afternoon and work until 11:00 or 12:00 at night) and a schedule imposed by the type of business I'm in.

Remember this rule about freelancing: The more time you put into your job, the more you will gain from it. Not just financially, although that's true too. But you'll also gain opportunities. So make sure you schedule at least 40 hours of work per week, preferably much, much more.

Leisure

Human beings need to rest. The hardest thing for me to learn as I took up sports in my late thirties was that I needed a day off. I wore myself out exercising and even fractured a bone in my foot because I didn't give myself enough relaxation time.

As you can probably tell from the above paragraph, I have trouble taking time off. I like being busy, and I like my work. But a person needs to recharge. Time off does that.

The time off can come in one hour per day or the standard two days per week. The key is this: You must schedule your leisure time weekly. Rest isn't something you do for two weeks out of every year. It has to happen on a regular basis to have any value at all.

But don't overdo your leisure either. I learned the hard way that I had to schedule my leisure time after my workday was over. I like to read. Early in my freelance career, I'd pick up a book at lunch, promising myself one more chapter, just one more chapter, until I finished the book. By then it was dinner and "too late" to start work, so I read another book. I lost entire weeks before I realized I couldn't read until the work was done. Then reading one more chapter became a reward instead of work avoidance.

You'll learn all of these things—what keeps you from work, what causes you to overwork, and all the other problems in between—over time. You learn what works for you and what doesn't, how to arrange your day, and what makes you the most productive.

But to start, make your list of priorities. Figure out how you juggled those priorities when you had a day job, then translate that juggling to your new freelance career. Add in the health care and the exercise (I know—you thought that could wait, right?), and keep track of your daily schedule to monitor how you're doing.

You won't get it right the first week or even the second. It'll take time to refine your schedule to fit your life and your priorities. Gradually, however, you'll find what works best for you and what makes you both the happiest and the most productive.

Chapter Three
Building Your Workspace

When I started the Guide on my website, I promised myself that I would answer readers' questions.

The first question I got came from Dave Goodwin: "I'm about to move into a new home, my first place with enough space for a dedicated office. Since creating the proper setting is the first step of any project, would you mind starting with your advice on setting up a proper workspace? I could be the first real-world test for your theories."

This is a tougher question than it initially seems to be. I want this Guide to work for all types of freelancers from plumbers to writers. Since I've owned or been a part of four retail businesses, and started two other businesses (not counting my own professional writing), I can help with more traditional businesses as well.

Workspace Outside of the Home

Recently, I met a contractor who now buys and sells distressed properties. He sat at a booth in our local Thai restaurant, phone in one hand, printouts of retail listings spread across the table, and a legal pad at his side. His laptop, closed, rested on the booth beside him.

He had stopped for lunch in the middle of a very busy day. He made calls, talked to potential clients, and scanned properties while waiting for his Pad Thai. After the food arrived, the restaurant's owner asked about the value of some property he had seen.

This question led to more questions, which led to a discussion involving me and my husband Dean. We learned a lot about the contractor's new business. He spent his days examining properties on a 100-mile stretch of the Oregon Coast.

He had three workspaces: his car, his home office, and wherever he found himself. Fortunately, in the 21st century, we can take the important parts of our office with us. The contractor illustrates my hesitation in tackling this topic. Workspace is what you need, when and where you need it. Workspace varies from profession to profession.

Pam, a housecleaner who recently retired, came to her clients. She carried her equipment in her truck and billed the clients who required a formal written statement from her dining room table.

Thomas, a gardener, also comes to his clients. He has two trucks, an equipment shed, and a room in his house for the bookwork. Last month, he informed me that he had just learned how to operate a computer. Now his statements, which had been typewritten and minimal (Thomas does not like being indoors), have a modern structure, with a place for the current amount, past due amounts, and balance forwards. His estimate form can be customized. The new computer also enabled him to get rid of his fax machine because he has finally learned the joys of e-mail.

Sue, who owns a collectibles store, works at the shop from 10:00 a.m. to 6:00 p.m. While the entire store is her workspace, she now has a dedicated area for eBay. On one desk, she has a computer and printer. Behind that, she has a flat table so that she can ship items without bending over too much or reaching up too high.

Unlike most workspaces of the self-employed, Sue's workspace provides no real privacy. She doesn't dare hide from the walk-in customers who might buy something from her shop. Her computer setup also houses a security monitor system so that she can watch customers even if she is momentarily unable to leave her desk.

These outside-the-home workspaces have some similarities and many differences. The main similarity is that they suit the owner's business. Pam, who rarely billed her clients since she got paid as she finished the day's work, didn't have a computer or a home office. She didn't need one.

Thomas needs the home office to keep track of all of his (hated) paperwork. Eventually, he hopes to hire an assistant to help him with that part of his job, so he has designed the workspace with the future assistant in mind.

Sue doesn't work at home. Her business has retail customers who walk through the brick-and-mortar store, and retail customers who buy from her online. She has to accommodate both—and keep an eye on the inventory during business hours.

Those of you currently looking for work have businesses that most closely resemble the contractor's. Your workspace exists in three locations: your home, your car, and wherever you stop. You need a cell phone and some way to remain organized on the road.

Very generally, then, what an office outside the home needs is:

1. A phone.

You must stay in contact somehow. Most of the self-employed who work outside the home have cell phones. Many of these phones are sophisticated high-end models that dispense with the need for a laptop. I know that Thomas synchs his phone with his new computer because he told me how much paperwork it saves him every single day.

2. As much privacy as possible.

Midway through a phone conversation that day, the contractor (who was one of those guys who spoke too loudly when he was on the phone) said to the person he was talking to, "I'm in a restaurant. I can't discuss this right now. I'll call you back when I get to my car."

Sue's eBay computer is in a cubby at the very back of the store. She can see anyone who enters the front door, but they can't see her or her computer, unless they go all the way back and step inside that cubby.

3. The tools of your trade.

Be they vacuum cleaners and dust mops, lawn mowers and clipping sheers, or a high-speed computer with the fastest internet connection possible, make sure you have the right tools at your fingertips. I've seen small business owners lose customers because the owner wasn't prepared to handle a problem or a new sale *right at that very moment*. Figure out what you need and be prepared.

4. An ergonomically correct workspace (wherever possible).

Those of you working out of your car can't do this, but the rest of you probably can. Thomas uses earplugs and braces to keep himself in shape. Sue has a shipping area suited to her height, with everything in reach so that she doesn't have to bend too much or lift too much. Treat your body well and you'll work more efficiently (and you won't get the kinds of injuries that often force the self-employed to retire).

As for the rest, I can't help much for those of you working outside the home. Your businesses have such different and individual requirements that I'll probably miss most of what you need.

Office in the Home

Most freelancers work out of their homes—or should. In the words of Randy Tatano, who has freelanced for NBC for four years, "The freelancers I've known who have had problems are the ones who set up fancy offices and buy all kinds of equipment. I'm sure you'll have a chapter on minimizing overhead."

An office in the home saves money. For those of you who are afraid to take the office-in-the-home deduction on your tax return because you've heard that it's a red flag for an audit, stop worrying.

If you follow these rules, you'll make it through any audit just fine. (Please do remember, however, that I am not an accountant or a tax attorney, so any tax advice I give here is based only on personal experience, which includes surviving two full audits and several small ones.)

1. Your home office must be a workspace only.

Don't store your Christmas decorations in the back corner, don't put the exercise equipment in the center of the room, and don't set up next to the washer and dryer. Your office must be a professional workspace, the kind you would have if you worked in a corporation. If you wouldn't put the kids' toy box in your office at your former day job, then you shouldn't put the toy box in your office at home, either.

2. If you must use part of the utility room (or the dining room) as your workspace, block your workspace office.

When I moved to Oregon, I had a small one-bedroom apartment. I used part of the dining room as my office and walled it off from the living room with bookshelves. The office space, while tiny, housed a desk, my computer and printer, my chair, two filing cabinets and my bookshelves. I couldn't see the living room from my office, and no one in the living room could see me. The only problem that office had was noise—I could hear everything in the apartment. Fortunately, I lived alone, so the noise problem was a minor one.

3. Figure out what you need and buy the best equipment you can—used.

I have a custom-made desk in my office. My husband found the desk used at an insurance liquidator's auction for $75. The desk is built for someone 5'5" (my height), so I don't have to elevate my chair and put little blocks under my feet to sit in a proper position at the keyboard. None of my file cabinets, mismatched though they are, cost more than $25. Some were free, since businesses often junk the things that they no longer need. Remember that your office is not a public space, so it doesn't have to be pretty. It just has to be functional.

4. Your home office needs a door, preferably one you can close. I didn't have a door that I could close in that dining room office, but I could have rigged one up with a beaded curtain or a blanket. But you need some way to shut out the world, to let your family know that you are working and *cannot be disturbed* except, as novelist Nora Roberts used to tell her children, in cases of fire or serious injury (she actually said arterial bleeding, but I think injury is a bit more prudent). If you live with others, keep your door closed when you're working. Open it only when you want company. Post your hours on that door, so that everyone respects them—including you.

5. Remove all distractions.

I took the television out of my office when I stopped writing non-fiction. (It was a good thing too, because I'm a political junkie and in election season, I can watch the cable channels 24/7.) Take the games off your computer and anything else that might waste your time. (I finally had to ditch Garage Band from mine because it kept me from writing.) Figure out what your business requires and put only those things in your office.

6. If your business is not something like eBay that needs a continual online presence, then set up a separate computer for your e-mail and your internet connection.

You can buy a good internet computer used (on eBay, in fact) for a few hundred dollars. It'll be the best investment you can make. E-mail distracts. Most computers are set up so that the system pings when new mail comes in. My Internet computer pings for e-mail, bongs for instant messages, and trills when my Facebook page updates. Those little sound effects are hard to ignore. So is the temptation to research something when you should be producing. Make a list and research later. Find a space for another computer and use it for the internet.

7. The same goes for the telephone.

If your business does not require you to use a phone most of the time, take the phone out of your office. Set times to make phone calls. Let voice mail pick up when you're working and return calls later. The fewer distractions you have in your office, the more efficient you will be. The more efficient you are, the more you'll get done—and you won't have to spend as many hours at your desk.

8. Make hard and fast rules that help you become more productive.

For example, I do not allow any fiction in my office except my own fiction. I am too prone to reading other people's work instead of doing my own. No novel without my own byline crosses the threshold. For some reason, non-fiction doesn't distract me, so I can keep all my non-fiction books inside my office. But fiction? Forget about it. You'll find your own time sinks. Ban them from your workspace.

9. Insurance.

Get a business rider on your homeowner's policy. Insurance usually doesn't cover business computers in the home and often won't cover any other business equipment in the home. So your family's computer in the kitchen is covered, but your precious work computer, where you make your living, is not—unless you spend an extra few bucks per month to insure it against disaster. (Also, if you have people visiting your workspace [your yoga studio or your therapy practice, for example], then you'll also need liability insurance, with a multimillion dollar rider. People can sustain lifelong injuries just by falling down stairs. You don't want someone to fall down your stairs and sue you for everything you own.)

10. Finally, make your workspace comfortable.

Make it a place that's your haven, somewhere you want to go every day.

Setting up your workspace is complicated, and you won't get it right at first. You'll have to re-evaluate it as you get used to freelancing and you identify what your needs really are. Be flexible. Try not to spend too much money. And make sure your workspace is yours, not someone else's.

Chapter Four
Business Plan

In some ways, this is an ironic chapter, because I have reached a point in my life where I've realized that most plans don't work. What I envisioned for myself as an 18-year-old wannabe writer has not happened. What has happened are things that I never could have imagined. Even my somewhat more realistic visions from my 25-year-old post-Clarion Writers' Workshop self have not quite happened the way I expected.

From the vantage point of 1985, I never would have thought I'd be sitting here.

Of course, if I took my 25-year-old self and showed her my life, she'd be awed and thrilled and she'd be happy she achieved it, although she would ask why I had not achieved some of her wilder dreams. Some simply aren't possible in 2010. I decided some weren't for me. And a few, well, I'm hoping I'll achieve them in the future.

So as I sit here, with a deep understanding of how futile planning is in a career in the arts, I also realize the importance of a business plan.

You may all go "huh?" in unison now.

Business planning is important, no matter what you do as a freelancer. Yet you need to be flexible and understand that your plan is simply that: a plan. And like all plans in the movies, it never quite goes the way the protagonists think it should.

Business plans come in a variety of forms. Some business plans are required. In the early 1980s, my then-husband and I wanted to open a frame shop and art gallery. He had a lot of experience with custom framing, and he'd operated a frame shop out of our home for a year. He had made some money. Then we figured (for reasons now lost to the mists of time) that we needed to open a storefront.

We did what all broke former college students do: we applied for a loan. First we went to our bank. Credit was as tough then as it is now, and so the bank (nicely, because banks were nice way back then) declined to loan us money.

So we went to the Small Business Administration and applied for an SBA loan for $60,000. (Boy, that number makes me shudder these days.) The SBA required financial records and a business plan. We had no idea what a business plan was. The SBA nicely supplied us with a form, which we filled out.

I'm sure some version of that form is online now. You can find other versions of business plan forms in accounting software and in self-help books. I'm not going to supply one here, but I will talk about it briefly. If you need something like that for your new business, then I would suggest you cobble one together from a variety of forms, just to cover all your bases.

In essence, what the SBA had us do was project five years of income. We had to justify that income—we couldn't just pull numbers out of our butt. We justified our projected income based on my former husband's sales for the previous year out of our home, and the yearly sales at the two frame shops that had employed him before he started the home store.

Then we had to extrapolate that income to a storefront, with advertising and good traffic. We had to show how other businesses in our area did—not just frame shops, but other businesses in the strip mall where we hoped to open the store. We had to understand the traffic patterns, the number of possible clients, and the way that all became sales.

When we finished our educated guesswork, we had to turn to our expenses. We knew what the rent and utilities would be. We knew what we would pay our single employee. We knew what our supplies would cost. Framing was easy—our expenses were a percentage of each order. The customer chose the design, and then we ordered the supplies. We had mat board and mounting boards on hand, but mostly, we had no up front supply costs. It was all sixty-to-ninety days after we ordered the material.

The only expense we had was the art itself, and we got a lot of the original work on commission. We bought posters at a discount so that browsers had things to frame, and we framed some of our favorites.

As for the equipment, we already owned the expensive stuff for the in-home business. So our expenses were pretty low. Where did that $60,000 number come from? Two years of operating costs, plus some cushion for our own salaries, etc.

The SBA came through with a loan…of $20,000. Which my ex promptly turned down, without consulting me. He then gave the business plan to his father, who funded us, which turned out to be one of those colossal mistakes, mostly because of our naïveté. I think now if we had taken the leaner, meaner SBA loan, we'd have worked harder, and we might still have a business.

Not, mind you, that I'd rather be doing that than this.

The SBA looked at our business plan, found problems with it, particularly in the overly optimistic estimates of income, and decided to fund us for a year. They then cut our salaries, and that's where they got the $20,000 number.

Which isn't bad. They were wrong on the income—we had a lot of traffic: my ex was good at what he did, and had a lot of loyal customers from the moment the shop opened. But they were right about the hidden expenses.

And that, I'm sure, comes from looking at countless business plans from countless businesses, all built on hope and fear and guestimates.

If you haven't opened your small business yet—be that as a freelance writer or a frame shop owner, a pediatrician or a tow truck driver—then write up a business plan as if you were applying for a loan. Download those documents, design the right one for you, then do the research and be honest with yourself.

Don't fudge the numbers. If you can't get the income to outweigh the expenses by being honest, then you probably aren't ready to go freelance. See the section on money management in this book, because it is in financial planning that most freelance businesses go belly up.

Full disclosure: I have never done that type of business plan for my writing business. I have done it for all the others, from Pulphouse Publishing to the collectibles store that Dean opened a few years ago (and sold at a profit).

Why haven't I done it for the writing? For two reasons. Writing, like many other businesses in the arts, is too by-guess-and-by-golly. I can tell you my sell-through for my short fiction (90% within a year of finishing a story; 99% within ten years of finishing), but I can't tell you how much a single story will earn. I wrote a story in August that got rejected (with a very nasty note) by the anthology editor who commissioned it, then turned the story around and sold it for seven times what the original editor had promised me. Some short stories have earned me tens of thousands of dollars. Others have earned a few hundred. Unlike a piece of glass or perfectly cut mat board, a short story has no fixed value.

And a short story earns for years, as do novels. I just resold two of my Grayson novels that I wrote ten years ago. When you sell a picture frame, you cannot earn money from the same picture frame years later. It's sold and it's gone.

I also can't tell you about the traffic a single story will get. I can point to similar stories, and the readership of various magazines, but I can't tell you how many of those people will read my story, and what it means if they do. It's easier with books—you can guess from previous sales what future sales might be like.

But books are not like pens. You can't mass-produce books. My friend Karen Joy Fowler had a string of well-written mid-list books that paid well, but not great. So you'd think, from her track record, that she'll always publish mid-list books.

One day, at a book signing, she looked across the bookstore and saw two signs. One read *Jane Austen*. The other, with an arrow pointing toward a back room, read *Book Club*. In that flash of inspiration we writers rely on, she combined both signs to *The Jane Austen Book Club*. Then she wrote a kick-ass novel, with that as the title.

The book arrived at her publisher's in the middle of the Jane Austen craze, as book clubs were gaining traction. Plus everyone in the publishing house loved the book. Word of mouth proved terrific, and *The Jane Austen Book Club* hit the *New York Times* Bestseller List, and got made into a movie.

In no way could Karen realistically have done a business plan that showed how *The Jane Austen Book Club* would take her little freelance business from a boutique store off the beaten path to a well-respected popular store on Fifth Avenue in New York City. No loan administrator would have given her a second look. No publisher would have believed her—not without reading the book itself. The title might've been great, but the book had to live up to that title, which it did.

So why am I, a dedicated freelance writer who knows her business very well, talking about business plans if I say they're not relevant for many businesses? Because that financial guestimation business plan, the kind you need to get a loan or to attract venture capital or to round up a few friends to give you back-up funds, is only one kind of business plan.

The rest of this chapter is about the other kind of business plan: the kind you draw up for yourself. Now I'm not talking about goals and dreams. There are other chapters on those topics.

What I'm talking about here is survival, plain and simple. Because without a business plan, your freelance business will not survive.

Again, I hear the chorus of "huh?" "Lady," you're all saying, "you started this whole chapter saying that plans go awry, that you can't foresee the future, that your freelance business doesn't have a formal business plan."

Yep. And yet I have an informal one.

Freelancers have two big problems: time and organization. When you quit your day job, you feel like you have a limitless amount of time ahead of you. You have all day to accomplish various tasks. But you lose the job's structure, so often days go by without accomplishing anything.

The same happens with organization. At a day job, someone organizes you—they tell you when to arrive, when to leave, when to eat lunch, where to sit, and what to do. When you freelance, you decide all those things. Which sounds lovely—in theory. In practice, it's a recipe for disaster.

To survive these things, you'll need discipline. You'll also need to learn how to structure yourself. And you'll need an informal business plan.

Your informal business plan is nothing like the one you'd prepare for the SBA. This plan is for your eyes only. But, like the SBA plan, this business plan must be realistic.

Your plan can only include things which you can control. For example, I know that 90% of my short stories will sell in the first year. Do I know which stories they are? No. Do I know which story will take ten years to sell? No. Do I know which story will pay me $10,000 and which one will pay me $100? No.

What I do know is that if I finish a story and mail it, it has a nine out of ten chance of selling within one year of the mail date. So I must (a) write short stories and (b) keep them in the mail.

I can control those two things.

I cannot control editors (dammit). Nor can I control readers. I can't predict which story will make my name and which one will disappear without a trace.

So, using what I can control, here's how I build my personal business plan: I decide how many stories I'll write this year. That

45

decision will be based on how long it takes me to write 1000 words, and how many words I will dedicate to my short fiction writing. So if I write 1000 words in an hour, then a 4000 word story will take me four hours minimum. Figure six to count in false starts, overwriting, rewriting, and general noodling. Most of my stories are longer than 4K, however, so I tend to figure as a good average 10K. I figure how many 10K stories I want to write, how many novels I want to write, and I divide by hours. I then figure out how much time I need to devote to writing each and every day.

(Like this: Let's say that my estimate shows me that I need to write 20,000 words per week for my writing plan. That means I must spend 20 hours per week at 1000 words per hour writing. If I write 500 words an hour, I'll spend 40 hours at it.)

I also need to factor in mailing time—and re-mailing time, since most stories do not sell on their first time out. Some writers set aside an entire workday for mailing once a month. I try to keep up with whatever I have on a weekly basis, keeping everything in the mail. That too becomes part of the plan. Nothing stays on my desk. Everything leaves the office, one way or another.

Your business plan should include hours to work each week, the amount you need to accomplish, and which projects you plan to do. You need to factor in things like time spent rounding up new work. (In a specialty store, that would be included in advertising and promotions; in writing it can be query letters and sending chapters to editors; in certain kinds of sales, it might be the number of cold calls you'll need to make each and every week.) You'll need to find your Goldilocks solution: you don't want to work too much, but you also don't want to work too little. You want your work schedule to be just right.

Even having concrete weekly goals is not enough to keep you producing day in and day out, particularly if you work at a solitary freelance job like writing. Your business plan should divide up by quarters (how much do you expect to get done by March 31?), and by year. You'll need a target for this year, for five years from now, and for ten years from now.

And no, your business plan can't include things like "sell more copies of books than Dan Brown." Or "turn your little coffee shop into the next international franchise coffee business (like Starbucks) by the year 2020." You can't control those things.

You can control how hard you try.

"But," you're all reminding me, "you say that plans go awry. How can you plan ten years out?"

You need to, to keep yourself on track. But you also need to revise your business plan regularly. If you take a left turn, as Karen Joy Fowler did with *The Jane Austen Book Club*, then you assess your business plan with the new direction in mind.

At the end of your year, reassess the plan. Did you achieve your daily, weekly, and monthly goals? If you didn't, why didn't you? If you did, were your goals too easy? Or were they just right? Did you work hard enough? Or did you hardly work at all?

Be honest with yourself.

Then write a new business plan, with new targets, reflecting your current realities.

I would suggest that you keep the plans in two files: one on your computer, and one in a hardcopy file folder. After ten years, it's amusing to look at old business plans. Some are very, very accurate. Some aren't. If you keep detailed notes, you'll know what works for you and what doesn't. You won't keep reinventing the wheel.

The nice thing about an informal business plan is this: you've created your own road to walk on. You're not flailing in the dark. You're actually on a path toward success. You may decide that particular path isn't for you, and you might blaze a new trail. But you'll be moving forward with a purpose, rather than hoping and waiting for someone else to do something that will propel you along.

Will you be where you thought you'd be ten years from now? I can guarantee that you won't. But if you follow your own plan, you might be in an even better position than you imagined you'd be.

And you will certainly have had an enjoyable journey.

Chapter Five
When to Quit Your Day Job

Every book on how to be your own boss has instructions about when to give up your day job. Each one of these books has a particular rule of thumb. Some say you cannot quit your day job until you have three months' salary in the bank. Some say three years' salary in the bank. Others say you need all your funding in place *and* at least five years' salary.

The sad truth of this economic downturn is that many people have already lost their day jobs and are trying to freelance just to make ends meet. Those people have major tasks ahead of them. They have to do all the things needed to bring some money in the house: register at the unemployment office, move money from long-term emergency savings to regular bank accounts, and cut the frills out of the budget. They also have to look for a new job, which takes hours every day.

Then and only then do they have time to freelance.

Even though these are the folks who inspired me to write this Guide right now and post it on my blog every week, this one chapter will have less to do with them than it will with the rest of you.

Those of you who've been forced into freelancing, don't let this chapter make you feel guilty. It's the rare freelancer who follows the advice I'm about to give.

Most of us jumped from the day job into freelancing because of circumstances or personality. Most of us became freelancers at exactly the wrong times in our lives. We were going through a divorce and making changes anyway. Or our freelance work overtook our real work time, so one afternoon we just quit. Or we moved to another community and didn't want the hassle of finding a new job (which, honestly, is a lot less hassle than freelancing itself).

Many of us figured freelancing would be easier than working for someone else, so we never searched for a job when we graduated from college. (Note to those of you thinking of this: Freelancing is *not*, let me repeat *not*, easier than working for someone else.) Or we had children so we figured that we'd make money instead of pay it out to day care or an au pair.

In other words, we incorrectly rationalized our choice to freelance and we jumped long before we should have. How did we survive? In a variety of ways, too numerous to mention.

Let me toss a few at you: We cut our budgets. We moved to more cost-effective housing. We had understanding parents/siblings/ friends with large bank accounts. We had spouses who worked. We learned the art of saving money—from clipping coupons to trimming the correct luxuries. We paid half the bills one month and the other half the next. (And dealt with the creditors calling every few hours.)

Eventually, those of us who survived as freelancers did several things: Our income caught up with and then surpassed our expenses. We learned how to thrive in a stressful environment (not kidding here—I know many freelancers who work better when the money is tight than they do when they have money in the bank). We learned how to be the best money managers in the world.

Money management is such a huge, huge topic that I have devoted a section to it.

Money management is the key to freelance survival.

But let's return to the topic at hand: When do you quit your day job?

The real answer, the true answer, is deceptively simple. It is this: you quit your day job whenever you damn well feel like it.

But that doesn't do you (or your family or your long-suffering spouse) any good. You want rules. You want advice. Those of you who are still employed and hating it want to know when you get to do what you want.

So…when do you quit?

There are a million answers to that question, and they're all individual. I can't tell you when to quit your day job any more than you can tell me what to write tomorrow. Even my rules of thumb would be wrong for most of you.

Instead, I'm going to recast the question several times in this chapter. Each refinement might bring you closer (or farther away) from quitting your day job.

Should You Quit Your Day Job?

For most people, the answer to that question is no. Most people can't handle all of the things it takes to be a full-time freelancer. Not that most folks aren't smart enough or talented enough or even ambitious enough. The difference between most people and full-time freelancers boils down to one thing: the ability to take risks.

Full-time freelancers are risk-takers. Most people aren't.

Most people value the safe, the secure, and the familiar. This always astonishes me, because safe and secure is usually a mirage.

When Dean and I traveled the country in the mid-1990s, talking to wannabe writers about the ups and downs of freelancing, we always made one point: Nothing in this life is secure.

I would use this example: The single proprietors I had once worked for, from the forensic psychologist to the real estate agent, all could have closed their businesses in the space of a week. Or my boss could have died, and the business would not survive him.

The wannabe writers who worked for small proprietors understood this. The wannabes who worked for corporations laughed. They *laughed*, and told me that their jobs were, by definition, secure.

Each time I heard this, I would stare at the speaker in shock, and then I would move on to a new topic. Because for many people at that time, jobs with large companies did seem secure.

But I had grown up in the Midwest. I had gone through college as the recession of the 1970s and early 1980s hit the car industry, starting a huge round of layoffs and plant closings. Once a week during that period, I manned the phones at a suicide hotline and fielded calls from people who had gotten laid off from their jobs, jobs they saw as a family legacy because their parents and grandparents had worked at the same plant.

That experience showed me that no job was secure. Jobs could—and did—disappear overnight.

Such a thing doesn't surprise those of you reading this now. The change of attitude began with Enron, a seemingly healthy corporation that one day told all of its employees to go home; and, oh, by the way, your pensions and your stocks are worthless.

The pensions and stocks were a new wrinkle to that problem I had grown up with. Even I was shocked about that. Because my

Depression-era parents had taught me that if you save your money, it's there for you in times of crisis.

Well, it is. Unless you let someone else manage your savings. But that's a topic for another day.

If the very idea of losing your day job makes your stomach hurt, you're not ready to quit. If the idea of being without a regular paycheck—of not knowing exactly when and where the money will come from one year, five years or ten years from now—makes you crazy, you should never, ever, quit your day job.

A lot of people have a small business in addition to their day jobs. They sell quilts or repair cars. They write novels or go on the lecture circuit. But they keep the day job because they like either the structure it gives or the regular paycheck that it brings in.

There's nothing wrong with that. Just because you make money from something you love doesn't mean you have to do that work full time.

Who Should Quit a Day Job?

If the first recasting of the day job question didn't scare you, and you still want to quit, should you? Maybe. If you're reasonably healthy, single, and have some money in the bank, go ahead and quit. Your decision will only have an impact on you. Then use the rest of this Guide and other books on starting your own business to help you set up.

However (and this is a big however), if you have dependents, you need to think long and hard about quitting that job. Children cost money. Spouses lose their jobs. Elderly parents need care. The entire clan—at least those old enough to vote—should be in on this decision together.

The last thing you want to do is come home one day and say, "Honey, I quit my day job. I'm going to freelance full time."

I know a lot of people who've done just that. And, as you can well imagine, it doesn't help the marriage any. Especially when the decision is made unilaterally and the family finances get rocked.

If you have a family and/or people who rely on your income, then quitting your day job and taking the risks to freelance full time must be a group decision. It should take a lot of planning, a lot of back-and-forth, and a clear understanding of what freelancing means. I would recommend that the non-freelancing part of the relationship read all of my Freelancer's Guide posts on my blog, as well as those business books I mentioned. Because a pat on the head followed by a *"do what you want, honey,"* is going to backfire big time down the road.

If your job provides excellent health insurance, you need to think twice or even three times about quitting that day job. Every freelancer needs health insurance. Let me repeat that: *Every freelancer needs health insurance.* I know too many people who quit to freelance with money in the bank, had a health problem which ate up the money, and went bankrupt within a few years—all because they never bought health insurance.

Health insurance is extremely expensive, and what you can buy as a freelancer isn't going to be as good as that provided by most employers.

If your spouse has a job with health insurance, then make sure you're on the spouse's policy *and so are the kids* before you quit your day job. Make sure the spouse's policy is as good as yours.

If you're not married and in reasonably good health, check the price of health insurance before you leave the job. All that careful planning that got you to the point of quitting probably didn't take the five-hundred to one-thousand dollars per month you'll need for a good health insurance policy.

The key for you here is simple: Never, *ever,* go without health insurance.

Finally, if you have a major job with a lot of seniority, you might want to think twice about quitting. Almost everyone quits the day job, finds out how hard the freelance life is, and goes back to the day job. Many try to freelance again, only to fail a second time, and return to the day job. It usually takes three or four tries before someone becomes a permanent full-time freelancer.

I worked part-time jobs just to pay the rent. Even my editing jobs were part time. I knew, for example, when I quit editing *The Magazine of Fantasy & Science Fiction,* that I would never get that job back. And I was okay with that.

Sometimes you can be rehired by your excellent company, but without the seniority. And loss of seniority can be a bad thing. It feels wrong to ask your boss if you can be rehired at the same seniority, pay and benefits if the freelancing doesn't work out. It's the rare boss who'll say yes. And if that boss is a mid-level manager, what's to guarantee he'll have his job when you throw in the towel six months down the road?

If you hate your day job and would never go back to it, then quit, no matter what your seniority (but think about that health insurance). If you don't care about being rehired at the same level, then quit. But if these things matter to you, then quitting is probably a very bad idea.

Should I Quit My Day Job Or Should I Downgrade?

Many of you don't know what I mean by downgrading. I mean this: If you have one of those high-level jobs that takes 80% of your time and chews up 98% of your stomach lining, you don't have time to develop your freelance strategy. You're just daydreaming about quitting that job.

You don't have time to do all the prep for quitting your day job. You think cold turkey would be nice.

But what about getting a lesser job, one with fewer hours and less hassle? If that job also provides health insurance, then you'd be easing your way into the full-time freelance position.

And, honestly, that new job will be a lot easier to give up when the time comes.

You'll probably have a cut in pay. (You'll get a concurrent cut in heartburn.) You'll have to deal with making less money, but you'll still have that regular paycheck. It'll be a good first test of your money management skills.

A lot of companies still offer a pre-retirement situation, one that allows the younger employees to advance while the older ones mentor and work fewer hours. See if your company offers that and if you're eligible. A lot of companies will also let you change jobs, even downsize, without any penalty to you (except in salary). That's worth investigating as well.

You still have a safety net, but you'll have more time. You'll also find out if you can manage to get your freelance work done with that extra time. And you'll figure out if your household can sustain a lower level of income.

Psychologically, this one's tough. People who identify themselves by their jobs and measure their self-worth by their raises and promotions won't be able to do this easily. It'll take a redefinition of self, and that's hard. Some people simply can't handle it.

But here's the hard truth. If you can't handle a decrease in salary or a lesser job, you'll never be able to handle working from home. Because most people you know will think that you have been fired or laid off, and that's why you're suddenly at home. After you've worked at home for a while, those same people will think you're not working at all, and will make mention of things like that.

When I was in my twenties, making a good living as a non-fiction freelancer, I found out that most people who knew me casually thought I was staying home for the kids. I had no kids. I still don't. But that never stopped people from making that assumption.

The Real Question: Should I Quit My Day Job?

You've read all of the above and still think you want to quit the day job. You're in the right emotional position and you have figured out a way to pay for your insurance. Your family is on board. Your home office sits empty, waiting for you to spend each and every day inside.

What do you have to do to make the actual leap?

First, you figure out how much money you need to live each and every month. Then you add half again as much for unexpected emergencies. Multiply that number by twelve, and that's what you need for a year.

Most experts feel you need three years of income in the bank before quitting your job. And that money does not include the emergency fund that you should have already put away. (Never mind that most people live paycheck to paycheck and never manage that emergency fund. We'll pretend that figure doesn't exist at the moment—or that most of us aren't part of that group.) Experts recommend that emergency fund equal six months (at the bare minimum) of your income.

This reserve money, by the way, must be in actual cash. Not in your home equity or in the available credit of your credit cards or in your stock portfolio. This money must be relatively liquid—something you can get your hands on quickly, something that won't decline with the vagaries of the market.

Let me use an example. Let's say it takes you $3000 to make your monthly bills with the mortgage, the new health insurance costs, and the groceries. Add another $1500 for unexpected emergencies, and calculate everything this way: It takes you $4500 per month to survive. That means you need to earn $54,000 per year to survive *after taxes*.

You don't know what your taxes will be? Look at what gets taken out of your paycheck. Then realize that you'll be paying for all of your social security. Right now, your employer pays half and you pay half. So it's even more than you think. Factor that in.

If you need $54,000 per year, then you'll need $162,000 to make your three-year-savings goal. Then you need to add in that emergency fund. Six months at $4500 per month comes out to an additional $27,000. All told, before you quit your day job, you'll need $189,000 in the bank.

See why most people never go full-time freelance?

Full disclosure time: I have never, ever, had that kind of money in the bank. Every single time I got rid of my day jobs, I had enough contracts to cover the job's salary. In other words, I had the promise of enough work to get me through the year.

Promises, by the way, are not hard cold cash.

I can live like this much more easily than I can go to a nine-to-five job. I'm much happier scrambling than I am doing someone else's bidding for eight hours per day.

I also realize I'm rare.

Most full-time freelancers had some money in the bank when they quit their day jobs. Usually three to six months worth. In our fictional example, that's $13,500 to $27,000—which are much easier numbers to achieve.

Often the folks who go full time do have working spouses, so many (most?) of the bills are covered.

So, ideally, you should have a lot of savings before you go full-time freelance. But as many people reading this guide already know, the ideal is seldom the reality. A lot of folks are surviving on their unemployment and hoping it lasts long enough for them to establish their freelance career.

Gosh, sounds like a lot of folks I know who became successful freelancers.

But this short topic is how to do quit your day job correctly.

And here's the most important part. You already need an established business practice.

Meaning, you should already have earned money at the thing you want to do as a full-time freelancer. If you want to be a full-time freelance writer, you better have sold more than one short story or one article to the local paper. If you want to set up your own legal practice, you better have clients who have already hired you and like you as their lawyer.

My ex-husband started a frame shop and art gallery about the time I went full-time non-fiction freelance. He had been framing art out of our back room. He was an artist when it came to cutting mats, find the right frames, and enhancing (and preserving) the art. He quit his day job because he was already earning the same amount of money in only a few hours per night. He knew he would make even more if he had a storefront—and he did.

He brought an established client base with him, and those people told their friends. The start-up was extremely successful. The transition was surprisingly easy. He made good money right from the start.

But the business failed because neither of us knew how to manage a business. We failed miserably, he and I. And the financial stress was one of the many nails in the coffin that had become our marriage.

I bring this up here because the stakes are very, very high. When you're single, you can make these decisions easily. But when you have family, you're taking an ever greater risk. You need to think through the ramifications of failure as well as the opportunities provided by success.

So…should you quit your day job?

Probably not.

But if you decide to do so, make sure you have these things in place:

1. **An ability to take risks**
2. **Health insurance**
3. **Familial support**
4. **Health insurance**
5. **Enough money to get through hard times**
6. **Health insurance**
7. **An established client base**
8. **Health insurance**
9. **An understanding that, the first few times you try to go full-time freelancing, you will probably fail**

Still want to quit your day job? Then good luck to you. A lot of us have done so. We've survived. You can too.

Chapter Six
Things You Need
Before You Quit Your Day Job

Let's assume that the previous chapter didn't convince you to keep your day job. You're going to take the plunge no matter what. Good for you. That's how most of us have entered this crazy profession. On the afternoon that I write this, I heard a woman on National Public Radio who confessed to starting her full-time freelance business when she lost her job in the 2003 recession. Then I picked up the April 2009 issue of *More Magazine*, and found a series of articles about women who started green businesses—often against all advice, often while in the middle of a job loss or downturn or personal crisis.

Most full-time freelancers you know didn't have that three years worth of income in the bank. Some barely had an emergency fund. A few didn't even have paying customers when they took the plunge.

Again, I'm not recommending this method, but I do know the realities of the world. And the reality of people who want to freelance is simple: if you really want to do it, you'll find a way to make it work.

So…in the previous chapter, I dealt with whether or not you should quit. In this chapter, I'm going to tell you the practical things you *must* have in place before you do quit.

(Those of you who've already quit that precious day job, you can still implement these items now. The sooner the better. Make a list and conquer one per day, if you can.)

The first few items on my list are in order of importance. After that, I'm going to place the items in random order, as I think of them.

1. You need to have the people you live with on board.

These are the people I'm describing as family. Your grandmother, hundreds of miles away in Iowa, doesn't have to approve; your wife, whose livelihood probably depends somewhat on yours, does. You cannot quit your day job by fiat. You must have your family on board.

Sometimes that takes work. Dean and I offer classes for established professional writers—not just full-time freelancers, but people who have already made money at their writing. (We only offer one course on business and publishing for beginners. Find the information on Dean's website, deanwesleysmith.com.) We offer one particular workshop for the professionals that role-plays the freelance lifestyle. Our theory is simple: If you practice freelancing in a reality-based role-playing situation, you'll know what you're getting into.

A lot of our students bring their spouses to that workshop. In fact, we ran that workshop just a year or so ago because the students who had done it before wanted to run their spouses through the simulation. Our weekend workshop for beginners would also give spouses similar information, without the role-playing aspect.

I'm not telling you all of this to get you to sign up for our workshops. I'm telling you this because it doesn't matter how much you try to tell your spouse what freelancing is like, your spouse won't understand until about a month in, when you haven't made a dime. Yes, you might have $5000 in accounts receivable, but all of those accounts are paying late—or in the case of the downturn in December/January/February of 2009, not at all.

Freelancing sounds good in theory, but it's difficult in practice.

Once you have your spouse/family on board, you have to continue to communicate, to make sure that person remains on your side. You and your family are in this together, even if everyone else in the household has a day job. You all need to know what's happening, why, and what to expect.

2. You need to know the exact state of your finances.

I mean you need to know, down to the penny, how much money you have, and how much of that money is liquid (easily available). You need to know how much money clients owe you and—this is important—approximately when they'll pay you.

In my business, writing, I have a vague idea when I'll receive payment for my short fiction. I mean vague as in—sometime in the next six months, I'll get a check. You can't plan for that.

I also know when money is due from book publishers under contract. Because book publishers always pay late, I add three months onto the due date in my financial calendar. That helps with my financial planning—and also makes it easier to cope with the chronically late payments.

My business also involves large sums of money that arrive without warning. Royalties land in the mailbox from unexpected projects, sometimes only a few dollars, and sometimes thousands of dollars. I never plan for those, but I don't treat them as windfalls either. They're part of what I earn, and they get banked until they have an assigned task.

I tell you this now because all freelance income is unpredictable. You don't have the clout of a major corporation behind you when you send your bill. You can cut off your service, but often that means little since the services provided by most freelance businesses aren't essential, the way electricity or cell phones are. So you have to realize where you sit in other people's financial payment schemes and plan accordingly.

In other words, just because you have $5000 in accounts receivable doesn't mean you'll receive all $5000 on time. You'll probably receive $1000 on time, $2000 within that three-month time limit I mentioned above, and the remaining $1000 in dribs and drabs over the upcoming year.

You must plan for that.

You also need contingency plans for when someone does not pay you. I don't mean how you handle the client, but how you handle your own finances.

Most people live from paycheck to paycheck. Freelancers can't afford to do that. We must earn more than we need because of that fictional example above. If we need $5000 to live, and we only get $4000 in a timely manner, we're in trouble. If we need $3000 to live, and we get $4000 in a timely manner, we're doing all right.

Which brings me too another aspect of what you need to know about your finances before you quit: you need to know exactly what your bills are every month. Use the highest bills you can find—the cell phone bill that your daughter added $100 extra in unauthorized text messaging charges, or the heat bill from the coldest month in the winter. *Those* are your expenses, not the summer heat bill and the cell phone bill the month you confiscated your daughter's cell as punishment. You need the highest bill as your example, not the lowest.

You also need to factor in those once-every-few-months bills, like the lump-sum car insurance payment or the tuition for your son's annual summer camp.

Then add in emergency expenses. Assume that you'll have to pay the deductibles on at least one of your insurances in the upcoming year. That might be anywhere from $500 if you have a low deductible, to $5000 if you have a medium deductible.

And finally, add in the cost of business travel and continuing education. Dean and I factor in about $1000 per month for that in our computations—figuring two freelancers @ $500 per month, or $6000 per year each in unexpected business travel or continuing education expenses.

Except for 1992 when we traveled every other weekend, we've never hit that amount. But it does build in an automatic cushion, one that can be used for other things, like an up-to-date computer system or just to build up savings until you actually gain that emergency fund I've been talking about.

Finally, know what your available credit is. You won't have a lot. Except for the blip of the last decade when a cat could get a credit card, you won't be able to get new credit. In the eyes of the banks, freelancers are unemployed. So all that credit you got as an employed person has suddenly become a luxury.

Once you quit, you won't be able to get a home equity line of credit or a third credit card. You won't be able to lease a car or qualify for a car payment. And you certainly won't be able to get a small business loan, especially if your business, like mine, doesn't require a storefront.

So take the available credit you have now as an employed person, and mentally cut it in half. You will probably lose some of it to a credit review or be denied the credit entirely when you try to use it (in the case of home equity lines of credit).

And then—this is essential—try not to use that credit. Again, I deal with this in the money chapters of the Guide, but here's the short version. Just because you're short $1000 now, doesn't mean that $1000 will come in before you have to pay your credit card bill. I know freelancers who had to stop freelancing because they racked up tens of thousands in credit card bills just paying their expenses.

Don't do that. Ever.

In short: You must know how much money you have (and how much is liquid), how much money you're owed (and approximately when it will come in), what your current bills are at their highest monthly rates, what your additional expenses are, and how much credit you realistically have available.

Put this information in some kind of accounting program and update it weekly.

3. You need to have all of your insurance in place.

You need health insurance, business insurance, homeowners or renters insurance, car insurance, and other insurance that pertains to your particular freelance business (if any). Purchase this *before* you go full-time freelance—and add it to your monthly/quarterly/annual expenses.

Things can and do go wrong. Believing that you're immune to disaster is the first step toward one.

4. You need to have a business plan.

Again, this is a topic I have explored in-depth in other parts of the Guide, but for the sake of this chapter, here's what you need: You need goals. Daily, weekly, monthly, and annual goals. You also need a five-year plan and a ten-year plan. You must keep these goals under your control.

(For example, we tell writers they can't control what sells. They can control productivity and quality. So no writer should make a goal like "I want to hit the bestseller list by the end of this year." But they can plan to write two novels this year.)

For more on this, see my husband Dean's blog posts on goal-setting from December, 2008. There are several. You can find them at deanwesleysmith.com.

5. You need a dedicated workspace.

As you set up your workspace, keep in mind something journalist Randy Tatano told me in an e-mail: "The freelancers I know who have had problems are the ones who set up fancy offices and buy all kinds of equipment."

In other words, keep your overhead low. In fact, unless you need a storefront, set up a workspace at home.

6. You need a schedule.

You had a schedule at your day job, but someone else imposed it on you. Now you need to design your own—and post it on the door to your (home) office.

Stick to this schedule, but make it realistic. For example, I'm not a morning person. (I can hear my husband laughing at the understatement.) I work best later in the day and like to stay up late at night.

When I first started freelancing, I set my writing time at 9:00 a.m. Usually, I rolled out of bed at 9:30, and didn't get to the office until 11:00, already behind and feeling bad.

Now I get up between 10:00 and 11:00 a.m., (usually closer to 10:00), exercise, do my e-mail and phone calls, have lunch around 3:00, and then go to the office for an extended stay. Aside from a quick dinner, I am in the office from the middle of the afternoon until the late night news.

This schedule suits me. I used to go to work at my day jobs in the morning, but I hated it. Since I'm self-employed, I can set up any schedule I want *so long as I follow it.*

And I do, religiously.

You need that schedule up front, and you need to follow it, or no one else will.

7. You need to budget time and money for continuing education.

Most professions require their practitioners to keep up on current trends. Often that requires a seminar or two during the year, as well as some materials. Schedule these when you're doing your budget and when you're setting up your day-to-day schedule.

You also need to keep up on the blogs for your type of business, subscribe to industry magazines, and read other industry publications. All of this takes time, but it shouldn't take *work* time, as it used to do in your day job.

Have the first year's dose set up before you quit that day job. And, remember, if you can't afford it—if you're not earning enough or if you don't have enough saved—don't do it.

8. You need to make an appointment to reexamine your goals every six months.

Freelancing is a fluid business. In the first six months especially, you'll learn what works and what doesn't. You might have to reassess your time, your budget, your goals, and your possibility for success.

Do this with your family—and be brutally honest. That's the only way this will work.

Set up the appointment, write it on the family calendar, and then keep that appointment. Do this at least twice a year. (Quarterly will work better for some families.) That'll prevent some panicked discussions about whether or not the freelancing is working (remember, honey? We're going to reassess in November), and it'll also prevent problems from getting out of hand.

9. You need to have a contingency plan...

...for everything. What happens if you can't pay your bills? What happens if you don't get enough work? What happens if you can't keep your schedule?

And the biggest contingency plan of all: You need to have a line—agreed to by all concerned—about when (if) you go back to a day job. You need to have all aspects of this plan in place—except for the day job itself—before you quit your current job.

That means you and your family have to agree on how much money you'll need to make, at what point you declare this first attempt at freelancing a failure, and what is not great but good enough by everyone's definition.

Remember what I said earlier: Most first-time freelancers go back to their day jobs. Most first-time freelancers fail. I did. Almost everyone I know did.

But that doesn't mean you can't try again when you have enough knowledge under your belt. The next time, you'll do it smarter.

As you can probably tell, freelancing is all about organization. Organizing your money, organizing your time, organizing your family—all in the best manner for you and your chosen profession. You can impose this organization *after* you've started to freelance. But those of you still contemplating the jump have an opportunity to do so *before* you leap.

Don't just quit and then figure out how to live your new life. Figure out what you need and want first, then figure out the best way to get there. Be cautious, be prudent, but most of all, be informed.

You'll have a greater chance of success if you follow the nine steps listed above.

Section Two:
Time Management

Chapter Seven
Time

Time. That's what any business boils down to. Time. I learned this quite young. I got paid by the hour (by the minute, really) at my very first long-term job as a waitress. That time clock, with its time stamp, tracked every single moment I was on the job. If I clocked in at 6:05 a.m. and clocked out at 1:55 p.m., I did not work eight hours. I worked seven hours and fifty minutes, and that's what I got paid for.

I really learned the meaning of time when I worked in radio. Everything in broadcast news is measured in seconds. Years later, after I became a science fiction writer, a television interviewer pulled me aside and said in surprise, "You're the first writer I've met who speaks in thirty-second sound bites."

Gosh, guess where I learned that.

I also learned to watch the clock. If the news had to be on at seven, you couldn't be five minutes late. It was seven or there would be the catastrophe of catastrophes—dead air.

Time isn't just about deadlines. Time is about efficiency. You see, we're only allowed so many hours on this earth. In fact, Clint Black has a great song about this phenomenon called "No Time to Kill," which I'd quote to you if there weren't copyright issues preventing it. No matter what we do, we don't get additional hours. Our days are 24 hours long, no matter what. The week lasts for seven days, no matter how hard we try to change that.

We can shortchange other parts of our lives to get more time. We can sleep less, spend less time with friends, or give up things we love, but those are only short-term solutions. If you do that for too long, you'll blow. You'll either get sick or have some kind of breakdown or (my explosion of choice) quit whatever it is that has taken all your time in a loud and dramatic fashion.

The best way to "gain" more time is to use what time you have more efficiently. There are a wide variety of ways to do that.

Here are some of the most common:

1. Work harder.

Years ago, a friend of mine who manages an entire division in a corporation told me that corporations factor in worker downtime. In other words (and I'm making up the statistics here, being too lazy to look them up), corporations figure that for every hour an employee is at the job, he works only forty minutes. The rest of the time is spent on the phone or in the bathroom or gossiping with coworkers. So in an eight-hour day, a corporate employee probably only works 5.3 hours.

When you work for yourself, there's no one to track your productivity. You can goof off until bedtime if you want—and newer at-home professionals often do. You think you have an entire day, and suddenly that entire day has gone by.

It's especially easy these days to waste time and feel productive while doing so. Twitter, Facebook, e-mail, and surfing the web feel like writing work to me, but if I spend all day typing Tweets and long letters to friends, I'm not getting any paying work done. Yet I've been writing all day long.

This is why I have no internet access whatsoever in my office. I won't even allow myself to bring my nifty new iPhone in here because that way lies inefficiency and financial death.

I have a separate office for everything that is not writing, from my phone to my laptop with its wireless internet connection to my television with its online capability.

In fact, over the years, I've weeded all distractions out of my office, like games on my computer and other people's fiction. Now if I want to waste time, I have to leave my office—a real clear sign that I'm not doing my job.

2. Work smarter.

This was the category that initially worried me as I wrote *The Freelancer's Survival Guide* on my blog. I couldn't write it any faster than any of my other projects. So I hoped that in the future all of the time I spent on the *Guide* would pay off.

As the *Guide* progressed, I had some intangible results, ones that matter. More people than ever now come to my website, and many are unfamiliar with my fiction. I get several letters per week from folks who've read the *Guide* who are now going to pick up a novel that I've written. So I'm gaining an added benefit here, one I didn't expect. I'm writing something that's turning into a loss leader.

A loss leader, for those of you unfamiliar with the term, refers to something a business gives away or sells at a discount that will bring customers to the business. I did not expect the *Guide* to be a loss leader.

Nor, honestly, did I expect it to generate much money in the website form. I initially wrote the *Guide* for people to read immediately because the recession was forcing a lot of people to go to work for themselves before they're ready. I'm trying to help with that.

So when I started the *Guide*, I fully expected it to be a complete waste of time and money (for me). I looked at it the way I look at the volunteer work I've done: as something I'm giving back to the community, not as something that will bring me any benefits.

The fact that there are benefits surprises me immensely.

And there have been a lot of benefits besides the ones mentioned above. I've learned about web publishing. WMG Publishing picked up the *Guide* and the short books excerpted from the larger volume. I made my advance off the website alone, and I have a new column, one that also talks about business, which keeps the *Guide* going. The time wasn't wasted after all.

Let's assume, however, that the *Guide* wasn't an experiment for me. Let's assume that it was something I had done before, as most of my fiction is. I would have done what most businesses call a cost-benefit analysis.

If I spend x time on this project, I should get y benefit from the project. Together x and y should equal or exceed z. If x and y together are less than z, then the project is not worth doing.

Let's put this in more concrete terms. If I spend a week writing a short story, and receive $100 plus publication in a reputable magazine, is that worth my time? Not usually. Because if I spent one week writing and only get $100 for my work, then I'm earning $2.50 per hour, which is well under minimum wage. The less tangible benefits would have to be off the chart for me to work for that amount of money. Honestly, I can't even think of what those off-the-chart benefits could possibly be for me to work so long for so little money.

One writer friend of mine, a long-time professional, told me that if he wasn't earning a minimum of $500 per day on his writing, he had a bad day. Imagine what his response would be if someone asked him to spend a week writing a $100 short story.

I have my own hourly number, under which I generally do not take a project. That hourly number often includes a pain-in-the-ass tax. In other words, I'll work for some difficult clients, but my fee is double or triple what it would be for other, more easygoing folks.

I also factor in time. I'll take a lower-paying job than some writers because I'm a fast writer. I'll finish a project four times faster than most writers, because of my broadcast training. I get things done. What this means is—to keep with our example—if someone asks me for a short story and can only pay me $100, I'll do a gut check. Does the story interest me? Yes. Do I want to be in that market? Yes. Can I write the story in an hour or two? If the answer to that final question is yes, then I'll take the project.

Often, however, the lowest paying clients are the ones who demand the most work.

So you, the professional, must work smarter. You must factor in *all* of the benefits for each job, and then give a realistic estimate of your time. If the tangibles and the intangibles add up to something greater than it would appear at first glance, then take the project. But if they mean that you'd be short-changing yourself—either in money or in time or in reputation—then turn the project down.

Here's the flipside. I've turned down projects that seem—on the surface—to be high paying surefire winners. I've watched the writers who've taken those projects suffer and lose money.

What happened?

Usually the pain-in-the-ass factor. The project, that should have taken three months, took three years. Three awful years of full manuscript revisions, four-hour conference calls that accomplished nothing, and a lot of wasted work. (Not to mention the hair-pulling agony of redoing a task over and over again for an unappreciative client.)

Nowadays, I can see these projects coming. I know which one will be a headache and which one won't. I've been doing this, as I said, for more than twenty years.

But I learned how to see these projects clearly because I made the mistake of taking some of them. I've suffered through them, and learned my lesson. I've learned that it's better to take the $5,000 project that requires two weeks of work than it is to take the $50,000 project that will suck two years from my life. You do the math. It's really not that hard, when you think about it.

In order to work smarter, you need to know what you want from your business and/or from each project that you do. For example, I want several things from my business. I want to continue my writing career. But I want to do it on my terms. I don't want to be a writer-for-hire, someone who writes what other people want. Nor do I want to be constrained by expectations. (I don't want to be pigeonholed.)

I want to continue funding my business. It must pay for itself and pay for my own living expenses.

I want to continue living in this little resort town by the sea, in my lovely home, with my wonderful husband. This life here in this little town costs me a certain amount of money every month—just like your life in your hometown costs you a certain amount of money every month.

So I have a monthly nut—the amount it takes me to live every single month. Multiply by twelve months in the year, then divide by 52. I now know what I must earn each week. (That's easier than trying to figure out if there are 4.5 weeks in a month or 4.3 or 4...) If I divide that weekly number by 40, then I know how much I must earn per hour, if I work a 40-hour week.

I now know what my hourly wage is. Then I must accurately figure out how much time each project will take. Take the amount that the project pays, and divide it by the number of hours it'll take you to finish that project. If you will earn your hourly wage plus some, take the project. If you will earn less than your hourly wage, turn the project down.

That's a simple formula, which you can adjust for intangibles such as bringing more people to your website. But if all of your projects pay mostly in intangibles, you won't earn enough to pay your bills.

Let's go back to the 5K/50K example.

Let's say you need $10 per hour to make your nut. (I know, most of you need a lot more, but $10 makes the math easy.) You figure the 5K project will take three weeks.

You need to earn $1200 to make your nut in three weeks. But for this three-week period of time, you'll earn $5000. Or to put it in hourly terms, you'll be earning $41 per hour when all you need is $10. That's $31 per hour *profit*.

But that 50K project: You thought it would only take one year, which means it'll pay off. You need to earn $20,800 in that year (52 weeks times 40 hours per week times $10 per hour). You'll make $50,000, more than double what you need. You'll earn $24 per hour—less than you'd earn on the short 5K project, but still good wages considering what you need to earn.

But if this 50K project extends over three years, then you will have lost $12,400 on this deal. (Your three-year nut is $62,400. You've earned only $50,000.) And we're talking if they paid up front. If the client pays the balance on completion, you might earn even less. Delayed payments cost you money in time and interest. Sometimes you don't even get the delayed payment, decreasing your pay rate even more.

Even if you got a lot of intangibles, such as good promotion and new clients coming to your business, they wouldn't make up for that devastating loss, which is more than a half a year's income.

Work smarter. Understand what each project will cost you in time, energy, and money.

3. Hire help.
I know, I know. In the *Freelancer's Survival Guide* online, I tell you not to hire an employee unless you need one.

But you might need one to help you become more efficient. Let's look at the 5K example. Let's assume you have one other project that also needs completion in that period of time. It pays $20 per hour and will take 60 hours total. That's an extra twenty hours during the week—so you'll have to work a 60-hour week for three weeks. Tough life.

Now let's assume that you must keep up this pace for the next six months. You can't afford a new employee at that rate, but you can afford someone to baby-sit the kids for a few hours during the week or someone to clean your house or cook your meals so that you're not constantly eating take-out.

Or maybe, like me, a 60-hour week doesn't scare you. But imagine if that stretches to an 80- or 100-hour week. At some point, you'll burn out. So you need to figure out how to cut your hours without losing income or clients.

Sometimes that means hiring a secretary or an assistant who comes in a few times per week. When the new owner of the collectibles store that my husband Dean Wesley Smith started realized that she needed to be onsite seven days per week, eight hours per day in this resort town's busy season, plus put items on eBay in her off hours, she realized she couldn't handle all of that for the required five months. She brings in another employee one day per week, and has added a computer in the store so that she can do eBay in her downtime.

She added a short-term employee for the season *and* decided to work smarter by adding eBay time into her store hours.

And that's what you have to do.

You need to figure out what your time is worth. You need to factor in the intangibles as well as the tangibles. (I don't take a lot of pain-in-the-ass projects; nor do I take projects that'll require me to leave home for months at a time.) You'll need to make sure you make your monthly nut plus some profit. And you'll need to factor in how much work you can actually do versus how much you think you can do.

(Usually self-employed people *overestimate* how much work they think they can do. They also overestimate how much work they think their employees can do, which leads to problems down the road.)

Here's the key to time: make sure you get paid your hourly minimum on every single job. No exceptions. That way, you'll always pay your bills.

Defend your time. Make sure those around you understand that you're doing paying work in those hours.

And finally, if you work harder and smarter and still aren't making your monthly nut, then you need to reassess your business. Because something isn't working. Either you're taking the wrong projects for the wrong reasons or you're not getting enough good paying work.

If you're doing this right, though, you should make a profit on most of your projects. People who know what their time is worth tend to do well in business.

Value your time. Charge for it.

You'll be glad you did.

Chapter Eight
Schedules and How to Keep Them

I often work with start-up publishers. I like their enthusiasm and their vision. After all, I once co-owned a start-up publishing company as well.

However, because I co-owned such a company, I keep a careful eye on the start-ups. I make sure that I can get out of my contracts easily if need be.

When I see potential trouble in a start-up, I let the owner know. If the trouble doesn't get fixed, I do an assessment: Can I live with that trouble? Will that trouble affect my work? If the answers are "yes and no," then I stay. If the answers are "no and yes," I try once more to solve the problems, and if that fails, I leave.

Over the years, I have left primarily due to lack of payment. Start-ups run through their money faster than anyone else. Several years ago, one start-up didn't have enough cash to publish an anthology to which I had contributed. The owner sent a letter saying payment would come six months after publication, which I found unacceptable. The owner, in other words, got all the benefit, and if that owner failed to pay, I would lose first publication rights to my story and never get compensated for them.

Besides, the owner violated the contract. I informed the owner of this, asked for my payment (which, supposedly on acceptance, was now overdue), and when the owner reiterated that no payment would come until six months after publication, I pulled the story. The book was already in production. That decision cost the publisher five times more than it would have if the publisher had simply honored our contract.

Such problems are common with start-ups. I've had to deal with at least one of these issues per year. The handwriting is always on the wall at that point. If the start-up delays payment, the start-up has money troubles. If a start-up has money troubles, *and continues to deny them*, the start-up will—and I mean *will*—go out of business.

In this particular case, the start-up I referred to was gone one year later. Half the authors in that anthology got their post-publication payment. The other half did not. The authors in the next anthology never did get paid.

Money issues are a place where problems become visible. Anyone who pays attention can see that handwriting on the wall.

But some time back, I had a different issue with a start-up. It had to do with scheduling.

This start-up—a small press—contracted to reissue several of my books. The editor who contacted me was one of the most reputable in the business. The press's owner had had a few business failures in the past, but I see that as a plus. The owner had managed to get start-up capital despite those failures. The owner also was a bright person who learned from mistakes. I think failure is a good thing if a person can learn from it, so I did not hold the failures against the owner; but I made a wary note of them, just as I would have if there were hints of money troubles.

This company had no money troubles. It was drowning in capital and had great plans for various projects. But I had a lot of trouble finding out when my books would be published. My editor couldn't get answers on that issue as well. And no one provided deadlines. I thought that strange.

Then came some personnel changes. My editor left. The new editor never answered e-mail. Neither did the owner. And I had some pretty serious questions that needed answering. Most importantly, I needed to know the publishing schedule because some of the books being reissued had co-publishing arrangements.

After months of no response from the publisher, I finally sent a registered letter canceling the contracts. I took longer than usual in doing so, simply because the problems seemed so unusual. But I was complaining to Dean one afternoon and I heard myself say this, "If I'm having trouble getting responses now before publication, when a publisher is *excited* about a project, imagine how hard it'll be to get a response if there's an actual problem, like a delayed payment or a botched cover."

That sentence decided me. I couldn't continue to do business with this publisher.

Eventually, the owner responded to my registered letter. The owner demanded to know why I hadn't e-mailed. I sent copies of all my correspondence. We had several back-and-forths, and things seemed to be getting resolved. Then I reiterated that I had needed the publishing schedule.

The owner asked me why I needed a schedule. I mentioned the co-publishing agreements, and then I stated what seemed obvious to me: all publishers had a schedule. This publisher just needed to share theirs with their authors.

"But," the publisher wrote back, "none of my companies have ever had any schedule, and we've done fine."

Suddenly, all became clear. The previous businesses hadn't failed from undercapitalization or from overextending. They had all failed because the owner had never, *ever,* had a schedule, and was now repeating the same mistake.

Needless to say, I stood by my cancellation, which turned out to be a good decision.

The poor business owner never did understand what had gone wrong, with me and with others. The company, while initially on solid financial footing, started having trouble. The troubles had nothing to do with the finances and everything to do with the lack of a schedule.

You see, without a schedule, other businesses can't work with yours. If you're a publisher, bookstores won't know when to order your books—and won't be able to depend on them to arrive on time. If you're a reader, you won't know when a book becomes available.

Five novels arrived in the mail this week, all of which I had pre-ordered, all of which I have been looking forward to for *months* and in one case, *years*. The books arrived on time, and I'm a happy, if overwhelmed, fan.

If you're a busy author, like me, you need the schedule so that you can meet your deadlines. If you're familiar with publishing, you can also see when things start going awry. Many years ago, an inexperienced editor at a major U.S. publishing house forgot to put my book into production. I noticed when the copy edit was late, then when the proof didn't show. I—and several other authors—had our agents find out what was going on. What was going on was that this editor was very incompetent, and once writers and their representatives started complaining, this editor got fired. My book was delayed for a year because someone hadn't met the schedule.

This book, called *Hitler's Angel,* ended up with a 500 copy print run in the United States because bookstores got confused. Most bookstores rely on their computers to track orders. The computers told the stores that the stores had ordered the book a year before and sold no copies. (Apparently the computers don't mention whether or not the book actually arrives.) So no major bookstore ordered the book.

The editor's mistake cost me thousands and thousands of dollars and doomed a good book for thirteen years. In 2010, John Blake in England published *Hitler's Angel* properly, with a good print run, reviews, and oh, yeah, an actual schedule. (The book will show up in the U.S. via John Blake in 2011—according to the schedule.)

A solid publishing schedule gives the author all kinds of flexibility, and when an author is multi-published, keeps books spaced a proper length apart (or not, if we're jamming something for attention).

Every publisher I've ever worked with, until this start-up, knew that a schedule was important. Not all publishers—particularly the new ones—could keep to the schedule, but they at least tried.

Recently, I had the happy surprise of encountering an extremely organized and scheduled publisher. I turned in a novel and got an e-mail from the managing editor, with all the important dates—when the revisions (if there were any) were due, when the copy edits needed to be finished, when the proofs needed to be done, and when the book would be available for pre-order. I about fell off my chair with delight and surprise.

Then I picked myself up, compared this publication schedule to my personal schedule, and informed the company of a possible problem—I would be traveling for weeks when one of the due dates hit. We adjusted everything within the hour, and the managing editor told me this was why the company sent out the in-house schedule, so they could adjust it to accommodate everyone concerned.

Wow! Such professionalism. In twenty-plus years of publishing and being published, I had never encountered such specificity before. I loved it, and I confess, I feel spoiled now.

Now you know why schedules are so important to publishing. But what about other businesses? Do they need schedules?

Of course they do. Everyone needs a schedule. If you don't have a schedule, you end up like that poor start-up above. After I left that start-up, I continued to pay attention; and I watched that poor business owner run from one fire to another, always trying to put them out. Detail after detail got lost as problems blew up in the owner's face.

Schedules provide structure. Sometimes that structure is as simple as business hours posted on the door of a retail store. Customers know when the store is open, and the owner knows when she needs to be there. But the store needs to keep to the posted hours. After a few tries, customers won't return to a store that's closed during its posted hours.

Dean just encountered this. He needed a new computer, and since there's a recession going on, he wanted to give his money to a local store, even though it would have been easier to order the computer via the internet. Dean told the owner he would show up on a particular Monday afternoon with a check. When Dean arrived, the store was closed. (A "Be Back Soon" sign was on the door.) Dean waited for twenty minutes, called the owner, got the store's answering machine, and gave up.

He left a message, informing the owner he had just lost a $2000 sale, then came home and ordered the computer off the internet. Weeks later, when Dean needed a cable for the computer, he tried the store again and found a different "Be Back Soon" sign. This time, he didn't wait. He went to another store ASAP, and will no longer return to this computer store.

The structure provides a framework for the entire business. It's up to the owner of the business to enforce that structure. For example, I recently heard of two different firings that occurred in our small town.

In the first, the employee showed up hours late for work, without calling. The employee did this repeatedly. After a year of this (!), the employee got fired. Was this the employee's fault? Of course. But it was also the business owner's fault for not respecting the schedule and the structure it provided.

Had I been the owner, and had my employee been that late without cause (a trip to the hospital; a car breakdown outside of cell phone range), I might have fired the employee on the spot. If the employee was particularly good, I might have issued a warning, and fired the employee the second time the employee was hours late. But I certainly wouldn't have waited a year. A year meant that the schedule had no meaning. Ignoring the problem gave the employee tacit permission to misbehave.

Another local business fired one of its three managers for failing to follow a different schedule. The manager would occasionally skip the night deposit, taking care of the deposit the next time the manager drove past the bank. Which meant that the books for the business were off considerably. It also meant that the manager had an entire day's receipts just riding around in the car. The manager was a nice person, without guile. It was just a case of being clueless. In this instance, the manager was clueless exactly twice: the first time, the manager got a warning; the second time, the manager got fired.

Schedules are schedules are schedules.

So...

You work for yourself. Why do you need a schedule?

You need a schedule to help you manage your time, to acquire discipline, and to meet deadlines. Once you become adept at your business, you will know how many hours something will take. You'll be able to schedule your time very well. You'll know *in advance* when you're overextended or under-extended. You'll know when you have to work extra hard and when you have some leisure time. You'll know when you need to hire help, even in the short term.

You'll also be able to compare your schedule with those of the people you do business with and come up with a joint schedule that suits you all. That's what I did with the publishing house that gave me its internal schedule, and what I tried to do with the start-up I had to leave. Because I'm very scheduled and I've been doing this a long time, I knew that my March, April, and May would be crammed. (They were.) I know that I need to work extra hard in June, July, and August because I'm going to lose two, maybe three weeks of work in September due to two trips (and all the planning that goes into such trips). I also know I'll be tired when I return, so I have to schedule lightly.

What level of schedule do you need? That's determined by your business. Most businesses need some kind of external schedule, marked by deadlines and contracts. But most employees—including you—need an internal schedule.

Just because a retail store is open from 10 to 5 doesn't mean the owner should spend the entire time behind the counter twiddling her thumbs as she waits for customers. She needs to have a schedule to change the inventory, to make bank deposits, to clean the store itself. She might put inventory up on eBay, which has its own scheduling demands, and she might have external deadlines imposed by the state and municipality in the form of tax documents. Even something with a seemingly simple schedule might be a lot more complex when viewed from the inside.

Other businesses work off appointment schedules or on construction schedules. Some have deadlines. Others have seasonal demands. All of them are valid. All of them create external schedules.

But external schedules mean nothing if you don't have your internal schedule under control. How do you do that?

You work backwards.

Think of it this way. When you went to your day job, you had a schedule. Let's say you had to be there at 9:00 a.m., and unlike the employee mentioned above, you couldn't be five minutes late without a phone call and a damn good reason.

So you figured the time in your head. You had a thirty-minute commute that could stretch to forty-five on bad days. You had to drop the kids off at school, which was fifteen minutes out of your way.

That meant you had to leave the house no later than eight o'clock. It took you an hour to get ready, counting shower and breakfast. If you lived on your own, you could get up at seven and make it. But you didn't. It always took an extra fifteen minutes to get the kids out of bed. Plus, you always hit the snooze button twice. No matter how hard you tried, you couldn't break yourself of that habit.

So, to be safe, you set your alarm for six in the morning, knowing you had built leeway into your schedule. You could oversleep an hour and still get to work on time. Maybe with practice, or as the kids got older, you could shave a half an hour off of that, and get up at six-thirty. Or maybe you convinced your spouse to take the kids. Then you could get up at seven.

We all make those kinds of decisions, every day. Now you have to make them for your business. Let's say yours is a deadline-oriented business, like mine. The external deadline is in stone. So you don't want to miss it, not even if you get the flu or you lose an employee or your computer dies.

So you move the hard deadline a month earlier or two months earlier, and shoot for the new date. Then you count backwards.

In your backwards count, you must be realistic. Let's go back to the getting-to-work metaphor. A friend of mine once told me he lived ten minutes away from work when there was no traffic. The problem was that the commute took thirty minutes when the traffic was going speed limit. If there was a jam, his commute took an hour. (This was why, he told me later, he decided to walk—he actually got there faster. But that's a digression about a health decision, as well as a scheduling decision.)

If you worked at top speed, you could probably get the project done in a month. But top speed isn't always possible. In fact, top speed usually leads to mistakes and burnout.

At your slowest speed, barely working at all, you could get the project done in four months. But that would be dull and probably counterproductive, since most of us who work on deadline get paid as the deadlines get met.

So how to find a happy medium?

First, buy a calendar. Write in holidays, days off, and vacation days. If you have chronic health problems, as I do, plan for those as well. (I usually plan for an unscheduled week off somewhere in a quarterly schedule.) Put in personal time, like parent-teacher conferences, the kids' soccer matches, dinner and a date with your spouse. Those days are days away from work.

Then figure you can finish the project in 75 days of steady work (add the one month at top speed to the four months of slow speed and divide by two. That gives you 2.5 months or 75 days). Count backwards from your early deadline, skipping the days off and half days. Circle that date on your calendar. That's your drop-dead start date. Do not miss it. You might finish the project earlier than your early deadline. Good for you. You've just become reliable.

But you might have to struggle to meet your early deadline because—guess what? Life happens. If you're struggling, you have some time built into your schedule. But your drop-dead deadline is just that. Something you cannot miss.

Play whatever mind games it takes to make your schedule work. And *write it all down*. The early deadline, the start date, the time you think it will take to finish.

Because you might have to juggle everything if another deadline gets into the mix.

This happened to me in April. I agreed to write a story that would take quite a bit of research. The editor implied that the story would be due in June. When I asked for his actual deadline, he gave me May 15. I looked at that, looked at my already-crammed schedule, and realized that I would have to work late into the night to get it done. But I could do it, research and all. It meant that I had to shave some things out of my schedule—mostly, following the news (which I do obsessively). No morning newspaper. No evening newscasts. No peeking at news websites. I took to listening to NPR on my iPhone because the app let me download and listen in the middle of the night if need be, or when I was taking out the garbage or feeding the cats.

I adjusted a few other deadlines closer to their drop-deads than I liked. And I didn't write ahead on the *Freelancer's Guide*, for instance, although I had planned to. But I managed to make it work. I got it all done, and done well.

I would have had to turn the editor down, though, if I hadn't already had extra time built into my schedule. And I would have lost some significant revenue.

Do what it takes to set up your internal schedule. I use calendars and computerized reminders. I also maintain a daily, weekly, and monthly to-do list. I frequently look ahead at my list, so that I make sure I'm on track.

I work on a project basis—sometimes working 12-hour days, sometimes working 6-hour days. (Occasionally slacking with 4-hour days). Others work on an hourly schedule. They sit at their desks from 9 to 5 just as they would if they had a day job. Or they give themselves a certain number of tasks to complete each hour.

That minute level of scheduling is an individual thing. But there are two things that must be absolute:

1. Your schedule must help you complete work.

That sounds so elementary. But if I had an hourly schedule, I'd subvert it and get nothing done. I learned that a long time ago. However, I love to finish things, so I try to finish as many projects as possible in the space of a year. I also like to challenge myself, so I make sure most of the projects are outside my comfort zone.

Long ago, I defined the things I could not cut from my schedule. An hour for meals. (Half an hour for lunch, if need be.) Reading. Exercise. A good night's sleep. An hour of TV per night. I could jettison those things, but not for long. Those were absolutes. And if I skipped some, like exercise and sleep, I wouldn't be effective at my job. So there are times I eat at my desk, but I skip an hour of

85

TV before I skip my daily run. (Dammit.) You have things like that too. Be honest about them. That'll help you keep your schedule and meet your deadlines.

2. You must enforce your schedule.

Just like that business owner who let his employee arrive late every day for a year (!), you risk losing control of your business if you think of a schedule as a suggestion rather than something written in stone. You'll run from crisis to crisis like that publisher I mentioned, instead of completing good and productive work on time.

Not to mention the fact that if you use a schedule as a suggestion instead of a structure, you'll be in a constant state of panic. Everyone from your suppliers to your creditors to your clients will be angry with you for neglecting one or another detail. Your business will suffer, even if you thrive on conflict. And, ultimately, you'll end up hating the job you created for yourself.

A schedule is as essential to a business as the skeleton is to the human body. Often outsiders can't see the schedule—or just get hints of it—but they'd know if it were missing. A human being would be a packet of flesh and fluids without the skeleton. A business is just a bunch of good intentions without the structure provided by a schedule.

Figure out your schedule—both internal and external. Refine it as time goes on. Figure out what works for you and what doesn't. Then implement it. Make sure that the people around you know about the schedule *and respect it*. You have to respect it as well. It's the thing that will make or break your business.

Why do you think I hadn't missed in seventy-one weeks of the *Freelancer's Guide? Schedule*, my friends. Some weeks, it was the only thing that got me to the computer—despite being tired or cranky or just plain reluctant. It got me to the computer tonight, even though I would much rather be working on a new project that has me all excited, or reading those five new pre-ordered books.

I have time for both of those things in my schedule. And I can get to them now, since this week's work is done.

Chapter Nine
Deadlines

Here's the problem with waiting until the last minute to do something: the day arrives and it is the worst possible day to do that thing. Take today, for example. I have a migraine, I didn't sleep much, it's the hottest day of the year so far, and we're moving. In fact, we slated today to do a lot of the major moving, so I've been picking, lifting, walking, and cleaning for the past six hours with only one break for dinner, which I *inhaled.*

I'm still cleaning—as I write this, the washing machine is humming and so is the dishwasher (with its third load)—because once you move something from Point A to Point B, you realize just how dirty Point A has gotten, and how you couldn't stomach putting that thing away in Point B until the thing is clean. So there will be more picking, lifting, walking, and cleaning tomorrow but at least tomorrow, I don't have to end the day writing this.

If I fall asleep while writing this…well, you'll never know, except that the "Gone Fishing" notice will be on the website tomorrow. The greater danger is that my brain will shut off, which it does with an audible clunk (at least, it's audible to me). Then you will notice, because my aphasia will kick in, and while I'll have perfectly spelled words in this piece, they won't be the right ones in the right order.

Normally, I work ahead of the deadline. I thought of doing that this week, considering we had the move today, but I figured I wouldn't need to do so. I hadn't counted on six-plus hours, a migraine, and heat. (Well, to the rest of you: warmth. It rarely gets above 70 here, and today it did. So for us, that's hot. For most of you in August, that's cool.) I didn't plan as well as usual.

I have had a couple of deadline issues this week. Writing isn't a science—if it were, every publishing company would only publish bestsellers. I always plan to revise or redraft (write new from scratch) whenever I turn in an assigned piece. So I try to turn in those pieces early, just in case something goes wrong.

This past week, my strategy paid off. I turned in a story which the editor hated. It's a damn fine story, but oh, did it miss the anthology's mark. It's already in the mail elsewhere. But now, I have to write an entirely new, more suitable story for that anthology. If I had pushed the deadline as I have with this column, I would have missed out entirely. I wouldn't get my second (or third) chance at the anthology.

Instead, I turned in my story two months early—three, if you figure that most editors build in a month's lag time for those silly writers who are always late. I will get my second chance.

There are other benefits to meeting a deadline early. One of my writer friends turned in her second series novel on time. Some other writer missed a deadline, so my friend's novel has been moved on the publishing schedule to a much better publication date.

Another benefit? More work. Often, I get extra work because I write well, quickly (some writers don't), and I meet deadlines. So, remember those writers I mentioned who are always late? If one of them misses a short story deadline, and the anthology editor still needs to fill space, he calls me. Sometimes I will have two and three stories in an anthology under various (and occasionally secret) pen names, mostly because other writers can't seem to get off their butts.

(Which might be a problem for me tonight as well, considering how my muscles have started seizing up.)

So, since I'm thinking about deadlines, let's take a look at them and how they apply to all freelancers.

In some professions, deadlines are easy. In retail, the only deadlines that happen every day are your opening and closing times. It's important to hold fast to those times, because you'll lose customers who get disgusted when you're not open at 10:00 a.m. (as you said you'd be) or have closed two hours early because you got bored. That's the quickest way to kill a retail business.

The other deadlines in retail don't apply to all shops. If you celebrate the holidays, then you need to get your holiday merchandise out by a particular date. (As I write this, the "holiday" is Back to

School, and all the shops are stocked with notebooks and pens and backpacks and gadgets that didn't even exist when I was in school. There will be a short breather (very short) and then the Halloween stuff will appear, and I will have to guard my pocketbook, because I tend to buy little ghostie and vampiry doodads by the dozens (and I don't want to move them from one place to another).)

Book retailers have to place new books out on the publication date—not before, and not after. Some books get embargoed, meaning the bookseller isn't even supposed to open the box until the day of publication. But those are usually highly anticipated books, and who can blame the bookseller for taking a peek for his own personal reading pleasure? Certainly not me.

But, for the most part, the deadlines in retail are the same deadlines that other businesses have: paying the bills, the employees, and the taxes on time. Otherwise, if you own your own shop, you work in a relatively deadline-free environment.

I can't think of many other professions that can claim that. Of course, many of those professions have a different name for the deadline. Doctors and dentists have appointment schedules. Deadlines don't come into play unless treatment needs proper timing.

Lawyers also have appointment schedules, but they also have real deadlines, particularly if they are trial lawyers. The court sets the deadlines and a lawyer misses them at his (and his client's) peril. That's why trial lawyers can disappear from their daily lives for months at a time as they prepare witnesses, go over evidence, and plan strategy for the really big trials. And many lawyers don't sleep much during that time either, because the lawyer has to be in his chair when court begins in the morning or he faces punishment from the judge for delaying everyone else.

A lot of professions have non-performance penalties. If you're a tax accountant and you miss filing deadlines, you can get fined. Contractors have time-overruns built into their bids, but if they go too far over, they risk fines or penalties or loss of revenue from the client.

Some professions are constrained by time on both ends. A contractor can't work 24/7 on a project, as Dean did on one writing deadline. The law doesn't allow it, for one thing (most towns have ordinances prohibiting noise during the hours between 11:00 p.m. and 7:00 a.m.), and generally speaking, the client wouldn't like it either. Not to mention the union regulations and the labor law restrictions on many folks who own their own businesses.

So when contractors bid on a project, they have to know reasonably well how much time that project will take. The deadlines matter for the client—so the client knows when he'll have use of his kitchen again, for example—and for the contractor. The contractor doesn't have just one client. He'll want to bid on other jobs that will follow this one. Let me tell you from experience, there's nothing more annoying than a contractor who can't get to your job because he hasn't finished the previous job yet.

Some professions, like mine, allow you to complete the job early. Those professions are like mine in more ways than one: our work is generally subjective. Architects deal with this. One wag, writing about New York City, mentioned that in New York, large projects have a pattern: The idealistic project, the sacrificial project, the realistic project, and the actual project. The idealistic project, he said, is the one that gets the ball rolling—the one that allows property to change hands, and the city government to change the ordinances. The sacrificial project is the one everyone likes, but is impractical. It might actually get underway, but gets stalled by lawsuits from former landowners or neighbors who hate the idea of anything going into that neighborhood. The realistic project is, then, the compromise between the first two—the one that the lawsuits settle on, the one that fits the land use designs. The realistic project is often so ugly that someone decides to hire one more architect to get one more design. And that design is always the actual project, because by then, everyone is tired of the process and ready to move on to something else.

If the job is small enough, the same architect works on all four projects (and expects the pattern). If it's large enough, the job might provide work for two generations of architects over the lifetime of the project. All of those architects, however, meet deadlines, set by the client or the city or both. The project itself will then have deadlines and so will the court cases.

Deadlines are, no matter what your profession, a fact of life.

So, then, why do so many people miss those deadlines?

I'm not the person to ask. If you'll look at the next chapter on discipline, you'll see that I've been meeting deadlines since I was in broadcasting. (Hell, I met them before that—I was one of the annoying kids who got my homework done early.)

Everyone eventually will miss a deadline. Life intrudes. Illness strikes, emergencies happen. A friend who had a strict deadline got seriously injured at a work-related event and that injury turned into a life-threatening series of complications. So instead of meeting her deadline early, my friend was two months late. Had she waited until the last minute to start, however, she would have been six to eight months late. The fact that she could work at all with all of the health problems was a miracle in and of itself.

What do you do if you're going to be late? You inform the client the instant that you know. No excuses. You explain the reason for the tardiness and apologize. Sincerely. Then you set a new deadline.

If you're in a profession where no new deadline is possible (the judge refuses to change the court date, for example), you come up with another solution. You might have to give up the job and give it to someone else who is as (or more) qualified than you are.

But the bottom line is simple: you keep your client informed of your progress. You never, ever, disappear or go dark. You never miss the deadline and then apologize. You tell your client what the problem is, and what your solution will be. If you turn out to be wrong—if you're able to meet the original deadline—do so. If you overestimated how quickly the problem would end, tell the client the moment you know and change the deadline again. Offer a refund. Offer to find someone to replace you. Generally, the client will refuse because the client wants you for the job. But sometimes the client has needs you don't even know about, and the client can't wait for you. Nor should he have to.

Accept that missed deadlines happen and plan for them. If you have the kind of business that takes half the payment on the beginning of the project and half on completion, realize that you might have to repay that first payment if you miss the deadline. (Or repay a percentage of it.) Try not to spend that payment before the job is done.

(This is why so many professions separate costs out by time. You pay by the hour, with a retainer up front. Or you pay expenses *and* the cost of the job. Expenses happen no matter what. The cost of the job might have to be repaid if the deadline doesn't get met.)

I've mentioned deadlines in previous chapters. I've stressed how important they are, and I'm sure you've nodded, agreeing with me, knowing that I'm right, the way your teacher is right when she wants the assignment on time.

But deadlines are more complicated than that. Because in the real world, deadlines add up to only one thing: your reputation. If you meet your deadlines, you have a good reputation. If you're early, you have a sterling reputation. If you're chronically late, no matter how good your actual work is, you'll have a bad reputation.

A freelancer with a bad reputation eventually becomes someone else's employee. In other words, a bad reputation will cost you your business. And the quickest way to ruin your own reputation is to consistently miss your deadlines.

I'm a few sentences away from meeting my deadline tonight. Self-imposed, yes. But worthwhile all the same. In some ways, I see these posts as an appointment with those of you who visit every week. Some of you visit as soon as I post, and some of you straggle in throughout the week. But you know I'll have something new on the site when you click to it.

That matters to me. It matters enough that I'm sitting in my office to the music of the dishwasher and washing machine (and now, the dryer) as I play Bach loud enough to wake the dead—or at least to keep me awake as I type this.

Keep your deadlines. Be on time for your appointments. Open your stores on time and don't close them early. Respect your clients. Then they'll respect you in return.

Chapter Ten
Discipline

I don't want to write this chapter. I have half a dozen reasons—some of them very good—as to why. First, my chronic illness has flared this week, so I'm struggling against my health. Second, Thursday is one of my annual days off, and I usually post the Guide on Thursday. If I were working a regular job, this day off would be on my calendar—and would have been since before I was hired. Third, I am moving my office and it looks like this week is D-Day for the desk, computer, printer, and calendar, the very things I use to write 95% of the time.

Those are the good reasons. Here are the whiney reasons: First, my office cat died two weeks ago. I really don't like going into my office when she's not there. Second, I gave up my non-fiction career for a reason twenty-three years ago. I don't like writing non-fiction. It's work. Fiction, on the other hand, is fun. Third, I've been doing this *Guide* for a while now and it's no longer new (or as my husband would say, it's not bright and shiny), so it's become a chore—something with a deadline that must be met, instead of something I look forward to doing.

I might admit the whiney reasons to friends. But here are the final reasons, the ones that come up when I'm tired and not feeling well, like today. First, I'd rather be reading. (Honestly, I'd always rather be reading.) Second, I want cake. (That's Thursday.) Third, I want to watch the news. And get e-mail. And go on Twitter. And surf the net. And, and, and….

I don't want to be sitting in my empty office, groggy from a nap that only left me feeling marginally better, writing part of a book that isn't under contract and might never be.

So why am I here?

Because I anticipated this day. Seriously. I knew this day was coming. And I planned for it.

Here's why I'm sitting in my empty office, groggy from a nap that left me feeling only marginally better, writing part of a book that isn't under contract.

You.

I have met my deadline on the *Freelancer's Guide* every week since April second. I post, you make comments and e-mail me. Some of you have donated to the *Guide*, and some of you have subscribed, so I have a very real obligation to hit the mark, week after week, until this project is done.

That's the main reason. In fact, that's the only reason I'm here this week.

That reason negates all the complaints I had in the first paragraph.

But the complaints in the second—the ones I call the whiney reasons—have come up before. And despite the fact that two of them sound project-specific, they're not. They come up, with different rationales, with every single project I work on.

I would always rather start a new project than work through the middle of another project. And the *Freelancer's Guide* is in the muddy middle. How far into the middle, I can't tell you. I can never estimate easily how much material I have left.

Besides, I love beginnings. Not the actual moment of work, which can be hard as I try to figure out how to approach the project, but grooming the idea and preparing it for the actual writing. That bright and shiny part of writing is appealing to me, and I always have more than one project going just to keep that bright and shiny part of my brain occupied.

I also work well at the end of a project. Gone are the days when I'd just skip the end. (I got tired of Dean looking at me and saying, "You skipped the last 10,000 words *again*.") When I know how something will end, I want it finished, and I work harder to get it done so that I can move on to the bright and shiny new thing.

Then there's the daily battle against "I want to read" and "I want to eat" and "I want to see a movie/news/TV." The battle against "I want to be doing something else, something that sounds fun, because right now, this project isn't fun."

Or as I usually say to someone who complains on television (and dammit, they can't hear me), "Wah."

Discipline gets a freelancer past all the complaints, but it's not the discipline you imagine from all those movies about military school or from watching Tiger Woods' (pre-divorce) interviews about his dogged determination to be the first on the course and the last to leave.

Discipline gets the job done, as Malcolm Gladwell noted in his controversial book, *Outliers.* The musicians who put in more practice hours have more success than those who put in fewer hours. Same with athletes, and same with writers and almost everyone else in the arts. Both Bill Clinton and Barack Obama spent more time on the campaign trail in their initial successful Presidential bid than any of their opponents did—both in hours per day, and days per week.

But *how* did they do that? How do some musicians, playing the same instrument with the same intensity as other musicians, manage to hit the practice room more often? Why does Tiger Woods work harder than *every other professional golfer* on the course—especially since he says, quite frankly, that it's the hours of practice that make him the golfer he is.

Let's stick with Tiger for a moment. My husband used to be a professional golfer, so golf is important to our household, and Dean has more insight than most about the sport. We've watched Tiger since he won the U.S. Amateur competition in the 1990s. Dean told me then that this kid would be a phenom, and he is.

More than a decade later, Tiger Woods can rest on his laurels, but he doesn't. He won the U.S. Open in 2008, playing for four days with a destroyed knee and a cracked bone. Golf days last six hours or so, and golf, for those of you who don't play or follow the sport, hurts knees more than any other part of the body because of an unnatural twisting motion that the golfer must make when he swings.

It takes discipline to go to that course every day in extreme pain, but you see it not just in Tiger Woods, but also in most athletes at the pro level. It's so bad in most professional sports that teams have doctors on stand-by to order a badly injured player off the court/field so that the injury will not become permanent and career ending.

What causes this attitude? Sportscasters call that "heart," but it's more than heart. We've all seen high school players with heart, players who will give their all when the time comes to win the big game.

But it's not the big game that matters. It's the practice. It's sitting down to play scales for the 50,000[th] time because you need to warm up your hands before getting to Mozart. It's the drudgery of the same thing every day, with no defined ending.

It's the ability to overcome the urge to grab the bright and shiny and interesting to finish what you've started.

It's—and I'm sorry to say this, folks—it's what gets you to your day job five days per week, fifty-two weeks per year.

The problem is that most people don't apply that same discipline to their freelance work. There are reasons for this, which I'll get to. And, before the comments come in, let me add that I do realize that most people at a day job are not working at their best. Maybe they never do as well as they could. Many never reach their full potential. Most don't even try.

So what is it that makes some people work hard at their freelance careers while others work hard enough to get by or can't figure out a way to work at all?

It's not discipline. It's figuring out how to get yourself to work.

Seriously. What gets most people to their day jobs isn't the job. It's the money they get from the jobs, money that lets them pay their bills and support their families. Sure, a handful *like* their work, but most like the paycheck and benefits better.

Here's the problem: there are no paychecks and benefits when you work for yourself. If that's your motivation for working, then you're not going to have much luck freelancing—providing you carry that motivation into your freelance work.

Let's boil it down a bit more. When you begin freelancing, you do it for the love. Often you wait for the muse or until you get an order or if a friend asks for your help with something that you're good at. Eventually, you make some money at this, and then you realize you might be able to make a living at it.

Already bad habits have formed. You start doing this as a hobby, *after* everything else of importance gets finished. It feels natural to do the freelance work last.

Other things are always important. Your daughter skins her knee, the phone rings, a friend needs help moving. You have to learn to make your hobby, or the thing you did only when you "had time," become your first priority.

How do you do that?

Unfortunately, I can't tell you. What you need to do is specific to you. There is no magic bullet, no one-size-fits-all answer.

But let me give you some ideas, based on my own experience.

And as I typed those words, I heard my writing friends giggle. They are all convinced that I'm the most disciplined person they know. They're wrong. In most things, I lack discipline entirely.

Unlike most of my writing friends, I have not held a full-time job for years. Why? Discipline. At some point, the paycheck isn't enough for me. I hate having someone tell me what to do, and that always triumphs.

Even the radio job that I loved didn't last long. I quit four separate times. Each time the station hired me to be *interim* news director, at my insistence. I didn't want the permanent job. So I stayed until someone new came on board, and came back as interim director when that someone new left. I remained at the station in between *as a volunteer*, working a few nights per week. But I didn't want to be an employee there. The only thing that broke that years-long cycle, by the way, was my move out of town.

Discipline has always been a major issue for me. I get bored easily, and I don't play well with others. So hiring a personal trainer, for example, would never work for me. I would do my best to circumvent anything the trainer told me.

In my forties, I had a piano teacher. I stayed until I learned how to play the instrument adequately. Then I realized I was seeing how much practice it actually took to convince the teacher I had spent days at it instead of an hour or two. Once I fooled her a few times, we were done.

This is why I never became a musician. I didn't have the discipline. And I love music. At one point in my life, I played 15 different instruments. (Only two of them really well.) I just don't love music enough to conquer my discipline problem.

I love writing enough to work through each issue as it comes up. How? By figuring out what stopped me from getting a day's worth of work involved.

Each time I solved one issue, another cropped up. Then I would have to solve that one. This pattern continues to this day.

When I discuss this with students, I tell them that gaining discipline is a series of mind games. Your mind will find good and effective ways to stop you. You have to figure out ways around them. The old cliché about when a door closes, go through a window applies here.

I can sense the frustration among you now. I'm not being specific enough to help. So let's go back through my initial points, above, and I'll tell you how I get around them. Maybe that will strike a chord.

First, health issues. I'll deal with this more in the illness chapter below. But in short, here's what helps me. I imagine making my excuses to a boss. If a good boss would let me go home sick or encourage me to stay away from the office, then I stay away from the computer. But if I can put in a day of so-so work, I do. I store up projects for days when my illness is present, but not so bad that I have to spend the day in bed. Those are the projects I do when I'm not feeling well.

Second, my annual days off. I have a few of them—birthday, anniversary, Christmas, and a couple of others. If I don't take those days, I'm angry at myself. Sometimes I take an entire week around it. That's just reasonable for any job. There's more on this in the chapter about vacations below.

Third, moving my office. I haven't done that for years. It's a good excuse not to work, except that I have deadlines, just as you would at a day job. I had to figure out a way to work while I'm in the middle of this transition. Because if it's not this transition, it's another transition. Life is full of them, and you have to figure out how to put in your freelance hours, even while everything changes around you.

But those are bigger events. It's the small ones that interfere with discipline. Let's address what I call the whiney complaints.

First, I would rather read. It took me an entire summer to figure out that reading, for me, will suck all my time out of every single day. I cannot start a book with breakfast or I will read until I go to bed.

How did I discover this? I had a day job that went part time. I opted to take the afternoons off. When the job had been full time, I read during my lunch break. So I continued this habit on the part-time schedule—and got nothing done.

I tried "disciplining" myself. I would put the book down and try to go to work, only to find myself reading again. "Disciplining"—forcing myself to quit—didn't work. No matter how hard I tried, I simply could not stop reading, even when I finished the book. I'd move to the next one.

So the key for me wasn't *quitting* reading. It was *not starting*. I set the books aside until I got x-amount of work done each day.

This isn't easy. It required actual hiding of the books. I enlisted my then-husband's help, making sure the books were out of sight.

Eventually, I learned that I worked hard and fast if I knew I could read when I was done. I got my work done, and then I read. Problem solved.

It sounds so easy, but it took months of trial and error. No amount of "forcing" myself got me to change my habits. I had to figure out where the problem started, and nip it in the bud.

Second, I want cake. (Don't we all?) That's usually a sign to me that I'm hungry. I need to figure out if I'm really hungry or—catch this—bored with what I'm doing. If I'm bored, I think I'm hungry, because that's one of the few things I will get up from my desk to deal with. If I need a meal, I eat. But my subconscious loves to trick me (and my hips) by convincing me to leave when I'm not through.

Often, the "I'm hungry" reaction comes when I'm working on something particularly difficult or something I don't want to do. Again, it took many months (and too many calories) to figure this one out. Now, before I get something to eat, I ask myself this: do I like what I'm working on? If the answer is no, I generally stay at my desk.

Note that I do not ask myself if I'm hungry. I've already identified hungry, and the answer would be yes. But I figured out that my subconscious has learned a mind game to convince me to get away from the computer, one that makes me think I'm hungry (or craving food, like cake) and gets me to leave *when I don't need to*.

We all have mind games like this, and they're hard to identify. The question should always be: is work going well? Because if it is, and I'm hungry, I have trouble tearing myself away. If it isn't, I'll make up any damn reason to leave my desk.

Third, I want to watch the news, download e-mail, look at the internet, do Twitter….in other words, do something else entirely.

This was almost as bad for me as reading was. I learned to keep my office spare. My computer has internet access and it also has e-mail access. I have shut those programs down. I've tossed away all games that were initially on my computer. There is no phone or television in my office. I have a stereo and a radio turned to a classical channel. No news of any kind allowed here.

Why? Because they all distract me. Rather than "discipline" myself to overcome the temptation, I remove the temptation entirely. In order to download my e-mail, I have to go to a different computer, one with an existing e-mail program, and download from there. I need to go to a different room to watch television. I can't even hear the phone ring in my office.

These were all tough things to learn. The internet is particularly sneaky because you feel like you're working when you're online. You are not working—even if, like me, a small part of your business comes through the internet. You're not doing your core business. I have a number of writing friends who refuse to remove the internet from their computer. Those friends get very little done. All of them have spouses who work, and so the writer doesn't have to bring in a lot of money. All of them frown at me when I suggest removing the internet from their writing computer.

Everyone has these leaks, as the poker players call them. A leak is something that drains your income, something that has nothing to do with your work. And it's often something you're not willing to give up.

You have to learn how to control this leak and make it work for you. And, here's the tough part: if you can't control it, seek help. I went into therapy a number of years ago to help with one of my writing issues, something that got in the way of my business. And much as I hate authority, I listened to that counselor, because being a successful writer meant more to me than the leak.

However, had we worked on my discipline issues with music, I probably would have blown off the therapy within weeks. I have never had the discipline there, and I really don't want it. Not deep down.

And that's the final issue. If you want a successful freelance career of any kind, you'll overcome the things that get in your way. You can't do it all at once. You have to tackle one problem at a time. But you're willing to work on those problems.

If you're not willing to solve the problem after years of trying, then you probably don't want this freelance career (whatever it is) as much as you think you do.

Discipline is not about forcing yourself to improve. It's about wanting to get better.

That's the difference between Tiger Woods and all those other golfers. Tiger wants to be the best, and he knows the only way to do that is to work harder than everyone else. But he doesn't define that as the best *right now*. He means the best *ever*. He keeps Jack Nicklaus's stats on his wall, trying to beat them. Tiger's not playing the current field. He's playing the entire field from the dawn of recorded golf history.

And he's doing a good job at knocking down the records.

But here's the key. He's not doing this for his fans. He's not doing it for his (late) father or for golf history. He's doing it for himself. Because he wants to. Because that's his goal.

So...

How do you get disciplined?

Here are a few thoughts.

1. Define what you want to achieve.

Not other people's goals for you. Not what your parents want or your spouse wants. What do you want? And how badly to do you want it? Will you die disappointed if you don't achieve it? Will you feel like a failure? Or will you shrug and move on to the next thing?

2. Make a list of the things that are in the way of that achievement.

If everything you list comes from the outside, then you have another problem. For example, writers often say they can't get published because the publishing industry is impossible to crack or they need an agent or they can't figure out how to submit their work. Those, my friends, are excuses. Other people have succeeded in your industry. Figure out how they did it, and then try it yourself.

By "what gets in the way," I mean what part of *you* gets in the way. What are you doing to block your success? How do you change that? Sometimes the change is minor, like asking yourself whether you are really hungry or you are avoiding work. Sometimes the change is major, like the one thing I mentioned (deliberately vaguely) that forced me to go to therapy. I couldn't change that one on my own—but it was *my* problem, and I had to find a solution. I just needed help doing so.

3. Change your thought patterns.

When you decide to go full-time freelance, realize that your hobby has just become your job. That realization alone will take time. Then figure out how to make your freelance work a priority in your own mind. Apply patterns from your day job to your freelance work.

Ask these questions:

-- What made you go to your day job every morning?
-- What made you stay there?
-- What made you work on days when you felt crummy?
-- What made you work on days when you had somewhere better to go?

And so on. Use those answers to design your freelance work.

For example, my husband Dean works hard when he's under deadline. He has trouble working when he has no deadlines at all. The key for him is to create deadlines—or to get someone from the outside (an editor, usually) to give him a deadline.

I didn't think I had that issue until I started the *Freelancer's Guide*. Then I realized that I never finish non-fiction unless I have a deadline. I don't like writing non-fiction. I love writing fiction and will do it without a deadline. But the deadline gets me to finish non-fiction projects—my two columns, some articles, and now this.

By meeting my deadline on this *Guide* every week, I've also established something else. I've got a streak going. I hate breaking streaks, so that's motivation to work on weeks like this one, when I could just as easily post a note that the *Guide* is on a one-week hiatus.

I learned long ago that I have to love what I'm doing to sustain the work. I loved working at the radio station, but hated it when I was in charge. So I kept quitting the paying work to go back to volunteering.

I love writing fiction, so I continue to do it, even when times are tough.

When I need to be disciplined, I have to find the love at the center of what I'm doing. Here's an example. I have tried to maintain a regular exercise program since middle-aged spread hit in my mid-thirties (thanks in part to that hunger thing, above).

I started with an exercise I love, swimming. But it was inconvenient. I had to drive half an hour each way to the pool. The hours were irregular, and I'd often lose too much work time. So I started riding my bicycle. I enlisted the help of a friend from the gym. I had to meet her at a designated time every day. That got me out of the house.

We couldn't sustain the rides. Then I fell off the bike and broke my arm, the second serious bike accident in my life. (The first, when I was nine, smashed my face so badly, I still have occasional dental surgeries to repair the damage.) I realized that cycling on the Oregon Coast along a highway with no bike lanes (there are none for more than 100 miles) is too dangerous for me.

So I decided to run. When I made this decision, I couldn't run for a minute without feeling ill. I didn't like it. I had never liked running. Worse, I got bored quickly.

But I love music. If a song that I like comes on the radio, I crank the volume. If I'm alone in the house, I dance. So I put my favorite CDs on my iPod, and promised myself I could run for the length of one song.

I couldn't, not for weeks. Eventually I managed. But I wasn't running because I liked running. I was using that time as an excuse to listen to my favorite music all by myself.

Two years later, I can run for 30 minutes straight. When I feel like it's time to find a new form of exercise, I realize it's time to change the music in my iPod. I'm bored with what's there. I would rather swim, honestly. I would like to be on my bike. But running works for me now. And I've become so conditioned to it that last week, when my iPod battery died, I played some music in my head and finished the workout.

Could I do that every time? Hell, no. But I know how to make myself go out for a daily run now—and how to enjoy it. Set the iPod on shuffle and see what songs come up.

It took me fifteen years to find a form of exercise I can do every day, rain or shine, one that I *will* do. And what gets me out there now isn't the exercise or the need for it.

It's the half hour of music. Which I love.

So the most important aspect of discipline isn't discipline at all. It's this:

4. Find the love.

Find what you love about what you do, and channel that each and every day. Acknowledge it, too. When I finish a run, I check in with myself. Inevitably, I feel better when I quit than I did when I started. I've told Dean that, and sometimes he's gotten me outside by reminding me of it. (I have to tell you, it sometimes pisses me off that I feel better *after* a run, when I felt so crummy before the run.) Celebrate your achievement, even if that achievement is just getting to your desk.

Celebrate with something you enjoy.

I used to celebrate a day's writing by reading. Then I started editing, and reading ceased to be a reward for several years. In those years, I celebrated with a good movie or a guilty-pleasure TV show. Now I'm back to celebrating with reading.

Which is what I'm going to do now.

Oh, by the way, I'm no longer groggy from the nap, although I still feel under par. I did run today, and felt better afterwards (dammit!). And I got this chapter of the *Guide* done, two days early. I'll post it late tomorrow, which will be one day early. Then I'll get my day off. With cake.

That's my reward, along with all the fun things planned for that day.

And that was more than enough to get me into my chair today—even though I didn't want to be here.

Chapter Eleven

Illness

How do you know when you're too sick to work? Seems easy enough to figure out, right? We're all adults. We know when we're sick. But for freelancers, that's a tougher question than it seems.

We all get sick. The serious things—pneumonia, bronchitis, certain types of flu—leave us too ill to get out of bed. They're not the problem to the freelancer. The milder illnesses are.

When you work for someone else, it's easy to know when to go into work. If you had one of those cushy jobs with paid sick leave and paid vacation, chances are you took more sick days than you needed. If you were feeling a little off, and you had the paid time coming to you, you took the day and stayed home. Even seasonal allergies might have warranted a little paid "me" time.

If you had a by-the-hour job without those benefits, you took as little time off as possible. At my last waitressing job, the boss actually had rules about when *not* to come to work. ("If you're contagious," she'd say, "you must stay home.") People who work by the hour usually need the money. They come to work when they can barely walk because they don't dare lose the hours.

Freelancing is closer to the by-the-hour job, but it's not quite the same. When you freelance, you get paid for piecework. In other words, the more things you finish, the more you get paid.

You finish more things if you put in more hours.

Seems obvious, right? But most people aren't used to being their own boss. Most people are too lenient with themselves. They lose entire days to headaches or the sniffles because they're not feeling "up to par." Days, even weeks, go by while the freelancer waits to feel better.

Here's an ugly truth: *When you work at home, you have no colleagues to distract you. You're constantly assessing how you feel, and always coming up short.*

That's right. You'll probably feel worse day-to-day when you work at home. Some of it is the solitude. Some of it is the lack of exercise. Some of it is the lack of fresh air.

When you go to a job away from home, you have to walk outside and drive somewhere. When I started freelancing, I'd stay in the house for days on end. It took me a while to realize that a walk around the block was often enough to make me feel energetic and healthy.

So…how *do* you know if you're too sick to work?

It's simple. Imagine the toughest boss you ever worked for. Then imagine telling him (and my toughest boss was a man) that you can't come into work today because…and fill in the reason here.

If you can't imagine yourself telling Tough Boss that reason, then you go to work.

It goes like this: "Hi, Tough Boss. I can't come to work today because I have a temperature of 102 and I'm heading to the doctor this afternoon."

Fine, good. My old Tough Boss would have let me out for that.

But imagine this one: "Hi, Tough Boss. I can't come to work today because I'm feeling sluggish."

Or…

"Hi, Tough Boss. I can't come to work today because I didn't get a good night's sleep last night."

Or…

"Hi, Tough Boss. I can't come to work today because I'm not thinking as clearly as I usually do."

One or two of those with the Tough Boss I'd had (back in 1980—this dude really lives in my memory) and I would've been fired. Fast.

A friend once told me that people who work at corporate jobs aren't productive every moment of every day. They talk to their colleagues on company time. They daydream. They do make-work to look busy. This friend was a corporate manager who estimated that a good 40% of the time, his employees weren't working at their peak.

On the days they came in feeling "sluggish" or "tired," they probably got less done.

When you work for someone else, you get used to days like that. You know you won't get fired (unless you have other problems with job performance). Your employer knew that was part of the deal when he decided to hire employees in his business. Every self-employed person knows that the hardest worker in the company is always the boss.

On those days when you would go into work with a mild cold or allergies, you did what you could. Sometimes, you got brownie points just for showing up and keeping your desk warm.

I was so used to working for myself that when I got my single full-time job back in 1984, I caused a huge stir in the office. I worked as an editorial assistant in a textbook publishing house. I got my day's assignments and usually finished them within the first hour of my eight-hour shift.

The other editorial assistants pulled me aside after a week of that and told me to slow down because I was making them look bad. I didn't get it. I figured I was there to *work*, so I worked. I could have done the work of all the editorial assistants and filled up my day. But that wasn't the corporate structure. So I did my hour's worth of work, and spent the remaining seven hours reading the books the company published. My boss promised to promote me if someone in editorial quit. Which no one had for nearly two years. After four months of that, I left the job because I was horribly, unbelievably bored.

(Years later, I got a great part-time job as a secretary for a forensic psychologist. He looked at my resume and said, "My biggest concern about you is that you're used to working for yourself. I'm hiring you to sit and answer phones. I'm afraid you might get bored." I told him about my experience at the textbook publisher and we both laughed about it. Then he agreed that I could write or read at my desk when he had nothing for me to do. Needless to say, that was the best day job I ever had.)

If you had one of those jobs that let you slack off with regularity, then freelancing is going to be a big shock for you. Unless you modify your behavior right now, you'll be one of those freelancers who gets nothing done for days on end, especially in spring allergy season or when the baby keeps you up all night.

No matter how dedicated you are, the reality is that there will be days when you feel sick, but not sick enough to stay home (from that imaginary Tough Boss). How do you do your best work when that happens?

Well, you don't. You figure out what tasks you can do. I'm writing this piece two days earlier than I planned because today, I'm surviving on Advil and caffeine.

I'm not thinking clearly enough to write fiction. So I'm doing tasks that I find easier than fiction writing. And yes, writing non-fiction is easier than fiction, at least for me. (Besides, I can always clean this chapter up later if I don't like what I've done.)

I've been feeling punk for three days now. I've photocopied contracts, put together files for a project that I'm working on with a publisher in Virginia, done research on the next story I'm writing, and cleaned up my office.

I know the pattern of my chronic condition, so I know that in a day or two, I'll be back up to my normal level of energy. Why waste my good days on tasks I can do when I'm not feeling up to par? I'm planning ahead by doing some of this work before it's due.

This is exactly what you would have done at your day job if you were feeling a little under the weather, but you still managed to show up. You'd have done the things you'd been putting off, things that required less effort than your daily tasks.

Just think of Tough Boss. Make your excuses out loud, and see if they'll fly with him. If they won't, then go to your office. Do what you can.

You'll be happy that you did.

Chapter Twelve
Burnout

Burnout is a difficult topic. Most people who suffer burnout don't see it coming, although their friends often do. In hindsight, the burnout looks inevitable. In the middle of the events that cause the burnout, it seems impossible.

First, let's talk about burnout itself. "Burnout" spelled as one word is a recent colloquialism used to describe a physical and psychological distinction. It's so new, in fact, that my favorite desk dictionary, *The Macmillan Contemporary Dictionary*, which I bought in 1979 while in college, doesn't list the one-word version. *Macmillan* says that "burn out" is to stop burning by lack of fuel (the fire burned out) or (second definition) to wear out due to heat or friction (the car's engine burned out).

Both are right if you think metaphorically, which is probably how this whole turn of phrase got started. Because, by the new century, burnout had become one word and it described a human condition: "psychological exhaustion and diminished efficiency," my *Encarta World English Dictionary* describes it, and says it results from overwork or prolonged exposure to stress. The synonyms include "to be used up."

Sometimes dictionary definitions are silly, but sometimes they're quite useful. I find these useful. Because to be burned out feels like you've been used up. It does result in diminished efficiency (such a bloodless phrase). If you think of it in terms of an engine, it does feel as if the engine has flamed out and there is nothing left.

I've been burned out a number of times in my life. I burned out at the radio station from sheer exhaustion. I got five hours of sleep per night. Normally I'm an eight-hour per night person. My husband and friends will tell you I'm unpleasant if I get six hours three days running. Imagine how unpleasant I was back then. I went on four to five hours of sleep for months. In those days, I didn't believe in naps. So I went to work at 5:00 a.m. for the 6:00 a.m. newscast, finished by 10:00, went out with the gang for breakfast, and walked home. Then I wrote non-fiction for three hours, and walked back to the station by 3:30 p.m. at the latest, to put together the 7:00 p.m. newscast. I left at 8:30, had dinner, watched a little TV, and tried to sleep by 11:00 p.m.

You'll note that there isn't a lot of downtime in that schedule. Nor did I take any days off. I wrote fiction on the weekends. In addition, I kept myself fueled through my normal afternoon energy low (which is now my nap time) by alternating caffeine and fudge on the half-hours. My addiction to both was so bad that when I retired (yep, another official retirement, this one at the age of 25), the crew gave me a *pallet* of fudge as a going-away present.

For years, I got tired just thinking of going back to radio. Whatever I had burned out hadn't been replaced.

I've had other burnouts, some much worse, one caused by a complete crisis of confidence in my writing combined with some very bad business decisions on my part. I also had health problems which didn't allow me to exercise which, I've learned, is a real key to my mental health. I remember working in that period, but it felt like I was working underwater—each movement slow and careful, my writing speed down to a tenth of normal.

I watched that working-underwater phenomenon happen to my husband Dean as our business Pulphouse Publishing collapsed in 1992. Dean had been working on the ragged end of exhaustion for nearly four years at that point, trying to do everything. Somewhere around 1990, we tried to hire a manager to take some of the burden off of him, but we couldn't find anyone competent whom we could afford. About 1991 or so, writer Christina F. York, a longtime friend, started giving Dean pamphlets and intervention materials on stress—what happens when you get stressed out, how to know which stage of stress you're in, the fact that stress leads to burnout—and Dean flung them aside. He knew that the burnout was coming; he just wanted to hold it off until he could afford to hire his own replacement.

That day never happened. Instead, a bad financial wave caused by the first Gulf War practically destroyed mail order in this country (and Pulphouse was primarily a mail order business). We compounded the problem by making bad financial decisions and we had to layoff the entire staff, everyone except Dean. I took the part-time editing job at *The Magazine of Fantasy and Science Fiction* to bring in a guaranteed monthly outside income.

Dean continued to work to save the business—or to save what he could of the business. His real goal was to prevent a bankruptcy because we didn't want to deal with the copyright issues. To make matters worse, his father died. So in the midst of grief for his father and grief for the loss of the business, in the midst of great stress, he had to try to get something done each and every day.

He could barely get out of bed, yet he managed. But I have vivid memories of him in this period moving like an eighty-year-old man with bad arthritis, forgetting where he was half the time as he tried to complete a task.

Burnout—when it happens—is real, and it takes you down hard. It happens to the strongest of us. (I call Dean my own personal Superman—he can keep up with 20-somethings in physical labor, even now, when he's three times their age.) In fact, it seems to happen to the strongest of us because we're the ones who don't rest when we need to, sometimes because we don't dare—we feel we'll lose what's important to us.

Dean's impending burnout at Pulphouse was obvious to everyone around him, but we couldn't figure out what to do about it. Years later, when I burned out, Dean tried to warn me it was coming. He saw the signs very clearly, but I didn't. I remember being surprised when the burnout finally happened.

So what are the signs of burnout?

1. Great physical exhaustion.

Not just a little tiredness, but the kind that prevents you from getting out of bed in the morning. Sometimes people who are this tired need to be hospitalized for exhaustion.

2. Emotional exhaustion.

People who are burned out feel like they can't deal with life the way they used to. Things that they might have ignored now make them angry. Extreme irritability, anger, negativity are all part of burnout. Also an inability to feel joy. The things that you used to enjoy are now burdens.

3. Pessimism.

Those of us who freelance are by nature optimists. We have to have hope or we wouldn't be able to do what we do. We might be cynics, we might seem a little rough around the edges, but at heart, we believe that things will always get better because if we didn't, we couldn't freelance. But in burnout, the optimism goes away. The world seems black. There is no hope. A once-hopeful person becomes an angry pessimist.

4. Inefficiency.

Someone who could get fifteen things done in an hour now can't finish any tasks. Work goes unfinished or simply forgotten. Fewer and fewer things matter—including work or once-beloved tasks.

5. Decreased social contact/ruined relationships.

Usually the relationships don't end because of a big dramatic scene, but because the burned-out person withdraws. Even in the closest relationships, like marriage, the burned-out person no longer has any interest in participating. Like everything else when you're burned out, relationships seem like too much work with very little point.

6. Increased illness.

You'd think that's just part of #4—a way of getting out of work. But study after study shows that the body under stress has a decreased immune response, so if a cold enters your town and you're burned out, you'll be one of the first people sick. My personal opinion is that it's the body's way of slowing you down; if it can't slow you down with exhaustion, it'll force you down. I don't know of studies to back that up, but I've seen it time and time again with my stressed-out, burned-out friends—and of course, it's happened to me.

If any or all of these things are going on in your life right now, you're burned out, and you'll have to make changes. Some of the changes are simple—but you'll have to force yourself to care enough to make them (which is hard).

To fight burnout, you need to:

1. Sleep eight hours a night.

Not ten, not eleven, because too much sleep over a long period of time can be as harmful as too little.

2. Eat well.

Nutritious food, not fudge on the half hour, but something small and healthy every few hours.

3. Exercise.

One thirty-minute walk per day will reduce your stress level, even if you don't have time to take the walk. Walk as you work on the problems in your life instead of sitting at your desk stewing about them.

Some experts on burnout recommend that you get rid of the thing that's stressing you the most—banish it from your life. Other experts say you shouldn't make important decisions when you're in crisis.

The problem for the self-employed is that our jobs burn us out. The Mayo Clinic has a great article on job-related burnout. (mayoclinic.com/health/burnout/WL00062). The article takes you through the symptoms, some of the causes, and suggests some solutions.

In this economy, however, those of us who have real-world jobs (jobs in which other people pay us) don't want to lose them. And those of us who work for ourselves might be struggling to keep our heads above water. Getting rid of our small businesses or changing jobs isn't an option.

So what do you do?

Figure out if the burnout is job related. It might be. If you own the business, you're in a position to make some positive changes. Money, or the lack of it, is often a huge stressor. See the section on money management for some help with that.

You might have some dysfunctional employees. Either change their behavior or get rid of the employees. Again, in this economy, it shouldn't be hard to find replacement workers.

Look at the other suggestions in the Mayo article: it might help you combat the work-related stress.

There's another factor in burnout that most people ignore: Success. While some of my burnout (and Dean's) has come from failure, most of it has come from success.

I can hear the chorus of *what?* from all of you. It's simple, really. When you're successful and you run your own business, you get busier. Because you've had lean times, you take as much work as you possibly can because you know lean times will come again. You'll work your tail off, and then some, trying to keep ahead of demand.

I burned out doing *F&SF* to the point where I—a voracious reader—didn't want to read a word. I only read for my job, and I was beginning to hate it. Fortunately, I could leave editing and did so with relief, although it took me years to be able to read for enjoyment again.

Dean burned out the year he got too many novel assignments and finished all of them—including five novels due in the month of May. It hadn't started out like that—he had taken a reasonable amount of work. But other people missed their deadlines and Dean was a fixer—someone who wrote novels when other people couldn't do the job—and he took on too many projects. Then one book got pushed back, two got pushed forward, and he had already had one due that month. Suddenly, he was writing all the time, not sleeping, and trying to keep up with everything else.

He wondered why he didn't feel like writing at the end of that year. I was amazed he could still move.

We were in a financial position with both of those cases of burnout—my *F&SF* burnout and Dean's big novel year burnout—so that we could take time off and assess what we wanted to do. I quit editing—it really and truly is not for me—and Dean eventually went back to writing, but on a saner and much more controlled schedule.

Not everyone is in the position to take time away and assess. Sometimes you have to make changes while in the middle of the burnout, and that's hard.

It's better to avoid burnout altogether. How do you do that? Well...

1. **Sleep eight hours a night.**
2. **Eat well.**
3. **Exercise.**

Seriously. You take care of yourself. But you also have to take care of your emotional health.

Go back to the earlier chapter on priorities. If you do everything in that chapter, you'll have a better chance of avoiding burnout. You'll know how to pace yourself throughout the day. In fact, a lot of chapters, from Priorities to Staying Positive to Discipline will help you prevent burnout.

Some of those things will help you even if you are burned out. One of the many websites on burnout recommends that you read inspirational texts. It doesn't mean that you read religious works (although that might help some of the believers among us), but books and articles by people who are upbeat or have succeeded in your chosen field. A study I saw recently said that people who listen to their favorite music for a half an hour per day are more upbeat than people who don't listen to music. I combine my music with my exercise, and it keeps me motivated. In fact, I don't worry about missing my exercise—I worry about missing my alone time with my iPod.

The best way to avoid burnout is to keep a balance in your life between work and play, between family and providing for that family. Find a way to maintain your joy in life, and have some downtime.

If you're already burned out, then you need to work on your recovery. Sometimes that takes professional help. A therapist got me through one of my worst periods of burnout. Sometimes all it takes is some judicious scheduling (including those personal hours) and an ability to say no to the wrong projects.

Burnout is a big problem. If any of the symptoms above sound familiar to you, you need to take care of yourself—before you end up in the hospital for exhaustion, before your good friends start giving you articles on the perils of stress, before you collapse completely.

People who run their own businesses are very vulnerable to burnout. If you're aware of that, you've take the first step toward preventing burnout.

You are a finely tuned machine, and the word burnout originated with machines; machines that eventually broke down because someone ran them too hard. You'll probably be vigilant against burnout when times are tough, but remember: you're more vulnerable to burnout when you're successful.

Plan accordingly—and take care of yourself. Your business will thrive if you do.

Chapter Thirteen
Vacations

When I discussed illness and the freelancer on my blog, the topic—which also dealt peripherally with taking time off—brought up another time-off question from several readers. Here it is, phrased by Jas. Marshall:

"When you're a freelancer, how do you take a vacation? When you are your own toughest boss, and you're pushing to produce more stuff so you can get paid, and so on…how do you justify even a single day off when 'I could be editing that novel to get it out the door' or whatever?"

When that question came in, I knew I was in trouble. Because I'm trying to keep this as general as possible about freelancing, not just freelance *writers*. Frankly, freelance writers are a different breed from other freelancers—and, I've been told, I'm a different breed than many freelance writers.

So I opened the question to freelancing friends on four different business e-mail lists that I'm on. The answers are self-selected (meaning this is not a scientific poll), but they're interesting and insightful.

What I asked is this: *A question for the freelancers on the list. When was the last time you took a real vacation?*

I deliberately did not define "real vacation," figuring people would do so for me. If their definition wasn't clear from their answers, then I sent a follow-up e-mail, asking how they defined real vacation.

I got some great responses. I couldn't use a few, however, because they came from people who did not freelance at all, but worked at a full-time job for corporations (usually in the arts). They felt slighted. "After all," they told me (rather grumpily), "not all

117

people with full-time jobs use their vacation time."—as I well know. My father never took his vacations nor did he use his sick days as long as he was a professor in the University of Wisconsin system (from 1967-1990; he retired at the age of 75).

But, as the original question implies, vacations and time off are tricky for freelancers. A friend of mine, who worked for decades as a freelance therapist, took at least two long vacations per year. She worked out of her garage, remodeled to be a comfortable space with an exterior door, and as a result, she rarely left home. Her work was so emotionally intense that if she didn't take time off on a regular basis, she would have burned out.

Then there's me. When I worked real jobs, I couldn't wait to get home so that I could read, write, and watch TV/movies (create and consume stories, as my husband says). Now I "work" every day at reading, writing, and watching TV/movies. When I travel, I'm storing up experiences for my work—and I'm usually reading and writing along the way.

My last (and only) real vacation came in 2005. I had had a series of health problems, some serious business setbacks, and some financial reversals. Suddenly a truckload of money came in, more than expected. Dean and I saved most of it, but we decided to spend a small fraction on a vacation. We meandered all over the West Coast. Our only deadline: tickets to see George Carlin in Las Vegas ten days from the day we left.

We explored, shopped, and saw friends. We bought books. We bought more books. I read books. I did not write. I slept. We visited casinos. Dean played poker. I read—and learned that people look at you strangely when you read books in casinos. We saw many different shows. We saw George Carlin perform what would later become his last HBO special.

It is the first (and only) time I have ever spent more than a week away from writing without going insane. That tells me just how exhausted I was.

Usually, however, I bring my laptop on any trip. I write. I read. I explore. I love visiting cities and seeing their history. But then I return to my hotel room and write about what I've seen. I *enjoy* this, and find it refreshing.

But that's me.

Now, let's hear from other freelancers.

First, the folks who do not make the bulk of their living writing (or editing) fiction:

Shanti Fader's freelance work includes proofreading, copy editing, transcriptions, online research, data entry, and jewelry-making. You can see her jewelry designs at tattedbutterfly.etsy.com.

"If you're talking about vacations taken from freelance work," she writes, "my last vacation was June of 2008, when I took off the weeks before and after my wedding. I told my regulars I wouldn't be available during those weeks, and didn't actively seek out any other work."

Glenn Hauman, who describes what he does as "whatever needs to be done" at the website comicmix.com writes, "'Vacation' is such a tricky word. There are lots of times I've spent an extra day in a city I had to go to because of a convention. Or in some cases, I'll drive, even though the convention is a good fifteen hours away by car. There are lots of times that I've had to scribble down a thought for later exploitation or take a photo for future reference. So if capturing an inspiration is work or taking the time to develop it out is work, then yeah. There are even vacation moments that turn into work—witness this year's Easter dinner which turned into three hours of tech support for a friend of my mother."

Randy Tatano, who works as a freelance broadcast news reporter, mostly for NBC, writes, "if I can't take vacations, you might as well shoot me. I'd rather cut back in other areas if I have to."

He and his wife generally take one or two trips a year. They just booked a trip to Europe for their 20th anniversary. He has advice for reporters at his blog, tvnewsgrapevine.blogspot.com.

Before Rick Dickson left his job as a liquidation consultant to become a full-time fiction writer, he took only one formal vacation in ten years. He describes his former consulting job like this:

"I was Richard Gere in *Pretty Woman*, except that I was hired by insurance regulators to pull apart dead insurance companies: find the money, prove where it went, and work to get it back. (Mostly profit-sharing, international fronting agreements, and reinsurance contracts.) Sadly, 'no,' I never got the girl."

As to why he took only one formal vacation, he says, "As a consultant, I had a lot of downtime between assignments. When you've got a job where the phone can ring at any time to the question, 'How fast can you be in **insert city name here**?', you need to consider these times to be vacation too. I did a lot of the local things…biking, hiking, flying, and playing tourist. The problem with scheduling a 'real' vacation was that I had to do that months in advance and always ended up needing to postpone due to a big client's emergency call (which meant those vacations never materialized)."

I can empathize. When Dean and I owned and operated our own publishing house, Pulphouse Publishing, we never had a real vacation either, although we traveled all over the United States. In those days, before cell phones were cheap and common, we would get off the airplane for a two-hour layover and spend most of that time on a pay phone. We spent a lot of time dashing from place to place, often to meet the needs of the business, and rarely with more than a few hours off.

Vacation time truly does depend on the type of freelancing you do. But most freelancers I know have the problems Rick and Shanti mentioned: Clients who expect the work done *now*. It takes a lot of juggling to get time away—even for your wedding.

Freelance writers, editors, and artists have other problems. We used to do this work for free in our time off.

As Gerald M. Weinberg, who has freelanced for more than fifty years, says, "By my definition, a vacation is an escape from work you don't want to do. According to my definition, I've been on a real vacation for a long, long time."

He's been spending his vacation time writing fiction and non-fiction. His most recent book is *Perfect Software: And Other Illusions about Testing*. You can find his many, many other publications and fascinating biography at geraldmweinberg.com.

He's not alone in this attitude toward freelancing. I share it. So does Laura Anne Gilman. Laura Anne used to be my book editor at Roc before she saw the light and gave it all up to write her own novels, the most recent being *Blood From Stone*. Check out her very excellent blog at lauraannegilman.net.

About vacations, she writes, "If you want the last time I took a vacation where I did no writing, no editing, nothing related to the day job, I think that was 2004. I was bored."

Dave Wolverton, who has written fifty novels under different names (the latest, *The Wyrmling Horde*), says, "I take a day off every few months, but I'd go nuts if I tried to take two days in a row. I have to be very sick to do that."

Dave keeps two websites in addition to all his other work — runelords.com and davidfarland.net.

Some writers aren't as happy about their lack of time off. Russell Davis, whose most recent novel (written as Cliff Ryder) is *The Ties That Bind*, wrote a succinct answer. He took his last real vacation in 1996 and, he editorializes, "that is pretty damn pathetic."

You can find his blog at westernsensibility.blogspot.com.

Some writers just flat out answered my question with dates and times. It amazes me how we can all remember that last "real" vacation—and how, for many of us, it was long ago.

Carole Nelson Douglas, whose most recent novel is *Brimstone Kiss*, writes, "My Last Vacation: February 1987, when my husband and I drove to Corpus Christi and South Padre Island after moving to Texas in 1984. We had to cut our vacation short and drive back to Fort Worth to get some sales figures my new publisher needed right away for a forthcoming book."

Carole also keeps two websites: carolenelsondouglas.com and dancingwithwerewolves.com.

Laura Resnick's answer was so succinct, I asked her to clarify. To my initial inquiry, Laura wrote, "July 2006." And that was it.

I responded: "No work, no writing at all? What kind of vacation?"

And she answered, "I stopped off in England for two weeks in July 2006, on my way home from Jerusalem. Spent the time visiting friends around the country. However, I did three days of on-site research for a book idea: We drove around, collected brochures, took photos, visited places of particular interest to me viz my short story idea. But I only count *writing* as work; I don't count touring a beautiful area with a particular agenda as work."

For my day-to-day business, as you'll see later, I only count words on the page as work too. But research is part of writing, and I would have counted Laura's trip as work. To each her own.

Laura, by the way, has written twenty books, including *The Purifying Fire*. She's on the web at LauraResnick.com.

Some writers couldn't remember the exact date of their last vacation. Irene Radford, who writes under various names (her latest novel *Faery Moon*, was written as P.R. Frost) and blogs at ireneradford.com, initially wrote that she and her husband Tim, "take day trips when I don't even look for bookstores to do drive-by signings. Other than that? Probably 1993 before I sold my first book."

But then, later e-mails revealed Irene to be in the same category as Dave Wolverton, Laura Anne Gilman, and I am. Irene said (and I love this), "Freelancing is as much a calling as a career. I cannot not write. I go insane if I'm not actively creating something in my head or on my computer. More than two days off and I start drifting away from conversations, seeing fictional landscapes instead of actual ones. My fingers itch for pen and paper or the touch of a keyboard."

While Irene wasn't exactly sure when her last vacation was, Keith R.A. DeCandido had to be corrected about the date of his, on a public forum. Keith, another one of my editors who gave it all up for the freelance life, answered my question on the board instead of e-mailing me directly. He wrote:

"You mean [a vacation] in which I didn't work *at all?* **thinks** Probably New Orleans in 1997, when I was working for Byron Preiss. For the week prior to the World Fantasy Convention, I did not work and didn't let the office know how to get in touch with me. It was bliss. Every vacation I've taken since has had a work component. (I went full-time freelance in 1998)."

After he posted that, another writer popped on the board with this addition, "Dude, that convention was in 1994," which surprised Keith.

Keith, whom you can find at kradical.livejournal. com describes his work as "freelance writing (of both fiction and non-fiction) and editing."

His most recent book is *Star Trek: A Singular Destiny*, but his most recent publication would be the ongoing *Farscape* comic books.

Keith's mother, GraceAnne Andreassi DeCandido, also freelances. She describes her work as a freelance writer, editor, and teacher. Her most recent publication is in *The Horn Book* magazine for January/February, 2009. Everything else she does is listed at well. com/user/ladyhawk/gadhome.html.

She writes, "The last real vacation I took was eight glorious days in Paris in 2006. The thing about both freelancing and teaching is that there is almost never a day that I cannot take a couple of hours and do what I want, but at the same time, I am never 'off.' Student e-mail must be answered even late on Saturday night; editing web site material gets done between larger assignments, and I am tied to the academic year tightly since I teach summers too. Those eight days were actually completely free of any work, and it was lovely. But it was a long time ago."

Most writers consider single days away from conventions vacations. The content of Mike Resnick's initial paragraph matches Glenn Hauman's almost exactly:

"Tricky question," Mike writes. "If you mean a day tacked on to the end of a convention, then January of this year. Other than things like that, 1984—we took 10 days in England, and I only spent one day visiting my British editors or doing any kind of business. Didn't do business *during* any of our safaris, but a lot of each turned up in novels and short stories and was always intended to."

Mike writes about six novels per year. His personal website is mikeresnick.com, and that's where you'll find the release dates for his upcoming books.

Michael A. Stackpole, freelance writer, game designer, and creative consultant, gets one vacation per year, a three-day fishing trip in Maine.

"The trick is this," Mike writes. "It's a family outing, and the last two years I'd not have gone if my father didn't need someone to drive him from Vermont to Maine—I would have let work interfere."

Mike, whose latest publication is *The New World*, adds, "Other than that, I really haven't had a vacation in the last 30 years."

You can find out what Mike's been doing for the last 30 years at stormwolf.com (and while you're there, check out his writing newsletter, *The Secrets*).

Jennifer R. Baumer, who hasn't yet succumbed to the temptation of a website, has published over 700 articles in local, regional, and national markets, as well as ghostwritten eight books. She went to Disneyland in March with her husband, but "I worked all through the weekend before and the Monday before we left and had a meeting the day after we returned."

She adds, "It's almost so hard to get ready for a vacation, finishing articles, dealing with deadlines from multiple projects and relaxing clients who panic, that sometimes it feels not worth it. Conversely, or perhaps exactly the same-ly, it sometimes seems easier and more relaxing to work some during that time than to have it preying on one's mind. (Fiction doesn't count—I wrote fiction both nights we were in the hotel at Disneyland and was perfectly happy.)"

But not all freelance writers have the same attitude toward vacations. Steve Perry, whose latest book is *Predator: Turnabout*, reports that he takes "the camper out once or twice a month for at least a weekend, three days if we can, and at least one longer stint every summer."

Then he adds, "I love my work, but I also want to have a life—what's that old saying? Nobody on their death bed says, 'Gee, I wish I'd spent more time at the office.' If all I did was write, what would be the point?"

You can find many more of Steve's opinions at themanwhonevermissed.blogspot.com (and while there, nag him to write more short stories).

Jane Yolen manages to have a life as well. She says, "I go to Scotland for four months every year. Have for 18 years. Yes, I still write, but half of every day is playing with friends. And when my kids come to visit, for the 2-4 weeks they are there, we play all day long."

Still, Jane publishes several books a year. This spring alone, three have appeared: *My Uncle Emily, A Dragon's Heart,* and *A Mirror to Nature.* You can keep up with her at janeyolen.com.

In her response to my question, Carrie Vaughn, author of the Kitty series, makes her priorities clear: "I've been freelancing since 2007, and I try to take a trip every year. I went to Belize for a week last March (2008) and will be going to Hawaii with my family in June. I also try to take an extra couple of days when traveling for work….I should mention that I love traveling and will take a trip before replacing a broken appliance."

Follow her travels and upcoming publications at carrievaughn. com.

For most freelance writers and editors, however, the biggest factor in taking time off is money.

John Ordover, another of my former editors who has gone freelance, writes, "When freelancing, I was less likely to spend money on a vacation because without a salary coming in, I never knew how long the money in the bank had to last."

John now owns and runs JJO Productions (jjoproductions. com) a media consulting and production company.

Alexandra Honigsberg is even more blunt. Alexandra is a freelance writer/editor, an adjunct instructor of Philosophy and Theology at St. John's University, and a freelance lecturer in those fields as well as a freelance musician, a corporate consultant in ethics, and an itinerant priest and chaplain of the Old Catholic Church with an emphasis on interfaith dialogue.

She writes, "I live so close to the bone that any trip is for something that is an absolute necessity and then I tag on a few days before/after for myself and keep a tight budget….I invented the freakin' Stay-cation. I live in NYC…so many fabulous free things to do. I've done all the touristy things in my town and many things off the beaten track as well…a meal in a cool ethnic restaurant can be a mini-vacation, a spa/salon day, a ride up the Hudson on the Dayliner with a picnic lunch, a cheap rental car drive up to Rhinebeck for the day, taking the scenic route…those are affordable ways that I keep my sanity…but no, no real vacations. Just not possible on what I've been making, so far, but hey, I'm still here, still in my great apartment, and still pluggin' away."

Her latest article, "The Un-Ethics of *Watchmen*" can be found on Glenn Hauman's Comic Mix website. Her latest short story, "In His Own Image," appeared in *Ravens in the Library*, edited by Phil Brucato and Sandra Buskirk. She's currently too busy to design a website (clearly!).

Award-winning editor Ellen Datlow keeps an eye on the bottom line for the tax man. She writes, "Even when employed, I'd add on days to business trips for vacation. I've rarely gone on trips that are exclusively for pleasure, other than trips with my family for special occasions—my parents' 50th and 60th anniversaries. But since most of my friends are somehow involved in the field, my visits to them are usually tax deductible."

Ellen blogs about her trips and editing at datlow.com. Her latest publication is *Poe*.

One of the friends who often provides the tax deduction for Ellen is Pat Cadigan, who moved from Kansas City to London some years ago. Pat, whose latest short story, "Truth and Bone," can be found in Ellen's *Poe* anthology, says, "The last time I went on a vacation that was totally a vacation was Thanksgiving, 1999. My son had moved back to the U.S. to live with his dad, so I took my mother to Kansas City so we could have Thanksgiving with him. This was only technically a vacation in that it did not involve any work. Traveling with my mother is not a vacation. I'd like to build a vacation into a business trip but I've never been able to afford it."

In the sf field, however, business trips are often to interesting places. Ellen and Pat went to Worldcon in Japan a few years ago. I went to Paris four times on someone else's dime (and worked hard, ate plenty, and fell in love with the city).

Award-winning editor, Gardner Dozois, whose *Year's Best Science Fiction* appears every June, points this out in his answer to the question.

He and his wife Susan "went to Australia…and toured there, but a great deal of the initial cost of getting there and back was defrayed by Clarion South, who wanted me to teach, so I guess that was work-related, or at least SF-related."

He has moved to full-time freelancing in the past few years, and adds, "We may well never be able to afford to have a pure vacation vacation again, although I hope to still be able to do some SF-related things like going to Worldcon, which can be valuable, as a place to scout for work. I picked up a couple of gigs from going to Denver in 2008, for instance."

Like Gardner, I got a lot of work at Denver's Worldcon, and I had a lot of fun too. I don't count such trips as vacations, but I do enjoy them immensely as a way to see friends, stay in touch with the field, and meet people.

But some freelancers quoted above would have counted the Worldcon time as vacation (no writing) and others would not have. It's clear that each freelancer designs her own career, making her own rules and figuring out what works for her.

Which is what any new freelancer has to do. You can work too much, especially if you're in a high-burnout profession, like therapy or broadcast journalism. You can also work too little.

You have to find the balance yourself.

If you can't afford a vacation, take a leaf from Alexandra Honigsberg's book and take a stay-cation. Not all of us live in New York City (sigh), but we all have interesting sights near our homes. I always take my birthday off, and usually, Dean and I go somewhere nearby and see the sights. Last year we went to Portland, only two hours away, and met up with my sister, showing her Powell's Books and then exploring Old Town, which I had never really visited before.

To answer the original question, "How do you justify even one day off?"

You shouldn't have to justify at all. People deserve time off. There's always one more page to write, one more project to finish, one more book to read. There's always a client with an emergency or a news story breaking somewhere. Sometimes you just have to shut off the cell phone, shut down the computer, and go to the beach.

Often, that's more than enough.

Section Three:
Money Management

Chapter Fourteen
Money

Money is a difficult topic to discuss. Most people don't want to think about it. Most of us don't know how to discuss it. Most of us consider financial information private—even more private than our sex lives (and you know how you are, you TMI people, you).

And yet money is probably the most important topic of all for freelancers.

Because money—the lack of it or, oddly enough, an abundance of it—is the primary reason most freelance businesses fail.

Consider this: In the United States, we insist on remedial skills for our children. At minimum, we want them to read at a high school level, to do basic algebra, and to write well enough to communicate their thoughts. They often don't achieve these minimums, which is why every president in my lifetime has had some proposal for "fixing" education.

No matter how education is fixed—and each generation has things it must put up with from its elders—it always fails in one big important area.

American public schools do not teach money management. Some private schools do. Colleges occasionally do, in their business schools. But oddly, I think, most colleges expect the business majors to have basic money management skills—and most of them do not.

Whenever my husband Dean Wesley Smith and I teach the Master Class, a class designed for professional writers who have plateaued in their careers, we begin with a financial quiz. We want to make certain that we use terms everyone understands. (Find information about our classes at deanwesleysmith.com.)

The classes, composed of already-established professionals, have an average age of 40. The quiz has ten questions—basic questions such as "define net worth" and "explain cash flow."

Most of the students fail. They get one or two questions right, and that's it.

One or two.

These are fully functional adults, many with day jobs. Most have children. Most have lived away from their parents and have managed their own finances since they were eighteen years old.

The public school's original rationale for failing to teach money management was that kids should learn how to handle money at home. Some kids do. Some get allowances to buy what they want, and when the money's gone, it's gone. Some learn how to save, either with an account or with a piggy bank. Some (if *Kiplinger's* is to be believed) even manage their own stock portfolios—or did, before the debacle last fall.

Most of us, however, got haphazard money management training at home. My ex-husband, for example, got an allowance. But when it ran out, his mother would just hand him a $20 to cover whatever he needed. By the time I met him, he didn't realize deep down that money was a finite commodity.

Even with that problem, however, he was better off than I was. My parents never discussed money. They encouraged fiscal responsibility, since they were both products of the Depression, and I do remember the day my mother took me to the bank to open my own savings account.

But when the school sent home a form for family information, my father refused to fill out the money sections. He wouldn't tell anyone what he earned. One of my grade school teachers made me bring the form back to my father and ask him again to fill it out.

My father scrawled "None of your damned business" across the form, and handed it back to me. I didn't find out what the man earned until he died, and my siblings and I made certain my mother had enough money to live on. She had more than enough—she was happy to tell us how much—and I was a bit stunned at the amount.

I learned that by the time I was thirty, I was out-earning my father. I had always thought my parents rich. My friends thought them rich. My parents just pretended very, very well.

(The reason we didn't have a second home at the lake like my wealthier friends [my mother told me when I asked] was because we didn't want one, not because we couldn't afford one. In fact, I never once heard my parents say that we couldn't afford something. My parents left me with the impression that we could afford everything. We just didn't want very much.)

Our perceptions about money—what we learned from our parents, our grandparents, our friends, and the world around us—have an impact on how we handle money. Most of us just do what we were taught. We work 9 to 5, have a "secure" job, and pay our bills on time. If we have investments, we hire someone to take care of them for us because (we were taught) it takes specialized knowledge to handle money.

Money management has become an arcane science in American society. We all get by, but only a few hold the keys to the kingdom.

We've seen, in the last few years, what giving the keys to that very important kingdom to people with specialized knowledge brings. It brings economic ruin and chaos.

I'm smart about money. I still make mistakes (jeez, do I), but I'm a very, very good money manager. I'd like to tell you I was always this way.

But I wasn't.

I learned about money from the school of hard, hard, hard knocks.

Let me give you a few examples.

I married the first time at nineteen. I had never lived on my own. You've already heard about my parents' magical approach to money. I spent my eighteenth year in a private college on a full scholarship—one that paid for room, board, expenses, *and* tuition. I didn't want for anything that year.

I gave it all up for love. So romantic. (So dumb. My favorite prof said, "Marry him after you graduate." My divorced older sister said, "If you want to sleep with him, sleep with him, for god's sake. You don't need to be married for that." In my nineteen-year-old wisdom, I thought she was being cynical. I thought my professor was "liberal." If only I had listened….)

The minister who performed the ceremony gave all of the starry-eyed young couples who asked him to marry them a questionnaire of his own devising. It went on for pages, and tried to ferret out compatibility.

He called us into his office in two months before the ceremony, and said he had never seen such a compatible couple. Our answers matched on 80% of the questions. But, he confided, he was worried.

The only area we didn't match on *at all* was money. We disagreed on every single question.

He said, gently, that this could be a serious problem in the relationship, and we might want to rethink the marriage. He thought some counseling on financial issues would be in order before we said "I do."

We disagreed with him.

He married us.

We divorced seven years later.

The main area of contention? Money. Not that we fought. We didn't. We just mismanaged our way into marital hell.

But the first steps in my financial education came in those years. For example, I was raised traditionally. I was taught that the man handled the financial affairs in the family, so my new husband handled the money. Until two years in, when we started bouncing checks. I learned that my ex balanced the checkbook "in his head." He never wrote anything down.

I spent Christmas through New Year's that year going over each and every bank statement, and balancing them by hand. I'm dyslexic. Sometimes it took me four and five hours *per statement*, and I had 24 of them to go over.

I couldn't find $200. It had completely vanished. So on the first banking day of the new year, I went to the bank with all my statements, and explained my problem.

The bank president took me aside (scaring the crap out of me) and offered to put the $200 back into my account. It turned out that an employee had embezzled from every mismanaged account she could find (ours being one of them), and the bank was reimbursing to avoid the information being made public. I had to sign a confidentiality agreement.

I could've blown the whistle on the whole deal. There would've been court cases and arrests and lots of publicity.

I didn't blow any whistle. I signed the agreement. We needed that $200.

Lesson 1: If you want your money handled well, do it yourself

Lesson 2: People with fiduciary responsibility embezzle. I was shocked. Shocked! [Note: this would not be the last time that someone embezzled from me. Sometimes you need to be hit over the head a few times before the lesson sinks in.]

Lesson 3: Desperate people can be bought off.

I became tight with money. I had leaks, though. I bought books as if I were wealthy. I ate out even when I was broke. I had to learn to budget for those things. More on that later.

As for my ex, we remained married for another five years. During that time we started and lost a business because we didn't know how to handle money (more on that later too). After that, we borrowed $500 from my parents so that my ex could take a class on finances. The class taught him to be a financial adviser.

The B student who never graduated from college. The man who balanced the checkbook in his head. That man took a two-week course at a hotel in Milwaukee, Wisconsin, so that he could work for a financial services firm, giving people financial advice and selling them securities.

I was appalled. I still am. My ex was (and probably still is) a good man. He had a great heart and really wanted to help people. He was also a great salesman.

But in those days, he was the last person to give anyone financial advice.

To his credit, he knew it. He read everything he could about finances and he bought one of the first computer games, one that simulated the stock market. We learned from that game how risky stock investments were.

Unlike most couples with one spouse working at the financial services firm, we didn't buy any of the securities my ex sold. We knew we didn't understand them well enough.

Lesson 4: The "experts" often know less about finances than you do.

In those years, as I realized I knew nothing about money at all, I did what I always do. I researched it. I became a business reporter because I could go to "experts" to ask them money questions—and get paid for it.

For nearly five years, I wrote articles on movers, shakers, and financial whiz kids for publications from *In Business* to *Entrepreneur*. I did not write financial advice columns. I didn't feel comfortable advising people about something I barely understood. I was attempting to get my own financial education, one expert at a time, and I was managing to get paid for it.

At the time, I did not make the connection between the experts I interviewed and my ex-husband, the financial services expert. I figured the experts I interviewed knew more about money than my ex and I did.

Now I wonder exactly how much smoke got blown up my ass in those years. Still, my financial education was (finally) beginning.

I do owe my ex and his money management skills a great debt, however. He found two thousand dollars in scholarships and other donations to get me to Clarion Writers' Workshop in 1985, and I will be forever grateful.

At Clarion, Joe and Gay Haldeman gave a three-hour lecture on money and business. In my six weeks at Clarion, those three hours were the only mention of the one thing that makes or breaks a writer's career. Joe and Gay filled those three hours with great advice. They had a long list of "dos" and "don'ts."

I took copious notes. I listened attentively.

Then, in the next few years, I proceeded to do every single financial thing that they said to avoid.

The one I remember the most: don't pay your bills with your credit cards in anticipation of a big check. Gay said that, and she may have actually shaken a finger at us as she did so. I do remember the serious frown on her face as she spoke.

Because…five years later, I paid bills with my credit card in anticipation of a big check. And when I found myself in serious financial hot water because of it, that frown on Gay's face came back to me.

Over and over and over again.

I wasn't being perverse. I wasn't trying to prove Joe and Gay wrong. I wasn't trying to ignore their advice.

The problem is that you can tell someone not to do something, and they will remember that advice. After they've made the mistake themselves.

Dean and I relearned that lesson when we taught the first Master Class in 1999. We told students not to make the same mistakes we did. We delineated what those mistakes were. In the intervening years, each student told us that they made those mistakes, and wished they had listened to us, just as I wished I had listened to Joe and Gay.

Dean and I tried to figure out how to give students actual experience with these problems without having the real-life consequences. Subsequent Master Classes have had a role-playing game that we call (unoriginally) the Game, designed to mimic the business conditions of a freelance life. Dean, Loren Coleman, and

I designed it. Loren, a well-known writer who also owns Catalyst Games, made it work. (He's our assistant at the Master Class; we couldn't do it without him.)

Now students tell us they wished they'd listened, but they do so far less. More often they tell us the mistakes they avoided because they "made" those mistakes at the Master Class.

I wish I could find a way to have all of you make the mistakes in a pretend environment. Because I know so many of you will read this section on money and finances and then remember the lessons *after* you've made the mistakes.

The only thing I can tell you is this: We learn by making mistakes.

I would not be good with money if I hadn't had the experiences listed above. And some others that I will discuss. Two failed businesses, several successful businesses. Living below the poverty line for two years straight and yet somehow managing to survive. Living well above the poverty line and not being able to pay my bills for the first time in my life.

Learning that making money was only the first step. Financial success did not mean, as a Clarion friend of mine once said, "Becoming rich and never having to work again." It meant learning how to live within my means—and figuring out what those means really were.

Learning about cash flow, and liquidity, and the difference between investment and savings. Learning how to differentiate uncertainty and risk. Learning how illusive security really and truly is.

Some of this came through life lessons. Some through reading. Some through watching and avoiding the mistakes of others.

I wish I had a copy of that quiz the minister gave me and my ex-husband. I'd post it here right now. Because you and your significant other, the person who will live or who is living this freelance life with you, need to take a quiz just like it.

If you haven't already figured out your differences about money management, you need to learn it. You need to figure out your own hidden preconceptions about finances. You need to learn exactly what you believe about money and what your significant other believes.

You also need to figure out—and this is extremely important—what your financial end game is.

Would you be happy making $100,000 year in and year out? $50,000? $500,000?

Or is there no dollar limit on your happiness? Is your financial end game tied to things instead—a paid-off house, a car you own, enough money to send the kids to college, and enough to maintain a comfortable (by your definition) lifestyle?

Or do you want a 24,000 square foot house like Dean Koontz just built?

Money doesn't buy happiness, but money can get in the way of happiness. You need to figure out all of this stuff, preferably before you go freelance. But if you're one of my readers who already freelances, then you should stop and figure out what your financial desires are.

Because they motivate you.

Let me give you one more personal example. In 1985, at Clarion, I would have agreed with my friend: I wanted to be rich and never have to work again.

Now I know that if I were filthy rich (J.K. Rowling rich), I would still work. I can't *not* work. I love what I do, and I'd do it even if I never had to make another dime. I'd be like Nora Roberts, writing several books a year, whether my fans wanted to read them or not.

Several of my friends would quit work if they achieved their financial dreams. They'd manage their money or tour the world or spend time with their grandchildren, like one of my favorite romance writers, LaVyrle Spencer, who retired in her sixties to spend her remaining years with her family.

You need to figure out what you want out of life, out of your freelancing, and out of your finances. That's the first step in this money discussion.

Figure it out before you read any farther. And then we'll talk some more.

Chapter Fifteen
The Freelance Equation

I remember the exact moment when I learned how pernicious expenses were. I was nineteen years old, six months married, and exceedingly naïve. My parents, as I mentioned in the introduction, never discussed money. Not ever. I had no idea they made house payments. I didn't know that electricity cost money. I had a vague idea that they paid for groceries because I watched my mom whip out the checkbook at the store every week. But the costs of daily living simply did not exist for me as I grew up.

I didn't live away from home until I got married. By then, I knew intellectually that people paid rent and utilities, but I didn't understand the implications of that. I remember being terrified to go to the phone company and sign up for service. The questions these people asked—people who didn't know me! They wanted to know where I lived, how much I earned, what my social security number was. I answered everything with trepidation, and for successfully completing their little application, the phone company gave me a black rotary dial telephone that was so heavy I could have used it as a cudgel to beat someone to death.

The apartment we rented on the eighth floor of a high rise (very Mary Tyler Moore, I remember thinking) included all utilities, but all utilities didn't mean telephone. (Honestly, I'm still confused about that one.) All utilities did include heat, electricity, and water. The city paid for garbage collection. (Hear that, State of Oregon? In civilized places, the city pays for garbage collection.)

We had to pay rent, which was (as I recall) a whopping $180 per month. We also paid for insurance, phone, and food. We did not have a car. I'm positive our monthly bills were less than $500. We had $3000 in the bank when we got married. $1000 of it went to first semester tuition; another $250 went to books. My then-husband and I both got jobs which, as I look at it now, covered more than the monthly expenses.

But...

We depleted the last big part of our savings at the beginning of the second semester. We had enough to pay for the third semester, and the fourth was going to be interesting.

Without the savings in the bank, I panicked. I always had savings. I didn't have expenses, I rarely spent my allowance (yes, I was one of those kids), and I got a good job at sixteen.

By late April, we had less than $1000 in the bank. I sat on the outside terrace at the Union South cafeteria at the University of Wisconsin-Madison on the first warm day of the year, and fretted about money.

Because at that moment, that very moment, I realized that no matter what I did, the expenses would recur, month after month after month. We had to have a roof over our heads. We had to have food. We could live without a phone, I supposed (but I didn't want to), but in no way was I going to go without insurance. (We went without insurance for one week as we switched over from our parents' plans to the university's plans, and I was convinced that that would be the week we were going to get the Martian Death Flu or get hit by a bus. Neither happened, of course, but I still vividly remember the fear I felt until the new insurance kicked in.)

Until I was nineteen years and ten months old, I had no idea that expenses happened even if you did nothing. Especially if you did nothing. As long as you ate and slept and had a place to do those two things, you were spending money.

That realization set me on a quest to earn more money and to reduce expenses. By May, my husband and I had become resident managers of an apartment complex, trading work for rent. I worked full time that summer for the realty company that managed the apartment complex. My husband became a full-time janitor at a building downtown. We saved enough for the next year's tuition.

We did fine, until we got the 1099 in January. The 1099 in which the realty company (quite properly) declared our rent as income to us. Income we had to pay taxes on.

I'm pretty sure that the guy who hired us explained all of this. I also know that to me and my husband, the guy sounded like the adults in *A Charlie Brown Christmas*. Everything the poor guy said went in as blah-blah-blah-blah-blah.

We survived. We made money. We started businesses and worked for a variety of people. I freelanced. We managed, just like most people do.

But we were frugal. Not that we had a choice. In the early 1980s, only the upper middle class and wealthiest Americans had credit cards. People with low incomes couldn't get any kind of credit, not for car loans and certainly not for home loans. We bought our first two cars used. A couple from our church co-signed our first new car loan, taking quite a gamble. (Fortunately, the worst of our money troubles happened after we got their names off that loan.)

If we wanted something, we paid cash for it. If we didn't have cash, we didn't buy. Many Fridays, I scurried to the bank to cash one of our paychecks so that we would have enough money to buy groceries on Saturday (our grocery shopping day). When we didn't have enough money for gas, we took the bus. When we didn't have enough money for the bus, we walked.

(Up hill, both directions, in the snow.)

I realize how all of this sounds now, but I'm not exaggerating. The culture has changed a lot in thirty years. Because of the recent economic meltdown, we're returning to a cash-based society, especially for our lower- to moderate-income members.

And personally, I think that's a good thing.

I write this on Wednesday. On Tuesday night, one of the network newscasts had an in-depth piece about the changes people are making to cope with the new economy. They talked with one young single mother (we must always have an example!) who had $5000 in credit card bills. She was paying them down slowly, with the help of a credit counseling agency.

The piece ended with her saying sadly that she only spends cash these days and if she can't afford something, she doesn't buy it. The implication was that we should feel sorry for her.

I turned to Dean and said, "So it's news now that someone is living within her means?"

He replied, "I was just thinking the same thing."

But it *is* news.

From the late 1980s on, we lived in a society built on easy credit. We moved from a cash-based economy to a credit-based economy. A lot of old-timers either laughed or complained when George W. Bush exhorted Americans to go shopping after 9/11, but he was serious. Because he knew, even then, that any decline in the spending habits of Americans would have a dire effect upon the economy.

We saw that dire effect from September of 2008 through February of 2009. Spending more or less stopped. And the economy spiraled downward. Spending has risen slowly since then, but I doubt it'll return to its peak any time soon.

People who were used to augmenting their salaries with their credit cards suddenly had to learn how to make choices about where to spend their money. Their 401Ks had already taken a large hit. Their home values declined. The loss of wealth in this country (hell, the loss of wealth in the world) in the last nine months has been staggering.

All of it has consequences. Everyone has to trim, from the major corporations down to the smallest households. Unfortunately, some of those cuts came in employment, which is why the unemployment numbers shot up so drastically. Many people who lost their jobs had no savings at all. Those who did have savings watched the money evaporate as it went to large credit card bills, adjustable-rate mortgages, and unbreakable leases on oversized cars.

The jobs ended, the savings vanished, but the expenses kept building up, month after month after month.

Sometime in December of 2009, Dean said to me, "You know, most of America is living the freelance lifestyle now."

And damn if he wasn't right.

It's the rare freelancer who has a reliable monthly salary. Most people who work for themselves have an irregular income. The income generally works like this:

Gross income – cost of doing business = net income

Some freelancers are lucky enough to count their own salary in the cost of doing business. *All* freelancers should count their own salary in that cost. But most do not.

Those who do not usually wait for the net income to pay themselves. That's how most freelancers live.

But in a business's early years, income generally works like this:

Gross income – the cost of doing business = zero

Or, worse:

Gross income – the cost of doing business = net loss

If you started your business with the three years of expenses as most experts recommend, then you probably have enough cushion to handle the second and third scenarios.

If that's the case, and you are lucky enough to have the first scenario, a net income, then you're supposed to take a (small) salary and thread the rest of the money back into the business itself or to continue to increase your rainy-day fund. Eventually, you'll end up with too much capital, and you'll need to invest in something other than the business itself.

That's a problem you want to trade up for, and we'll deal with it later. But for now, let's deal with scenarios two and three.

If you started your business haphazardly, the way most freelancers do, you don't have a cushion at all.

How do you survive?

Good question. The correct answer is that often your business doesn't survive.

There are many reasons why, but let's do this in general, starting with the third scenario.

If your business operates at a net loss month after month after month, then you have to make drastic changes. You must decrease expenses without harming the business itself (and that's a real trick) and *at the same time*, you must increase income.

If you can't do both, then your business is doomed.

This is why most freelancers fail the first time they go freelance. The freelancer *underestimates* the cost of doing business and *overestimates* the income he'll receive from his work.

That scenario leads to an inevitable monthly net loss.

And here's where the perniciousness of expenses comes in. If you can't pay June's expenses, then you won't be able to pay July's expenses. If your expenses are, say, $2000 per month for your business (regardless of *personal* expenses, which we haven't even discussed yet), then by the end of July, you're $4000 in the hole. On the first of August, you'll be $6000 in the hole.

It's easier to come up with $2000 than it is to come up with $6000. And if you couldn't come up with the original $2000, then it's unlikely you'll ever find the $6000.

141

And none of that counts the cost of deferring expenses. Every business adds a late charge onto the bill. Usually those are ten percent of the bill. So by August first, you'll owe $6400 (you're not yet late for August, so that $200 hasn't tacked on).

A lot of small business owners deal with June's (drastic) shortfall by charging it on their credit cards. Then they have a similar shortfall in July and face another in August.

Charging expenses compounds the problem, quite literally. Instead of the 10% late fees charged by the service providers, the freelancer who can't pay gets charged anywhere from 15 to 20% on the money. So they'll owe either $6600 or $6800 on the first of August. Not counting the monthly payments, which you can't charge, but which either come off another credit card or from some other loan source.

Eventually, credit dries up. It's not as easily available now as it was a year ago, and I suspect it'll be even harder to get a year from now. As a culture, we're returning to the tight credit markets of the late 1970s.

If you borrow without making changes to your business, always hoping that things will improve, you're dooming your business. Things will not improve, and you'll have to close the business (or drastically reduce it) and return to a day job.

If you return to a day job with all of those business expenses filling your credit card, you'll need a rather large salary to pay off the debt and pay your living expenses.

This is not a gamble that anyone should take, yet so many do. When I was a young writer, I was in a business-information-sharing group with other young writers. One writer had the promise of a Hollywood deal. He charged his living and business expenses on his credit cards, expecting a big payoff in the near future.

Unfortunately, he did not understand the nature of the writing business or the unreliability of Hollywood promises. Before he had to return to a day job, he had racked up $50,000 in credit card bills. I can't even imagine what his monthly payments were, and how many years it took him to pay off that one mistake in judgment.

So how do you deal with scenario 3? Let's look at it again.

Gross income – the cost of doing business = net loss

First, you have to catch this problem in the very first month that it occurs. You can't let it compound for even one more month, as I mentioned above. Because expenses continue, month after month after month. They grow like snowdrifts in a blizzard, and it seems like nothing you can do will stop them.

That's not true, of course. You can stop them.

Your first step to solving this dilemma is to take a clear-eyed view at your entire business, and ask yourself some questions.

1. Was the business undercapitalized in the first place?

In other words, did you start with less money than you needed to run the business? If the answer is yes, then that's where the problem began. Most businesses fail due to undercapitalization. You start behind, and you never really catch up.

But if you weren't undercapitalized, then you need to figure out what happened to the money you had when you started. So you ask the next question:

2. Are your business expenses too high?

Did you rent an office when you could make do with an office in the home? Do you have employees who are doing work that you could do but prefer not to do? Are you paying those employees too much? Are you paying them benefits? Are you paying too much for materials?

You need to evaluate each expense with an eye to getting rid of it altogether. The only standard you have now is this one: *Can you run your business without spending that money?*

If the answer is yes, then the expense is unnecessary.

Watch out for the "yes, but" answers. Those are the most pernicious. "Yes, but my business won't be as efficient." "Yes, but my products won't be of the same quality." "Yes, but Suzy has worked for us for ten years."

Believe me, I've lost entire businesses because I didn't realize that "yes, but" is the worst possible answer. It makes you keep the expense even though you know you shouldn't.

If any part of the answer is yes, then you must cut that expense immediately.

I do realize that cutting expenses immediately is often difficult for many companies. The company signed a lease, for example, or made a contract with a supplier. Each lease and contract should have an early termination clause. Those clauses often contain penalties. Examine if that penalty will cost you less than maintaining the expense for another year.

Or negotiate with the company holding the lease or contract. Often the penalties can be waved or paid over time, mitigating the worst of them.

Put yourself in survival mode here, and cut, cut, cut. As many leaseholders are learning in this recession, it's better to get some money on a broken lease than no money on a delinquent one.

Cut your expenses to the absolute bone.

If that doesn't mitigate your net loss, then you have to ask the next question:

3. How can I boost the business's income?

Often you can do that by becoming more efficient. As a business grows, it occasionally creates a lot of make-work. Make-work seems like real work, but actually has nothing to do with income generation. By trimming make-work and concentrating on real work, you can usually boost your business's income.

Another way to boost income is to examine all of your income sources. Examine them this way: time spent versus income generated. Often one income source takes less time and generates more income than other income sources. Trim the income sources that take a lot of time and bring in very little money in favor of income sources that take less time and bring in more money.

A third way to boost income is to try something new— generate a new income source. If this takes capital (money), now is not the time to do it. But if the change takes no capital and very little time, then it's worth the try.

However, if you can't decrease your expenses and you can't increase your income, ask this question:

4. Is the problem cash flow?

Cash flow is exactly what it sounds like: how quickly money arrives at your business. For example, if Client A owes you $2000 and pays within thirty days, then Client A meets your monthly expenses. But if Client A is suddenly paying on sixty days instead of thirty, you can't pay your monthly expenses either. You'll, of course, charge Client A for his late payment, but as you've learned with your own paying of expenses, the late fee doesn't matter until you've actually written (and received) the check.

I would hope that Client A isn't your only client. If he is, then you need other clients to cover the shortfall. If he is one of many clients, then maybe you might be able to cover the shortfall using money from other clients.

A cash-flow problem can be as serious as no income at all. Because it snowballs in just the same way that a net loss snowballs. If you're not charging Client A enough in late fees to cover your own late fees, then you'll be losing money on Client A's business.

So many freelancers just hope that Client A will go back to paying on 30 days. But Client A might be in financial trouble. Client A might be going out of business.

And unfortunately, the freelance or small business often gets paid last in those situations. You're not the person who is getting Client A's rent so that he can keep his storefront open, nor are you the person getting Client A's utility payments to keep his lights on. You're down the food chain, and you might never see a dime.

When a client starts paying late, you have to worry immediately, and start planning for the loss of that income *immediately,* or the loss of Client A's business might mean the failure of your business.

Finally, if the problem isn't cash flow, and you can't decrease expenses or increase income, then you have to ask this question:

5. Is my business going to fail?

Be realistic. The answer is probably yes. If it is, cut your losses *immediately*. The last thing you want is all the debt incurred by the continued monthly expenses. Shut the doors, turn off the lights, and search for a day job.

Freelancers who don't have a storefront often have the most trouble with this because their expenses seem low. They'll hang on to the freelance gig too long, hoping for improvement.

You have to be an optimist to be a freelancer, but in this situation, your optimism will hurt you instead of help you. You need to be a clear-eyed realist here, or maybe even a pessimist.

Chalk this attempt up as a learning experience, cut your losses, and go back to your day job. Continue freelancing on the side. Then figure out what lessons you've learned, fix the mistakes you've made, and when you're ready, try again.

Those of you in scenario 2 need to do the same self-examination that the people in scenario 3 have done. But first, let me remind you what scenario 2 is:

Gross income – the cost of doing business = zero

Scenario 2 is nasty. Because nowhere in that cost of doing business do most freelancers include a salary. The cost of doing business equals the gross income of the business, with nothing left over.

So how does the freelancer live? By finding a supportive parent, spouse or friend. Someone who'll pay the living expenses while the freelancer conducts her business.

This scenario takes horrible advantage of the parent, spouse, or friend. In reality, all the freelancer has in that instance is a spouse who indulges them. If the freelancer gets a divorce or if (God forbid) the spouse dies, then the freelancer is immediately thrust in scenario 3.

If you've lived the scenario 2 lifestyle for years now, it's time to reassess. You need to do the same analysis outlined for people in scenario 3. You have to change that zero at the end of the equation to a net income, and you have to do it before life circumstances force you to make the changes or to shut down the business.

Chapter Sixteen
Definitions

Some of you are doing the equations above and think you're doing fine, yet if you look at your bank account, you realize you're not doing well at all. The problem might be in the definition of terms. Let's go back to our equations again:

1. **Gross income – cost of doing business = net income**
2. **Gross income – cost of doing business = zero**
3. **Gross income – cost of doing business = net loss**

And now, let's do what we should have done in the first place. Let's define terms.

Gross income is all of the income that arrives at your business, from the smallest pennies to the largest checks. **All** of the income, without exception. If you earned the money through your freelance labor, then it gets counted as part of the business's gross income.

We are only discussing the income that comes into **your business**, not the income that comes into **your household**. For many freelancers, that's a tough distinction. Early on in freelancing, the money you made at your part-time work was bonus money, used to splurge on dinner or perhaps buy a nice pair of diamond earrings for the wife.

I would hope that before you became a full-time freelancer, you learned how to separate your freelance income from your belief that it's all bonus money and yours for the taking.

If not, you're already in a world of hurt, and probably don't even realize it.

A lot of freelancers, however, only count their **primary freelance income** as gross income, and that, too, is a mistake. For example, fiction writers make a lot of money from a variety of sources, from New York publishing houses to audio sales to foreign sales. Some writers believe that checks under $100 are bonus money. Others think that sales from other countries are bonus. If you make money in a way that is somehow tied to your business (selling extra copies of your own books on eBay, for example), then that money is all part of your gross income.

I can hear some of you complain now. You don't want to keep track of the tiny checks, or the twenty bucks someone hands you for a hard-to-find copy of your novel. Too bad. Set up your accounting system so that you can keep track of every dime. Even if it isn't important now, it will become important later.

The **cost of doing business** is precisely that. How much does it cost you to run your business?

Break this down into finite units, depending on your business.

If you have a retail store or an office outside the home, I would break this down into the smallest possible unit: How much does it cost you to run your business **every single day**?

Some businesses can get by with knowing that figure for the entire **week**.

Most businesses keep track of costs by the **month.**

A few keep track by **project**. (How much did it cost you to do that particular client's job from start to finish, including overhead?)

For this piece, I'm going to go over general **monthly** costs. I do realize that each freelance business is different. I can't write a piece that will include all the expenses plumbers incur and a piece that will include all the expenses criminal defense attorneys incur.

But I can speak about expenses in general.

Overhead: overhead is the general recurring costs of running your business. Remember that I mentioned I realized that even by breathing, we were all incurring expenses? To a business, that's the overhead.

Overhead includes those expenses that happen **even if you're earning no money at all**. Those expenses include (but are not limited to):

--Rent
--Utilities, including telephone and internet (and cable, for those of us who are freelance storytellers or freelance reporters)
--Salaries (your salary as well as the salaries for any employees)
--Vehicles/large equipment (trucks, tractors, large machinery, etc.) (I'm figuring that you're amortizing the cost of these machines over the year, instead of writing off the cost of purchase in the month it occurs.)
--Office equipment (computers, printers, photocopiers, etc.) (Again, see the note for #4.)
--Supplies (The monthly things you need to keep all of that running.)
--Maintenance (from equipment maintenance to janitorial services)
--Business insurance(s)
--Taxes (All of them, from sales tax to property tax to social security tax.)

Costs per project: People who own storefronts usually don't have this issue, but the rest of us work on a piecework basis. We don't get paid a salary (except through our own business). We generate income by finishing projects. Each project will have general, predictable costs, and several unpredictable costs. All projects also have basic costs that most freelancers ignore. These costs include (but, again, are not limited to):

1. Materials specific to the project. For example, a friend of mine makes quilts. She has fabric, thread, batting, and all the other things she needs for the average quilt, but if someone wants a quilt made from a specially imported silk, that silk would be specific to this project.

2. Gas/transportation/travel expenses/meals. Any errands you do associated with this project and this project only; you should include a per diem (per day) expense for the vehicle used or the exact mileage and cost of gas. (For example, most writers never count their mileage to and from the post office as part of the expense of a particular project. But they should.)

As for travel expenses and meals, the IRS has rules as to what can be deducted. But we're not discussing the IRS here. We're talking actual cost. So include the full price of business travel per project, as well as the full cost of each meal.

3. Cost overruns: You should know how much each project will cost to complete. Projects sometimes cost more because the client demands something new or because the project is bigger than initially predicted. Those overruns need to be included in cost per project.

Note: I should include time as part of the cost per project. I am not going to here, because we're discussing actual cash outlay. But time is an important part of project costs, and I will get to that in another part of the Freelancer's Guide. To order the full Guide, see the end of this short book.

Right now, however, we're talking internal costs and I trust I've taken care of the cost of your time in overhead with the inclusion of your salary (hint, hint).

Other important business costs. This category, important costs, often includes the expenses that make or break your business. These costs include (but, again, are not limited to):

1. Continuing education. Many professions require a certain amount of continuing education from the practitioners so that they can keep their licenses. Many state bars require continuing education from attorneys. Most hospitals require continuing education from their doctors (and damn, I wish that was all hospitals).

Freelancers should always continue educating themselves about their businesses. Sometimes that means attending a class. Often it just means keeping up with the current materials—books on the latest trends, subscribing to the trade magazines, etc.

2. Advertising/The cost of finding new business. Not every business has or needs an ad budget. For example, freelance writers never advertise on the radio. Plumbers sometimes do. Lawyers never used to, but they seem to own late-night television now. (Do they think the sleepless are more inclined to sue?)

But we all have to generate new business, whether that's through designing and maintaining a website or handing out business cards at the local Rotary luncheon. This doesn't go into overhead because, for most of us, it's not a consistent expense; but it does have to go somewhere, which is why I put it here.

3. Advice. Many freelancers engage the services of other professionals to help with particular business matters. They hire freelance accountants to handle their year-end taxes. They hire attorneys to handle a particularly annoying problem. They hire real estate agents to help them buy a new office complex. Freelancers can often go months without paying for advice, but they rarely go years without it. Again, amortize the cost of the advice, and include it in your monthly expenses.

Of course, those are not all of the costs of doing business, but that's enough for a general start. You know what your business entails. Sit down and make a list of all the costs—again, from the smallest expense (the cost of the newspaper you buy for fifty cents every day at lunch) to the largest, and then break down those expenses by month. That will give you the monthly cost of doing business.

Subtract that cost from your monthly gross income, and you'll get (I hope) a **net income.**

Notice how many fixed costs there are to running a business? More than most people expect, especially when they started making quilts for friends and then decided to go full time with an entire business.

For first-time freelancers, the expenses are often a big shock. When you work a day job, you never think of the overhead expenses. The office exists. The lights are on. The phones work. Those things don't really matter to you, the employee, so long as you get your paycheck on time.

As a full time freelancer, you're now responsible for the phones, the lights, and the office, as well as everything (and everyone) in it. That's quite a change, and it's often a difficult one.

Now let's note what I did not include in expenses.

I didn't include your house payment or the payment for the car your spouse drives exclusively. Nor did I include the cost of your kid's ballet lessons.

Personal expenses come out of your salary. Got that? They don't come out of the cost of doing business. Here's a pretty solid rule of thumb for you: *If you can't legitimately deduct the expense from your business's income tax, then you can't pay for that expense with business funds.*

Think of it this way. If you still had a day job, would you ask your boss to buy your groceries? Your boss would laugh at you and remind you that's what you get a paycheck for.

I can't be more specific than that. If you're a fashion designer, then clothing is a business expense, just like theater tickets are when you're an actor. Each business is different and has different needs. For me, books are a legitimate business expense. But all books wouldn't be a legitimate business expense for a gardener. Only books on gardening and related topics would be a business expense for him.

Why am I telling you this? Because freelancers horribly intermingle their personal finances with their business finances. You have to keep them separate.

I know most of you work at home. That's where the trouble starts. You work at home, your family lives there, and you think nothing of intermingling your expenses with theirs.

You can't intermingle. It has to remain as separate as it was when you had a day job.

You're going to have to start thinking in percentages. Figure out what percentage your office is of your house's square footage. For easy math, let's say that your office is 25% of your family's house. You only use that office for your business. You don't store exercise equipment there, or keep your son's drum set in the back closet. Just your business.

Then 25% of your house payment is your rent for your office. Just like 25% of the electric bill and 25% of the water bill and 25% of the heating bill make up your utility costs for your office. Got that? Be scrupulous about this—and take pictures of your office, so that at tax time, you can prove that you use that office *only* for your business.

(Please remember here that I am not an accountant or a tax attorney. I'm just a humble freelancer with too much life experience not to share some of it.)

Try to have a car that you only use for your business. Otherwise you're going to have to figure out usage, either by project or by daily use. You'll need a contemporaneous log. That goes for other items with shared uses. Try to keep shared items to a minimum.

I know you can't always do that, but do your best. And when you must share, be very, very clear about how much you used that item.

The personal-items problem is the very reason I'm telling you to take a salary from your business. It makes things very simple. The easiest way to do this is to keep a separate business bank account and never, ever, use it for personal items. Write yourself a salary check every month, and put that money in your personal account. Treat it the way you would treat your paycheck from your day job. When that salary money is gone, it's gone—even if there is extra money in the business account.

Believe me, that accountant you hire at tax time every year will be much happier with you if you do things this way. So will the IRS auditor if you ever have to face that music. (And let me tell you, as a person who has had two full audits, it's really not as bad as the press makes it out to be. Yes, it takes time from your life, but if you're organized and diligent in your record-keeping, you'll survive just fine—and live to freelance another day.)

If you subtract those costs of doing business from your gross income, and come out with a net loss, then you need to make changes. The change you cannot and should not make is to cut your own salary.

I'm sure many of you wondered how, month after month, a full time freelancer subtracts the cost of doing business from his gross income and comes out with nothing. The way most full-time freelancers make that second equation work is by cutting out their salary and letting their spouse handle the personal expenses. *All* of the personal expenses.

The freelancer's business—without the cost of the salary— breaks even. Which means that, if you add the salary back in, the business is operating at a net loss.

Which cannot and should not be sustained over time.

I've gone for pages now and I have not discussed that lovely phrase, "net income." So let me simply say here that most long-term full-time freelancers have a rather large net income. We wouldn't stay in the business if we didn't.

But a net income creates its own problems.

Chapter Seventeen
Net Income

The Freelancer's Survival Guide was born on my blog. As I wrote the chapters, readers asked questions and made comments. Many of the comments are based on readers' experiences. If you're interested in the wisdom of others, go to kristinekathrynrusch.com and click on the *Freelancer's Survival Guide* tab. That will take you to the table of contents. Hit the posts marked "Money" and read the comments.

One of the most frequently asked questions I received as I wrote the posts on money was how can you learn this financial information on your own—without making the mistakes—when there are very few books published about freelancing and money. Most of the books that I know of are out of date, thanks to the so-called New Economy.

However, most of my information that hasn't come from personal experience has come from observation. Not just observation of my friends and business associates, but observation of others as well.

And the week I wrote the chapter on Income provided yet another opportunity for that kind of observation. I wrote these chapters during the summer that Michael Jackson died.

Mixed into the increasingly lurid coverage of Michael Jackson's death was the coverage of his finances and his estate. This information is available on the web. Read it. Listen to whatever you can. Because you can learn from celebrities, who are mostly freelancers. Michael Jackson certainly was.

Estimates put him at $400 to $500 million in debt at the time of his death, yet he has an estate that will increase in value over the years—and has increased in value just since his death. Artists, writers, musicians, take heart from this and keep your copyrights, get royalties, and make sure you're paid for your work without losing rights to any of it. Those rights are what made Jackson's debt vanish quickly, and left his heirs with a large fortune.

Jackson mismanaged his money horribly. The state of Jackson's finances reminds me of the state of another entertainer's finances at the time of his death. Elvis Presley had spent every dime of his fortune and then some at the time of his death. Like Jackson, he sometimes spent more than he had. Yet now the Presley estate is one of the largest entertainment estates in the world. What happened? Priscilla Presley took over and managed the money properly.

You can read about the changes, the legal fights, and the money management in an out-of-print book called *Elvis Inc.: The Fall And Rise of the Presley Empire* by Sean O'Neal. Find this book. It'll make fascinating reading while you're looking at the financial coverage of the Jackson estate.

And as you're reading about Elvis and learning about the Jackson estate, realize that these two men made money outside of the mainstream. They were *entertainers*, not brokers or money managers. They made money from their art, and their estates continue to make money from the work that these people produced in their lifetime.

Which brings us to…

Income

Remember my initial freelancer's equation?

Gross income – cost of doing business = net income

First, a reminder: **Gross income** is all of the income that arrives at your business, from the smallest pennies to the largest checks. **All** of the income, without exception. If you earned the money through your freelance labor, then it gets counted as part of the business's gross income.

Net income is the money left over after you pay the expenses. **All** of the expenses, including a salary to yourself and your employees. (Note that I didn't do much on employees in the Expenses chapter. I cover employees in the complete *Guide*.) Sometimes that net income is tiny and sometimes it's very, very large.

Because freelancing is often so unpredictable, you may not know on January 1 that you will make a large net profit by December 31. Most freelancers plan for the bad times, but they have no idea how to plan for the good times.

In some ways, that's what happens to millionaire lottery winners and others, like artists/entertainers/athletes, who can make six- to seven-figures more than they expected in a single year. Even contractors can do that, by getting a plum project in an upscale housing development—although that's less likely these days than it was in 2005.

Before you get into the enviable position of making a large net income (and you will, if you're good at what you do, you work hard at what you love, and you keep your expenses under control), you must learn how to handle large sums of money.

How do you do that without the large sum of money? Easy. You follow what others have done. I read a lot of celebrity and sports news because, mixed in with the gossip, is valuable information about failed investments, horrible risks, and terrible tax problems. Those are all relevant to you now.

In addition, I read the financial press. The business section of my newspaper, the *Wall Street Journal*, and a lot of financial magazines. As I do this, I remember that I used to be a business reporter, and I had only a marginal understanding of what I was writing about. So I take everything I read with a grain of salt. If I don't understand what the article said, I look for some other way of gleaning the same information, and I try to figure out if the reporter filter is inaccurate (often it is).

Reporters, even business reporters, rarely specialize in high finance. The people who claim to do well in high finance don't always do well either. The financial gurus on the business channels like CNBC missed the upcoming housing bust, which I find laughable. My business-oriented friends and I all saw it coming. It was obvious—the elephant in the room, if you will. Yet the so-called experts missed it and the inevitable economic downturn.

Read books about the history of finance. Books about the Great Depression, about stock swindles, about banking schemes, about times of great worldwide financial success and great worldwide financial loss. Start with John Kenneth Galbraith's tidy little book on the beginnings of the Depression, *The Great Crash of 1929*. History really does repeat itself. We just witnessed it.

Finally, read books by self-made millionaires. Folks like Warren Buffet are willing to share their insights. You don't have to do what Buffet does—and probably shouldn't—but you should learn his attitudes about money. He's extremely good at handling it, and he understands what it can and cannot do for you.

The problem most people have with a sudden net profit is that they see it as a windfall. They don't see it as something that needs to be managed, just as something that can be spent.

I mentioned the millionaire lottery winners who go broke within a few years. Everyone wonders how they do that, but it's really very simple. They spend every single dime, save nothing, invest nothing, incur great expenses, and fail to understand that money—even a great deal of money—is finite.

Michael Jackson died $400-$500 million dollars *in debt*. Figure out how he did that. It wasn't all amusement parks and facial reconstructive surgery. He lost more than he made year after year after year—and he made more per year than most people ever make in their lifetimes.

Here's what you don't do when you have a large net income—which I'm going to call a **net profit** from now on, because that's the correct business term.

You do not go on a mega-spending spree.

You can go on a small spending spree. Buy your wife an expensive pair of earrings. Buy your kids some great new toy. Buy yourself something small that you've always wanted, but see as an indulgence.

There. Now you're done spending. You've rewarded yourself and your family, but not in a great big way.

Because—here's the raw truth of it, folks—that small spending spree is a taxable event. The money you just spent is money you'll have to pay taxes on. It's not a business expense. It's a bonus, and if any of you have ever gotten a bonus at your day job, you know that the bookkeeper already took payroll taxes out of the bonus before giving it to you.

How do all these lottery millionaires and first-time celebrities get in tax trouble? Simple. They forget that they must pay taxes on their net profit (which they saw as a windfall). They spent all the money, and then the tax bill occurred.

If you figure federal taxes at one-third of your net income (which is how the IRS does it [roughly]), then you would owe over $33,000 on a net income of $100,000. See how quickly that adds up? And how difficult it is to catch up, particularly if your net profits don't happen year after year after year?

So…you have a net profit. You rewarded yourself with a tiny spending spree. Or not. Preferably not. But people do like celebrating when they come into money, so if you're one of those folks, then celebrate by spending a teeny tiny amount of money.

After your itty bitty spending spree, set aside one-third to one-half of the net profit to pay the taxman. The IRS wants you to pay for large tax bills quarterly, and that's a good idea.

Here's why.

Net profits aren't always predictable, as I noted above. Most people underestimate how much they'll earn once the profits start rolling in. So if you set aside one-third of the money you got on the first quarter's net profit, then forgot to do so for the second quarter, received a bigger-than-expected net profit in the third quarter, and no net profit in the fourth, you could easily be behind on your tax bill. That one-third of the first quarter's profits won't be enough to cover the entire year.

Better to pay that one-third in at the end of that quarter. That's called an **estimated tax payment.** You don't get penalized for estimating wrong, unless you continually underestimate and underpay, year after year after year.

Remember, I am not a tax attorney, nor am I qualified to give tax and legal advice. I'm just giving you my opinion here.

And my opinion is to pay those estimated payments to the best of your ability. If, at the end of the year, you discover that you overpaid your estimated tax, you can get a refund, just like you did when you overestimated your withholding payments from your day job.

If you underestimated, you need to make that payment in full when you file your taxes. And if you seriously underestimated, you can make payments, but you have to pay interest and/or penalties.

Don't underestimate. Set aside *more* money than you need for taxes, and pay your quarterly tax bills from that. Keep that money in a liquid account, like a money market savings account or a one- to three-month certificate of deposit, especially earmarked for taxes.

At the end of the year, do your taxes and make your payments. If you have money left over, great. Set it aside for next year's taxes, or invest it as you're going to invest the rest of your net profits.

So you've had your eensy weensy spending spree and you've paid your taxes, and you still have money left over. You can do a lot of different things with it.

You can pay yourself a large bonus, taking all of the leftover money—after you've taken tax payments out of that. If you do so, realize that you're going to pay taxes twice on that money—once on the business receipt of the money and once on your personal use of that money. In other words, that's probably not the best use of your money.

First, I would reinvest in the company. I would upgrade something like a bit of machinery, or something to a better product. I would not incur monthly expenses doing so—which means I wouldn't get an office outside the home or hire an employee.

I might simply park that money in some kind of savings account as an emergency fund. Over time, you'll get a large emergency fund and you'll need to diversify. But if it looks like the large net profit is not going to be a recurring event, then save as much of that money as you possible can—in *low-risk* savings.

Be smart about it. Don't put all of your money in the same institution. As people learned this past year, banks do fail, and even though the FDIC insures them, sometimes it takes weeks to get all the money that you're owed. Spread your liquid savings around various banks.

Watch your level of risk. Here's my theory of investing. My job—my writing career—is high risk. I do not have a day job and a salary paid by someone outside. I'm dependent on myself to make money.

So I keep my net profits in low-risk investments. I plow a lot of money back into my business. I have much more liquidity than the "experts" say a person should have. And I have no stocks. I never have. They're too high risk—and were, even in the tech bubble of the 1990s.

I invest in real estate—and that took a hit in this recession—but I'll continue to do so as time goes on. Why? Real estate isn't as high risk for me as it is for most people. I used to work in real estate. I handled rentals. I've never expected property values to rise continually. I've always expected—and planned for—the ups and downs.

I'm sure each and every one of you has expertise in an area outside of your freelance business. You might consider your secondary investments there. But again, watch your risk.

For example, between us, Dean and I have run or been involved in at least ten different bar and restaurant businesses. We would never own one. Running a restaurant takes diligence that we would not have as investors—and we don't want to run the business ourselves.

Dean recently started a retail business to sell collectibles, which he knows quite a bit about. We invested heavily in that business and sold it for a profit as the recession was getting deeper. We always planned to sell the business. We knew how much money we could make. (We actually made more.) But again, we both knew retail and we knew our limits.

Those are not traditional investments—stocks, bonds, etc.— but we don't live a traditional life.

So…to put it all in a nutshell:

If you have what you believe to be a short-term net profit:

1. **Set aside your taxes.**
2. **Save for future emergencies.**
3. **Reinvest in your business.**
4. **Stash the remaining money in a low-risk investment, maybe even something liquid.**

If you know that your net profit will continue and might even grow over the next few years:

1. **Set aside your taxes each time you register that net profit.**
2. **Save for future emergencies. Set a limit on that savings account.**
3. **Reinvest in your business.**
4. **Diversify. Keep some money liquid. Then invest in something quite different from the business you're working in. Again, keep your investments as low risk as possible.**

Let me define **risk**:

Risk comes in many forms. Not just in the possible financial loss that can occur when your investment goes south, but also in the possible loss of time. I wouldn't own a restaurant, not just because the financial risk is great (it is), but also because a restaurant needs hands-on management to make sure it maintains its profit margin. I don't have that kind of time.

Dean was willing to invest a great deal of time for his collectibles store, knowing that investment of time was limited to

12-18 months. It paid off, even as the economic downturn started, because he knows the collectibles business and the local business environment very well, and because he has run other profitable retail businesses in the past.

It was a nice break from his writing, and he used it as such. He does that now and then, which makes me, the financial conservative, very, very happy.

When you invest—in anything—*research that investment first. Know your level of risk. Know the possible downside to the investment and monitor that investment closely.*

I can't tell you how many people I've talked to who never once looked at their 401K until stocks fell dramatically last September. These people let other people invest for them, had no idea how their money was being used, and believed those "estimated rate of return" figures some broker spouted off when they joined the 401K. Some people I talked to last fall had thought that the stock market was a risk-free investment. I still shake my head over that.

Managing money takes a lot of time and effort. The more money you have, the more effort it takes.

The people who lose their wealth do so because they let someone else manage their money. Those managers embezzle (Bernie Madoff and all the lower level pond scum that are filling the news these days) or mismanage the money. If the managers were wealthy, for the most part, they wouldn't be doing the day job of managing other people's money. It's that simple.

That doesn't mean that financial managers are worthless. But most people use them incorrectly.

Never lose control of your money. Keep track of every single dime. If you made a risky investment, fine—as long as you know the risks going in. The last thing you want to do is be surprised, as so many Madoff investors were last fall. One day those sad people were comfortable or even rich. The next day, they were broke. All because they forgot the basic rules of investing: *keep an eye on your money, ask questions, and diversify.*

I can't be much more specific than this because everyone's risk tolerance varies. Everyone's knowledge of money management varies. Everyone's expertise varies.

But if I've gotten you to be conservative with your profits, I've done my job. Don't hide your money under the mattress. But it's okay to park the money in a low-yield money market account (or several accounts) while you're deciding what to do with it. Research everything and go into each investment with your eyes wide open.

The best thing you can do is start researching how you want to invest *before* you ever have a net profit. If it's too late for you and you've been running profits for years, then start your research now.

Yes, managing your money takes time. But that's one of the problems you trade up for. You want to spend time allocating your profits. It's a much better way to spend your days than trying to keep yourself from sinking in too much debt.

Chapter Eighteen
Income Streams

I know a lot of freelancers who have one client. Just one, who pays a lot of money to the freelancer, and that single client keeps the freelancer in business. It's a freelance arrangement, because the freelancer works from home, handles her own taxes, and is usually paid by the task.

One client and one client only is the riskiest way to run your freelance business.

If the client dies, has financial troubles, or shuts down his business, your business disappears along with it, just like your day job would disappear if you worked for a sole proprietor at, say, a dentist's office.

If the client dies—even if he dies suddenly—you're actually better off than you would be if he has financial troubles or if he shuts down his business. I hate to be crass about this, but if your single client dies and you're quick about billing, your final bill will be paid by the estate.

If your client has financial trouble, you'll probably be one of the last people paid. Or you might get paid, but only when the client needs you. Chances are that you'll get stiffed on your last few bills, and you'll never be able to recover that money.

Getting stiffed is part of doing business. The key is to minimize the losses.

If your client goes out of business—especially if it's sudden— you're probably out of luck. Not only will you never see the final payments on your last few bills, you will lose the income source for your business forever.

Just like employees at a restaurant that locks its doors one night and never reopens, you'll be outside in the cold without your final check, looking for a new job.

How do you solve this problem? Simple.

Work for more than one client/company.

That way, if your main client shuts down, you'll have income while you're getting through the tough times. You'll have income while you're looking for someone to replace that really big client. While you'll be struggling to fill that financial gap, you won't be going from large checks to no checks. You'll have something to tide you along the way.

Sometimes, however, entire industries shut down. The tried-and-true example, used in every single economics class I ever had, is buggy whips. When Henry Ford invented the automobile more than 100 years ago, he destroyed the buggy whip industry.

Before cars, you'll recall, people rode horses everywhere. And often, they rode in a carriage with either a single horse or a team of horses pulling a carriage. This, by the way, is the reason we still use the term "horsepower" as a measure of the power of a car's engine. The term "horsepower" was an advertising term for early automobiles, telling prospective buyers that the new car was the equivalent of 5 horses or 50 horses.

Horses didn't go away. People still ride them, mostly for pleasure, although some do so as part of their job. Carriages didn't go away. Every major city in the U.S. has a horse-drawn carriage ride around some romantic or historic part of town. But buggy whips—I've only seen one in use in my entire life, and that was for show.

Many in the carriage industry moved over to building carriages for cars. (That's why your car's middle is called its carriage.) My grandfather, a rural mail carrier who started his route with a horse-drawn carriage, kept his horse until the horse died, long after my grandfather moved to using a car.

But buggy whips were an accessory, replaced year after year, and were a hugely profitable industry. The whips were also specialized—can you think of another legitimate use for them? I can't, off the top of my head—and over a relatively short period of time, whips went from something most households owned to something of a curiosity.

An entire industry wiped out in the space of about (I'm not looking this up; you can) twenty years. It declined within five years of the day Henry Ford introduced the idea of credit into the economy, making cars affordable to everyone. (But the introduction of credit into American life is a topic for another day—and a different guide.)

Have I seen industries go away in my lifetime? Yes, dozens of them. Some were blips—how many of you have a dedicated fax machine these days?—and some were essential, like daily milk delivery. In the early 1960s when I was a little girl, we had an aluminum box outside the front door of our 3-bedroom ranch house, and every morning (or at least once a week), a delivery man put a glass quart of milk inside the box. I have no idea how my parents paid him or when that service ended. I only remember it because I got my butt paddled one day for putting garbage in that box (a bag of dog poo if I remember right) and the look on my mother's face as she pulled that garbage out of a place that was built to house milk.

Every industry changes. Every industry goes through boom-and-bust cycles. One industry's bust is another industry's boom.

For example, realtors are hurting right now. A few years ago, realtors could sell a shed with an outhouse and call it a fixer-upper. Now, perfectly good homes are not selling at all, which means that realtors are suffering great losses in their income. Those realtors who understand boom-and-bust cycles saved during the boom, and those savings are helping them ride out this bust. But several others are probably looking for a new profession right now.

On the other hand, an entire industry is growing right now. People who clean out empty houses and prepare them for sale have more work than they can handle. With the rise in foreclosures, former owners have left their homes in a hurry and often in a disaster. The cleaners make sure the house is show-ready (as much as possible). Often the bank hires the cleaners in the hopes of making the property presentable and saleable.

Sometimes, however, work in all industries simply stops. It has happened to me at two different times in publishing. The first time is too arcane to explain here, having to do with distribution system changes and an industry reacting in fear.

But the second time is memorable, and easy to explain.

I work for a variety of publishers. Nine years ago, all of my publishers were in New York City. When 9/11 happened, several of my publishers were only a few blocks away from Ground Zero. They were closed for a month, unable to get to their offices.

Other publishers lost key people, or had people on family leave because those people had lost a loved one. For six months after 9/11, my husband and I didn't receive a single check from a large New York City publisher, even though we had several due—in *September*.

Business simply stopped for a few months—at least in New York.

Fortunately, I have other publishers in France, Germany, Israel, and Russia, just to name a few places. They didn't stop publishing—although for a while, science fiction and fantasy publishing in Germany went through such a bust that German sf publishers weren't buying any books from anyone.

So I learned. I have different publishers—different clients, if you will. But I also work in a variety of related industries.

For example, I write science fiction novels. Those sell to one set of publishers. I write fantasy novels. That's a wider set of publishers. I write mystery novels. Yet a different set of publishers. And romance fiction—a fourth set of publishers.

I continue to write non-fiction, even though I complain about it. I sell that to magazines and online publications. I write short stories, which sell all over the country to magazines, online publishers, and anthology publishers.

I also sell books and short stories overseas. Each publisher in each country represents a different client.

I also teach. And I give speeches. Mostly, I charge a nominal fee. (I've learned that people don't value something they don't pay for.) I don't make a profit on that, but look at teaching as paying forward. Other professional writers taught me, and I can't pay them back. But I can teach newer professional writers as a way of continuing that giving.

I look at speeches as a bit of promotion and as a way of giving to my readers. I don't do many speeches, and I suppose a time will come when I will have to charge the going rate, just to keep the demand down. But right now, I choose not to.

However, both of those skills—teaching and speechifying—could become additional income streams if I need them some day.

So, the lesson here is simple:

Diversify.

Offer more than one product (short stories, novels in different genres) to more than one market. Use all of your skills, not just a few, and you'll make more money.

I can't tell you how many opportunities have come my way because I work in more than one part of the publishing industry. When I went to the World Science Fiction Convention in Denver in

2008, I got offered three different editing jobs. I turned them all down because I don't want to edit any longer. But I had worked in that part of the industry for so long and people liked what I did well enough that I still get job offers for that work, more ten years after I quit.

When possible, get paid more than once for the same work.

That's not possible in every industry. But in a lot of freelance industries, you produce a product that you might be able to sell in more than one place. For example, I have an entire inventory of stories and novels that have sold in the United States. I can remarket all of those stories and novels overseas. I can also resell those stories and novels to different U.S. markets, depending on the rights I initially sold.

The nice thing about writing as opposed to, say, plumbing, is that my work from twenty years ago still generates income. If you have a freelance gig like mine, figure out how to make your past work earn for you and how to make your current work do double and triple duty.

Keep good records.

It's easy to keep track of everything if you only have one client. But if you have dozens of clients and hundreds of products, like I do, the only thing that will keep you afloat is excellent record-keeping. If you work alone, then your record-keeping system can be as idiosyncratic as you are. If you have employees, you'll probably need to develop set systems for record keeping.

I keep an extensive tickler file (a reminder file, for those of you who haven't worked in business), and I use it not just to keep track of my own deadlines, but also my clients' deadlines. In other words, I keep track of when money is due and how much to expect, so that I don't have to dig through files or back e-mails to find information.

I keep my records by project and by client. For example, if a book sells in the United States, that's one project and one client. If I resell that book to Germany, then I create a new file for that project with a different client.

Then I have my Accounts Receivable file. I know who owes me money and how much. I'll discuss this more in-depth in the billing chapter, but suffice to say that my record-keeping keeps my business afloat.

Finally, **keep track of industry changes.**

Right now, huge changes are going on in publishing, mostly because of connectivity, social networking, and the web. I am doing my best to explore new markets created by these changes. I don't automatically close my mind to online publishing, as so many of my colleagues have. They're afraid of theft. I'm more interested in expanding my audience.

My *Freelancer's Survival Guide* blog was an experiment in new media. Cutting out the publishing middleman is appropriate for some projects—like this one, which is timely. However, I need to be paid per project, and that's why I put the donation button up.

Right now, I'm exploring various venues to get my out-of-print novels and stories back in the hands of readers. I haven't decided if I'll republish some of them or if I'll find a publisher to do so. I also haven't decided if I'll use my own website as a forum for those stories.

But these opportunities exist now. They didn't exist ten years ago. Ten years ago, an out-of-print novel remained out of print unless a new publisher was interested or a writer hit the *New York Times* list with a similar book.

A lot of my colleagues are stuck in the past. They won't publish anything on their websites. They won't join social networks. They won't explore online markets. They're overwhelmed by the changes or they're not working to understand them.

Most of what I hear from these folks is uninformed fear. And that fear may limit or curtail their careers in the future.

On the Fourth of July weekend in 2009, I received two different business opportunities, one through a Facebook contact and one through Twitter. Both opportunities wouldn't have come to me if I weren't exploring these new social networking sites. Both opportunities turned into income.

And—honestly—even if they hadn't, I was happy to have the chance. I always feel that way about new opportunities. The chance is important, whether or not it ends up going my way.

Let's go back to the buggy whips, carriages, and the introduction of cars. I'm sure a lot of carriage makers went out of business in those years as well. But the far-sighted ones learned how to change one part of their industry to suit the newfangled machinery.

That's what every small business owner should do. Keep up

with all the changes in your industry and see how you can profit from those changes. In the beginning, the profits might be small. But in the end, you'll be ready to make the changes long before everyone else in the industry, and that will help you survive.

So, in short, here are a few things you need to do to maximize profits for your business:

1. **Have more than one client.**
2. **Diversify.**
3. **Get paid more than once for the same work (if possible).**
4. **Keep excellent records.**
5. **Take advantage of changes in your industry.**

The more sources of income you have—whether it's an abundance of clients or an abundance of opportunities—the more chances you have for success.

I told you above that you need to be a realist and/or a pessimist when you're looking at your expenses. When you look at potential income, you must be an optimist. Always assume that a new client will be interested in you, or that you can learn the new computer program that will allow you to streamline your business.

Approach each new thing, client, or opportunity with an open mind and an eye to the future. You'll be much more successful if you do.

Chapter Nineteen
Billing and Toughness

Billing and toughness.

Those two things go together. In order to have income, you must charge for your work. Once you set the price, you must demand payment in some form or another. If you don't get that payment, you must go after it, somehow.

First, let's discuss setting price.

Oddly enough, this is often the toughest thing for the freelancer. You must set a price for your work. This price must do three things: it must reimburse you for your time and effort, as well as whatever costs you already have in the project; it must be within the range of whatever the customer can afford; and it must indicate value.

The last is the most nebulous. But when Dean and I started teaching our own writers workshops, we learned what this means.

We started our workshops as a way to pay forward. Other professional writers had helped us along the way, and we couldn't help them in their careers. So we pay forward, to the other professionals and up-and-coming writers who need help.

Initially, we did a lot of work for free, or for the expenses (and somehow, what we got paid never did cover expenses). These workshops, while giving us some practice, never really attracted the writers we wanted to help. Sometimes one or two of them would come, but the majority were people who had thought of writing, but weren't writing.

We used price to weed out the wannabe writers who weren't serious. But we had other considerations. The workshops had to pay their own expenses. And we had to keep the price relatively low, because most professional writers and serious writers trying to become professional often didn't have much money. We certainly didn't in their shoes.

So we set the price as low as we could and still cover expenses. We had to donate our time to do this—and once in a while, we still miss. Last fall, for example, after the Master Class for professionals who need to jumpstart their careers, we were $3000 in the wrong direction. So not only did we donate our time, we lost $3000.

Not the best way to run a business.

Fortunately, we don't make our living teaching. If we did, we would charge a lot more. For example, a writer I know who has published no novels and maybe twenty short stories (who would, in short, be a candidate for our Master Class if he were so inclined) makes his living teaching and charges $5000 to $10,000 *per student* for his weekly workshops. We charge $2500 for two weeks, and that includes room and breakfast.

The price difference comes from two areas. He needs the money to make his living, and he doesn't care who comes to his workshops. In fact, most of the people who do come are upper middle class and retired, and see the workshop as an adventure vacation.

We make our money writing, and we care who comes to our workshops. We screen heavily—and even at our discounted prices, a lot of our students struggle to get the time off and to pay for the workshop itself.

Note the considerations in setting price.

Each freelance group sets price differently. Contractors bid for projects. The bids are estimates, but they become binding when the client takes the project. Anything over the estimate becomes a cost overrun that the client must approve.

When a contractor bids, he's setting his price based on several factors: the cost of materials, the cost of labor, the cost of overhead, and the cost of intangibles (discovering, for example, that the floor he was going to use as the base for the new wall is rotted and must be replaced). The contractor must also make a profit, or he will go out of business.

Contractors have another consideration: contractors bid against each other. So the contractor must factor his competitors into the mix. The cost of materials should remain the same for all the contractors. The cost of labor should be similar. And all of the contractors have to factor in the intangibles.

The only areas where the contractor has discretion are the cost of overhead and the profit. However, the contractor can only trim his overhead so far. Sometimes a contractor will forgo the profit to get the job, with the guarantee of being the sole contractor on future jobs. In those jobs, the contractor will add the profit back in.

Over the years, contractors have learned to shave expenses in other areas. They work with their suppliers, getting excellent deals which bring down the cost of materials. They decide when they can use cheaper labor—or just do the job themselves.

All of these things factor into price. And it becomes a real balancing act. Most independent contractors go out of business because they undercharge too much. They get the job, but just like our Master Class last year, the job costs them more money than they expected. They don't make overhead and they certainly don't make a profit.

Contractors aren't the only ones who get paid for the job. Plumbers and a variety of other service providers do the same, with the same considerations.

Consultants have an even more difficult task. They ask to be paid for their intellectual ability in a certain area—again, the ability to do a job. But often there are no materials. There are no other employees. There's only one person's knowledge, and the value it imparts to the client.

Lawyers, psychologists, money managers, all must set their fee, whether it's an hourly rate or a fee per job or—in the case of agents (from book agents to insurance agents to real estate agents), a percentage of the gross money they bring in for their client. In many of these fields, there are reasonable and standard rates. But the more in demand the consultant is, the more she can charge. Starting in these fields, however, can be difficult, because the consultant's worth is, at that point, unproven.

When we owned the collectibles shop, we had other considerations on setting price. We sold comic books, marbles, cookie jars, jewelry—all kinds of things that people collect. (Dean collected them and finally decided to use the shop to sell off his collections. It didn't work because he bought new collectibles while there. That is, it didn't work, until he sold the store.)

We had owned many of the items that we sold for decades. Some of the items had risen in value; some had lost value. Dean set the prices because this is his area of expertise. The shop was in an antiques mall at the far end of the tourist town where we live. (You can still visit the shop, which has been run by its new owner for longer than we had it. Pop Culture Collectibles, in Streetcar Village, Lincoln City, Oregon.)

Dean knew his customer base, and that set not only the prices, but also which items he had in his store. He knew most of the traffic would come from tourists looking for souvenirs, so he needed to provide cheap impulse buys. Some of the traffic would be true collectors, who would find the one item they needed to fill out their collections. For them, he needed to offer that item at its value or higher, so that he could negotiate the price down to something they'd be willing to pay. Collectors will often pay more than something is worth so that they can finish their collections.

Other collectors would want an item, but would be like Dean himself: they wouldn't buy that collectible unless it was beneath the price listed in the various price guides. So for them, he needed collectibles priced enough under guide to be tempting, but the price had to be high enough so that Dean made a profit on the item.

Finally, he would have repeat customers—also collectors— who checked the store every month or so to see if something new came in, so that they could add to their collections. Often these collectors fell into the last category. But their presence meant that Dean's inventory had to change on a regular basis.

So he had to price to move product out the door.

So the prices in his store varied from extremely high to extremely low. His main thought with the store—our original reason for owning it—was to move product. So most items were priced under market value. But he had a few that he knew only the specialty collectors would buy, so he priced those at or above market value.

And then there were the truly special items that he had in the store mostly as decoration. In other words, he didn't want to sell those items, but he wanted people to see them.

Those items had the price that Dean called ridiculous. The ridiculous price was so high that he would part with the item and feel good about the item leaving his life. Needless to say, he didn't sell many of those, but when he did, he laughed all the way to the bank.

Most writers reading this are feeling a bit confused at the moment. Writers don't set price the way that retail store owners do. Writers mail their materials to a market that will pay them an established rate. From many writers' points of view that means that the magazine or the book publisher sets the price.

But that's simply not true.

Writers place a value upon their work in a different way. The value for their work comes in the markets they pursue.

For example, pay rates for short stories vary from payment in copies of the magazine (in other words no money at all and very little value) to thousands of dollars per story.

The competition for the thousands-of-dollar markets is high; the competition for the pays-in-copies markets is extremely low. Even as a beginning writer, I refused to submit stories to the pays-in-copies markets. My theory was—and is—this: I'm a professional. I get paid for my work in actual money.

I started then and continue to mail my work to the high-competition, high-paying markets. Those markets often invite high-end contributors, so the room for an unsolicited story is quite small—maybe one or two slots per year. Some years I hit that slot, some years I don't, but I always try.

Then I work my way down, figuring out two things: Price and audience.

Why audience? Simple. As I grow the number of people who like my work, I can increase the price I demand for that work. I become one of the invitees instead of someone knocking on the door trying to get into the highest paying markets.

The attitude remains the same for my work with book publishers. I factor in the time it takes me to write a novel, what I need to pay my bills, and how much profit I want *at minimum*. (Of course, I will take money above the minimum, so setting the minimum price is the best.)

I'm fast and prolific, which gives me the luxury of taking some lower-paying project because I want to write it. If I only wrote one book every five years, I would have to demand a higher price for it—if I were a full-time freelancer. (Most people who write one book every five years have day jobs.)

How do I demand price? In the book publishing industry, price is negotiable. The publisher makes an offer for my work. The offer includes a price (among other things). I then accept the price or negotiate it upwards. The publisher has a limit of what he will pay me on the upper end, and I have a limit of what I will accept on the lower end.

Sometimes we come to an agreement, and sometimes we don't.

Occasionally, I screw up. A project takes more work than I expected, for example. In one case, I had deliberately priced myself out of the market (I thought), and the publisher exceeded my price. I was stuck with a project I really didn't want to do. I learned, in that instance, to set the bar higher for a project I don't want.

Note: rarely do I say no to a project I don't want. I want the publisher to return to me with other projects and/or to consider future projects I send him. So instead of saying no, I set my price so high that the publisher will decide to hire a different writer. This is the writer equivalent of Dean's decorative collectibles. My problem early on was that I didn't set my price high enough to laugh all the way to the bank.

Sometimes, the publisher screws up. He pays me more than the project could ever earn. This usually happens on projects that originate with the publisher and he asks me to do the writing. It does happen with my original work, but rarely. Usually the publisher and I know what the market will bear for that work, and we both set our prices accordingly. I set mine by demanding an up-front payment of a certain amount, with a royalty in case the book does better than expected. He sets his with that upfront payment and with the price point he puts on the later book.

Which brings me to the *Freelancer's Guide*. I could have written 50 pages, added a proposal, and marketed this book to the top non-fiction publishers. If I had done that, I would have had a dollar figure in mind for my advance payment. If no publisher offered that, I wouldn't write the project.

For years, I had thought of doing that but never did. Part of that was because, as a full-time fiction writer, I never made the time for the speculative non-fiction work. All of my non-fiction these days is commissioned.

I have received a lot of non-fiction book offers in the past twenty-five years, and I've accepted none of them. Mostly I've priced myself out of the market on purpose. In the one case where the publisher accepted my price, I would have completed the book—except that it was a rush job, and a legitimate family emergency arose. (I had to go to Hollywood to work with a production company for two weeks, and two days before I was to leave, my mother died.) No money had changed hands. I begged out of the project, and the publisher found someone else to write the book.

When I realized in March of 2009 that the *Freelancer's Guide* needed to be on the market *right now*, I still could have gone to a mainstream publisher. "Right now" would have become a year later, but the book would still have had its uses. And a book publisher in today's market would have understood the need for such a project.

Instead, I decided to answer the siren song of "now" and use the opportunities available to me as a freelancer in the modern market to publish the book immediately.

I was thinking of my audience, mostly. Just like Dean and I do with teaching, I wanted the *Guide* to benefit people who are struggling right now and trying to succeed in a new profession. (Many longtime professional freelancers started in recessions or [if you read history] the Great Depression. If you can't find work, you create your own.)

Even with this self-publishing option, I had a variety of routes. I could have posted the *Guide* as proprietary e-files. People who had e-readers could download the book for a price that I would set. But many people don't have e-readers, although most people have computers. So I could have posted the *Guide* privately on my website. It would have taken a password to access the *Guide*. I could have set a price for that password.

But I had two considerations against that option: first, most of my new audience wouldn't have discretionary income. I want to reach the folks who were living on unemployment benefits, suddenly and frighteningly unemployed, and looking at all of their options. Those folks couldn't pay for the *Guide*.

The other consideration was pure marketing: People now know me as a fiction writer. No one knows I wrote non-fiction for years unless I've told them. So the value of the *Guide* would be hard for the customer to determine without actually reading it. I could have given the first installment away for free and made people pay for the rest, but that automatically limited my market.

So I decided to publish on my site. But I had the internal problem of the deadline. I don't write for free. I never have. I need some kind of payment for my expenses (which are my time, my webspace, my research [which can be extensive], and my overhead). So I put up the donation button.

Even then, I could have set price. PayPal gives me the option of accepting a set fee for the donation. I decided to let the consumer choose what price she paid for the *Guide*. And I was up front about that.

Here's how I see it: Those of you who donated (thank you) are paying for more than my expenses. You're buying free copies of the *Guide* and giving them to the people who actually need it. In other words, you're making the "free" part of this *Guide* possible.

Setting price is probably the most important part of your freelance business. It's also the most difficult. You will miss on occasion, especially early on. Chalk that up to a learning experience—and don't make the same mistake again.

Here are the factors to consider as you set price:

1. **Your expenses.**
2. **The amount of time the project will take** (or that you've already invested).
3. **The cost of materials** (if any).
4. **The cost of labor besides you** (if any).
5. **The minimum you need to make on the item/project to make a slight profit—or to gain an intangible, like getting the client to return.** (In retail, that's called a loss leader; you give something away for free, so that the client will purchase another similar item at a much higher cost.)
6. **The maximum you can charge a client without chasing the client to something or someone cheaper.**
7. **The profit** (and there needs to be a profit most of the time).

Let's assume you've established price for your various wares/ services. You know what you'll charge. You've even been a good freelancer and agreed upon price with your client before you take the job.

Now the difficult part begins.

Not the actual work. Freelancers love the actual work; that's why we're in this crazy business.

The hard part is making sure we get paid.

Early on, most freelancers are reluctant to discuss payment. Most believe that setting price, signing a contract, or settling on a bid, is more than enough. Unfortunately, it often isn't.

In the area of payment, the only self-employed person who has an advantage is the storeowner. The moment a customer enters a store, she knows that she has to lay down some cash if she wants to remove an item from that store. The item usually has a price sticker, or sits on a shelf beneath a properly displayed price.

The only people who walk out with an item they haven't paid for are shoplifters, who can be prosecuted under various and sundry criminal statutes, depending on the price of the item or items they steal.

If only the rest of us had it so easy.

Here's a fact: People hate to pay bills. I know I do. Just today when I was in the post office, a woman joked about not paying her bills next month because she was tired of their constant demands.

When you agree to perform a service or do a job, and you have not received full payment from your client up front, your work has become a bill.

Now think of this bill from the client's point of view, because you are a client of various services and a purchaser of many wares. Your monthly bills are paid on a schedule (on time, I hope). They're also paid according to importance. Your bills get paid in a certain order. So do everyone else's. Including your clients.

And unless you're providing an important *continuing* service, you will automatically rank lower than the rent, the utilities, and the groceries. The good clients pay you no matter what. The well-intentioned clients pay you when they can. The bad clients pay you when they get around to it. The horrible clients don't pay you at all.

You will get all four clients in your business. The key is to make sure the bulk of your clients are good clients. Realize, however, that good clients can become horrible clients if something awful (like a recession) happens. I'll talk about the warning signs of that impending catastrophe a little later.

When they start, most freelancers assume all of their clients will be good clients. Many freelancers rely on the contract they have with the client to set payment times. Most contracts—and all jobs requiring a bid—have dates certain for payment. If that payment isn't met on that date, then the contract is void.

(Conversely, the freelancer also has dates by which the service or job must be finished. If the freelancer misses those dates, then the contract is void as well.)

The **good clients** mark those dates on the calendar, and meet them without any prompting at all. Provided you do the work as agreed (and of course you do), checks show up in your mailbox like clockwork.

In all of my years in publishing, only a few of my clients have paid on time. Even though publishing contracts have a date certain for payment (usually triggered by turn-in dates for my side of the work), most major publishers pay three to six months after they're legally obligated to do so.

It took me a long time to figure out why.

Like any corporation, large publishing companies have different departments to handle different tasks. When I turn in a manuscript, the editor immediately puts in for payment. But that request for payment goes through several hands before a check ever gets cut. Then that check must find its way to me.

These systems benefit the corporation. The longer it hangs on to its money, the more interest it can earn from that money. (This practice used to be even worse in the 1980s, when personal savings accounts paid 5% on deposits—and businesses earned even more.)

Some of these delays are the cost of doing business. You have to expect them. And, if you do a lot of business with a certain client, you learn how long their in-house process is. Sometimes you can expedite that process. But rarely can you avoid it altogether.

That's why so many bills that you received have a net 30 days payment request on them. That's a tacit acknowledgement of the fact that you won't pay the bill the day it arrives. You must pay it within thirty days. That's considered reasonable within the business world. You'll learn what "reasonable" is in your freelance world within a short period of time.

However much we wish otherwise, good clients are rare in all businesses. The most common client is the **well-intentioned client**. These people pay their deposit and then might not pay another dime for months, maybe a year, although they mean to.

How do you get a well-intentioned client to pay?

There are several ways.

First, you invoice. Most freelancers never invoice. Many writers haven't written an invoice ever, yet they bitch when they don't get paid. An invoice, sent monthly, is an excellent reminder of payment due.

That invoice should be net 30 days like most invoices. It should also carry a notice: *Any payment made after 30 days will receive a 1 percent surcharge.* (Or a late fee of no more than 10% of the bill, which you should delineate out. If the bill is for $250, then the late fee should be no more than $25 and can be as little as $2.50.)

This is an easy way to notify the client that you will charge more if payment is late.

Often that's enough to get the well-intentioned client to pay within thirty days.

Second, make a courtesy call. Yep, call someone about the payment and *ask for it*. Calling a client about a late bill is uncomfortable for you, but even more uncomfortable for him. He's well intentioned, remember, and will be embarrassed by his own behavior.

If you've invoiced the client, remind him that he had to pay within thirty days. Call within the week of the missed payment and say that you'll waive the late fee if the check arrives immediately.

Chances are, you'll get money within the week.

Usually, those two things are enough to get a well-intentioned client to pay. Remember that the timeline varies from profession to profession. Unfortunately, in my profession, net 90 days is customary. So I initiate a version of this system after three months, instead of after just one.

The timeline also varies from job to job. If you're a contractor who must finish a house a month before the annual beginning of the rainy season, then you might invoice every week or two. If the client gets behind…

Well, let's discuss clients who pay very late in a moment.

Just remember: the best thing to do is believe that all of your clients are well intentioned. If you believe they're all good clients, you'll get burned a lot early on. If you believe they're all well intentioned, you'll invoice and you'll keep an eye on payments.

Invoices, by the way, can be generated for all types of businesses. All it really takes is a piece of paper with the name and address of your business, the date, the date of service or job turn-in, the amount, a running total (in case the client doesn't pay the previous invoice), a 30-60-90 day clock, and a notice of possible interest or late fees if the client is delayed in payment. Most accounting software has an invoice that you can tailor to your business.

Print out two copies of the invoice and save one paper copy for your files. If you have a computer crash like I did a few weeks ago, you'll be happy that you did. (Not everyone backs up their data on a daily basis, so you'd miss some invoices.)

Set up a business calendar with client payment dates marked in red. I mark the date the payment is due, the date I expect the payment (which is often different—by the aforementioned 90 days), and the date when I will consider the payment overdue. My computer calendar has reminders, so I will get notification, which does spur me to action.

That's a simple system, and one that works for a freelancer who works alone. I'm sure there are as many systems as there are freelancers. The best thing to do is have a system in place that works for you.

Well-intentioned clients can become good clients with some diligence on your part. The well-intentioned client who doesn't have financial troubles will get into the habit of paying you regularly because you're one of those people who nags about money.

The sad truth of the matter is that the old cliché is right: the squeaky wheel does get the grease. And if the client knows you'll want payment on time (or at least within 30 days of invoice) or you'll constantly remind them, they'll make sure the reminders never happen.

But a financial reversal can change any client—good or well-intentioned—into a **bad client**. Here's where the freelancer gets in trouble.

Again, put yourself in the client's shoes. His income gets reduced due to the bad economy. He pays the essential bills—rent, power, water—and puts everything else on a sliding scale. That scale is determined by need, but also by what Mark Terry called in the comments section of my blog, the PITA tax.

I love that term. It's the pain-in-the-ass tax. If the client knows you're going to bother him when you don't get paid, you'll move up the payment ladder. You're a potential pain in the ass. And in billing, pains in the ass get paid.

Unfortunately, it's the silent, polite freelancer who loses out here.

If you assume your good client will continue to pay you on time, you're very trusting. Someday you will pay for that trust. As I once told a freelancer friend of mine, the secret to getting paid is to be first in line, especially as money troubles hit. I've been paid by more failing businesses than most of my writer friends. I'm familiar with the signs since I've had businesses that fail. And when the signs become obvious, I'll push harder and harder for payment.

We've all been in the client's circumstance. We all know that some bills slide, and then slide some more; and sometimes they never,

ever, get paid. The quieter the freelancer is, the more likely the money will run out and the freelancer will never get paid.

The bad client promises payment, yet never comes through. Ninety days pass, then 100 days pass, and still no payment, not even if you send invoices with late fees and make the follow-up phone calls.

So...how do you get paid?

You stop working. It's that simple. To use the contractor example from above, let's assume the contractor must frame in a house before the rainy season. The client hasn't paid the incremental fees on the contract. (For example, ten percent when the foundation gets dug, plus expenses [I'm making these percentages up; I know they're not accurate]; another ten percent when the foundation gets poured, plus expenses, and so on.)

The contractor tells the bad client that the house won't get framed in until all invoices are paid. The client might lose the entire house to wet, mold, and other problems if the contractor stops.

I haven't dealt with one thing that needs a mention here. Any agreement you have with a client needs consequences—on both sides. Never assume that the client understands your work methods. Have it all in writing up front.

Remember this: *It's better to have everything in writing—clear writing—than it is to have a spoken gentleman's agreement.*

Recently, I have had to withhold manuscripts from publishers while I awaited payment. I've had to do this before in recessions or economic downturns. In one recent case, the contract was invalid until I got my first payment. In other words, the publisher and I had no agreement at all until money changed hands. I didn't turn in the completed manuscript until I got paid because the contract wasn't valid until the client paid me up front.

Other writers with the same house had no trouble turning in their manuscripts. But I've had work published without payment only to then watch the publishing house collapse. The work is published, those publication rights exercised (which means I lost those particular rights), and I never received compensation.

So I'm tough about being paid. Even with friends.

In another instance, a reputable small company bought a story of mine and gave me a contract that guaranteed payment on acceptance. I didn't receive any money. I nagged and invoiced. Months later, I saw a prepublication galley of the book with my story in it. I called the people in charge, reminded them that they had no rights to the story because they hadn't paid me, and they told me they weren't going to pay until after publication.

That was not in our contract. They wouldn't budge. Neither would I. (Ten other writers gave in, feeling sorry for the publisher.) The contract was void. They had lost the right to publish the story. I pulled the story from the anthology a month before the anthology was due to appear. The company had to reprint the text, junking a lot of paper. It would have been cheaper to pay me.

But, last I heard, no one in the anthology has been paid (two years after the publication) and the company never paid the printer either. The handwriting was on the wall. That company is officially on hiatus (unofficially out of business). Even if it comes back, it will never regain its good reputation.

I sold that story to a different market, making triple what the first publisher had promised. And I got paid on acceptance.

I made money in that transaction. I'm the only freelancer who did.

Because I'm tough.

I expect my business to be treated like any other business. I expect payment for my work. I expect that payment on time. I will modify my on-time expectation to include what is reasonable for the client's usual payment schedule. But…I will charge late fees. I will nag if I'm not paid. And I will withhold work or withdraw work if no payment is forthcoming.

Often I do the tough jobs myself. Some companies have employees who make the tough phone calls or write the difficult letters. But in any one-(wo)man operation, the proprietor writes the dunning letter and makes the dunning phone calls. And pulls the plug on projects until the money arrives from the client.

Sometimes the money never arrives. That turns the bad client into the **horrible client**. The key here is to make certain that the horrible client doesn't owe you too much money, which is why you get tough with the bad client. You're cutting your losses early.

You have to assume that all bad clients will become horrible clients. You must make sure that whatever money the bad client refuses to pay now is the only money they owe you. Because you could go ten, twenty or one hundred percent deeper in debt. I've known freelancers who have done three or four jobs for once-good clients before the freelancers realized the client hadn't just become bad, he'd become horrible.

That's how you go out of business—you're not getting paid. You're doing someone with a failing business a favor. And the best thing you can do for someone whose business is failing is pull out of the slide. Maybe that will be the wake-up call the client needs. Maybe then that client will take drastic action and pull his business out of the slide. Or go out of business before he drags others down with him.

Once you become convinced that the horrible client will never pay his bills with you, you have a choice.

You can continue to pursue the debt, which may mean that you'll have to hire a lawyer, go to court, and maybe get in line at a bankruptcy proceeding, as an unsecured creditor.

Or you can write the debt off.

I try to never get into this situation. But in the few times things have gone this badly for me, I've declined to go to court. Why? By the time I have to hire a lawyer, the chances of me getting any money from the client are slim. If the client is in bankruptcy, I am a minor unsecured creditor. The secured creditors get paid first. The unsecured may get a share of what's left or nothing at all.

By this point, I will have wasted years and gallons of stomach acid on something that will give me no financial return at all. Better to chalk it all up to experience and move to the next project.

Again, I'm not an attorney, nor am I a tax accountant. But I do write off losses in the year that loss occurs. And sometimes I make more money on the write off than I ever would if I had to pay a lawyer, go to court, and squeeze some pennies out of the deadbeat client.

Be practical, and remember what your time is worth. You're always better off doing new work than you are chasing after deadbeats (no matter how furious they've made you).

How do you know a good client is going bad?

First, pay attention to the world around you. As the economy slipped into recession, the business sections of newspapers told the story. It's been clear for years now that the housing bubble would burst. It's also been clear that American car manufacturers were in trouble. When the credit crisis hit, all businesses that couldn't exist without a business line of credit would struggle to stay alive.

If you had any of those businesses as clients—or if you had clients in related fields—you should have been making certain you got paid up front. You also should have been limiting the amount of work you did in those markets, maybe cutting them altogether and finding new clients. (Remember how I recommended diversification? This is why.)

I follow the news religiously. It keeps me on top of my game.

But that's a global way of staying on top of things. Even when the national economy is rosy, people still go out of business. They mismanage their accounts. They overextend. They produce a crummy product or take too many vacations.

Payments will get slower and slower. They might even become late for the first time in your relationship. When you call to check on something, the client will ask you for a favor. Can you do something now for payment later?

In these circumstances, the answer is—and should always be—no.

You have your own business to run, your own bills to pay, and your own family to feed. You must keep clients on a businesslike relationship. That's why so many people recommend that you never go into business with your friends. Because friends are the hardest people in the world to say no to.

Chances are that you will lose the client's business, maybe forever. But if things have gotten so bad that the client can't pay you for work already completed, then he's probably going out of business anyway. Maybe not this year. But next year. And you don't want him to take you with him.

However—and this is a big however—know what is customary in your business. A friend who has no connection to the publishing industry told me this story: One of her friends self-published a non-fiction book and somehow managed to get the local chain bookstore to sell it. The book sold out. The self-published writer demanded payment from the bookstore immediately.

All bookstores pay on net 90 days—sometimes on net 120 days. Chains never pay before that 90-day window.

This self-published writer wanted the money immediately. When she still hadn't seen a check after thirty days, she sued.

She lost, of course.

My friend talked about the injustice of the big chain bookstores, when in reality, her self-published friend knew nothing about the business and acted inappropriately. The self-published writer cost herself a lot of grief and money when she could have simply learned a bit about the business and gotten her small check.

So…before you decide that someone is a horrible client,

make sure you know the norms of the business you're in. Check your contract/bid/ binding agreement. You might have signed something that allowed a later-than-usual payment.

Before you blame the client, make sure the mistake is not your mistake.

And remember, sometimes that mistake is being too lenient from the beginning.

I've learned to be tough with money. I've had clients go bankrupt. I've had friends take advantage of my generous nature. I've had good clients turn horrible.

I've also trained well-intentioned clients to be good clients. I've waited for payment from companies that have had odd downturns (9/11 was an obvious and serious one). I've been a freelancer for most of my adult life, and I've always made a living.

Then again, at any sign of trouble, I'm always the first in line.

Chapter Twenty
Employees

Really, this chapter shouldn't be titled "Employees." It should be titled "People You Hire to Do Stuff for You." But that's too long and a little too wordy, even if it is accurate.

You see, the word "employee" has a specific meaning in the culture and under the tax code. According to the dictionary, an employee is someone who is paid by someone else to do work. Which is a lot like "people you hire to do stuff for you"—just as wordy and almost as vague. (Maybe I should have written "to work for you," but I digress.)

In the culture, however, an employee is someone who goes to your place of business and works for you there. You schedule that employee for a certain number of hours, pay that employee a set wage per hour or a set salary, deduct all the applicable employment taxes, and give that employee a few perks like a paid vacation or sick leave or a bonus.

According to the IRS—and remember, I'm not a lawyer, a tax accountant, or even a tax expert—an employee is someone who does their work at your place of business (or your home) for set hours and a set rate of pay. This can get dodgy, and we'll get to that later. But there are strict rules in the tax code that define employees, and if you ever hire someone, you'd best check out what those rules are in case you need to follow them.

Because the word "employee" has so many fraught meanings, I'm only going to use the cultural one. For example, Dean and I have no employees—at least this year. However, we hire a woman to clean our house weekly and a gardener who beautifies our yard biweekly. The day after I finish this chapter, we'll hire movers to lug books and furniture from one building to another. In May, we hired a real estate agent to sell two of our properties, and I hired a literary agent a few years ago.

Actually, I've hired several literary agents over the various decades, and I'm not sure I can give you an accurate count of how many literary agents actually represent my work—not without some research, considering I have an agent in every country in which I'm published, plus a few in countries where I hope to be published. I have had, over the years, a Hollywood agent and a series of lawyers for a variety of different tasks, ranging from divorce to incorporation to real estate.

So how many people currently work for me? Dunno. Two more tomorrow than today (those movers) and two less by the weekend than tomorrow (again, those movers). If I had to give you an educated guess, I'd say that I have seven people working for me in the United States at this very moment. (More like twenty people, if you count all the folks who are working for me overseas.)

None of these people are employees by IRS rules. Most are consultants or people I hire for a specific task (the movers). Most of the house cleaners I've had over the years are employees of some other business—a house-cleaning business that I hire, just as we're hiring those movers through a moving company. The moving company handles all those nasty employee taxes and the IRS rules, and those fees are probably included in the hourly rate I pay to have those two strong guys to lug boxes of books from one building to the next.

But…I have had real employees, as many as nineteen, back when Dean and I owned Pulphouse Publishing. Only a few years ago, we had a full-time employee at the collectibles store. That was a condition of deciding to own the store—an employee to handle the traffic, so we could travel and continue writing.

With that employee came all kinds of pain-in-the-ass stuff like the aforementioned taxes and IRS documentation. You could spend two hours per day filling out forms, if you're so inclined, which we weren't. So we hired a payroll service to handle all the employee payment matters. We could have hired a bookkeeper, but the service was cheaper.

Back when I was an employee, I handled the employment taxes and all of that stuff for my employer. (Yep, dyslexic old me. That worked well [and yes, that was sarcasm].) It was that experience that made me a convert of temp services, employment companies (like moving companies), and payroll services.

Anything to avoid filling out those forms ever again.

But I get ahead of myself—although not by much. I needed to establish my employer credentials before I write this part of the *Guide*.

Because this first part of the employee chapter should help you decide when (if) you should hire an employee.

The real answer to when you should hire an employee is: never.

Labor costs are usually the greatest expense in any business. The problem with employees is that they're people. They're people you'll get to know and probably befriend despite your best efforts, so even if they cost you more money than they're worth, you'll be loathe to fire them or lay them off when the time comes.

So...you're better off doing the work yourself.

However, that's often unrealistic. Most businesses need a few employees to run efficiently. And it's a balancing act to figure how many you actually need.

Most employees want to do the minimal amount of work for which they'll get the most amount of money.

Most employers want the maximum amount of work for the least amount of money.

You can see the conflict here.

Most first-time employers believe that an employee will work as hard as the employer does, which is a huge mistake. Clearly, most employers don't remember their own employee days—days when they arrived at work exhausted, left early, got the minimum done (or less than the minimum) and foisted the bulk of the job on someone else—or worse, didn't do it at all.

Here's the most important thing to remember about anyone you hire for any task: *No one else will care about your business as much as you do. No one else will work as hard as you do. No one else will ever have as much at stake in your business as you do.*

If you remember all of that, you might survive having employees. But if you forget it, you could be in big, big trouble.

So let's deal with the tough question first: *when do you need an employee—and by employee, I mean the kind that the IRS recognizes as an employee?*

You need an employee when you can no longer function alone as a business operator. You need help to run the day-to-day aspects of your business. You need to be in two places at once, each and every day.

If you have more work than you can possibly do by yourself, even putting in extra hours and streamlining your production, then you'll need an employee.

The first thing you need to figure out is whether or not your need is permanent. Are you in a busy cycle that will go bust in a few short months? Or has your business increase become a fact of life?

If it's a busy cycle, you can (and should) hire help through a temp agency. The agency will vet the employee, pay the employee's wages and taxes, and make sure the employee meets your schedule. Should you dislike this employee, the agency will provide someone else.

That's the best possible short-term solution, and something you should do before you ever hire an employee yourself, because too many small business owners hire an employee only to discover that they hate having someone else on site. Or there are other problems, which we will get to later.

But let's say you're not on a busy cycle. Business has improved enough that you can't provide the same quality product (or service) without some help.

Now you need to figure out if you need full- or part-time help. Be conservative. The fewer people you hire means the fewer people you fire.

Yep, you'll fire people. You'll lay them off. You'll cause distress in their lives—and in yours.

I've fired more people than I want to think about. I even fired volunteers, back when I worked for the listener-sponsored radio station. And why would you ever fire a volunteer—someone who gives of their time and talent?

Often, I fired the volunteer for cause: they stole from the station, they repeatedly insulted or abused the other volunteers, they repeatedly said inappropriate things on the air. But twice, I fired volunteers *for not coming to work*. Go figure that. Those two people volunteered their time, made a commitment, and then didn't show up. When they did bother to come to the station, they were offended when we (in the form of me) told them we didn't need them any more.

After doing that at the ripe old age of 23, I thought I could fire anyone.

I was wrong.

It's different when you fire a friend or someone whom you like who simply can't perform the job at all. And you will fire people. People who embezzle. People who don't bathe (yeah, that was an uncomfortable conversation). People who show up late *every single day*.

Worse than firing, though, is laying someone off. Income necessitates layoffs—or to put it more clearly, *lack* of income necessitates layoffs. Consider that 600,000 people lost their jobs to layoffs in January of 2009 alone. Most of those companies that laid the employees off still exist. The companies were just trimming their bottom line—because as I said, the biggest expense in most businesses is labor. People, in other words.

People with sick kids and elderly parents. People who do their jobs well, but cost a lot of money in wages and benefits. People who have mortgages and car payments and grocery bills. People whom you will get to know very, very well.

If you can't imagine firing employees, if you can't imagine laying off people who do their jobs well, then you should never, ever, hire an employee.

Here are some other tricky things about employees: Lots of federal, state, and local rules and regulations govern your relationship with those employees. Some of those rules govern how you pay them. Some govern the taxes. Some govern how you treat the employee at the job. Some govern what benefits you can legally give. Some govern how you fire people.

All have an impact on you. Employees can and do file grievances with the state for a variety of things, some valid (like sexual harassment) and some not. Suddenly your business isn't quite yours any more.

For example, I have a hell of a potty mouth, and whenever I've had employees, I've cleaned up my language so extremely that I could be talking to a nun without embarrassment. Why? Because some of the language I use can, in some states, be considered harassment, religious persecution, unfriendly workplace, all of that stuff.

Stuff you'll have to consider, just because you hired someone else to sit in your place of business.

I've already alluded to the paperwork, which is enormous, even for one employee. When I worked as an editor for Mercury

Press, my boss complained about where I lived. Mercury Press (which owned *The Magazine of Fantasy and Science Fiction* at that time) was based in Connecticut. I lived in Eugene, Oregon, which was in Lane County.

And Lane County had some kind of tax on employees—a transit tax, if I remember correctly—that Mercury Press, in Connecticut, had to pay. It wasn't the money that bothered my boss. It was the paperwork, which was nonstandard, and took hours every month to fill out.

The rest of what I'm going to say about employees you probably know, but you haven't thought about from an employer's point of view. And you need to.

First, you must hire an employee. Again, you must follow federal, state, and local guidelines to do this. You cannot discriminate by race, creed, or gender. And you cannot discriminate against anyone with disabilities.

Again, let me use a Mercury Press story. Connecticut has some of the most stringent disability laws in the nation. Because Mercury Press had three employees, it had to have ramps and bathrooms that accommodated the disabled. Never mind that two of the three employees worked out of state. My then-employer had to completely remodel his office building to comply with what were then new regulations. It cost thousands.

You need to know what your state regulations are—and what the federal regulations are—before you ever hire anyone. Especially if your store or office is old and lacks proper access.

If you work at home, realize that there are regulations governing businesses with employees in the home. You also could be subject to a lot more harassment suits and other problems just because of your business's location.

(And think about this: do you really want to fire someone who then gets angry and knows where you live? Just a thought from someone who once received a death threat from a volunteer she fired for cause.)

Let's assume you go through a legal hiring process (yes, there are rules for hiring), and find someone you hope will be a good employee.

You need to know how many hours that person will work and how you will pay them. Will you pay them hourly? If so, you probably need some form of time clock. The honor method really doesn't work, unless you're there to supervise. If you pay them hourly, what will you pay for overtime? (Realize again, that each state has rules governing overtime pay.)

If there will be a lot of overtime, consider putting that employee on a salary. Here's the secret to salaried employees—the employer should get 50-60 hours of work out of 40 hours of pay. Of course, the employee gets some perks as well—usually benefits like medical insurance, paid sick leave, paid vacation, a 401K—things that compensate for that unpaid overtime. (Those of you who still have salaried positions, have you ever noticed that the first people laid off in any company are salaried employees who never put in more than 40 hours, and often put in less? There's a reason those folks get let go first—and it's because they're not giving a good benefit for the buck.)

This may sound silly, but I can't tell you how many first-time employers haven't considered it: *Make sure the salary or hourly pay rate you offer is one that you can afford.*

Before you set the rate of pay, make sure 1) that it meets the state minimum wage (which is often greater than federal minimum) and 2) that the pay rate is what you're giving the *employee*, not what you're paying out of pocket.

I heard a collective "huh?" from those of you who have never hired anyone. Let me remind you of all that paperwork and taxes I discussed earlier. Now go look at your last paycheck from your last (or current) job. See the withholding? See the Social Security tax? See all those little notations, the dollars that never make it into your pocket?

When you're the employer, those aren't just numbers on a pay stub. That's money you have to pay. And you don't just pay part of the Social Security. You pay all of it (double what you see in your own pay stub). The withholding goes into a special tax account. The Social Security payment does as well.

So when you promise to pay someone $10 per hour, make sure you can afford that money—including the tax payments on the hourly wage. Or the salary.

The tax troubles you hear about—the scary ones, where you hear about the IRS bolting the door of a business—usually involve nonpayment of employee taxes. Those are the easiest things to skip in the short term, and the things that have the most consequences in the long term.

So make sure you can afford your employee before you ever accept a single résumé for the position.

Also remember that you're obligated to pay this person. Let's say you agree on a two-week pay period. You must write that check at the end of two weeks. Your employee's payment comes first—again, because of the laws governing this. You can't (or I should say shouldn't) withhold payment because you can't afford it or because some client didn't make the payments he promised. You must meet your employee obligations according to both state and federal employment laws.

So you better be able to afford that check every two weeks, like you promised. The minute paying your employee looks dicey, you need to consider laying that employee off.

Yep. It's tough. And it gets tougher.

Because once you've hired that person and you've agreed to a pay schedule, you also need to define the job that person will do. Part of defining the job is scheduling work hours.

You have become a supervisor as well as a business owner. You need to make sure your employee arrives on time, that your employee does the work assigned, and that your employee leaves on time. (The opposite of the employee who never shows up to work is the one who takes advantage of that hourly overtime rate to rack up a lot of extra money.)

You have to teach the employee to do the job properly—which in the short term will cost you some productivity (and that can be a problem, since you're hiring this person to help your business become more productive)—and you'll have to make sure the employee behaves properly (dresses appropriately, has good phone manners, has clean hands [in the case of restaurants], doesn't cheat, lie, or steal… you name it, you have to watch for it).

You have just hired a person to save you time and here they are costing you time. And they'll continue to do so. Employees are rarely self-motivating. Most only do what they're told.

So when you're considering hiring an employee, you will need to factor in your lost time. If that employee doesn't bring in double or triple what they earn, they're not worth the time and effort you'll put into them.

I could go on and on. I've been an employee and an employer. I have a ton of horror stories—and none of them match the horror stories of my friend, a former manager who worked in high tech.

Having an employee is the most difficult part of owning a business.

So why would you want one?

Oddly enough, most business owners see employees as saviors, as people who will take some of the burden off.

That can't be farther from the truth.

But the very real fact of owning a successful business is that you can't—and shouldn't—do everything. You will need help.

Fortunately, as I mentioned, there are a ton of services that can provide you with that help. The Internal Revenue Service just doesn't call the people who provide these services employees.

They fall under other categories, often self defined. Agents, contractors, consultants. We hire them all the time and think nothing of it.

However, they do work for us. We hire them to perform a task—or, as I said earlier, we hire them to do stuff for us.

Under the dictionary definition, they're employees as well. Remember the dictionary defines employee in a variety of ways that all boils down to this: someone whom someone else pays to do work.

That's it.

So, as a generic term, throughout this chapter, I'll call them workers. I'll try very hard to use whatever term applies—lawyer, bricklayer, plumber—but if I need a general overall term for someone who is not required to be at your place of business twenty, thirty, or forty hours per week to do their job, I'll use the term worker.

Got that?

English can be such a confusing language.

Anyway…here goes.

You think you'll never hire an employee—and maybe you won't. If you're really creative and understand the employment laws in your state as well as the applicable parts of the tax code, you might not have to hire an official employee. You might find ways around it.

If you do have to hire an employee, do the things I mentioned above.

Otherwise, hire a worker.

We've all done it. We have a lot of people in our lives who work for us. Doctors, lawyers, tutors, Pilates instructors—all of them get hired to do stuff for us that we can't do ourselves.

Notice that most of them fall into the professionals category. They provide a service that you pay for, just as you, as a business owner, provide a service to someone else. They get paid for their time or they get paid by the job, but the key part of their job is to provide a service and/or work product *for you*.

That doesn't preclude them from providing a service and/or work product for someone else. In fact, they probably do because they have a business to keep up as well, and unless you're a regular customer, you don't give them enough work to keep their own business running.

Think of all the people you've met who provide a service on an as-needed basis. Caterers, plumbers, dog walkers—if there's a need, someone will fill it.

And you can hire that someone, for a set fee or by the hour or by the job. The method of payment is always different. Some require a retainer to "retain" their services, after which they bill by the hour. Some require half up front. Some require ten percent. And some ask that you pay the moment the job is finished.

The methods of payment vary as much as the service providers do.

Here's what they all have in common, however.

You pay them in exchange for work they do for you.

Pay attention here: You pay them.

You hire them.

On this project, or for this area of your business, *they work for you*.

It's a tough distinction to make and people forget it all the time. Not just business owners, but regular people. People who go to the doctor or hire a real estate agent. Those people sometimes forget who is in charge.

And it's easy to forget. When you go to this kind of service provider, you are hiring that person for their expertise. If that person is renowned in their field, then that person will be pricey and probably a bit arrogant. But you're still the one paying the bills. You're still the person who hired the service provider, no matter how renowned, how respected, or how revered.

You must remember that.

As I mentioned, a lot of people work for me. I run my own cottage industry here, and have done so for decades. I have learned I can't do without some service providers.

For example, I have had my house cleaned since I was twenty-nine years old. I couldn't afford the house cleaner back then, not really, but I hired her. I was working eighteen-hour days. My apartment (it wasn't even a house) was a sty. I can handle clutter, but I can't handle dirt. So I had a choice: Sleep or clean.

I choose sleep—which meant that once per month (which was all I could handle at the time), an employee of the local house cleaning service ventured into my dusty, cluttered apartment and tried to make some kind of order out of it. She at least kept the filth at bay.

As I made more money, I moved from once per month to once per week. When the money gets tight, I scale back to twice per month (and regret it every time). But I haven't gone without a house cleaner in more than twenty years.

Everyone else on my workers' list is expendable. I can—and have—done without if I absolutely have to.

Because here's the truth about employees and workers: with only one exception that I can think of right off the top of my head, they're all expendable. I can do the work myself if I have to. I can learn the job. I can figure it out. I'll botch it up (particularly if it's plumbing), but I'll learn it.

The exception? Doctors and medical specialists. I can't learn that job. I don't want to learn that job. But I do as much as I can by being an informed consumer of their services.

I also believe in second opinions. And third opinions. And fourth opinions. Because the era of the Doctor As God has gone by the wayside. Doctors are human. They come in competent varieties and incompetent varieties. You don't want to find out they're incompetent after the surgery is completed. You want to know up front.

So…let's remove doctors from our list for the time being. (I know: you're still reeling—doctors? In the worker category? But… but…. Remember. You're hiring them to do work for you. That work might be surgery to alleviate your back pain, but you're still hiring them—and you have the right to hire someone else if you don't like the doctor or if you notice that he never washes his hands. Okay?)

Let's go back to my original point, made before I mentioned doctors:

You can do the work yourself if you have to.

You can build your own house, lay your own pipes, install your own electrical systems. Yep, you might have to take classes. You might have to read some books and you might need some certification, but you can do it.

Just like you can represent yourself in a court of law. Anyone can, for any reason. It's just better to hire a lawyer for his areas of expertise. But you don't have to.

Just like you don't have to have a real estate agent to sell your house. Or to buy one. Dean and I have done our own real estate transactions. We've also hired realtors. Sometimes it was easier to do the transaction ourselves. Sometimes it was better to have an expert run us through the system.

And this brings us to book agents. You don't need one to sell a book. I know, I know, all the publishing houses tell you they won't look at books that aren't represented by agents. Yet every day in this country, writers sell books without an agent. How? By writing a really good book and mailing it.

In fact, the main job of a book agent is not book sales. It is all the other stuff—the stuff that really does require an expertise, like contract negotiation. I can and have sold books myself. I've negotiated the contract myself. I've sold books overseas myself. (It's easier now than ever, thanks to the internet.) But I still have an agent. Why? Because I like relying on his expertise.

I'm still in charge, however.

I know the writers who are reading this are reeling, just like you doctor disbelievers did earlier. Writers who are having trouble with the concept of agent as a worker (and not as a savior, a god, or a miracle worker who will rescue you from anonymity and make you famous) need to read my husband's blog titled "Life After Agents." You'll find them on his website, deanwesleysmith.com.

All of these people and more, from the movers we hired (because Dean wanted to save both time and his back) to the pesticide guy who'll come next week to get rid of a hornet's nest on the front lawn, are workers. They are people you hire—and if you hire them, then you are in charge of them on this project. And you should know what they're doing and why.

Let me give you an extreme example. You're on trial for a murder you did not commit. The very famous (and expensive) defense attorney you hired says that, based on his experience, you shouldn't fight the charges in court because juries are notoriously fickle. You'd be better off pleading to a lesser charge and only going to jail for a few years.

Are you going to listen to that? Are you going to jail for a crime you didn't commit? Of course not. You'll fire that attorney and hire one who'll work for you to the best of her ability, one who'll do everything she can to make sure the charges get dropped.

Too often, I see people in important situations bow to the expertise of the worker they hired without questioning that worker, without researching anything, and without understanding what they've just agreed to. It might not be something as dramatic as a murder trial, but it might be just as important, like the treatment for a certain kind of illness or a way of handling finances for their business.

I hate to tell you this, but the reason so many people got scammed by Bernard Madoff and other Ponzi schemers of his ilk is because those people did not do their due diligence. They didn't monitor his activities, or question his results, or (in many cases) even look at their statements beyond looking for the percentage profit. And that's just an invitation to some con man like Madoff to steal everything the client owns.

How do you hire a worker of any kind?

1. You figure out what you need that person to do.
Simple as that. You figure out the job first. You might be wrong. You might not know all that the job entails. But you need to know what the job is.

That sounds elementary, and it often is. You need someone to fix your car because it won't start. You need someone to get rid of the hornet's nest in your front yard. You need someone to check that gash you just got on your knee and see if you need stitches to help it heal.

Occasionally, however, the task isn't simple. You need a divorce, which is complicated without children, but a nightmare with children. You need someone to rent out the various houses you own in another town a hundred miles away. You need a mechanic to service the five vehicles that make your catering business run.

Sometimes the work you want these people to do will extend over years instead of hours. Sometimes you'll end up with a working relationship. Sometimes you'll want an overseer—someone who will recommend other professionals to help you with the tasks at hand. A divorce attorney will recommend an accountant to keep your finances in order as things get rough. A U.S. book agent will partner with a French book agent to sell your work into France. A Hollywood agent might recommend a publicist to make certain you get the most promotion possible on the job you've just gotten, and so on.

You need to know what you want going in, so that you don't spend a lot of money on goods and services that you don't want. For example, if the man I hire to get rid of the hornet's nest tells me that carpenter ants have burrowed into my house, then we'll discuss whether or not we need to solve that problem. If a plumber tells me that the pipes in my house are all rusted and we need to replace them (and I've seen no evidence of rust), then I would call another plumber for a second opinion—and a second estimate of the cost of repairs.

You need to know how much you're willing to spend, how hard you're willing to work with your new worker, and approximately how much time the task (or tasks) will take.

You must also be flexible. Since you're hiring someone else to do this task, you might not be the expert here. You might not know exactly what the job entails. Be willing to learn. If the person you're considering for this task tells you different things than you've assumed, take the time to double-check your assumptions and his.

2. Research everything.

Don't rely on the "conventional wisdom." Conventional wisdom is often wrong. Facts, not assumptions, rule.

The first thing to research is the task itself. Is it something you can do? If not, why not? If you prefer not to—or in the case of my house cleaner, something you'll never do but you want done—then by all means hire someone. But make sure you have researched the job, and examined your reasons for asking someone else to do it.

The second thing you must research is the person you want to hire. Too many people hire the first person who offers to work with them. This is particularly bad in the writing business, when unpublished writers hire the first agent who says they'll represent that writer's work. In writing, I've learned, the agent you hire when you're unpublished is often *not* the agent you want once you become published.

Book agents are not regulated. No one oversees the industry, which is why there are so many con artists in the business. Writers give their entire financial future over to these people without a bit of research—rather like the folks who hired Madoff. And you saw how well that worked out.

But don't smirk. How many of you have gone to the very first specialist your doctor recommended for your latest medical problem? Just because your general practitioner recommended the person doesn't mean that specialist is for you. Research. There are more and more organizations that track doctors, hospitals, and medical professionals.

If the worker you want to hire is in a regulated industry, like a contractor, make sure there are no outstanding complaints against that person. If they're not in a regulated industry, check with the Better Business Bureau in the worker's state to see what kinds of complaints have been lodged.

Word of mouth is also valuable, especially in a small industry or a small town. But remember, people are people are people. Which means that they might hate someone you like and vice versa. Talk to people who are clients of your worker and talk to people who refuse to hire him. See if the complaints are valid, but make sure that the people who love his work are informed people and not people who close their eyes to any potential problem.

So many serious problems could have been avoided if only the business owner researched the worker they were hiring.

In the end, however, the choice is yours. And the responsibility lies with you. If the financial manager you hired absconds with your funds, it's ultimately your responsibility for hiring him—and for not firing him at the first sign of trouble. (And believe me, in cases of embezzlement, there are always first signs of trouble. And second signs. And third signs.)

When you're in business with someone, you have to trust them. But you don't have to blindly trust them. You must protect your own interests first.

3. Agree to terms up front—and make sure those terms are in writing.

You and your worker have to know what the job is, an estimate of the costs, and how long the job will last. You also need a termination clause. Thirty days notice? Two weeks? Make sure that it's a mutually agreed-upon termination clause and valid for both sides (in other words, if he doesn't like working for you, he can quit). You need everything in writing so that you don't get into a he-said, she-said legal situation.

You don't need a contract—and many of your worker relationships won't have contracts. (I don't have them with my house cleaner, for instance.) You still need a dated piece of paper detailing what the job is, who does what, and when. That will be enough to get rid of a he-said, she-said problem should the matter ever go to court.

And relationships do go sour. Sometimes you will go to court. You might not initiate the proceeding. The worker might. But you need to be protected. So keep invoices, that piece of paper delineating the work, and any other information that pertains to the job the worker does. Chances are you won't ever need that file. But the time might come when you just might.

4. Supervise.

You don't have to hover. But you need to check up on your worker on a regular basis. If you listened to the Madoff coverage, you would have heard from people who fired Madoff or didn't hire him at all. Why? Because when they asked him what the details meant on his statements, his answer was a version of "Trust me, you don't need to know." (What I used to call the Don't-Worry-Your-Pretty-Little-Head factor.) Any client who claimed they needed to know got released by Madoff. Any client who didn't like Madoff's answers fired Madoff.

But a surprising number trusted him. And got screwed.

You need to keep track of everything your worker does. You need to get solid answers to your questions. If the answers don't come in a timely manner, push. If they don't come at all, fire this service provider and hire someone else.

Over the course of your business's lifetime, you will hook up with a bad worker or two. It's inevitable. The key is to cut that person loose before they do a lot of serious damage.

5. Be Fair.

If the worker does a good job, do what you can to hang on to that person. Sometimes you'll pay a bonus. Sometimes you'll recommend him to someone else. (Be careful on that one; you don't want your worker to get too busy to do a good job for you.) Sometimes you'll give him extra work when times are tough to hang on to him in the good times. Be fair to the good worker and he'll work harder for you.

6. Remember that life happens.

Good workers may become chronically ill. They may get in bad situations. They may have all-consuming clients and cases that have nothing to do with you. Sometimes your excellent worker becomes a bad worker. Or no longer has time for you. That's okay. (And if they're really good, they'll tell you up front.) Then go through this process again and hire someone new for this particular job. Maybe, if your favorite worker's life situation improves, you can hire her for the next job.

7. Question, question, question.

If something doesn't sound kosher, it probably isn't. For example, in book publishing, publishers often tell writers to hire an agent. That would be like me telling my housekeeper that she needs a secretary before she can work for me. How she runs her company is her business, just like the way I run my writing career is my business.

If someone you want to hire tells you that you must pay in full up front before the job is even started, run from this person. A percentage (even half) is fine up front, but not in full. Not ever. You need a way to guarantee that the job gets completed.

I can think of a thousand examples like this. If you don't know what's reasonable and customary in the worker's area of expertise, *find out before you hire him*. If something doesn't seem right, then put the brakes on before you enter into a relationship with that person.

Remember that I told you to be flexible? That also means you need to be flexible about who you hire, what you hire them for, and when you hire them. Go on your timetable after you're fully informed.

Hiring people, whether they're employees or workers, is a lot of work. But it can be worthwhile. I had the same house cleaner for more than twenty years before health issues caused her to retire. My house was never cleaner. And she introduced us to her husband, a handyman who improved our property a thousandfold.

Yes, I've had bad experiences with workers and employees alike. But the good experiences outweigh the bad.

Before you hire anyone, remember two things:

1. You can do most anything yourself. So ask yourself why you need to pay someone else to do this task.

And...

2. No one else cares about your business as much as you do. No one else ever will. So don't expect an employee or a worker to do as much as you do. It's not fair to either of you.

Finally, my advice on all things: the more informed you are, the better off you'll be. That goes for employees, workers, finances, and just about everything else covered by this *Freelancer's Guide*.

Stick to that principle and you'll do well—even when hiring others to help you keep your business afloat.

Chapter Twenty-one
Advertising

I have had this topic in my topics list for nearly a year, but it became relevant when I got my third request to put an ad on my website. For once, I didn't dismiss the request with a polite note. I actually considered it and as I did, I realized the reason I hadn't written about advertising was that I was considering it from a very 20th century perspective.

A little background:

As you know, I've held a wide variety of jobs. Some of those included selling advertising and placing ads. If you have a business, somehow you have to get word of that business out to the general public or to your possible clientele, which is even harder than it sounds.

If I were writing the *Guide* just for freelancer writers, I would call this topic self-promotion. But I'm not and besides, my opinion on the whole writing/self-promotion thing is evolving as well. It's a brand new century, and nearly the second decade in that brand new century, and things they are a-changin'. Rapidly, in fact. So rapidly that I think I need a scoreboard to keep track.

Even my handy dandy dictionaries can't keep up. When I was growing up, everyone thought advertising was a dirty word, an occupation practiced by sleezeballs who wanted to manipulate you into buying something you didn't want. Somewhere, back in the dark recesses of my memory, I recall hearing about "subliminal advertising"—secret messages embedded into things like films that would force young innocent creatures like me to go into the lobby and buy greasy, fat-covered popcorn.

I knew a few ad execs back in the day. They didn't have a lot of self-respect. In fact, they didn't have a lot of respect for anyone.

(The TV show *Mad Men* captures some of this attitude.) By the mid-1980s, advertising became a profession like any other—that whole smarmy manipulative thing was just accepted or tolerated or perhaps better understood—and more importantly, it became something in which seasoned professionals helped the little guy (read: us) improve or sell or grow a business.

Writers, artists, musicians all bemoaned the fact they couldn't get advertising. Store owners complained that advertising was so *expensive* and, worse, they were expected to design their own ads. Local radio and TV stations had advertising departments that would write and develop your ad for their medium, but, whoa, could you tell the locally produced ad from a national ad. The locally produced one was generally awful. Cheesy, cheap, and unprofessional.

I guess we all learned how important the advertising professional was.

About ten years ago, we entered the brave new world of advertising on the internet. There was a big debate about whether or not websites for places like CNN.com should run ads from somewhere else. There was a concurrent debate about whether or not internet advertising was effective. And yet a third debate about how to measure its effectiveness.

Then there was the age-old argument about whether or not the new entertainment form (the internet) would ruin advertising for the older forms. This debate happened as radio came in ("It'll take ads from newspapers!"), and as television came in ("It'll take ads from radio!"). Ads have migrated to the internet, and they haven't hurt the other forms. Other things have decreased the effectiveness of advertising in those forms—the decline of local radio, the decline of the newspaper, and the advent of the DVR, enabling people to fast-forward or skip through commercials.

But here's the dirty little secret about advertising that I learned back in the 1980s, long before the advent of the internet. (She writes with some perplexity, feeling old.) Not all advertising is effective for all products.

Yep, unlike the myth, advertising is not a one-size-fits-all proposition. You see it with movies. With the exception of a truly big-budget film, all movies from major studios get the same kind of treatment. A big advertising campaign in all media for a week, sometimes two, sometimes three weeks before the movie's release. After that, the ads die off, and the movies rely on word of mouth.

The big blowout ad budgets used to bring the movie goers in during the all-important opening weekend, and those opening weekend numbers were used to calculate a film's success. It would take a week or more for the public to understand that the stinker really stank and attendance would drop off. By then, the movie's advertising had done its job and given that movie a #1 status or the biggest weekend for that particular genre or whatever—some kind of tagline that could be used to advertise the DVD when it came out six months or a year later.

Now the big blowout ad campaigns work less effectively because of Twitter and other social media sites. The first attendees will often tell later attendees that the show is brilliant or it stinks.

But let's go back to the days before Twitter. (She writes tentatively, feeling old.) Just because movie A and movie B had the same advertising in the same markets didn't mean that movie A and movie B had the same kind of opening weekend.

Some of that might have been the names associated with movie. Movie goers used name-brand recognition just like everyone else. Until the last decade, a movie with a bona fide movie star usually had a set opening number. (Until too many stars made too many stinkers.)

Some of the difference in the opening weekend had to do with the audience itself. No matter how hard movie studios tried, they couldn't get single young men ages 18-35 to go to a romantic comedy, even if those guys were on a date. Nor could they get women ages 35-50 to go to a violent action movie or carve-'em-up horror flick, even if they were accompanying their teenage sons.

The advent of multiple TV markets made it possible to advertise the chick flick on Lifetime television and the horror flick on Spike TV. All of those ads might have been produced with equal care, and they all might have aired on the three major networks, but they'd air in different timeslots. The chick flick ad would air during *Desperate Housewives*, the horror flick during *Lost*. Targeting the correct customer base is all-important in advertising because we've all heard the phrase "wasting advertising dollars."

Advertising dollars are limited, no matter what business you're in. And each dollar spent on ads should bring in at least "x" dollars in revenue. (I'm sure there's a real formula for this that I am not going to look up.)

Big businesses like the movies have done studies of their

demographics, the effect of advertising on those demographics, and an understanding of what kind of response each form of advertising has for its business.

You, as a small business owner, can't do that.

In fact, some small business owners forgo advertising altogether.

And that's a mistake.

Somehow you have to stand out in all the noise. If you have opened a retail shop, you need to let potential customers know you exist. If you're a lawyer, you have to distinguish your practice from all the other legal practices out there.

Artists (and by this I mean writers, visual artists, musicians) have a two-pronged problem. We want people to buy our product—the stories, the art, the music—but we also want to let potential clients (publishers, design studios, music labels) know that we will do good contractual work.

Any business can do a lot of free advertising through networking. (To see how to do so effectively, look at the section on Networking.)

But let's talk about paid advertising for a few minutes. When should you do it? Or should you do it at all?

The answer is yes, no matter what your business. You need an ad budget and you need to know how to use it.

Advertising is, according to that handy dandy *Encarta World English Dictionary* so thoughtfully provided by my software company, "the promotion through public announcements in newspapers or on the radio, television, or Internet of something such as a product, service, event or vacancy in order to attract or increase interest in it." There are some sub definitions, but you know those.

Let's take the main definition and look at it. The key words here are "promotion" and "attract or increase interest."

People can't go into a store they don't know exists. They can't buy a book they've never heard of. They won't attend a concert if they don't know when and where or even if it's being held.

I can already hear the professional writers sputtering. *I've had books published*, they say, *and no one spent a dime advertising it.*

Really? Did that book get reviewed? Did the publisher produce galleys? Because all of that costs money, and that money comes out of—you guessed it—the advertising budget.

It's the rare book in the modern era that doesn't have some form of advertising budget, however small.

It's the rare business that thrives on word of mouth only.

So how do you go about advertising for your business?

1. Figure out who your target audience is.

Do you need street traffic—strangers coming through the door to buy your product? Or do you need clients? Do you need to appeal to a handful of big organizations (like some artists often do)? Or do you need to appeal to as many people as possible?

You can't figure out advertising until you know whom your ads need to reach. Sometimes an article in a trade journal is a lot more effective than an outrageously expensive ad during the Super Bowl.

Do this work first or you'll waste every single ad dollar you ever spend.

2. Set an ad budget—and stick to it.

You might only be able to devote a few dollars toward advertising, but every little bit counts. And remember: free is good. When my ex and I owned the art gallery/frame shop, we gave away free framing services (limited to certain inexpensive frames and mats) in exchange for promotion. Local restaurants participate in cook-offs and other events sponsored by the community in the hopes of drawing in new customers. Right now, our local businesses are doing a weird free promotion that has caught my attention. They are taking a dressmaker's dummy, putting a t-shirt or a sign around its neck, and placing it outside the business for two days. That dummy has been all over town, wearing t-shirts for the local gym and for a local bookstore. It's a creepy-looking thing, done up with a sense of humor, and it does catch your attention. One business even gave the dummy an arm (it didn't have one) and had it point at the business from the parking lot.

I have no idea whose idea that was, but it works for anyone driving down the main drag of our little town.

Merchants often go together to buy ad space. The strip mall that includes the collectibles store that Dean started does group advertising every quarter, at a fraction of the cost an individual ad would have. The ad is also bigger and more noticeable.

3. Be creative. Be different.

In the 1990s, Debbie Macomber was the first writer to make bookmarks with the cover of her novel on them and send those bookmarks to bookstores carrying her book. Now everyone does it, and bookstores often toss out the bookmarks without ever setting them out. Talk about a waste of advertising dollars. But when Debbie did it, hers was a unique product, the only bookmark at the checkout, something for the reader to look at *even if they weren't buying one of her books*.

Brilliant stuff. She's always been on the forefront of writer marketing, and her look is always creative and always different.

The worst thing you can do in advertising is exactly what everyone else is doing.

4. Get the most bang for your buck.

That's hard, because you're going to lose some money as you start out. Because I had sold ads for newspapers and written ads for radio stations before my ex and I opened our frame shop/art gallery, I knew that ads had varying effectiveness. We had an ad budget, unlike other retail stores in the same strip mall, and for our first foray into advertising, we placed two ads, one in the local morning paper and the other on a local radio station. Then we quizzed every single customer who came into the store: where did you hear about us? We got two answers.

The first: *I heard about you on the radio.*

The second: *I saw your sign as I drove by and decided to stop.*

The newspaper ad was a complete and total waste of our advertising dollars and we never ran another. But we ran radio ads on various stations, particularly when we had sales, and those ads brought in a wide variety of customers.

One reason was my experience. I wrote our radio ads. Each radio station insisted on having their own disk jockeys read the ads, and we heard through the sales force (and I heard from the djs) that they loved our ads because they weren't cheesy or hard to read. There's a trick to writing for radio and in them thar days (she writes, feeling old again) I knew it cold.

Obviously my skills at newspaper ads were less effective.

Keep track of the results of your ad buys. I do that even now, even when I'm not spending the money. Some years ago, my publisher ran an ad for one of my Smokey Dalton mystery novels in the *New Yorker*. This was a quarter page ribbon ad, running next to the letters column, where most prominent book ads get placed.

The ad made no difference in sales. None. No blip on Amazon.com, no increase in sales on my royalty statement. A complete waste of advertising dollars.

My British publisher Max Crime sent out review copies of my novel *Hitler's Angel* in June and that book got favorably reviewed in one of England's largest newspapers, *The Daily Mail*. Sales of that book jumped through the roof that very weekend, and so far those sales have continued at the greater number.

Even if no one else reviews the book (and other publications have), that single review was worth every single review copy the publisher sent out. That was an effective use of advertising dollars— probably more effective than taking out a paid ad in *The Daily Mail* itself.

5. Don't do the same thing over and over again.

Yes, continue with the effective advertising, but mix it up. Debbie Macomber may still be doing bookmarks for all I know, but she has entire other promotion schemes for her books now. A local mattress business here in Oregon has run the same TV ad for years now, and even though I can recite the damn thing word for word, I really don't pay attention to it any more. Why should I? I know what it says, and it didn't draw me into the business in the first place. Why would it draw me after repeated daily listens? I don't patronize a business just because the ads have worn me down. I doubt you do either.

6. Remember that advertising creates or increases interest in your good, service, event or company.

"Creates" or "increases." "Creates" is important, because in the beginning, no one knows who you are. But "increases" is equally important, because after time, you cease to be the hot new thing. People forget. Or they assume you'll always be there.

Consumers and clients have finite reserves as well, and if they go to a new business that has "created" interest, they may forgo yours just because you no longer have their attention.

You need to recapture it in an interesting, non-annoying manner.

How do you do that?

It differs from business to business, service to service, event to event. It also differs from year to year. I'd have given you different advice on where to advertise your business ten years ago than I'd give you now. The world is changing, the way people find out about new products, services, businesses has changed, and the way advertising works has changed as well.

7. Remember that time is a precious commodity—for you and everyone else.

If you want a minute of someone's time, you'd better earn it. That doesn't just apply for televised ads. It applies to anything you do to promote your business or your work.

For example, I do very few book signings at bookstores. Most of those signings simply aren't worth my time. The bookstore puts out a few copies of my book, does no advertising outside of the store (and sometimes not even in the store), and I sign a handful of copies. Some bookstores will return unsold *signed* copies for full credit to the publisher, so the books don't even remain in the store as autographed copies.

But I will always say yes to a book signing at North by Northwest Books run by Sheldon McArthur here in Lincoln City. Shelly used to run the Mystery Bookstore in Los Angeles; indeed that's where I first met him, when he sponsored a signing for one of my Kris Nelscott mystery novels. I was on a publisher-sponsored book tour, and even then, Shelly's work stood out. I signed fifty copies of my book, half or more of which went to affiliated bookstores in California. At other stores, even big chain stores, I only signed about ten copies.

Now that Shelly's semi-retired, he's opened a small bookstore here to keep his hand in. But when he does a signing, he goes all out. He promotes it both locally and nationally. He sends out a mailing to his most valued customers all around the world. He writes reviews and pays for ads in the local paper. He puts flyers all over town. And he contacts individual book buyers who he believes might like my work, even if they've never heard of me.

Shelly has sold more copies of my books than anyone except my publishers. And that's not an exaggeration.

So when he calls and asks, I'm there. And when I need a bookstore to order books for me, I go through Shelly. I also promote him on my website (note who got mentioned by name in this section of the *Guide*?) and I send tourists down to his shop whenever I get a chance.

My annual two hours in Shelly's store are never wasted. And I know, since he asks me back whenever I have a new release, that he feels he's getting something out of my signings as well.

Publicity is a good thing for a freelancer. When the right people know about you and your business, they'll knock on your door. The key is figuring out how to reach them. And that might take a t-shirted mannequin beside the highway or it might take a free download of a song off your album. You need to figure that out. And if the first thing you try doesn't work, try something else.

Just remember: be yourself. You're the best advertisement for your business. And remember that advertising is only effective once if the product is bad. Once you get someone to try a bad product, no amount of advertising in the world will make them return to that product. Word of mouth can be good, but it can also turn against you. Make sure you do the best you can, no matter what.

That's the best advertising of all.

Earlier in this chapter, I mentioned that I'd been thinking about advertising in a very 20th century manner. I've been thinking about a lot of things in 20th century manner, which makes sense, considering I spent 40 years in the 20th century, and only 10 in the 21st (so far). But everything is changing rapidly (particularly in my profession, publishing) and keeping up is becoming a challenge.

Witness advertising. Everyone is trying to find a new way to do it—and by new, I mean effective. Of course, that's been the quest from the beginning. What works? What doesn't? What does it cost?

What caused me to finally start on the ad topic was an e-mail. I got a request to put a paid ad on my website. I've gotten them before, and dithered. This time, I didn't dither.

I questioned and thought, and thought some more.

I've had a website for at least ten years. In the beginning, that website was a "static website," back before anyone even used the term. It was a strictly informational place. If you wanted to know what else I published, you went to that site. If you wanted to know what's coming up, you went to that site. Nothing more.

I was an early adapter on a static website, but a late adapter to an active website. Some of that came from a fear of flame wars. In the early days of the internet, listserves, and e-mails, flame wars (or fights for those of you not into the jargon) happened a lot, and over the most trivial things. People would object to a word or an idea and then scream about it, sometimes defaming you all over the net.

Which, since the net's audience was small back then, wasn't that big a deal. But it felt like a big deal.

So my initial foray into putting actual content on my website was tentative, with comments section turned off. I didn't want flaming to dominate my site. After a while, I polled some friends and asked how bad the flame wars were on their websites. Most long-term bloggers had the occasional good discussion, but no real flame wars. The days of constant flaming seemed to be over.

So I turned on the comments section, and haven't regretted it for a moment. My columns on other sites have generated some flame wars—one war started by a semiprofessional flamer (a person who goes around agitating people), but so far, nothing untoward.

I no longer see my website as a static place that informs people of things. Now it's an interactive site where I learn as much (I hope) as y'all do from me. I also use it to inform you of my books and stories, as well as about things that interest me.

For example, my Recommended Reading list came out of editing. The thing I loved best about editing was sharing new writers and new stories/new discoveries with like-minded readers. The thing I liked least about editing was being limited to a genre. With the Recommended Reading list, I thought, I could just point out good things to read from any place and any genre and any time period.

It has worked that way, and I know I get a slightly different audience to that list than I do to the *Guide*. What I didn't realize until earlier this year was that I was providing free advertising to people whose work I like. A *New York Times* bestselling writer, who happens to be a friend of mine, contacted me after seeing my recommendation for his novel (which I read in proofs that I got from a local bookstore) and asked if the recommendation could be used to sell the book to bookstores. Of course, I said yes. I've gotten that request a few other times, and I know that several other writers/publishers have quoted from my list without asking permission because they know the list is public, and they can do so.

But the Recommended Reading list does not exist so that I can get free books (although I occasionally do) or to promote someone for the sake of promoting them. It exists because I like sharing things that I consider very, very good. And that's the only reason.

I also share other fun things—an occasional movie or a song

or links to someone else's website. The website has become an extension of me, but the me that you find at a convention, not the me that my closest friends know. (I doubt you folks want to know my cats' latest antics or what I had for breakfast.) When I'm here, I talk about things I'd talk to you about if we were sitting around a bar after the sessions ended. Or I have a formal discussion, like I do when I give a speech or speak on a panel. Of course, I mention my own work. That's one reason I'm there. But the other reason I go to conventions is to have fun. And that's become a reason to hang out on my website as well.

I did monetize the website when I started the *Freelancer's Guide* because I wanted to write this, and I didn't want to wait for money from the publishing industry. So…when I got this e-mail about putting a paid ad on my site, I actually considered it. The first few e-mails I got, some as long as a year ago, I dismissed with a polite letter. I felt uncomfortable even considering advertising.

When I got this most recent request, I discovered I had moved past uncomfortable.

But I was still uncertain.

So I contacted other professional writers on various listserves and asked them what they thought about taking ads on my website. The first three answers I got reflected my ambivalence.

One writer said that my website advertised *me* and I shouldn't confuse the issue with running ads for other products on the site.

Another writer said that I should consider the ad, but be very cautious because it would reflect on me.

And a third writer told me to take the money and run.

All of this made the issue as clear as mud. I had already come up with those answers and, depending on the moment, vacillated between all three of them.

Then I got an e-mail from Cindie Geddes. Cindie makes her living as a non-fiction writer, but she's also a hell of a fiction writer. You can find out more about her work at cindiegeddes.com.

Cindie wrote, "I'm a lover of technology and love blogs as much as I do essays, magazines, books, etc. (Don't tell.) Anyway, when I see a few tasteful ads on a site (IF I even notice them) it tells me that the site has enough popularity and/or credibility for someone to be willing to pay to put ads on it. It shows a level of professionalism. And since I'm reading it, it's obviously run by someone I like and I think, 'Yay! Someone else has good taste like me' and 'Yay, this person I like is making money, so they can spend more time on content I like.' In talking to friends who don't write or produce web content but do consume web content, the reaction was universally the same (unless the site is for a charity, oddly enough, or a politician)."

She then pointed me to blogger Allie Brosh. Allie Brosh dealt with the whole advertising question in April, and in a very creative way. Instead of asking other bloggers what they did, she went directly to her audience with a little quiz. That quiz showed that she was dealing with some of the same questions I had. (hyperboleandahalf. blogspot.com/2010/04/someone-should-probably-kill-this-post.html.)

I read the posts (and explored the site. Interesting stuff there), then I finished reading Cindie's letter. She closed with this,

"You've been making a living writing. You have a Donate button. Ads fit perfectly with what you do. Hell, with all the opinions you're getting, you could do a blog on the benefit or problems of taking ads on your site."

Bingo! And that's when the mud cleared. Or whatever tortured metaphor you want. Because I remembered what ads are. They piggyback on existing content that has an audience. Ads use that audience to try to cobble together their own audience, one that will purchase the product.

I looked at the other posts from the other writers, and realized I disagreed with one of them. The one that said my website advertised *me* and should just focus on me.

That thought had bothered me from the start, but I didn't know why. After Cindie's letter, I could articulate it and here's how I did. Oprah Winfrey is starting her own television channel soon. Oprah's channel will take ads, just like her magazine does.

Just like the radio stations I worked for did.

Just like the magazines I worked for did.

My website is not an advertisement. If it were, you folks would leave after one visit. It's a channel, a program, a magazine. It's content. The moment you don't like the content, you'll switch to another channel, go to another blog, do something else.

In other words, a website—like so many other things in this culture—is entertainment. And in a consumer culture, we fund entertainment with advertising.

I do promote my own stuff on the website. But I also promote other people's things as well, and not just in the Recommended

Reading. I promote magazines when they're publishing my work, and I promote book companies that publish anthologies or that publish my novels. I promote artists who do great book covers. I'm constantly pointing to other content. Sometimes for free, and sometimes for the price of buying my own work.

An ad fits into that. A paid ad.

However, in order to run a paid ad, I had to set up some mental ground rules. If my website were an actual company, those mental ground rules would be written down. Every company I worked for that took ads had rules, and the advertising department had to live up to those rules.

My mental ground rules for advertising are:

1. The advertiser can't offend me.
That sounds weird, but I mean it. If someone wanted to put an ad for an adult film company on my site, I would say no. If they killed baby seals to make fur coats, I would say no. If their product was in any way offensive or the website that promoted their product was offensive, I would say no.

2. The advertiser couldn't be political.
I have a lot of friends in politics and, much as I love y'all, I'm not taking on your political ads. My website is a politics-free place, and it will stay that way.

3. Nor can the ads be for a religious organization.
The same rule applies as it does to politics.

4. In fact, anything controversial will stay off my blog._
And, by the way, the person who defines "controversial" is me. You readers might feel something is controversial, but I might not agree. I get the final vote.

5. The ad has to be relatively unobtrusive.
I asked the ad rep for some sample ads on other websites. He pointed me to one at the bottom of a post. Since I was traveling, I didn't explore the whole website, so I was under the impression that the ad would run under *every* post. That would have been obtrusive, and I would have said no to that. But that's not what the ad rep

wanted. He wanted it at the end of one post, and one post only. I accepted the ad. Go to kristinekathrynrusch.com and find it. I dare you. (Okay, I'll reveal where it is later in this chapter.)

6. Unobtrusive means no pop-up ads, no music, no flash, no video.

Allie Brosh mentions this on her blog. She writes in her post on the ad, "You will never see me write a paid review of anything. I will never molest you with pop-ups or pop-unders or anything that flashes or moves or causes my page to freeze. There will be no pop-ups or moving things. None. Ever."

I agree. And as for paid reviews—nope. Never did it, never will. If I recommend something, it's because I like it, not because someone paid me to tell you about it.

7. I will not take ads for my static websites.

I have a site for my "Diving into the Wreck" universe (divingintothewreck.com), and I'll soon have sites for my Fey universe and the Retrieval Artist universe, as well as a few others. Those sites are pure information and advertisement for my series. They're not active, and they do exist just for those products. I'm not going to confuse the issue with other ads. But on this site, and any other active site I start, I'll take paid ads if someone wants to place them on the site.

That's my short list, my mental list, for any potential ads. I'm sure that if I get more ad queries, I'll end up with a longer list.

I know the radio stations I worked for took paid political advertising, within limits. Those stations also had time limits, word usage rules (no swear words, for example), and balance issues. One radio station's hard and fast rule: they would not take public service announcements for a product that was the subject of a paid ad somewhere else.

At the newspapers, the ads had size limitations. The magazines I worked for insisted the ads were "camera-ready," meaning that the ads could be inserted into the magazine's proof copy without any work by the magazine at all. (The newspapers and radio stations I worked for would often prepare the ad for the client.)

If you're going to take ads for your blog or your magazine or your video, you'll need your own set of ground rules. And the first, of course, is whether or not you'll take advertising at all.

I put a lot of sweat and angst into that question. I peppered the poor ad rep with a ton of e-mails. I finally accepted the ad, and got payment via PayPal.

And once I accepted the ad, I had to laugh at myself. All that angst, all those questions. You can find the ad at the bottom of a post called "Detail," which I put up on August 30, 2008. Two lines and a link to a page in Vista Print's catalogue. It'll stay up for a year.

I felt a bit ridiculous. But I'm happy I did the assessment. Because it clarified some thinking for me. And it got me to wondering: is this what the first radio stations went through one hundred years ago as they decided to take advertising?

I'm feeling my way around in this changing technological universe. And so, clearly, are other content providers, as Allie Brosh's post shows. We'll all decide what's best for us, and for our business.

And that's what freelancing is all about.

Chapter Twenty-two
Expanding Your Business

Recently, I have lived in a constant state of panic—and weirdly, that panic exists mostly in my own mind. From the outside, everything is going well; extremely well, in fact. But inside—well, a few mini volcanoes are going off—all of them triggered by the digital revolution.

I had already come to terms with the fact that I have more story ideas than I can write. Somewhere in the past, I figured that the marketplace would take care of some of them—meaning that the marketplace would deny me the opportunity to publish some of those ideas. In fact, the marketplace has closed the door on a number of projects, deemed unworthy by major New York publishers to be taken to readers.

I don't give up, but with so many projects, some have taken the back burner while others—more viable by publishing standards—rose to the forefront.

And then the digital revolution happened. This *Guide* happened. Kindle, Nook, and smart phones happened. Suddenly, I can publish what I want. Five thousand readers might seem small to New York, but to my little cottage industry, five thousand readers is huge.

All of those story ideas on the back burner? They're crowding the forefront of my brain, boiling over, and causing a mess in my writing kitchen. (Or to stretch the metaphor in another direction: they're children who used to sit quietly in the back of the room and are now crowding the front screaming, "Me first! Me! Me!")

Add to that my entire backlist of already-published material, most of which I control all the rights to. Over three hundred short stories and more than two dozen novels.

Not to mention all the work that's already in play, stuff I'm currently writing and stuff I have committed to write. Plus the teaching that I do because I believe in paying forward (I can't pay my wonderful teachers back, so I'm paying forward by teaching the next generation), and the reading I do to keep up, and the stories I watch on TV and movies—again to keep up—and the music I listen to because I love music (and without it, I would not exercise) and the newspapers, the magazines, the blogs, and…ack!!!!!!!!!!!!! Internal panic ensues.

Now, I'm very, very disciplined and very, very good at time management. I make lists, I know my priorities, I meet my deadlines.

But I want to step into this brave new world of publishing, and to do so I need to make choices. First, I need to prioritize my projects. Then, I need to make a budget of both time and money (projected incoming and projected outgoing). Then I need to figure out my timeline. And finally, I need to factor in where (if anywhere) I need help.

Let's start with the last thing first. Do I need help? (Okay, you wags. I mean *employees*, not, y'know, professional help of the kind you're thinking of.)

There are some things in my business that only I can do. I'm not like Alexander Dumas or James Patterson: I can't farm out my ideas with a great outline to other writers and be happy with the result. I recently said the same thing to an editor who proposed just such a project: I have learned through several long hard lessons that I don't play well with others when it comes to the actual writing.

So all those new backburner projects currently bubbling over from volcano #1? My problem. Something I'll have to solve through time management and discipline and sheer joy. (Can you tell I'm looking forward to this?)

But that pesky backlist. I don't have time to put it online—not and write new material. If I wanted to retire right now, I could, and live off my backlist, thanks to the brave new world of publishing and some other changes in the industry.

Of course, once I figure out what I want to do with that backlist, I could hire someone to do the actual conversion to online formats for me. The question is: do I want to do that?

If only it were so easy. In a magical world—the ideal world—the world of expectations, I could just hire someone and all of my problems would be solved.

But I've run enough businesses to know it doesn't work that way.

So I have to do a cost-benefit analysis. Is it worth my incredibly precious time to train an employee who may or may not work out? Is it worth the money to hire someone? And if I do hire them, where would they work? Do I bring them into my home office? (Okay: that sound you just heard? Me, screaming. Apparently no. They can't work here, in my home.) Do I let them work in their home office? (Nope: can't supervise very well there.) Or do I rent an office for them to work in?

Given my personality, my choice is the office outside of the home. I can supervise and I can keep them out of my home. But… an office costs money. Rent, utilities, insurance, as well as the employee's salary, and furniture for the office, a topflight computer so they can do the work, and here it is again…time. I'd have to stop in every day to make sure they're getting the job done.

The very idea of all of this makes me tired. I really don't want an employee at this stage of my career.

But what that means is that all of my volcanic plans must take a backseat to time—my time—and my focus. If I'm going to do this myself, then I need to carve out some time to do so, and I need to realize that going it alone will make the changeover much slower.

Again, I'd have to do a cost-benefit analysis. Can I make more money going it alone? Will slow get the job done—without the office expenses, without the employee hassle? Will I be able to make the change?

Is the change worthwhile?

And if I decide that the change is worthwhile, is it something that needs to get done now, this instant, or something that can stretch out over several years?

All personal questions about my business, all with both empirical answers (timeline, money) and personal answers (figuring out what I really want). Let me state here and now, however, that my decision to do work on future projects means that I will not approve fan fiction and I don't want anyone to do the work for me "as a favor." I license my copyrights and my worlds, and I am not in any way giving anyone blanket permission to work in them. (Remember? I do not play well with others.)

My analysis here is a textbook example of what all businesses go through when they want to expand. So let's discuss expansion.

First, let me deal with the elephant in the room.

Unsuccessful businesses often expand to increase revenue. It sounds counterintuitive, but some businesses can only get capital (investment money) if they have a new project to spend the money on. This leads to businesses that get stretched too thin. When you hear that a business was a house of cards, and once one card fell the entire thing toppled, you can pretty much guarantee that the business expanded too quickly—whether internally (hiring too many employees, rushing out too much product) or externally (opening too many storefronts). If you're thinking of expanding to get more capital because you're already under-funded, stop now. That way will guarantee the collapse of your business. All you're doing is holding off the inevitable.

Now that we have that out of the way, let's discuss successful businesses.At some point, every successful business will reach a point where expansion looks like a good idea. But is it?

The first question you must answer is this: *Can your business continue to thrive without expanding?*

Most businesses can thrive without growing. Even though growing seems like a natural state, it is sometimes the death of a healthy business. The owners get spread too thin or the expansion doesn't work out or the economy has a downturn. The expansion might actually weaken the business itself.

Does your expansion have its roots in changing neighborhoods or changing technologies? If you own a storefront, would you be better off in a different neighborhood with more traffic? Or another neighborhood with a different kind of traffic? Is your neighborhood aging or going downhill, facing economic changes or a retooling? You need to consider all of that before moving your business to a larger space or adding another storefront in a different location.

Changing technology is another matter, and it happens to be the one I'm facing. My business would thrive just fine on the old technological model. But will my business thrive in five years? Ten? If I believe that the new technologies are essential to the publishing industry, then I need to jump on the wave now. I won't be an early adapter—that's Michael A. Stackpole, J.A. Konrath, and others—but I'd be in the early wave. Already I'm getting e-mails and tweets from around the world, asking for digital copies of my work. Imagine how many I'd have to fend off if I refuse to cross into e-publishing.

I've analyzed my industry and feel *for me* that working in conventional publishing and e-publishing will be beneficial. (Remember, I have a mountain of real-world publishing experience, as the former owner of a publishing house, a former editor, and a non-writing-related small business owner. In other words, I have a lot more experience than most writers going into this, not counting the goodwill from my writing career.) Now that I've figured out that it's beneficial, I need to figure out what works for me in my expansion.

But moving into new technologies might not work for your business. The technology might be a fad—something that seems like a good idea, but doesn't catch on. Remember, we have had video phone technology since the 1980s, but it's taken 20+ years for the technology to garner even marginal usage—and that's via computer, not through a landline. If you had been an early adapter of video phone technology for your business, or running a communications business with video phones as a main selling point, you would have lost money, particularly if you adapted that tech in the late 1980s.

Sometimes letting others adapt early is the best response. They'll work out the bugs, and take the risks. The key for any business that feels it must grow and change due to changes in technology is research.

Before I made the decision to add digital to my writing business, I did two years of research—and I'm still doing research. The Freelancer's Guide blog is part of that research. But I'm reading about digital, trying some of the products on a consumer basis (I have a Kindle and an iPhone, and have already had some hands-on contact with an iPad), and continue to look at pricing, as well as successful—and unsuccessful—adapters of the new technology.

Research—as I say almost every week—is an important part of your business.

If you are going to expand due to new technologies, you also have to look into the future. If it takes 20 years for these changes in your field to establish itself—like a video phone—will you be around to capitalize on it? Do you want to be self-employed in 20 years? Will you be retired? Can you imagine yourself selling the business and moving on to something else?

If any of those things are true, *and* you don't need the new technology to maintain your thriving business, then technological expansion might not be for you.

Other things to consider as you expand:

1. The financial cost of expansion.

I delineated my costs above. I'd need an outside office and an employee. Here in my tiny town, I'm looking at a minimum of $24,000 per year in additional expenses for just those two things. Will the expansion bring in $30,000 in its first year so that I can afford that change *and* make a profit? Or would I be hurting my business with the expansion by breaking even on the new office space and the new employee? Or would I lose money?

Be harsh here, because these decisions are the ones that will make or break your business.

2. The time cost of expansion.

I mentioned this above as well. Expansion takes time out of your business day. When you're already pressed for time, such a change can be disastrous. Figure out your hourly wage. Even self-employed people can break down their earnings into an hourly rate. Once you have that, then factor in the time it will take you to establish the new office (say) or train the new employee(s) or learn the new technology.

Will the profit you make off the expansion be worth the money lost because your time is spent on the expansion and not earning as you have been doing? In other words, can you afford to lose 10-30 hours per week of your time to establish this new side of your business? Can you make a profit on the expansion by doing so? Or can it wait?

3. If your math proves that expansion is worthwhile, are you better off making a slow expansion or a rapid one?

Sometimes it's better to lose a month of work time all at once and get the new part of the business up and running. If you extend that month over a year (an hour here and an hour there), you might lose the advantage the expansion would bring, or you might actually increase your costs in both time and money. Again, it depends on the type of expansion you're planning and the type of business you're running.

Whether or not to expand your business is the second most important business decision you'll ever make—right after deciding to own your own business in the first place. Look at expansion as closely as you would look at leaping from your day job to working for yourself. Use all of the tools I mention in other parts of the *Guide* as your blueprint for expansion. Because expansion is like starting a new business. You'll fundamentally change the business you've started *and* you might jeopardize it.

Plan carefully before you make the decision.

And here's one other thought on the expansion. If you're at all in doubt, if thinking of expanding makes your stomach hurt, then don't do it. Your gut sense on this is as important as all of the number crunching, the facts, and the figures.

If you have made your business successful through hard work and perseverance, then your subconscious knows as much or more about that business than your conscious brain does. Your gut is an informed gut, and if it's worried that an expansion will fail, then maybe you're missing something important in your very logical plans.

Never take a leap as important as expanding your business without being fully confident in your decision. You must believe that your business will be *more* successful if it expands. Not a little more. A lot more.

Because an expansion will cost you more in time and energy than you will plan on. Any change does. There will be unexpected results—good and bad—from that expansion. You won't be able to plan for everything.

You will have to know you're making the right decision.

I know that moving into e-publishing is the right thing for me. But I'm not yet ready to commit to a path on how to achieve it. I have more research to do, more numbers to crunch. I have to decide if I need an employee or if I'm simply pushing myself too far too fast.

I have a lot of exploration to do before I commit to a path for my business expansion. I've been around long enough to know that research and planning are the only things that will make this decision work.

In the meantime, I have a novel and several short stories to finish. I have some backlist that I will e-pub, slowly.

My business is thriving and I'm enjoying it. Even with the panic attacks. For once, I'm panicking about having too many opportunities rather than not enough. And that's a change from 20 years ago. A good change.

One I can appreciate as I look toward the future of my industry, which seems brighter than ever before.

Chapter Twenty-three
Incorporation

One of the topics people asked me to cover in the blog version of the *Freelancer's Guide* was incorporation.

I agonized over writing about incorporation and twice crossed it off my list. I am not a lawyer, nor am I a tax expert. I really didn't want to tackle the topic. But I talked with a few people about whether or not I should write about incorporation, and all of them seemed enthusiastic.

A few suggested I contact my "panel of experts" to discuss incorporation. While I know dozens of attorneys, many of who are tax attorneys or copyright attorneys or corporate attorneys, I don't feel right asking them to comment for this article.

I know what they'll all say. It depends on the business. It depends on the financial situation of the business. It depends on the structure of the business. It depends on whether or not you want investors, what your tax liability is, and what it might become.

It depends, it depends, it depends.

It also depends on which country you're in. Since I've received donations for the Guide from Japan, England, the Netherlands, and Canada (to name only a few), I don't want to spend a lot of time on a topic that I know only from an American perspective.

So I'm going to handle this very complicated topic in a very simple manner.

First, let's discuss business structure.

Most freelancers are sole proprietors. They run their own business by themselves. They own it, they run it, and they manage it alone. They file a Schedule C on the United States tax form. They use a simple accounting system. Often their business doesn't even have a name, except their name. People in the arts work this way, often.

So the tax document is filed under the owner's name. Business cards have the freelancer's name on them, and maybe a description of what the freelancer does.

That's it. Simple and easy. For most of you, this is a fine system. No need to mess with it.

But let's say you decided to name your business Green Frahg Productions. You have become the owner and operator of Green Frahg Productions. You want all bank accounts, receipts, bills, payments, everything financial to funnel through Green Frahg Productions.

There are many ways to do this.

To open a bank account in the United States under the name Green Frahg Productions, you'll need a DBA document. That's a Doing Business As form which you can get from your bank. You'll need to file that form with the state. Once you've filled out that form with all the pertinent information, you can then open your accounts under the name Green Frahg Productions.

It's really that simple. Each state has different regulations. Your banker will tell you what the regulations are for your state. I have a hunch it works this way in each country as well.

You'll be on the DBA as the owner and operator, but Green Frahg becomes the public face of your business, not you. The check for any purchased material will come to Green Frahg Productions. The only problem comes in signing the contract. *Someone* has to sign as a representative of Green Frahg, and that someone is you.

A DBA is the simplest way to assume a name other than yours for your business. A corporation is an extremely complicated way, and if you want a corporate identity only for the name, then you don't understand corporations.

Under U.S. law (and under the laws of many other countries), a corporation is a separate entity. In other words, it exists, as a person exists. In the U.S., we're constantly arguing about what that means. The major Supreme Court case this year, *Citizens United v. Federal Election Commission*, that caused so much controversy is a case about (among other things) the definition of a corporation under the law. These things change all the time, and there are books upon books upon books defining what a corporation is, what its tax liability is, and what regulations it must follow.

Not to mention that, inside the United States, corporations can take various forms. Some have limited liability. Some are public—

meaning that anyone can buy stock in them (through the correct channels). Some are private. There is subchapter this and structure that, and they all follow different rules.

One thing each corporation holds in common is this: if you decide to incorporate, your paperwork will increase exponentially. You'll have to have board meetings. You'll need to document everything. Your finances must be handled a certain way. Your taxes must be handled a certain way.

If you fail to follow those rules, you are legally liable for all kinds of nastiness. Taking on a corporation is a mighty task, one you shouldn't do lightly, if at all. It's certainly not something you can decide on your own. You'll need to hire an attorney to help you incorporate. Make sure that the attorney you hire is a business attorney who handles corporations routinely.

You'll also need a certified public accountant to help you set up the books of your corporation. Those books must be set up to a particular standard, and that standard has to be maintained.

If you have stockholders, then you'll need to do reports, filings, disclosures and all kinds of things like that. Corporations, in case you can't tell, are a gigantic pain in the butt.

So…if corporations are a pain, why do people incorporate their businesses?

For a variety of reasons. Many will incorporate to minimize their personal tax liability. If your business starts making *profits* in the hundreds of thousands, then you might want to consider incorporating. Your tax liability (in the States) *might* go down. It might not. I know people who have so badly mishandled their corporations that their tax liability went up.

If your business is a risky one, then you might want a corporation to stand between you and any legal liabilities. If you're afraid that you could get sued routinely for standard business practices, then you might want to incorporate.

It sounds like I'm talking about criminal businesses here, but I'm not. I'm talking about a business, like a gym, where injury might be common, and lawsuits are expected. People hurt themselves all the time on gym equipment, and it doesn't matter how often you explain how to use the equipment correctly. People will sue.

If you own the gym as a sole proprietor, then any legal damages could come out of your own personal wealth. Your kid's college savings might go instead to the dumb guy who decided he could bench-press an extra 50 lbs and broke bones doing so. Yeah, you warned him, but you didn't take the weights away from him. And the jury found for the dumb guy. Your kid suddenly isn't going to college.

Unless your gym is incorporated and—here's the rub—it's the right kind of corporation, in which case you might be protected. Some corporations aren't protection against a lawsuit like that. Some are. The ones that are will act in this way: the court will take the damages from the corporation's finances and leave yours alone.

Again, it depends on what you need the corporation for.

So if you are thinking of incorporating, either to protect yourself from huge tax bills or to protect yourself from standard (and expected) lawsuits that are the cost of doing business, do these things:

1. Research, research, research.

Read up on corporations. Then find the right people to talk to. Research the attorneys you might hire. Research the accounting firms. Figure out what you really need *before* you ask for help.

2. Hire the correct attorney and listen to what she has to say.

Ask the right questions. Tell her exactly what you want the corporation for. Ask her about taxes, liabilities, benefits and drawbacks to the various corporations she proposes. You might want to see a second and third attorney to get their opinions as well. You don't want to have the wrong type of corporation when all is said and done.

3. Hire the right accountant and listen to what he has to say.

He's going to help you set up your finances. He's going to set up your accounts, and he's going to tell you how the accounts work for your type of corporation. Follow his instructions and setup *to the letter*. If you don't do this, you could be subject to extra taxes, fines, and all kinds of ugliness.

4. Keep a wall between you and that corporation.

Don't blur your finances. Don't blur your taxes. Don't tell people you are the business when you are not. Think of the corporation as another person and don't ever, ever, steal that other person's identity.

5. If you have shareholders, keep them informed.

The law requires this, of course, but so many small corporations don't do it. *Do it.* That prevents shareholder lawsuits.

If all of this talk of tax liability and rules and thick books and lawyers and accounting regulations and lawsuits scares you, good. It should. Because incorporating is a big decision and not one you should take lightly.

It's a decision that most of you should not take at all. Be happy with your DBA or your unnamed sole proprietorship. Plug along at your small business, and keep it small.

Once you become a corporation, you're playing with the big boys; and believe me, they play nasty. Stay out of their game if you can at all avoid it. If you decide to join them, then be prepared—and follow the rules.

You'll be glad you did.

Section Four:
How to Negotiate Anything

Chapter Twenty-four
The Rules of Negotiation

My ex-husband used to say all of life is negotiable.

That attitude fascinated me and repelled me at the same time. I loved the way he could get bargains, and I loved the way he refused to hear the word no. But I was raised by people who didn't negotiate. For all I know, my parents spent full list price on their cars.

The price was the price, my upbringing said. When someone told you the rules, you followed them. You didn't negotiate them. You didn't ask for the price to come down. You didn't try to get something special for yourself.

Who did you think you were, anyway? Someone *special*? Someone to whom the rules did not apply?

My husband, Dean Wesley Smith, also loves to negotiate. He hates to spend full price for anything. Early in our relationship, I argued with him as he tried to negotiate the price of a television set in a Fred Meyer store. Fred Meyer, for those of you who don't live near one, was once considered a lower-level department store. Now it's mid-level. It sells everything from food to electronics to clothes to furniture, but not as cheaply as Wal-Mart or Target nor as expensively as Macy's. What Fred Meyer shares with those places is this: the listed price is the price. If they want to discount the item, they put it on sale.

Dean never believed that. He knew that the salesperson on the floor couldn't negotiate, but the manager could. So Dean would see the last television set or the single remaining display model or a huge number of televisions, none of which were moving, and he'd ask for the manager. Then Dean would offer to pay half price and take the item away immediately—no box, no nothing. Just cash.

Nine times out of ten, the manager took him up on the offer. Or she'd negotiate in return. *I can't sell you that television at half price, but I can sell you this one for even less.*

Some places—like car dealerships—expect you to negotiate. When
I lived in Madison, Wisconsin, there was an appliance and electronics store
called American Furniture and Appliances, run by a guy named Lenny.
Everyone in town called the place Crazy TV Lenny's because that was the
moniker that he gave himself on his wild TV ads. (For an idea what this
guy was like, see the Ted Danson character in *Made in America*.)

My ex and I often shopped there, and I let my ex handle the
negotiations. His mother gave us $200 every Christmas, and we
managed to stretch it a long way—often through my ex's negotiating
skill at Crazy TV Lenny's.

Even there, I had trouble listening to the negotiation. But I
knew it was appropriate.

It wasn't appropriate (or so I believed) at Fred Meyer. So
on that night more than twenty years ago, as Dean started into his
negotiations, I hissed at him: "They don't negotiate here."

He waved me off.

"Seriously," I said. "They won't let you do that here."

Finally, he turned to me and snapped, "Kindly shut up."

Which I did, surprisingly enough.

And we walked out with a much-needed $500 television that
we only paid $200 for.

You can negotiate anywhere. The worst thing they can say to
you is no.

Back then, my problem with face-to-face negotiation was
a case of terminal embarrassment. I didn't want to call attention to
myself in public in any way. Some of this came from my shyness, but
some of it came from my upbringing. My mother worried constantly
about what other people thought, and it rubbed off on me. It still takes
a conscious effort for me not to worry about what other people think.

I figured if it was bad form to negotiate, then people would
remember, and ostracize me.

Only no one has ever remembered Dean badly for negotiation.
In fact, the places he's negotiated things have remembered him, and
have often offered him other deals. They *respect* him, which was
quite a lesson for me.

The other lesson about face-to-face negotiation that I learned
from both men is that both of them negotiated with a smile and a
shrug. They charmed the salesperson, making the salesperson feel as
good about the sale as they did.

Now, no one has ever called me charming. Strong,

opinionated, blunt, difficult, smart, and truthful, yes, but charming—
never. And honestly, while I care what people think as a default mode,
I mostly don't care if they like me. I am what I am; take it or leave it.

The charmer makes each person feel special. And the charmer
can be a chameleon, becoming all things to all people.

Sadly, I don't have the patience for that. A charmer can
negotiate face-to-face from a position of weakness.

I can't—at least not face-to-face. I can negotiate from a position
of weakness in writing or through an intermediary. More on that later.

I can, however, negotiate face-to-face if I believe it's a matter
of fairness. Which was why I had no trouble as a sixteen-year-old
asking for payment for my high school newspaper column. It seemed
logical to me that if everyone else at the paper got paid for her work, I
should as well. I presented it that way to my teacher, who presented to
the paper. I didn't try to charm anyone.

I've done that many times over the years. I do it from an
informed perspective. I find out what others get paid for the same
work and ask for that rate for myself. Or ask for an increase based on
past performance.

I have no trouble doing that. It's based on rules, you see, and I
can do rules face-to-face.

But things like negotiating at a car dealership or in a store
have no rules, so I'm at a loss. I don't do it, but these days, I'm happy
when Dean does—and occasionally I suggest it to him. Then I leave
the vicinity. Because I can't stay calm while he does it. I panic or get
embarrassed, even now.

Which is why I initially put off writing about negotiation.
I don't do it well face-to-face. I think of Dean or my ex-husband. I
think of all those other people I've known who are experts at getting
the best price for the best product, and I know I'm not like them.

However, if you were to ask anyone who does business with
me, they'd call me a skilled negotiator. In fact, I've had a number of
people tell me I'm such a good negotiator, I should do it for a living—
as a book agent, for example. (Which means they aren't thinking
things through. Why should I make 15% off someone else's work,
when I can make 85 to 100% off my own?)

How can I be known as such a skilled negotiator when I can't
dicker with a car dealer?

Simple: I know my strengths and weaknesses. I also know
what I want.

The rules for negotiation are pretty easy:

1. Know What You Want.

That sounds elementary, but most people don't know what they want before they enter into negotiation. In the TV example above, Dean and I were broke, with only about $250 to our name. Our television had died a spectacular death (involving sparks and explosions), and we needed a new one. We wanted the best set we could get for our money. Me, I would have just looked at $200 TVs. Dean looked at all the TVs to see which he could bargain down to $200. He got us the better deal. But we knew our limits. We couldn't spend more than $200 and still get groceries. I'm sure the store manager had some kind of limitation on his end as well—probably the cost of the item versus the cost of the space it took on his shelf.

2. Ask.

You won't get what you want if you don't ask, so what's the risk? The worst thing the other party can do is say no.

3. Be Prepared To Walk Away.

You won't always get what you want. But you should never settle for less than what you need. So many people get caught up in the negotiation they forget that they can simply say no and leave. You can always try another day.

4. Stay Calm.

Negotiations are for rational people, making business decisions. The moment you feel yourself getting angry or panicked or embarrassed, end the negotiation. Calm down. You have to be able to think clearly, and you won't be able to do that if you're emotional in any way.

5. Never Reveal Your Entire Hand.

Even if you're desperate—especially if you're desperate—don't admit it. Don't tell the salesperson that you only have $200. Don't say you'll do anything to be published or start your business or go on TV. The moment you reveal your deepest needs, you give the other party a hook that will guarantee that they'll triumph in the negotiation. Make sure that you keep your reason for making the deal—whatever it is—completely to yourself.

6. Don't Flip-Flop.

If you say you'll walk before you spend $250, then walk. Make promises and keep them. Or you lose your standing in the negotiation, and your word means nothing.

All of this is deliberately vague, because negotiation happens in a variety of circumstances. You negotiate salary when you get a job, as does your future boss. You negotiate when you propose marriage to someone—you are making an alliance, after all, and you discuss what that alliance entails. You negotiate when you rent an apartment or buy a house. You negotiate when you order in large quantities from a supplier. Most of us even negotiate traffic tickets ("Honest, officer, I didn't see the speed limit sign. It's hidden behind a bush.")

Each of those negotiations takes different skills.

So for the sake of the *Guide*, I'll examine the most common types of negotiation you'll do when you're in business. These include—but are not limited to—contracts and financial dealings. I'll also discuss negotiations with potential clients and with potential employees.

All of these take different approaches. For example, fiduciary negotiations might be short-term, like my high school column for the local paper. But contracts exist for a specific period of time—anywhere from six months to ten years or more. You need to think about all aspects of that as you negotiate, not just your short-term goal.

Then there are different methods of negotiation. Many of us hire a negotiator—be that an agent or an attorney or a publicist—to do the actual talking for us. But a negotiator needs guidance, and ultimately, they're following *your* wishes. So I'll discuss when you need one and when you don't. And, when you do need one, what kind should you hire? A charmer, a shark, or a combination of both?

Negotiation is a deep topic. The first thing you need to do as we delve into it is figure out how good you are at negotiating. Can you negotiate face-to-face? Is it easy for you to ask for what you want? When you do ask, do you get it nine out of ten times, or do you alienate the people you talk to?

Before you enter a negotiation, you also need to figure out something else: the power relationships.

In each relationship, one person has more power than the other person. Most recently, I heard this premise expressed in a fairly mediocre Matthew McConaughey movie called *The Ghosts of Girlfriends Past*. Michael Douglas, in the Jacob Marley role (and frankly, the best thing in the movie), tells McConaughey that the person with the most power in any romantic relationship is the person who wants it the *least*.

If you think about that, that's true. The person who is the least involved controls whether or not the relationship continues. The other person, the person who wants it the most, must abide by the wishes of the person who doesn't want it quite as much.

But, as McConaughey learns in the movie, romantic relations aren't (or shouldn't be) about power. They're about a lot of other things, not the least of which are love and friendship and valuing the other person.

I didn't tell you this just for your sappy movie lesson of the day, but for that one little nugget of truth spoken by Douglas's character. In any negotiation, the person who wants it the least has the most power.

Job seekers are discovering this right now. They really, really, really need a job, any job (the higher paying the better) so that the bills get paid. Employers, on the other hand, aren't sure about the wisdom of hiring yet another employee, so employers approach the negotiation with ambivalence.

When ambivalence meets desperation, one of two things occurs. Either the ambivalent person decides it's too much work to hire someone—particularly when a lot of job seekers answer an ad—or the ambivalent one takes advantage of another person's desperation. Desperate people say things like, "I'll do anything," or "Just hire me, please." And that leads to being underpaid for the job or overworked, just to please the boss—if, of course, the boss chooses to hire.

The set-up question for this often comes early in the interview, by the way. It's the "What kind of salary would you like?" question, which was a question I always hated as a job seeker and refused to answer. What I would say was either, "You stated your pay rates in the ad, which is why I answered it" or "Perhaps you should tell me what you're willing to pay." The first answer shut down that fishing question; the second threw the ball back into the interviewer's court.

When I mentioned that question at weekly writers' lunch the other day (in connection with writing about negotiation), a woman who has worked at middle-management jobs her whole life said her answer to the question was similar to mine: "What are you willing to pay?"

But the best answer came from a man who worked in the highest level of management for decades, getting six-figure salaries in the computer industry. He said whenever he got asked that question, he would respond, "We can discuss that later. Let's see first if we're suited for each other."

Invariably at the end of the interview, when the company indicated that they wanted to hire him—and he wanted to work for them—the company would ask again what kind of salary he wanted. He would respond, "I'd like to get more than I'm being paid now."

Of course, they'd ask his current rate, and choke when they heard it. But, he said, they always paid him. By the end of his high tech career, he often got paid more than his bosses.

That's a skilled negotiator.

Note in his example the fluidity of the power relationship. In the beginning, the power seemed to belong to the hiring company. Then they asked the salary question. He made it clear that he wasn't even sure he wanted the job. The power relationship became equal at that point. The discussions continued, and eventually, the company decided that they wanted him. He then had the power in the relationship—he could say no. And he stated his terms which were "Pay me more than I'm getting now."

In other words, he didn't need them, but they needed him.

So many people can't do that because they need the job itself. So you have to understand when you enter into that negotiation that you (the potential employee) automatically have less power in the negotiation. You *need* the job. They *want* an employee, but they don't necessarily want you.

You need to convince them to hire you without being desperate about it. And you probably won't be in position to argue over salary. Which was always my position when I was looking for a day job. I never wanted a day job, so I only applied when I needed one. Look again at my answers to that question. "What's your salary range?" Or "I saw your range in the ad, and that's why I'm here."

In other words, I took salary off the table, let them know they could afford me, and then we figured out if they wanted to hire me. (And if I wanted to be hired. Even desperate, I knew there were jobs I couldn't [or shouldn't] do.)

I've watched this same dynamic play out with writers over

the years. Freelance fiction writers, who have struggled for years, often accept the first offer they receive on a book. In publishing, the first offer a new writer gets is a low-ball offer. The editor expects the writer to negotiate. In fact, the editor who makes the offer *wants* the writer to negotiate because, if the writer doesn't, the editor knows the writer will hate the publisher later. The writer will end up blaming the publishing company for "screwing" him when, really, the writer screwed himself by not negotiating.

But in that early publishing relationship, the publishing company does have more power. They have it in two ways: they have the resources to publish the book; and they've become the vehicle for fulfilling a writer's greatest dream. It takes guts and a firm belief in one's self to walk away from that, but the writers who do benefit later on.

In the writer/publisher relationship, the power shifts over time. An established writer will often not get book offers because the editor is afraid to anger the writer with a low-ball offer. (I always say, *Make the offer, and let me make the decision.*) Established writers have a lot more clout than new writers.

I think that the only time writers and publishers reach parity is in the case of established writers who are negotiating with their publishers. They're negotiating over the book itself, and the power lines are equal. The writer wants the sale, yes, but only under certain conditions. The publisher wants the book, yes, but only under certain conditions. And the writer and publisher must then negotiate the best deal for all involved.

Bestselling writers and writers with hot properties, however, have all of the power in the publishing industry (many of them just don't realize it). They command higher advances, promotion budgets, and so on. They get offers from other publishing houses trying to steal them away, although these authors sometimes won't get offers from the houses that want them because those houses really and truly can't afford them. And everyone, everyone, wants a piece of those authors, so the authors can set their price.

Power fluctuates. You just have to know what yours is when you enter into a negotiation. Now let's look at negotiations themselves.

Chapter Twenty-five
Negotiating for the Short Term

In the last chapter, I mentioned how Dean negotiated for a television set. That was a short-term negotiation. We needed a TV, we had limited dollars, and we wanted that TV immediately. So we went with a set price in mind. Dean got us the best TV he could find for our limited dollars.

End of negotiation, end of situation.

You encounter this all the time as a freelancer. Someone wants to hire you for a short-term project. Or you want to work on a short-term project. This is a one-time thing that has absolutely no resale value. That's important because in many kinds of freelancing, your work can be sold and resold for years to come. Artists, writers, and musicians in particular face the resale issue, but not in every case.

So let's put this in a musician's ballpark. A few blocks from my house is one of the best blues clubs in the Northwest. Up-and-coming groups play there as well as long-term professionals and extremely famous blues musicians.

The gigs are short—one or two nights—and since no one is allowed to record while the musicians are playing, the gigs have no resale value at all. It's just a group of musicians playing to a crowded club.

Sometimes when musicians play bars, there are contracts. Sometimes there aren't. In this hypothetical case, let's assume there are no contracts involved. Just a handshake.

Musicians can get a flat fee for playing. They can get a flat fee and a percentage of the cover charge (if there is one). (A cover charge, for those of you who don't know, is the price you pay just to get into the club. Some clubs charge these every night; some never charge it; and some charge it only when there's a big name group playing.) Musicians can get a flat fee and a percentage of the bar's earnings that night. They can get a flat fee, a percentage of cover, *and* a percentage of the bar's earnings. Or they can get a percentage of cover and the bar's earnings. Or just a percentage of cover…

You see how this goes. It's all negotiable.

A brand new torch singer with no following at all might ask for a percentage of cover and the bar's earnings, but that's probably not wise for the bar or the singer. Because a brand new singer has no following, charging cover is probably a mistake—unless the club is so exclusive that playing there is an honor that will launch the torch singer's career. Even then, the torch singer should probably negotiate a flat fee. After all, this is a limited engagement and attendance will probably be down. The torch singer has a better chance of making her expenses with the flat fee than with a percentage.

However, the established professional probably wants a combination—a small guarantee (in other words, a flat fee) plus percentages of the cover and the bar's take. The small guarantee pays for everything should it be a stormy night or the advertising failed and the club didn't fill up.

The Big Names have an appearance fee that is non-negotiable (except for real friends). That gets paid no matter what. Whether it comes out of cover or the bar's earnings, it doesn't matter. The appearance fee gets paid. However, some Big Names want the appearance fee and a percentage of cover and the bar's earnings.

If you look at this, you realize that when a club books a Big Name, the club could actually lose money on the appearance. Why would a club do that? To bring in new customers, and hope they become repeat customers.

(This happens in books as well, which is why bestselling books are often sold at a discount. That's to bring people into the bookstore with the hope that they'll buy other books.)

But let's go back to our brand new torch singer. She can ask for the same appearance fee as the Big Name, but she won't get it. In fact, she might get laughed at. She can take the flat fee the club offers. She can take a percentage of cover and bar, with the idea that she might not make any money.

Most beginners wouldn't ask for the Big Name's appearance fee, not because they're afraid of being laughed at, but because they wouldn't think of it. Fine. That's probably good.

Okay. So we know what the power relationship is in this instance. But now let's look at the other part of the negotiation.

1. **What Does Our Torch Singer Want?**

She needs to figure out what she wants more than anything else. Is this club prestigious? Will it launch her career? Or is it just a local club in a small town that really has no importance at all?

If it's an important club and she wants to play the club more than anything else—money, hours, anything—then she has to make sure she has to keep that firmly in mind before she negotiates anything.

But let's assume this is a local club. Now she has to figure out what she wants to get paid. Let's also assume that the gig is two nights—Friday and Saturday—with no hope of renewal. She needs to find out how much the cover is, if there even is a cover, and what the bar expects to earn. Sometimes she can do that in her head—the number of seats in the club times the cover price plus the cost of one drink. If that number turns out to be much higher in a full club than the flat fee, she might want to ask for that. Of course, the request assumes she'll fill the club, which she probably won't, considering that it's a local club and she's an unknown.

But she is taking a risk with the club owner and they both have a stake in a good outcome. It might be worth the gamble to her.

Let's assume, though, that her rent is past due. She needs money more than anything else. She needs the flat fee at the very minimum.

Our torch singer has decided she needs a flat fee to play at the local club on Friday and Saturday night. That's the bottom line of her negotiation.

2. **Ask.**

But she needs money, and the flat fee is a small amount—say $100 for two nights. She gets the practice, and she's not going to say no to the $100. Does she tell the club owner that at the beginning of the negotiation? Of course not.

She has done her research, though, and she has learned that this club doesn't charge a cover when the performer is unknown.

So she goes into the negotiation knowing her limits: she can't ask for a cover percentage and she needs the flat fee. But it would be nice if she made more money than that flat fee.

She asks for $200 flat fee. That's double what was offered, but it's worth a try. But it would be better for her to ask for the flat fee plus a percentage of the bar. Because if she's good and word gets around, Saturday's bar take should be pretty high. She's taking a risk along with the club owner. She's not costing him extra money if no one comes to her performances, and she's making money if people do.

So she asks. What's the worst thing the club owner can say? All together now…the worst thing he can say is no.

3. Be Prepared to Walk Away.

In this particular instance, our torch singer is *not* prepared to walk away. She needs the money. But she doesn't tell the club owner that. The nuclear option is not available to her.

He's probably willing to walk away. So if he says no to her request for a percentage of the bar, she should laugh, tell him that $100 is fine, and shake hands.

4. Stay Calm.

She needs that $100. Is she nervous? You bet. Can she negotiate? I hope so. But she's a performer. She can probably pretend calm when she doesn't have it. If she can't pretend, then she should take a few deep breaths and make sure she thinks about each sentence before she speaks.

Because at her level of the career, it would be foolish for her to hire a manager to do the negotiating for her. Better that she learn how to do it on her own than sacrifice $15 to $20 of that much needed $100 for someone to speak for her—when she wouldn't get much out of that deal anyway.

5. Never Reveal Your Entire Hand.

Let's assume the deal's done, the hands are shaken, the torch singer is going to play the club. Should she tell the club owner that she needed that $100 more than anything? No. Should she tell him she never planned to walk away from the gig? No.

Because she might negotiate with him in the future, and she doesn't want him to know how good she is. She doesn't want to give him any insight into her ways of thinking. It doesn't benefit her—and he probably doesn't care anyway.

6. Don't Flip-Flop.

She's committed to the gig, shaken hands, and agreed to a fee. So she shouldn't arrive on Friday night, see that the club is full, and ask for more money. Nor should she back out of the deal, even if she finds out later that the club owner usually pays first-timers $500. She made the agreement; she should stick to it. If she doesn't like the deal, she needs to remember that *in future deals*. This one will be over in two days, she'll have some practice singing sexy songs in a dark club, and $100 toward her rent. That's what she negotiated, and if she's not satisfied, she needs to make sure she never agrees to this kind of deal again.

Which brings us back to point one. In future deals, she'll remember this deal and make sure she never takes a fee this low again—or does more research and finds out what others get paid—or agrees to only one night at $100.

This deal doesn't hurt her long term. She has only short-term considerations: a two-night stint, a flat fee, a few songs.

Chapter Twenty-six
Understanding Contracts

Negotiating for the long term is dicey. If you make a mistake, you don't have to live with it for a weekend. You might have to live with it for years.

So before we discuss the specifics, let's talk about the emotions of negotiation.

On one of my e-mail lists, we're discussing taming your inner 12-year-old in a business situation. You know what I mean: the core you, the scared or angry or shy person hidden behind your adult façade.

Too many of us let our inner twelve-year-olds rule our lives. My inner twelve-year-old is very shy. When I was twelve, I had switched schools from a pampered elitist school for the children of college professors to a public junior high school where the students occasionally carried knives. I was the victim of a horrible crime right after my twelfth birthday and was both traumatized and terrified throughout much of the year. For the first half of that school year, I came home from school and watched television until I went to bed; I didn't interact with anyone at all. People threatened me by their very existence. I survived by trying to predict their behavior.

And by being polite—very, very, very polite.

Extreme politeness is my default mode when I'm panicked. I'm very polite.

Fortunately, extreme politeness plus a need to predict behavior have made me a good negotiator. I plot out my moves and the other person's responses as if I'm plotting a Choose-Your-Own-Adventure novel. If other person does A, then I'll do A. If they do B, then I'll still do A. If they do C, I'll do B or K.

I rarely get surprised.

The problem for me in early negotiation—and in current negotiation if I'm not careful—isn't my inner twelve-year-old. It's my dreams. And dreams can catch anyone unaware.

If you're freelancing or thinking about freelancing, you love what you do. (If you don't love it, I have to ask you: why freelance?) In fact, you love what you do so much you've probably done it for free.

Money is rarely the freelancer's prime motivation. If it were, then people like Stephen Spielberg and Stephen King would retire after making their early millions. Even Donald Trump, who claims he's interested in money, is only interested in money as a way of keeping score. He would have quit long ago if getting rich was his only motivation.

When you are doing something as a living and you would do that something for free, you have a conflict in the area of money. More often than not, you're willing to undervalue your product. And that's something you need to watch out for.

The flipside, however, is that when you get paid a lot of money for doing what you love, you'll continue doing that something. You won't be a rich, idle person, because you're not doing that something for the money. You're doing it for the love.

While this all may seem like a tangent to negotiation, it really isn't, for several reasons. First, you need to know what your dreams for your business are and were, so that no one that you're negotiating with can hook you in those dreams. Second, you need to keep what you value the most about your work firmly in mind. And third, you have to know what your minimum nut is for your business.

Once you have those numbers, you're still not ready to enter into the kinds of negotiation I'm going to talk about in this chapter. You'll also need to be completely aware of your inner 12-year-old and her tendencies. (My inner 12-year-old, when uncomfortable, either retreats entirely, gets very polite, or becomes unbelievably [and uncontrollably] rude.) You'll need to know your dreams. And you need to know what you want to accomplish in this particular negotiation.

I ran you through some of that in the last chapter about short-term negotiation. That negotiation I described was relatively simple, with very little on the line. The cost of making a mistake in that negotiation was no more than a weekend's worth of headache.

This chapter will deal with contractual negotiations.

Every freelancer will deal with contracts at some point or another. If you have a storefront, you'll make a contract for rent. If you provide product on a regular basis to other businesses, chances are you'll enter into a contract with them. If you hire independent contractors, you'll enter into a contract with them.

Most of us have gotten used to scanning the legalese we see online. We download something, we check "agree" at the bottom to expedite the process. But we've just agreed to something, and really, we should know what it is. Online, there generally is no negotiation. Either you agree or you don't get the service you want. But saying no is a viable option, one many of us don't take enough.

Contracts are negotiable. Sometimes you have a take-it-or-leave-it contract, like those agreements online, but that still means you have a choice. You don't have to sign.

In the past year, as I've read more and more articles about the foreclosure crisis, I've been struck by some similarities in the stories of borrowers who ended up underwater in their mortgages or who couldn't make their payments. Many of them thought that they *had* to sign the contract for the house purchase when they were presented with it. Several of them, particularly people dealing with some companies that specialized in fraud, didn't even know the terms of the contract until they'd signed it.

Most of these people in these articles were blue-collar workers, many of them without a high school education. But a large number were college graduates who had somehow never gotten the message that you shouldn't sign something you don't understand.

I'm assuming you guys know that.

But how many of you, when faced with pages and pages of contractual agreements, signed anyway? The day Dean and I completed a refinance on our house, we annoyed the people at the title company something awful. We refinanced in the middle of the housing boom, taking advantage of loose credit because as freelancers we hadn't been able to receive a bank-funded mortgage in periods of tight credit. (The previous owner carried our contract initially.)

Dean and I both insisted on reading the documents before us. We're good at scanning contracts—Dean went to law school and I've been reading these puppies for years—and we went through them relatively quickly. Still, the woman with the title company kept looking at her watch and hurrying us along, telling us that some of the documents weren't very important.

We refused to sign one document because it changed the terms of our loan, the terms we had agreed to when we made the deal. In fact, it changed our loan from a fixed-rate mortgage to an adjustable-rate mortgage.

We made her draw up the paperwork all over again.

That document was slipped into the middle of about 100 pages of material.

I wonder how many other people that happened to, people who hadn't read the terms of their mortgage contracts.

There's nothing wrong with an adjustable-rate mortgage—if you know you're signing for it, and you plan for the adjustment when it occurs. Or if you believe you can sell the house before that adjustment occurs. (In today's market? Yeah, right.)

But so many people got caught unaware—which is as much their fault as the fault of the lender. Know what you're signing.

And know that you can walk away from any deal, so long as the contract is not signed *by both parties*. It's not a valid contract until both parties have affixed their legal signatures to the document.

Here are some quick-and-dirty things about contracts that will make your life easier in dealing with them. And before I get to them, this is the point where I must remind you that I am not an attorney and I am not giving you legal advice. I'm writing from my experience here, and I'm giving you free advice, friend to friend. Realize that my advice could be wrong. (Hell, all of the advice in the *Guide* could be wrong. Take everything I say with a grain of salt.)

So, here goes:

1. Contracts are complex legal documents.

Some are complex and incomprehensible by design. The harder it is for the layman to understand the contract, the more chances there are for that layman to get screwed. There is nothing simple about a contract. Even simple two- and three-line contracts have pitfalls in them—usually through something that's been omitted. Just because a contract looks simple doesn't mean that it is.

2. Every word in the contract is important. Each section is there for a reason.

Dean and I get into fascinating arguments about publishing contracts over this very point. Dean went to law school. He knows that some clauses in publishing contracts are completely unenforceable, so he sees no problem in signing a contract with the illegal, unenforceable clause.

I always remember the second part of two: *Each section is there for a reason.* So if the lawyers who drew up the contract knew that the clause was unenforceable (and if a guy who went to law school but never became a practicing attorney knows that a certain clause is unenforceable, then guaranteed the lawyer who put the clause in knew it as well), the question becomes: Why did the lawyers put the clause into the contract?

Usually, in publishing (and I can't say this about other industry's contracts with certainty), those clauses are there to make the ignorant do something. In the publishing contract, the ignorant one is the writer. So the clause is often to the publishing company's benefit and it demands that the writer do something that isn't in the writer's best interest. The writer doesn't have to do that thing, because the clause is unenforceable under the contract. But I can guarantee you that if that clause is in the contract, then some writer followed "the rules" set forth by the contract, even to the writer's detriment.

So remember, everything in the contract is there for a reason—even if that reason is only to force compliance on someone who doesn't know any better.

3. Each clause in the contract has an impact on the other clauses in that contract.

An attorney friend of mine once described a contract as a story. You don't know what it all means until you get to the end.

The upside of this is that often you'll run into "deal-breakers" in the negotiation: a negotiator on the other side won't change clause A no matter what. But if you change parts of clause C & D, you'll negate A.

I learned this early on negotiating a short story contract. The contracts person told me that Clause A was unbreakable, "But," he said coyly, "other writers have changed Clauses C & D." I read C & D and realized he was doing me a favor. He essentially gave me a way around clause A without causing him grief with his bosses and which led to me signing a much better contract.

4. Contracts bind you and the other party to a certain series of actions over time.

Contracts without a strict time limit aren't valid. In perpetuity is not a time limit. However, the time limit can be a moving target. In publishing, that moving target is often tied to the number of copies of a book sold. So if fewer than 100 copies are being sold per year, then the ticking clock of the contract sets in. In other words, the agreement between the parties may end if the book sells fewer than 100 copies for two years running. (Or some such thing.)

5. Contracts happen over a period of time.

Why did I stress that twice? Because most people look at contracts as a short-term thing, and they're usually a long-term thing.

Let's look at our torch singer from last week. Let's say she signed a contract with that blues club, one that guaranteed her five performance weekends per year at the club at $200 per appearance. Let's say the contract is a five-year contract.

All well and good. If she's a mediocre musician or a hobbyist, she should have no problem with that.

But what happens if her career takes off in year two? She's filling concert halls and making $20,000 appearance fees wherever she goes.

Except for that tiny blues club, which still pays her $200 per appearance, and will do so for three more years. Because she signed a bad contract. One that probably seemed good at the time.

(There are ways that a contract like that can be broken, but I'm not going to deal with them here. Generally speaking, though, if you signed a contract and so did the other party, the contract is a binding legal agreement, even if you don't like the terms two years in. In other words, you're stuck.)

6. Contracts are about control.

Control of money, control of a person's time, control of a particular property. The best contracts define the limits of that control in all areas. You may not like the definitions, but the fact that they're spelled out makes the contract understandable and negotiable. It's the simple contracts with only a few lines that get litigated most when there's a dispute over control.

7. Contracts are about the best- and worst-case scenarios.

I remember the first time I read a publishing contract. It mentions fire, flood, bankruptcy. It defines Acts of God. It discusses what to do if the publishing house goes out of business, if the writer dies, or if everyone gets sued. All the worst-case scenarios are there, including some I never thought of.

But so are the best-case scenarios: payouts if the book sells better than expected, things the publisher is obligated to do when success happens, things the writer is obligated to do.

Those lines excite writers. They think those lines mean that the publisher has changed his mind and committed to a better program for the book than initially promised. Nope. Those lines are there so that it's clear who is in control of what should the book succeed beyond anyone's wildest dreams.

8. Make sure you understand the contract you're signing.

It sounds so basic. I even mentioned that in the chapter above. But don't sign something you do not understand. Ask stupid questions. Repeatedly. Refuse to put your name on the document— even if there's a time crunch—until you understand every word. Better yet, don't sign unless you understand the contract's *story*, what the entire document means as a whole, not just as a sum of its parts.

Yes, I know. You didn't go to law school. Me either. But I was a reporter. And the one thing that being a reporter taught me is to question, question, question.

Contracts aren't set in stone. They can be redrafted, rewritten, redrawn. And sometimes they should be.

Whom should you ask for help with that contract? Well, that depends. Generally, you shouldn't ask the person you're negotiating with. But you shouldn't always ask your local attorney, either. Because every industry has its own jargon. Publishing contracts use words that mean something different than the same words in a real estate contract.

Lawyers have specialties for a reason, and that reason is often to understand the intricacies of that specialty. I would never hire a real estate attorney to negotiate a book contract. Nor would I hire an intellectual properties attorney (who can handle a book contract) to negotiate a car loan agreement.

And even then, no matter whom I hire, I have to know that person is doing a good job. So I need to know something of what I'm signing. The more educated I am about the contracts I sign, the better off I am.

It just so happens that I love contracts and contract negotiation. I'm fascinated by it, and I collect tons of information about publishing contracts. I knew more about publishing contracts than the agent I fired a few years ago—and he'd been in the business as long as I have.

I like publishing contracts because they're a means to an end. That end, for me, is to get my work in print. But I'm wary of contracts too, because I've seen bad ones ruin careers.

Right now, if you're paying attention, you're watching bad contracts ruin lives. The foreclosure crisis is built on terrible deals enshrined in bad contracts.

Contracts are central to our business lives. Yet most of us know nothing about them, and certainly don't know how to negotiate them.

Now that you've read this chapter, you need to start familiarizing yourself with the contracts that are essential to your business. Start walking through the business sections of bookstores, look for trade journals in your field, become a devotee of places like Nolo.com. Read the free legal advice that floats around the web. Go to places where people discuss the business of doing business. Start collecting information on your specialty. It'll benefit you more than you realize.

Most of us think, "I can't understand this" when it comes to contracts. Yet we have to understand it. Let me give you a tip from Colonel Tom Parker, who managed Elvis Presley—first to Elvis's benefit (in the early years) and then, when it became clear that Elvis knew nothing about money, to Parker's benefit (in the later years). Parker acknowledged that he made mistakes in negotiating contracts. He would find the clause that caused the mistake, tape it to his refrigerator, memorize it, and vow never to make that mistake again. (In later years, he put those clauses in his own contracts, and used those clauses to his own benefit.)

You will make many mistakes negotiating contracts. You won't understand all of what you sign early on. Expect to make the mistakes. Learn from them. Make sure you don't make those mistakes twice.

Chapter Twenty-seven
How to Negotiate Your Own Contract

The same day that I posted the previous chapter on my website, a writer asked for help with a business ethics question on one of my writer e-mail lists. Turned out her question wasn't about ethics at all. It was about a contractual relationship, a relationship defined by the contract. The answer to her question was in that contract, and negated the ethical dilemma entirely.

What was fascinating to me—and a bit appalling—was how many people answered her question as she posed it, without first wondering if she had some sort of document or contract in place. These people answered very firmly about their opinion of the ethics of the situation, when they didn't understand the situation at all.

They put me in mind of those old Holiday Inn Express commercials, in which some person steps up, gives authoritative advice that's often wrong, and then is asked if they're an expert on the situation. "Nope," they would say, "but I did stay at a Holiday Inn Express last night."

(I always wondered why the Holiday Inn Express people wanted us to stay in a place that proudly knocked off a few IQ points each time someone slept there. But hey, what do I know?)

I was rather stunned by the discussion on the list, since everyone on the list is a bright and educated person. But only one person (besides me) out of at least a dozen respondents even considered the contract, which makes me worry. These are folks who are supposed to know their freelance business, and they all made rookie mistakes that would have hurt them terribly if that "ethical" question had been theirs. The person who asked the question thought she had gone to a knowledgeable group—and it should have been— but instead she got a cross-section of America.

Most people in this country believe that business and financial matters are better dealt with by someone else, someone who is not them. Eventually, that willful ignorance catches up with everyone—and not in a pretty way.

I'll deal with the "someone elses" in the next chapter. In this chapter, I'm going to, in very vague terms, tell you the things to consider in negotiating your contract.

Before I do, I want you to do two things. If you haven't read the previous chapter, read it now. And I want you to remember that I am not a lawyer and I am not giving legal advice. I'm telling you how I believe the average person should think about contracts, but I'm not guaranteeing results nor am I saying that I'm always right. Essentially, I'm trying to give you a few tools so that you can go out and learn this stuff yourself.

And, if you'll note, I've often used that disclaimer or a similar one in the financial and legal chapters of the *Guide*. Because I'm protecting myself here.

Some people believe that guides like this are an implied contract. If these people follow what they believe to be my advice and the result bites them in the ass, then their first response would be to sue me. My disclaimer, here and in the other chapters, is there not for those people, but for any attorney that they might hire. Essentially, I'm putting the world on notice that I am not qualified to give bona fide legal advice. You're taking my advice at your own peril.

Got it?

In other words, I just did a quasi-legal document—a disclaimer—to protect me in a worst-case scenario. I've done it before, not just in the *Guide*, but also in teaching situations. If you want an expert on contracts and contract law, take classes from real attorneys. Read books written by real attorneys. Go to websites hosted by—you guessed it—real attorneys.

But I'm giving a layman's guide to negotiation, trying to give you some broad strokes and ways to think about negotiating which is (I know) something most of you have done your very best to avoid up until now.

And that's your first mistake.

Because contracts are negotiable. In fact, most anyone who offers a contract *expects* negotiation. And not just any negotiation, but informed and intelligent negotiation.

I've known many writers who've signed horrendous contracts because the writer didn't understand that the contract should be negotiated. The writers were afraid that if they tried to negotiate, the other party would take the contract away from them, and they'd lose the deal. So they signed.

After they signed, all of those writers had two experiences with the contract. First, the editor for the publishing house made a veiled reference to the contract, telling the writer that they "didn't get the best deal." That's editor-speak for "Oh, crap, at some point you're going to hate me, even though it'll be your fault."

Secondly, years later, those writers complained and complained and complained about being screwed. Sadly, they never realized that they had volunteered for the screwing by failing to negotiate.

So when faced with a contract, *expect to negotiate.* That expectation will take some of the anxiety away from the whole contract experience. You know—and the person you're dealing with knows—that you both are going to discuss terms before you both sign the document.

Believe me, it's a relief to the other party when you do negotiate. Everyone wants the best possible deal in a negotiation. But if you want to work with that person or deal with that person again, you want the best possible deal that will result in other deals in the future.

When you sign a bad contract without negotiating, the other party thinks that you're naïve or really inexperienced. They hope, after you both sign, that you're just plain stupid. Because if you're stupid, you'll never wise up and you will continue to work together. If you're naïve or inexperienced, at some point you'll catch a clue; and rather than blaming yourself for failing to negotiate, you'll probably blame them for "giving" you a "bad contract."

Which means that the working relationship won't last past that moment.

People who are really worried about the future relationship will stop you just before you sign an un-negotiated contract and tell you to change a few things in the contract. Those things will be to your benefit. What's happening here is that the person you're negotiating against has just hit you with a cluestick. That person—who is your adversary in the negotiation—knows it's to his best

interest to have a long-term relationship with you, and is trying
to protect that relationship, since you don't know enough to do it
yourself.

As I write these words, I realize that a bunch of you who
are reading this chapter have just realized that once upon a time,
you were hit with that very cluestick. And most of you never caught
the clue. You just thought the other person was being nice, when
really that person was protecting their business interests. If that
person screwed you too badly—and early-stage contracts are always
balanced heavily toward the person issuing the contract—then that
person knows you'd never work with them again.

If you've been hit with this particular cluestick and only just
now realized it, get thee to books on contracts and negotiations and
develop some backbone. Seriously. Because the only person you're
hurting is yourself.

Not everyone you negotiate with will take care of you in a
negotiation. In a one-time negotiation, where you know you don't
want to or never will work with the other person again, the contract
can be hideously one-sided. I've watched Dean be utterly ruthless
in such situations, to the point where I have to leave the room (that
damn politeness again) because I really want to tell the other person
that they're being screwed.

Dean is a much harder businessman than I am in these
situations. He figures if the person he's negotiating against is utterly
clueless, then he'll get what he wants *at their expense*. I once asked
him why he's willing to do that. His answer? "They came to me."

And in each case that I observed, the other person had come to
him. They initiated the relationship; they brought the product/service/
idea to him, and expected him to pay them for it. The fact that they
did not negotiate in that situation wasn't his problem. It was theirs.

As an aside, lest you think the man is heartless, let me tell you
that he never approaches someone and demands that they do business
with him. And I've watched him over the years pay out much more
money than he ever should to keep people in their homes, help with
medical bills, and make sure they get fed.

But if someone tries to do business with him and *initiates
the relationship expecting to be paid*, he will be ruthless. He
expects the other person to be the same. If they're not, that's not his
responsibility.

I'm not that person. But I've let him be that person as my proxy. More on this in the next chapter.

So, now you've decided to negotiate. But how do you do it? Let's go back to the rules of negotiation. They are:

1. **Know What You Want.**
2. **Ask.**
3. **Be Prepared to Walk Away.**
4. **Stay Calm.**
5. **Never Reveal Your Entire Hand.**
6. **Don't Flip-Flop.**

Those tips all apply to long-term negotiation as well as short-term negotiation.

But here are some things that make negotiations over a contract different from any other kind of negotiation.

1. The contract will bind you for a certain period of time.

That period of time might be one week; it might be ten years with the possibility of renewal.

When you negotiate, that time limit needs to be first and foremost in your mind. You need to understand all the implications of it—good and bad.

Let me give you two examples. Dean, who is a great negotiator, didn't trust my experience back in 1990 or so. I knew rental agreements and the pitfalls therein. He signed an agreement for Pulphouse Publishing for a long-term lease (five years, I believe), thinking it protected him by keeping the rent at a low, low price.

I had seen too many cases where long-term rental had hurt the business in question. I got my start in real estate in 1979, when the rental market became quite competitive. Rental places offered long-term leases, but no real deals. By 1981, as the recession deepened, many places forfeited their leases, and the rental companies lowered their rates for commercial properties. Sometimes they gave months away for free just for signing up. The companies that signed the agreement in 1979 paid five times what a company did in 1981.

That was part of my argument to Dean. He said he could live with that risk. But the other part of my argument was we might go out of business, and if we did, we would still be on the hook for that five-year lease. At the time, our business was going gangbusters. He did not believe that we would be gone within two years.

We were. And we were stuck with that lease. Fortunately for us, the landlord never fixed up the property and a friend got injured because of his negligence. That allowed Dean to negotiate a settlement, negating the rental agreement. But he wouldn't have had to do that if he had negotiated the term of the agreement down to a year or so, renewable on the same terms.

Who was right in this instance? Neither of us, really. Because had the business remained successful, then Dean's gamble would have paid off. Commercial real estate rental rates in Eugene, Oregon, climbed in that five-year period, and if we had to renew every year, we ran the risk of having our rent hiked dramatically.

The time limit on a contract can benefit you and it can hurt you. What looks like a good deal now might be a bad deal in the future.

It's up to you to imagine all the scenarios outlined in that contract, and decide if you can live with them ten, twenty, fifty years from now.

I deal with this a lot with writer friends. At various points in the career, writers can be short of money. Early on, writers are often broke, and that's when they sign bad contacts—particularly with Hollywood.

"Small Hollywood money," as one of my ex-agents called it, can run anywhere from $10,000 to $150,000. Those figures sound like a lot to most people, but to the suits in Hollywood, that's pocket change. I've had friends get "mediocre" Hollywood deals that ran from $200,000 to $700,000. And of course, the "good" deals go higher than that.

The key to Hollywood deals isn't the money. It's the terms of the contract. Often those $50,000 contracts have some nasty, nasty clauses. Clauses that say no matter what, the 50K is all the writer will ever get. (There are other nasty clauses not relevant here, but man, could I tell you stories…)

I've known a lot of writers who are really, really broke who need that $50,000 desperately. And before they sign that contract, I ask them this question, "Will you be happy twenty years from now after that project you got paid 50K for has become a blockbuster movie? Everyone else on the project will have made millions and will continue to make millions. You will have 50K that probably disappeared within the first two years you had it. If you can live with that scenario, then sign the contract."

Because, folks, the worst-case scenario in a contract like that is *success*. Most people step back, think about it, and decide to negotiate—trying to get some fees from later parts of that pie. But I have known a handful who either gambled that the 50K was all the project would ever make or who needed the money so badly that they knew, even twenty years hence, that they could live with the decision.

All of those factors influence negotiation.

You need a lot of imagination when faced with a contract. You have to imagine the worst-case and best-case scenarios for you. And you need to know how you'll feel about them for the duration of that contract.

In other words, you need to know yourself very, very well.

In most instances, I could walk away from that 50K no matter how desperate I was, because I know I'd be angry about it (with myself) twenty years from now. But in a circumstance that's life or death—paying for a surgery, for example—I'd accept that 50K in a heartbeat, and deal with the consequences later.

It's all very fluid.

What you need to figure is where you're at now, where you hope to be in the future, and what impact the decisions you make today will have on that future.

Because once you sign the contract, it's binding. And if you think negotiation is hard at this stage, imagine doing it—as Dean did—after the contract was signed and agreed to, and your circumstances changed for the worse. Then the negotiation is really, really, really hard—and might even take you to court. If you do go to court, and you have a valid contract signed by both parties, then you'll lose the case, guaranteed.

Negotiate up front when it's expected and it's relatively easy.

2. Focus on what you want.

When you enter into a contractual negotiation, know what you want and protect it. Don't get sidelined by other things.

For example, I want control over my work. I will walk away from contracts that take the control away from me—unless I'm asked to work in someone else's universe, like Star Trek or Star Wars. In those cases, I know that I'm entering a world that someone else controls, and I'll forfeit rights that I'll fight to the death for over my original work.

I've walked away from very lucrative contracts because I would lose control over my original work. I've accepted financially small contracts that have given me a lot of creative control. Control of my own work matters the most to me.

Other writers want publication more than anything. I watched a writer sign one of the worst contracts I'd ever seen because he was desperate to be published. When told how bad the contract was, he claimed he knew, but didn't care. Publication was the only thing that mattered to him.

Know what you want out of that agreement. Know how far you will go to protect what you want as you negotiate that agreement. Make sure you protect what you want *throughout the term* (time limit) of the agreement.

Everything else in the agreement is gravy, then.

3. Make sure you have a way to terminate the contract.

Often the termination clause benefits whoever drew up the contract. I've seen rental agreements in which the landlord can terminate the agreement with 24 hours notice, while the renter had to give six months notice. (Those agreements were so egregious that the State of Wisconsin stepped in and mandated a 30-day termination in all rental agreements, but each state is different.)

I've seen publishing contracts where the publisher can easily cancel the contract but the writer has to jump through so many hoops to cancel it that it would take months to even try.

Make sure the termination clause is clear and equitable. By equitable I mean that it's either very hard for both sides to terminate or very easy for both sides to terminate. But it shouldn't be easy for one side and hard for the other.

4. Money.

Most people mistakenly think that contracts are all about money. But remember what I said in the previous chapter. Contracts are about *control*.

So…

5. Make sure you know how you'll get paid or how you will make the payments.

That sounds so elementary, but it's not. Many contracts may promise a lot of money, but if you read the fine print, you'll realize that certain payments will get made if and only if other conditions are met. Some of those conditions might be extremely unlikely to ever occur.

For example, Hollywood contracts often promise to pay a percentage of "net profits." But anyone peripherally attached to Hollywood knows that "net profits" never happen. Creative bookkeeping will make certain that even the highest-earning films make no net profit, although they'll have a gross profit.

So the contract promising to pay x% of net profit really promises nothing.

Publishing has its own accounting tricks, which I could spend the next several weeks enumerating for you; everything from basket accounting to high discount rates.

Yet there are reasons to sign such contracts and often those reasons have more to do with what you want than what you'll get paid. You might get other clauses in the contract that will make you feel better about dodgy payment practices.

6. Control as much of the contract as possible.

Remember, that's what you and the other party are negotiating—who controls what. Try to keep as much of that control in your court as you possibly can. But realize where you stand and whom you're negotiating with. For example, if you're negotiating a contract to sell your work to the movies, realize that you don't have the deep pockets to make the film yourself. You will have to relinquish some control in those areas so that the film will get made. Just like they'll have to reimburse you for your property if they really, really want it. (And want to control it.)

7. Once you both sign, negotiation is over.

It's your signature on that document. That means you agreed to the terms therein. You *agreed*. The time to change the terms is before you sign. If you complain afterwards, you won't get any sympathy from me or anyone else who understands contracts. Because understanding that document is your responsibility, and you must understand it before you sign it.

Even more important, you must know you can live with the contract's terms for the duration of that contract, be it six months or sixty years.

If you sign it, you're responsible for every word in it. You've made your bed, as my mother used to say—and the contract is proof of that.

I could go on and on and on forever. Contracts are exceedingly complicated. Law schools spend several semesters on contracts. But, in short, here are some of the basics of contract negotiation (covered above):

1. **Expect to negotiate a contract.**
2. **Imagine how the terms of the contract will impact you over the lifetime of the contract.**
3. **Focus on what you want.**
4. **Make sure you have an equitable way to terminate the contract.**
5. **Make sure you know how you'll get paid or how you'll make payments**
6. **Control as much of the contract as possible.**
7. **Once you both sign, negotiation is over.**

Good contracts, bad contracts, beautifully negotiated contracts, un-negotiated contracts—ultimately, what happens with those is all up to you.

Expect no help with contracts. Learn it all yourself. I'll deal with this aspect more in the next chapter, but remember this: *You are responsible for your own career*—the good and the bad. Just you. And that responsibility extends to the agreements you make, and the contracts you sign.

Chapter Twenty-eight

When to Hire Someone Else to Negotiate Your Contract
or
Agents, Lawyers, and Business Managers (Oh, My)

In the previous chapters, I've talked about the things you need to know about yourself and your business in order to negotiate anything from a weekend gig to a long-term contract. I've mentioned managers, agents, and lawyers in passing—people whom you can hire to negotiate for you—but I've pretty much skipped over what they do, in favor of having you do it yourself.

In fact, if you read the entire *Freelancer's Survival Guide*, you'll see me recommend time and time again that you should do most of this stuff, from the financial to negotiation, yourself.

Yet I have a book agent, and quite often I bring him into a book deal for the express purpose of negotiation. He negotiates the deal for me.

Does that make me a hypocrite? Am I telling you to do what I say, not what I do?

No. Just this week—which is, for those of you reading this late, the week between Christmas and New Year's 2009-2010, I negotiated a contract all by my lonesome. It was a short e-rights contract for a novella that a publisher wanted to include in an anthology. The contract was purposely short and very vague (see the previous chapter on why someone would want to do that), and I made it less vague. But I still left in points that a hard negotiator would have changed.

Why? Because, in this case—and this case only—it was in my best interest to keep that contract simple. Normally, I would have negotiated that little contract bloody. But I saw a greater benefit in keeping the contract loose on both sides than I did in pinning everything down.

Also this week, I've read a contract of Dean's, giving him some feedback (which he really didn't need because he's so good at this stuff), and helped him design an agreement for another project he's working on.

And that doesn't count the several approaches I had from people who want something—a free story (no), a guest appearance (maybe), or some other thing that will require negotiation.

Normally, I handle so many negotiations that I barely pay attention to how many. I'm used to it now. These past ten days have been relatively slow in the negotiation department.

Finally, this week, I'm reading—slowly—a book contract for one of my pen names. The contract is with a brand-new company for me, and is the fourth iteration of the agreement. We've been negotiating since the first of November, or I should say, my agent has been doing so, while keeping me informed.

The day before Christmas, he e-mailed me the latest iteration, with all of his e-mails and the company's responses, so that I could see what had been done so far. I'm reading this version over the holidays, with the idea that there will be one, maybe two, maybe three more iterations before we're done.

My agent is a good negotiator, a man with a law degree who has a fondness for contract law and for publishing contracts in particular. He's good and sharp and catches things I might miss (or might not care as much about as I should). But in all of the contracts that he's negotiated for me so far, I've added language, cut language, or asked for things he never even considered. I'm very, very hands-on, even though he's the one interacting with the company.

I'm walking all sorts of negotiating lines in what is a relatively slow week, from negotiating contracts myself, to making agreements by e-mail, to making some verbal agreements, to hiring someone to do the negotiations for me. That's normal in a small business. Negotiation is, as I've said before, part of everyday life. You need to get used to it.

The trick is to know when to do the negotiation yourself and when to hire someone. Once you hire someone to negotiate for you, you must manage that negotiator properly.

First, let's discuss knowing when to hire someone. I discussed this briefly when talking about a torch singer who was asked to play a local club. I showed the torch singer's various considerations as she negotiated her fee and her performance time at that club.

As to whether or not she should hire someone to negotiate for her, I said this:

At her level of the career, it would be foolish for her to hire a manager to do the negotiating for her. Better that she learn how to do it on her own than sacrifice $15 to $20 of that much needed $100 for someone to speak for her—when she wouldn't get much out of that deal anyway.

Many of the considerations for hiring a negotiator are present in that short paragraph. Let's look at them.

1) What can a negotiator bring to the table?

That's always the first question you should ask. Sometimes all the negotiator brings is *a calm, disinterested voice*. And in some cases, that calm, disinterested voice is worth every penny you spend on it. A person who is not emotionally involved should—and let me emphasize *should*—see things a bit more clearly and hear what the other party has to say, without bias.

This calm disinterest is often why many organizations hire arbitrators to help negotiate contracts between say, a union and a company. The arbitrator will not negotiate for either side, but will facilitate negotiations. In these instances, each side has its own negotiator and the negotiator works through an arbitrator, to keep things as calm and above-board as possible.

Generally speaking, you as a freelancer don't need that high level of expertise. But you do need to figure out what you need. If a calm voice is all that's necessary, then you might not need a professional negotiator at all.

Let me stop one more time here and say this: *a professional negotiator has a different name in different businesses*. Lawyers can be professional negotiators. Most people in publishing rely on agents. People in Hollywood have tiers of negotiators from agents to managers to lawyers. Singers often have managers. But even your accountant can and will negotiate for you with the IRS, if need be. So negotiators come with all sorts of professional labels. For the purpose of this chapter, I will call all of them negotiators.

What else can the negotiator bring to the table? *Expertise.* It might take the negotiator five minutes to negotiate a contract that you'll struggle over for days, simply because the negotiator is more familiar with the language of that contract than you are.

A negotiator can also bring *clout.* Some negotiators—agents and managers in particular—have a reputation all their own, over and above yours. That reputation should augment the negotiation in a good way. In other words, if you're a beginner like that torch singer, a high-powered manager might—might—get you more money just because he's on board. He might be able to get you into meetings with prospective clients that you wouldn't otherwise get.

A negotiator also has the ability *to say things you can't.* That might sound silly until you think about it. I would love to tell a publisher that he should pay me more because I'm pretty or famous or a damned fine writer, but it sounds better when my representative says it. Right now, as a woman who has worked in this field for twenty years and has many accolades as well as an excellent track record, I'm a lot more comfortable doing this part for myself. But even now, I don't say, "I'm a bestselling, award-winning writer. You should pay me more." I'm a lot more subtle than that. But I do make sure that the party I'm negotiating with has the facts before she begins bargaining with me, so that when I get to my way of dealing with this (which is, "It's not standard practice for me to accept a fee that low, or this particular term in a contract."), she knows I'm coming from a position of strength.

Early on, you might have to hire that strength. Or someone willing to make that statement for you.

There is a downside to everything a negotiator can bring to the table. Right now, I'm only discussing the upside. But you'll have to factor it all in, including the screw-up factor which is this:

The more people you bring into a negotiation, the more likely it is to go wrong.

A long chain of negotiators (often seen in Hollywood—the lawyer talks to the manager who talks to the agent [or doesn't, as the case may be]) can turn a negotiation into one ugly game of telephone.

And in the end, the only person who'll suffer for it is you.

But I get ahead of myself.

In answering the *what does the negotiator bring to the table* question, you have to be realistic. Often, a negotiator adds nothing to a negotiation. If you're savvy about your own business, you probably have all the skills you need to negotiate; and bringing someone else in just muddies the waters. In the case of our torch singer, a negotiator wouldn't bring anything to the table except calm, which wasn't worth the fee the torch singer would have to pay for that calm.

So, before hiring a negotiator for a particular job, make sure the negotiator adds value. So many people have someone negotiate just because that person is on the payroll or that's what they have this particular worker for, without thinking about whether or not the negotiator is even appropriate to the circumstance.

Think before you act. And think twice (or maybe three or four times) before you hire someone.

2. In this instance, make sure the negotiator is worth his fee.

Again, you're looking at value, but you're looking at it from a slightly different perspective. If you look at the case of our torch singer, you'll remember she really needed the money from that gig to pay her rent. Taking ten to twenty-five percent of the fee away to pay a manager at that point would have been financially devastating for her.

It's better for her to do the negotiation herself and keep the money than it is to bring in a third party.

This is a two-pronged decision, by the way. I have a rule of thumb for my business. Under a certain dollar amount, I generally handle the negotiations myself. Over that amount, I *consider* bringing in my agent. I don't always do so.

But it's only a rule of thumb. If there's something I really, really, really want in that negotiation, something that's so important that I'll walk if I don't get it, I'm more likely to bring in the third party to negotiate for me. Partly, this is so that I won't tip my hand. Partly, it's to keep emotions out of the way, and partly, it's because I'm a pessimist. In that particular instance, I expect to walk away. I don't want to be the one to tell the company that we can't come to an agreement. I want my representative to do that—because that falls into the category of something I would rather have someone else say for me than saying it myself.

When you're considering the fee, you have to look at the value the negotiator will bring. I once had a writer friend tell me he was "training" his accountant to work with someone in the arts. In other words, my friend was paying someone who brought no value to the table and who, in fact, was costing my friend not just money but time as well. The accountant had no expertise in the area that my friend needed and therefore was making a boatload of money that my friend could have easily kept for himself.

In the case of our torch singer, the manager wouldn't have gotten her any more money. He probably wouldn't have gotten a better deal. He would simply have finalized the negotiation and taken anywhere from ten to twenty-five percent to do so. If she hired a manager in that instance, she was throwing her money away.

Let's look briefly at the flipside: my book contract. My agent has put in a lot of work negotiating boilerplate and other points to the contract. A great deal of my time over the past two months would have gone to minutia that I would have negotiated as well, but I didn't have to. It's been worth the fee.

However, I am reviewing that work right now, and will add my own opinions shortly. But in value, which I'm equating with service in exchange for money, I'm getting my money's worth.

The tricky thing is that each negotiation is different. Even my rule of thumb doesn't always work—which is why I look at it as a rule of thumb instead of something hard and fast.

In short, I bring in a negotiator *only when I need one*. I don't use a negotiator just because I happen to have one at the ready. I use one only when necessary.

Here's the other side of negotiating: so much can go wrong. You will make mistakes, as I've said before. But it's better for *you* to make the mistake than your negotiator.

Because if you're truly hands-off in negotiation, you might not know about the mistake until the negotiation is over and you've signed the contract. And that, my friends, is not your negotiator's fault. It's your fault.

Let me quote a comment left when I made the first negotiation post on my website. It's from Randy Tatano, who works as a freelance broadcast news reporter, mostly for NBC.

He wrote:

Well, on the topic of hiring someone to negotiate, a news anchor I know hired an agent to negotiate her next contract. Her agent took such a hard line that management called her bluff and she ended up out of work. She had absolutely no desire to leave but apparently didn't convey that well enough to her agent.

On the other side I was trying to hire an anchor once and the agent was so incredibly obnoxious I moved on to someone else. I was trying to negotiate and meet the guy in the middle but he wanted to play hardball.

What surprised me about these instances is that both anchors were extremely likable people, yet hired agents who were so difficult to deal with. And, as you pointed out so well Kris, anyone who negotiates for you needs to know exactly how you feel.

He's right. Too often a negotiator, who thinks he's acting in your best interest, can really cause damage to you and your business. Whose fault is that? Not the negotiator's. It's yours. You might have hired the wrong person, brought the negotiator into a situation he had no business being a part of, or failed to communicate what you really wanted from that negotiator.

As I was getting ready to write this chapter, I found all kinds of horrible stuff about the people you can hire to do tasks for you. The universe seemed to serve up these stories. Some will factor in later in this chapter.

But let me share one right now. In the *Washington Post* on January 5, 2010, toward the end of an article about the IRS regulating tax preparers ("IRS to Regulate Paid Tax Preparation," by David S. Hilzenrath), I found these interesting statistics: In 2006, employees of the Government Accountability Office, posing as taxpayers, had tax prep chains fill out tax returns. "All 19 preparers made mistakes, the IRS reported. Only two of the 19 arrived at the correct bottom line."

Ten of the 19 didn't report income they'd been told about and "several" didn't ask about income other than wages—in other words, stuff you as a freelancer would earn.

A 2008 study got similar if slightly better results. Seventeen out of 28 preparers got the bottom line wrong, leaving eleven instead of two to get the results right.

The IRS estimates that somewhere around 1 million people prepare taxes for a fee, and many do that without being tested. As IRS Commissioner Douglas Shulman said, "In most states you need a license to cut someone's hair, [but today] most tax-return preparers don't have to meet *any standards* when they sit down and prepare a federal tax return…." (Emphasis mine.)

What is it with this country and its regulations? My ex-husband got a job as a financial adviser without finishing college by taking a two-week course, and with our own finances in such a mess that *I* wasn't taking advice from him. Book agents across the country have absolutely no regulation, and yet writer after writer puts their entire livelihood in an agent's hands, often without oversight.

Now this about tax preparers. Since I only had someone prepare my taxes once—and that was because I was broke and in those days tax preparers were the only ones who could e-file and I needed the damn refund yesterday—I never investigated this in-depth. (And essentially, Dean and I handed the tax preparer the finished tax return. She just e-filed it for us.)

Apparently, in the United States of America, you have to follow rules for everything *unless* you want to handle other people's money. Oh, I can't tell you how deeply that appalls me.

Yet time and time again, people tell me how happy they are to hire someone so that they don't have to think about business. And I think when they say that, *You need to get out of business now and go work a day job. Because you're setting yourself up to get screwed.*

So…after reading the *Guide*, you're smart enough to track your own finances and to bring in a negotiator only when you need one.

But are you smart enough to supervise that negotiator properly?

What? What's this "supervise" word? Isn't the negotiator the expert?

Well, no. It's your business. Therefore you're the expert. The negotiator is just your mouthpiece.

Let's go back to Randy Tatano's comment from above. Look at this part of that comment:

…a news anchor I know hired an agent to negotiate her next contract. Her agent took such a hard line that management called her bluff and she ended up out of work. She had absolutely no desire to leave but apparently didn't convey that well enough to her agent.

There's a lot in that tiny paragraph. I'm not going to make any assumptions about the anchor here because I don't know her. But here's what I get:

The anchor wanted something in her next contract. Maybe she wanted more money, maybe she wanted a better on-air time. Maybe she wanted a half-hour monthly program showcasing her talent. Who knows?

But whatever it was, she told the agent—the negotiator—about it. What she did *not* say was that this particular thing that she wanted—for the sake of argument, let's say it's more money—was flexible. In other words, it was not a deal-breaker.

Clearly, though, the agent did not know that. He thought the goal of the negotiation was to get that extra money—not to keep the anchor's job. So when management didn't cough up the extra cash (or whatever it was), the agent walked. (See the chapter on negotiation options.)

Only the client didn't want to walk. She wanted to keep the job.

What we have here, folks, is a failure to communicate.

And another problem.

The agent acted without consulting the client. He walked without telling her, and she lost that job.

Did the agent do a bad job? You could say so, since the anchor didn't get whatever it was that she wanted. But I'll wager that the agent did a fine job. The problem here, as I see it, is with the client.

Because she did not communicate her needs up front to the person negotiating for her.

I've had agents go off half-cocked on me, especially when I was younger. (And I even had an agent who called me "hon," which should've been a red flag that he didn't respect me, but I was too young to realize it. Besides, back then, every man who was more than ten years older than I was called me "hon" or "dear." I had no idea that an employee shouldn't do that.) I had one who set my bottom line at $15,000 per project. That agent rejected projects without telling me. And when I found that out, that agent no longer worked for me.

Now my poor current agent suffers from my past mistakes and those of the people I hired. I must seem a bit paranoid to him. I keep track of everything from rejections to offers. And I keep the most track during negotiations.

How do I do that?

Simple. I have a hard and fast set of rules. And they aren't for the negotiator. They're for me.

Before anyone enters into a negotiation for me, I go through these steps:

1. I figure out what I want out of the negotiation.

If I were that news anchor, I'd figure out which I wanted more—the money (or whatever it was) or the job. In her case, it was clearly the job. So that's the primary goal of the negotiation. I would tell the agent to make sure I keep that job, no matter what.

2. I figure out how far I'm willing to bend.

No matter how much I want the job, am I willing to sell myself short to get it (or keep it)? Do I have other prospects that are as good or better? Do I really want to work with these people? How much leeway do I have in this negotiation? Can I walk?

3. Are there any deal-breakers?

For me, there are always deal-breakers. There are clauses in publishing contracts that I will not sign, even if I'm on my last dime and starving to death. As I mentioned in earlier chapters, most of those clauses have to do with control, not with money. If my name (or one of my names) appears on the work, then I'd better approve of that work. And that's my bottom line.

4. What kind of tone do I want to set?

Randy alludes to this in another part of his comments. He says, *On the other side I was trying to hire an anchor once and the agent was so incredibly obnoxious I moved on to someone else.* I prefer a civil tone in my negotiations, but I've been known to hire sharks on occasion—folks who are just vicious in negotiation. (I even got rid of one shark for not having enough bite.) Sometimes that hard line is very important to me. Sometimes the tone has to be very, very soft. Again, it varies according to circumstance, which is often why I handle some negotiations on my own. The *tone* is too difficult to explain easily, so I just do it myself.

Once I've figured out what I want, I must communicate all of that to my negotiator. I used to do that on the phone or in person, but soon learned that in business as in life, people hear what they want to hear. So now I write this all into a letter or into an e-mail, so that the negotiator can refer to it during the negotiations.

Then before anything goes any farther, I make sure that my negotiator understands my needs and *agrees with them*. This sounds so silly, since the negotiator is essentially an employee, but often the negotiator, hired for his skill, forgets that.

The agent I had who set the $15,000 limit forgot who was in charge. That agent believed I needed to write slower, and in order to "force" me to write slower (since I clearly wasn't doing it on my own), the agent set that arbitrary 15K limit on my work, thinking if I got paid that as a minimum, I'd slow down. Now, honestly, how many of you can live on 15K per year? I certainly can't. In all fairness, I had told the agent *on one project* that I would take no less than 15K, and that agent heard me set that as a limit for all of my projects. But I know that agent had been trying to get me to slow down for some time, and this was a case of hearing what you wanted to hear.

See why I write things down?

I've had negotiators tell me that they'll never take on a negotiation that they can't walk away from. Which tells me that these are people I don't want to hire. Because I don't always want to walk from a negotiation, just like that anchor didn't above. Which means that this type of negotiator is wrong for me.

Once I'm convinced the negotiator and I are on the same page, then I let the negotiator do his job. But I keep a watchful eye on the proceedings. And here's the real key:

The negotiator must check with me before making any decision.

I *never* give the negotiator the ability to make choices for me. That means that the negotiator *must* present me with any offer that crosses his desk, even if he does not approve of that offer.

I've had negotiators tell me that "we got this offer, and I don't think we should take it." In that case, I have the negotiator tell me what the offer is and why he thinks I shouldn't agree to it. I always listen, but I don't always act on the advice.

Because it is my business and I know what I want from that business, much better than the negotiator ever will.

Sometimes, of course, I should have listened. But more often than not, I ended up making the right choice—because I had possession of all the facts.

I keep track of the negotiation.

I stay in the loop. Even thought I've given my negotiator the outlines of what I want, I know that negotiation is not a linear process. First, I need to know that the general terms are agreed to by both sides. But a negotiation can go awry on the smallest of details, some that don't appear until late in the contract phase.

So I keep track.

When my negotiator thinks we have a deal, I get all aspects of that deal from him, and then I examine that deal with a fine-tooth comb. As I mentioned above, I often find things that were missed.

In some cases, I find things I just don't understand. I research them. First I ask my negotiator what he believes they mean. Then I look into it myself.

One agent that I hired hated this about me. We received a contract for a book deal that I really didn't like, but he felt we should accept it because the publisher had gone to the trouble of issuing the contract. That contract had a few deal-breakers in it for me, things I had mentioned to the agent up front, things he couldn't get the publisher to budge on. The contract came, I asked again, the publisher wouldn't budge, and I refused to sign. The deal was off.

The agent got angry with me, and that was the end of our relationship. He did not have the ability to walk away at all stages of the deal, and that harmed my business.

But I remembered the primary rule of negotiation:

It's my signature that goes on the contract; I'm the one who must live with the deal—not the negotiator. So therefore, if I don't like it and I can't fix it, I don't agree to it.

Period.

End of story.

So I get a preliminary final contract and I go through it carefully. Often I'll negotiate other points—through my negotiator, of course. And I outline those points as carefully as I outlined the early stage of the negotiation.

I tell the negotiator if there are any deal-breakers in the final points. I tell the negotiator if I'd sign the contract *as is*, but that I'd like these points if we can get them. I'm very clear about where I stand at that point in the negotiation, so that the negotiator is clear too.

Finally, because it bears repeating, *I never agree to a deal that I do not understand.* I can't tell you how many times I've had a negotiator tell me to trust them, they did the best they could, and the deal can't get any better. (That early agent actually said, "Trust me, honey.") All of that might be true—the negotiator may have done the best they could. The deal might not get better. But often the things I ask for in the latter stages of the negotiation *never even came up* in the early stages. The negotiator might not have gotten a better deal *because the negotiator didn't know he should try.*

If you keep track of the negotiator and the negotiation, you will be able to tell how good a job your negotiator is doing for you. You'll know, for example, if the other party is getting angry at your negotiator (as in Randy's example, above). In that case, you might be able to step in and salvage the negotiation. I've done that once or twice.

You'll also find out if your negotiator is as big an expert as she claims to be. A friend of mine hired a book agent who had worked as a book editor first. That agent claimed to know contracts.

By the time my friend got the final contract, that agent had added a mountain of clauses. (Added clauses are in bold.) *All of those clauses benefited the publisher, not the writer. All* of them. That agent knew contracts, all right. She knew them from the publishing side of the equation, not the writing side, but she didn't understand the legal language at all. If she had, she would have known that she was hurting her client, not helping him.

Unfortunately for my friend, he had a trust-me agent. (I wonder if she actually patted him on the head and said, "Trust me, honey.") And he trusted her instead of his writer friends who told him not to sign that contract, and who told him to negotiate a better one. As a result, this friend has signed the worst contract I have ever seen for a novel in my thirty years of publishing. And the sad part is that the worst clauses were added *by his negotiator*.

See why I tell you that you must know more about your business than anyone else? Why I tell you to understand what you sign? Yes, that means you must know a bit about the law as it pertains to your business, about the contracts that you will inevitably sign. As you can see from the examples from the newspaper, you must also understand the tax implications of your business, and how to handle your own money.

And you must supervise your employees—including the "experts" that you hire. The most important one to supervise (after your accountant and people who actually touch your money) is your negotiator, be she a lawyer, a manager, an agent, or your second in command.

You can't become a freelancer to avoid the business world. When you're a freelancer, you need to know more about business than everyone around you.

You must remember that your negotiator represents *you*. Your negotiator speaks for you. If you want her to speak in harsh tones, then hire a shark. If you want her to speak in soft tones, hire a more personable negotiator. Do not hire a pushover. Ever. Which means that you will occasionally have run-ins with your negotiator. If there is a run-in, make sure you win. If the negotiator balks, then you fire that negotiator and hire a different one.

Negotiators work *for you* and *must* have your best interest in mind.

Note I didn't state the cliché and say that they should have your best interest at heart. They have their own best interest at heart. Ultimately, a negotiator is in business for herself. But if she wants to do a good job for you, then she must do the job you hired her for *and nothing else*. And she must know where she stands.

So let me reiterate.

If you decided to hire a negotiator, then here's how you supervise that person:

1. **Communicate what you want out of the negotiation in writing.**
2. **Make sure your negotiator understands what you want before proceeding with the negotiation.**
3. **The negotiator cannot make decisions on her own. She must check with you before agreeing to anything.**
4. **Supervise the negotiation. Be hands on.**
5. **Make sure you understand all the details of the negotiated deal before agreeing to anything.**
6. **Remember that *you* are bound by the deal, not your negotiator. No matter what your negotiator recommends, you do not sign (or agree to) the final deal unless you understand it and can live with its terms.**

You can fire a negotiator in the middle of a negotiation. (Be aware that it might have an impact on your bargaining power, however.) You can step into that negotiation at any point and do all the work yourself. You do not need someone to negotiate for you. And if you do hire someone to negotiate for you, make sure she negotiates *for you*, and not for herself or someone else.

This short book on negotiation has given you a lot to think about and a lot to remember, I know. Negotiation is both an art and a science, and it's critical to all forms of business. Learn your own strengths and weaknesses in negotiation. Once you know what they are, you'll know when to hire help and when to forego it.

But even if you do hire someone to speak for you, stay informed and make sure she's speaking your words, not hers. Because a negotiator can screw up a deal badly without even realizing it, as in Randy Tatano's example. A negotiator can also bind you to a deal you don't want, as in my friend's trust-me agent case.

In both cases, those negotiators were poorly supervised. In the case of the anchor, it's up for debate whether or not she should have hired that particular negotiator. In the case of my writer friend, he hired a bad negotiator who made the situation much, much worse. He would have been better off signing the publisher's boilerplate contract without any negotiation at all.

So hire someone to speak for you with trepidation, knowing that the negotiator can muck things up. Make sure you're hiring that person for the right reasons. And keep a close eye on the proceedings.

You'll be happy you did.

Section Five:
Networking in Person and Online

Chapter Twenty-nine
Networking Definitions

Sometimes the topics that I've overlooked in my single-minded attempt at finishing this Guide astound me. This topic is one I hadn't thought of. I should have thought of it; I discuss networking with my writing students all the time. In fact, I network each and every day. But I hadn't considered it a stand-alone topic for the *Guide*, even though I mention networking in many of the chapters.

Writer Carolyn Nicita e-mailed me with the idea, only she labeled the topic "Support Groups and Professional Organizations." She also gave me a list of such organizations and groups, as well as subjects to discuss—which I greatly appreciate. Her list is comprehensive and helpful, and made it clear to me that I wouldn't be able to cover this in one single chapter.

Why did I choose "Networking" as my topic instead of "Support Groups"? Because networking has become extremely important to modern business in a variety of ways, from the support groups and professional organizations that Carolyn mentioned to seminars and continuing education to becoming active on social media and the web.

"Networking" is a very modern term. As I started this chapter, I grabbed the dictionaries around my desk and looked through them for the word "networking." I didn't expect to find that word in the *Webster's Collegiate Dictionary* (Fifth Edition) that my grandparents bought my father the year he entered college (1936)—and of course, I didn't find it in there. I did find "network," however, which had three definitions: a fabric or structure of cords or threads that cross each other at certain intervals and are secured in their crossing with knots, etc.; any system of lines that interlace like a net; and—the dictionary is very specific here—in radio terminology, a chain of stations.

Meaning that the word "network," when used to define broadcast media, was very new in 1936. Of course it would be. I hadn't thought about that much. Then I picked up *my* college dictionary, the *Macmillan Contemporary Dictionary* from 1979. I expected to find "networking" in there, but it wasn't there at all. But "network" was, of course. And in its definitions, I found the first reference to people: "interconnected organization or system—'a network of spies.'" I also found that they'd added to the radio definition (of course), by including television and by defining how those networks interlinked—through coaxial cables.

By the mid-1980s—*Webster's New World Dictionary*, for those of you keeping track—nothing had changed. I expected "networking" by then as well, but I was early. After all, the desktop computer had just arrived into American homes. I got my first in those years.

If I hefted my butt out of my chair and high-tailed it upstairs to the computer with my internet connection—on a DSL line, thank you, which these old dictionaries had never heard of—I could tell you to the year when "networking" became a noun. But I'm not going to be that efficient. The word "networking" appears in the dictionary built into the rather ancient computer that I write on—a 2005 iMac.

The Encarta World English Dictionary has six definitions of network—and the second is all about people. ("A large and widely distributed group of people or things such as shops, colleges, or churches, that communicate with one another and work together as a unit or system.") The 2005 definition also includes computers—of course—and "telecommunications" systems designed to exchange information.

So the definition of network has grown in the past 75 years. As that definition grew, we added the new term "networking." Encarta's definitions clearly show that the word came from computing. The first definition—"the linking of computers so that uses can exchange information…"—shows the word's history and most important usage (at least to the people who wrote the dictionary).

The second definition is the one that applies to us: "The building up or maintaining of *informal* relationships, especially with people whose friendship could bring advantages such as job or business opportunities." (Emphasis mine.)

Why did I start with dictionary definitions? Because words tell us a great deal about ourselves. Words that exist in English but don't exist in, say, Russian show us the difference between the cultures.

And words that have come into use or whose usage has changed within a single generation tell us about our culture.

I'm sure people networked in 1936. I'm sure they called it something else. (And, by the way, none of my dictionaries use "network" as a verb. When did that happen? Since 2005?) I'm equally sure that the networking that occurred in 1936 was not on the same scale that people network on today. The opportunities simply weren't there. People had relationships within their communities, but the chance to network with people from all over the country, let alone all over the world, belonged only to a few.

If you read about the early history of broadcasting—one of my favorite topics, actually—you learn that the live radio broadcasts that our grandparents remember from World War II came about because of a change in technology, and a small group of reporters who all knew each other. They got thrown onto the air *because there was no one else to do the work*, not because they were particularly good at it.

Early networks often work that way. Only a handful of people might have the skills to do a particular job, but those people might not be known to each other. So friends hire friends and then offer on-the-job training. It's human nature.

In early 2010, on *The Late, Late Show with Craig Ferguson,* Ferguson held a fascinating hour-long Tom Snyderish interview with British actor Stephen Fry. In the middle of that wide-ranging discussion, they talked about Twitter. Ferguson had recently joined Twitter; Fry was an early adopter who talked about the early days of Twitter.

In the beginning, Twitter grew by word of mouth—friends verbally told friends about it. Broadcasters started discussing it when celebrities started having "races" to increase the number of people following them, but the culture didn't take Twitter seriously until the Iranian elections in the summer of 2009. Iran closed its borders to outside journalists and censored broadcasts that left the country, but didn't shut down its cell phone networks—at least not right away. Real live news, from regular people, filtered through Twitter onto the net, and then out into the world.

A network that most people had initially seen as frivolous and a joke had suddenly gained international importance—and for many people, particularly those in Iran, life-or-death importance.

The world has become very small and the networks very large. My Facebook friends include people from Russia, Germany, France, Spain, South Korea, and Colombia, as well as Canada, the United

Kingdom, Australia, New Zealand, and the United States. Have I met all of these people face-to-face? No. But I have met most of them either through my website or their website or Twitter. I've done business with quite a few of them, even though we've never spoken on the telephone and we're on different parts of the globe. I've read their work; they've read mine. We actually communicate in ways unthinkable as recently as fifteen years ago.

And I'm benefiting a great deal from the networks that have come about via the internet. I've sold short stories because of Twitter, novels because of Facebook. I've worked with movie production companies through e-mail, and done broadcast interviews via Skype. I've been in touch with bookstores in Australia that carry my work and done online interviews for their websites. I've gone to conventions overseas because the organizers can reach me via my website, and I've been paid for overseas publications through PayPal, so I don't have to go through the rigmarole that banks require on any check received in another currency.

Networks are important, not just in established businesses like mine, but also in growing businesses. The woman we sold our collectibles store to in 2008 had a bumpy first winter, not just because it was the middle of the Great Recession, but also because she relied on the old-fashioned way to do business—word-of-mouth in our small tourist town.

She had repeat business from tourists who had come through the year before, and she had business from some local ads, but not enough to sustain her through our slow times. She was good at money management, and she had low expenses, so she made it through, but she learned quickly that she needed to do more.

My husband Dean Wesley Smith had taught her how to put collectibles on eBay, but she hadn't wanted to do the work. Not because she was work-averse—she isn't; she's a very hard worker—but because she wasn't that comfortable with computers.

Still, a hard winter will convince anyone to make a few changes. So she put a few items on eBay, and then a few more, and then even more. Slowly, she has formed an online network of people all over the world who are interested in the items she puts up for sale, from toy trains to cookie jars. She's known for quick service and quality products, and she's making it through this winter just fine.

The network of local shop owners helped her as well, answering her questions about working online, and forming a group that shared the cost of local advertising. She has a network of suppliers that she's established, people who comb junk shops and garage sales for that one special item. Her networks are helping her grow her business.

But there's a downside to networks as well. They can be time-consuming, and they can be destructive. Carolyn's points, from her e-mail, concern support groups and professional organizations, but they can apply to all networks in one way or another.

She mentions these:
•**How to know when you need a group.**
•**How to know when you need to get out of a group you're already in.**
•**How to cope with infighting and sabotage in your group.**
•**Legal and financial ramifications.**
•**Opportunities.**
•**Resource-sharing.**
•**How to know if you're a groupaholic.**
•**Goal and dream sharing.**

I'm also going to deal with two personality types:
•**The master networker who has no work to stand on.**
•**The excellent craftsperson who can't network to save her life.**

There are a lot of other topics as well, which I know I will touch on as I get deeper into this subject.

I'm going to structure networking into a variety of components.

First, I'll deal with in-person networks: support groups, professional organizations, seminars, conferences, and continuing education. I'll deal with the upsides—the interaction, the contacts—and the downsides.

Then, I'll deal with social media networks. I've solicited help for that chapter, even though I'm active on Facebook and Twitter, as well as here on my own blog. I also belong to some listserves, many of which have existed for a decade or more. I have a LinkedIn account, but I don't make the best use of it. And as someone reminded me on my Facebook page just the other day, I need to tend to my page on Goodreads.com (a page I didn't start; someone else did). I'm sure that there are other social media networks I know nothing about and which might be helpful to freelancers reading this. So if you know of any, come to my website and use the contact button to let me know. When I update the *Freelancer's Guide* (which I will do regularly), I'll add your information.

Finally, I'll deal with peripheral networks—networks that get built without you even realizing you're building them. The store owner above had no idea she was building a network of train collectors when she started selling toy trains on eBay. Now she's linked to several of those collectors all over the world.

I know many people found my blog not because they were fans of my fiction but because of all the business networks out there. Because of the Guide, I have built some peripheral networks—inadvertently. And if I need help with real estate questions or computer difficulties, I actually have some people I can turn to outside of my friends and acquaintances. I'm also building some non-fiction business relationships due to the *Guide*, and gaining contacts throughout the non-fiction online community.

That's an unexpected bonus of this Guide, certainly not one I planned on. I'll be discussing those peripheral networks last. Again, if you have any insights, do let me know.

Interestingly, I'm going from this writing session into a weekend's worth of networking. Dean and I are holding a workshop this weekend with the help of editor and writer Denise Little. These opportunities can be difficult and tiring, particularly for writers, who are an introverted bunch. But they can also be invigorating and uplifting, a chance to move forward in unexpected ways.

I'm sure the weekend will provide more insights for the Guide. Weekends like this one often do.

Yet even with the workshop, I wouldn't have thought of this topic without Carolyn. Which is a prime example of how networking adds value to a business.

And here's another way. I left in my dithering about the definitions of the word "networking" because it provided another example of networking itself. After I published this chapter in my blog, writer Michael A. Burstein posted this comment:

Kris, FYI, the Oxford English Dictionary gives the first in-print use of the word 'networking' defined as 'The action or process of making use of a network of people for the exchange of information, etc., or for professional or other advantage' from 1976. Here are their first two citations:

1976 C. L. ATTNEAVE in P. J. Guerin Family Therapy xii. 227 'Network' is a noun referring to entire social or family network as the unit of intervention… The techniques..described by Speck and Attneave..are those of assembling the social network, which they prefer to call a process of retribalization rather than 'networking'.

1979 Working Woman Oct. 4/2 The way networking works in real life for both men and women goes something like this: when you need help, someone you have known over a period of time, for whom you have done services and favors of friendship, takes your need as the opportunity to return them.

I find it interesting that the 1976 reference actually talks about researchers who wish to use a different term than "networking."

The OED also notes the first use of the word "networking" at all as dating from 1940, and referring to radio or television broadcasting.

As for the word "network" being used as a verb, well, they give a reference from all the way back in 1845, but the definition is "to cover something with a network" and is a transitive verb. "To network" meaning "to engage in social or professional networking" is cited as first appearing in print in 1980, in of all places, a book called "Networking" by M.S. Welch.

And why am I here to share all this? Because

of my desire to network with you, so many
years ago…

As I had written that initial passage, I had wished for an OED,
but I've never bought one. The next thing I knew, Michael popped up
online, after having checked his. Networking, benefiting us all.

Chapter Thirty
Continuing Education

I'm starting with continuing education because that was what was happening in my life as I wrote this chapter. As I mentioned above, Dean and I were teaching a continuing education class with editor Denise Little. Dean and I teach quite a few continuing education classes for professional writers. (You can find out more information about these classes on Dean's website, deanwesleysmith. com.)

Dean and I often say to writers that money should flow *to* the writer, except for continuing education. In that area, the writer needs to spend money to expand her horizons. I think that's true of most professions, although I'm not entirely certain. I know that some professions require an annual fee to remain current—dues of some kind—and others require an annual fee plus proof of continuing education (certain medical professions, for example [and thank heavens for that!]).

The reason we have to tell writers that money should flow *to* them and not away from them is that in writing (and I suspect many of the arts professions), scam artists have learned that the practitioners know little about business. It's easy to convince a young professional writer or a wannabe to spend money on something that the writer should either get for free or should be paid for.

A professional should continually update her knowledge in one way or another—whether through formal classes provided by the bar association or in a continuing education track at a university. Continuing education might also be workshops and seminars or trade magazine subscriptions and related books on the subject. The professional who does not continually educate herself in the changes in her profession gets left behind.

There is no set rule of thumb on continuing education. Some states mandate the amount of continuing education some professionals receive to maintain their license. (For example, the forensic psychologist I worked for had to have [I believe] fifteen hours of continuing education over two years to maintain his license. Minor, in the scheme of things.) Most professions have no such requirement—and freelancers often don't.

As I mentioned above, some continuing education comes in the form of books, trade journals, websites—all things you can consume at home or during off hours at work.

Continuing education provides countless opportunities for networking. Sometimes the networking comes from the instructor himself—his resume, and his track record for success through his programs. Sometimes (often) the networking comes from the other professionals at the seminar. People trade business cards, make contacts, and discuss business in the line for coffee during the break, over lunch, and in the elevator on the way to meetings. I've made a lot of contacts that way, some of whom I'd forgotten by the time I got home, and some who have become lifelong friends.

(A tip: when you receive a business card from someone at a conference or seminar, write a note about your conversation on the back of the card. You'll be glad you did. By the time you get home, you will have 10-20 business cards, and no real way to remember who is who if you don't make notes. I learned that one through hard experience.)

First, let's talk about how you evaluate a continuing education program outside the home.

1. Figure out where the holes are in your knowledge base and find a way to fill them.

What don't you know, or what don't you know well? That part's pretty self-explanatory. Let's assume you need a better way to do bookkeeping in your business, but you don't want to hire a bookkeeper. You've never kept books for any business, and the computer programs you can download seem unbelievably complex. You have no idea whether you need double-entry bookkeeping or what even the "accrual" bookkeeping method is.

You need to ask yourself: can you learn this on your own, or do you need guidance?

Some things are relatively easy to learn on your own. But some things require assistance. What those "things" are vary from person to person. Only you can answer the above questions. You also are the only one who knows if you can go to the weekend seminar on bookkeeping sponsored by the local chamber of commerce or if you need a full-on course at the local community college.

If you need the course, take it. You'll probably find yourself with other professionals—or maybe budding accountants who might become good bookkeepers when you're ready to hire a few years from now.

The seminar at the local chamber might serve you better, however, and you'll get to know the other business people in your area. You'll gain contacts as well as knowledge.

2. Do a cost-benefit analysis.

Two factors should go into your analysis of cost: time and money. Let's take money first, because that's the most obvious part of a cost-benefit analysis. First, what will it cost you *not* to learn the information? Will it harm your business financially?

Obviously, not knowing how to keep the books for your business will hurt you in the long run. So you need to learn how to do it. Let's assume that a weekend seminar in your hometown costs $50 (including lunch), a bookkeeping course at the community college costs $250, and the best bookkeeping software with tutorial costs $100. (I'm making these numbers up.)

Clearly, the seminar is the cheapest. But will it give you the most bang for the buck? Will you have to buy software anyway? If so, your cost just went up at least another $50. (The recommended software without the tutorial.) What will you gain from the seminar that you won't gain from the software itself?

The answer used to be pretty simple: In the past, you were on your own with software, and a seminar would give you people to consult. But now, with websites and FAQs and help lines, you might get the information help you need to understand the software—or not.

If you're mathematically challenged, you might be better off in the class. (I'm not suggesting the class because you're mathematically challenged and don't understand that $250 is more than $50—if that's your issue, you shouldn't be in business at all.) But if you didn't do well in math at school or you left before you had second-year algebra or you cribbed your homework off the kid next to you and never really learned anything past basic arithmetic, then a class might be the best thing for you. The teacher will help you, step-by-step, because that's what she gets paid for, and you'll have months to learn something that has given you fits in the past.

The toughest part of the cost-benefit analysis is the time factor. Some of us—particularly those of us who run our own businesses—simply don't have the four hours per week for sixteen weeks that a course at a community college would require. Some of us will have trouble carving a weekend out of our schedule for the seminar. For some businesses, weekends are the busiest time of the week. If you don't have an employee to cover for you, you can't go.

But will you spend more time struggling to learn the computer software in an unfamiliar discipline? Are you willing to take that risk? You have to answer that as you make these choices.

Fortunately, none of these choices are life or death. If you try the software first and it doesn't work, you can go to the weekend seminar. If you're more confused after the seminar than you were with the software, then you might have to take a class. Of course, all of this will lose you time and money—you're now at $400 plus the weekend plus the sixteen weeks of class plus the time you lost trying to figure out the damn software.

Sometimes the cheapest route turns out to be the most expensive. Sometimes the shortcut you take to save time doesn't save any time at all—and may even cost you more time than you ever bargained for.

3. Evaluate the seminar/class/workshop/conference.

Who are the instructors? Are they well respected in their fields? Are they people you can learn from?

And here's the biggie: Are they people you *want* to learn from?

I learned about the differences between instructors in my twenties. I have said, ever since I can remember, that my goal in life was to be a professional writer. I defined professional—even as a kid—as someone who made her living from writing.

Early on, I believed that you could not make a living as a fiction writer, so I went into journalism. That belief was a faulty one—fiction writers can and do make a living, and can, in fact, make a much better living than journalists (particularly nowadays).

Even though I was a history major in college, I took creative writing courses, and felt vaguely dissatisfied throughout without knowing why. I graduated, mailed out my fiction, and developed a relationship with Ellen Datlow at *Omni Magazine*. She apparently felt as frustrated as I did at my inability to break into her magazine, so she sent me the information on Clarion Writers' Workshop, which was then held at Michigan State University for six weeks over the summer.

I applied; I got in; I attended. I learned more in six weeks than I ever learned in my college creative writing courses. Of course, I was learning from published professionals (not all of whom were earning a living, but I didn't know that at the time). I grew and developed as a writer, and within six months of my return had sold my first professional short story.

But I was still a journalist, and one nice thing about being a reporter is that you can get paid to seek the answers to your questions. I wanted to know why I learned more at Clarion than I did in my prestigious university's writing courses. I interviewed the director of Clarion, and I interviewed the director of creative writing at the university—and learned something startling; something that made me, young firebrand that I was, furious.

I asked both directors the same set of questions. What I remember asking of the university creative writing director was a do-you-beat-your-wife question—why isn't your program turning out professional writers? What I really asked him—I was a diplomatic little thing—was for a list of the writers who had gone through his program who made a living at writing.

He said they didn't keep those records.

I asked why.

He said because that's not the point of the program.

Feeling a bit stunned, I asked, if you're not trying to create professional writers, what are you trying to do?

He said that they were trying to get as many of their students into qualified MFA programs in creative writing as they possibly could.

"Okay," I said, "but then what? Don't you know who graduated and became a professional writer?"

He explained to me, as if I were stupid (which I guess I was), that the point of an MFA in creative writing was not to become a professional writer, but to go on to get a doctorate in writing, so that the student could then become a professor of creative writing at a prestigious university. He had the figures on that success rate, if I wanted to see it.

I don't remember if I did or did not. I did want to fall off my chair. I was furious—at him, and at myself. No one had told me the goal of the university's creative writing program before. Of course, I hadn't asked, either. I had wasted years—literally years—of my education, being taught by instructors whose goal for me was different from my own.

Of course I learned more at Clarion, which was designed to help young writers become professional. I had finally found the right classes and the right instructors.

Not that there is anything wrong with becoming a professor. I come from a family full of them. I'm one of the only people in my family who does not have an advanced degree in something or other.

But I never wanted to be a professor. I wanted to be a professional writer. And I had gone to the wrong instructors at the wrong school who proceeded—innocently enough—to teach me the wrong trade.

It took me years to realize that the mistake had not been theirs. It had been mine. (Even though I was raised by a professor who repeatedly said that no one should go to college to learn a trade. I guess that cluestick continually missed me.)

Now when I want to learn something from someone else, I research their credentials first and foremost. I would have told the young me to skip the MFAs and the PhDs even if those professors had earned those degrees at top-ranking universities (which many of my instructors had). I would have told the young me to go to science fiction conventions and writers conferences and attend panels/workshops run by writers who were making a *documented* living at their profession. By documented, I mean that they had a bibliography—works in print, that I could find and read and evaluate.

I still attend seminars. I often go to writers conferences as an instructor so that I can sit in on panels by other professional writers and learn from them. Dean and I spoke at the Space Coast Writers' Conference in Cocoa Beach, Florida, a few years ago because of the roster of guests and because we wanted to visit Cape Canaveral, which we did. The added bonus of that writers' conference? The attendees, many of whom worked at NASA during the glory years of the moon landings. Boy, did I learn a lot. Boy, did I enjoy myself. Boy, did I make connections.

Other things to evaluate: Will you get time with the instructors? Will you learn from the other attendees? Will you have incidental costs—hotel rooms, plane fare, meals—or will a seminar/class in your hometown do just as well for you?

4. List your reasons for attending.

Some freelancers become conference/workshop junkies. I'll discuss this phenomenon in full in a later chapter, but make sure you're not going "because everyone else is" or "because you don't want to miss anything."

It's perfectly fine to go to a conference because you need to get out of your routine—all of us, particularly those of us who work at home, do that on occasion—but make sure you're not doing that too much. (And realize there might be cheaper ways to break your routine than flying across country for a conference.)

5. Plan your continuing education year.

Use your calendar and figure out how many hours you can devote to outside learning—conferences, classes, seminars. Do this before looking at the conference listings for your profession. Then stick to that timeline. One year Dean and I made the mistake of traveling 26 weekends. That hurt our business and it hurt us. We had reasons for each conference we attended, but those reasons were not enough to justify that much time away from our businesses.

There's a reason that the professions that require a certain number of hours of continuing education require those hours over a two- or three-year period. To require the hours in one year makes it hard for the working professional to meet the requirements and make a living. Remember that as you set up your timeline.

6. Step Out Of Your Comfort Zone.

If you do attend a conference/workshop/seminar, make sure you do more than go to panels and sit quietly in the back. Meet the other attendees. Go to meals. Go to the pre-banquet happy hour. *Talk* to people. Exchange contact information. You can and will learn from the attendees.

It always stuns me that a small handful of writers attend our classes and never come out of their rooms. They do the homework, do the writing, and do the reading, but they don't meet their fellow attendees. Those fellow attendees may go on to be bestselling or award-winning writers, well-known editors, or influential publishers.

All of those things have happened to our past students. You never know which contact will prove valuable in the future.

Dean and I use the workshops as well. The reason I wrote the *Freelancer's Guide* on my blog is because of contacts I made at a workshop nearly twenty years ago. Michael J. Totten and Scott William Carter came to a workshop Dean and I were running every week in Eugene, Oregon. Michael and Scott were college students then. They've gone on to become professional writers who know a lot about computers.

When Dean and I decided we needed to know more about websites, blogs, and internet business, we asked to meet Scott and Michael in a nearby city. We bought them dinner, and for four hours, they told us what we needed to know to start. We have been talking to them off and on for an entire year, sharing information and learning.

Learning we would never have grasped if we had dismissed them as just college students and wannabe writers all those years ago.

When you go to a seminar, be professional. Dress well. Be polite. But talk to people. And more importantly, listen to them. You'll be surprised what you learn.

Continuing education is a very important part of your business. Without it, you will stagnate and your business will stop growing. But don't let education overwhelm your business. Remember why you're doing this and make each educational project work for you.

Chapter Thirty-one
Lies, Scam Artists, and Bullshit Meters

Irony of ironies. If it hadn't been for networking, I wouldn't have lost an hour of my work time saving one of my best friends from a scam artist. Not that he would have fallen prey entirely. My friend, whom I met in college, works in one of those professions where, if you add the word "thriller" to the end of it, you get a bestselling book category—for *some* of its practitioners, anyway. For every Robin Cook or John Grisham, there are a slew of wannabes or almost-beens who write good novels, but never really make a living.

But everybody thinks these writers make a living—meaning everyone outside of the publishing profession, everyone who reads one of those hyphenate thrillers. The other side to those thrillers is that people who have degrees and/or expertise in the professions that inspire the thrillers believe they have experiences and/or the knowledge to write a better thriller than the current practitioners of the genre.

My friend has more than enough experience to write a good thriller, and better chops than most. He was a good writer in college, and with some practice, might write a fine novel someday.

He dreams of it. And lo and behold, through a continuing education brochure in connection with his current business, he gets offered the chance to take a seminar on writing the thriller. He'll be able to write this conference off as a business expense for his current business. (Or hell, I don't know, he might even get the entire thing paid for by his employer.)

So, bright man that he is, he asks me—in a private message on Facebook—if I've ever heard of the people putting on the seminar. Smart question. He follows that with a second question: is it worth studying with these people?

My answer to my friend, after a bit of digging, was an unequivocal no. Two of the people putting on the seminar are legit—they've published books in the hyphenate thriller genre—small books, not bestsellers. But the person who will "train" everyone to break into publishing, the person who talks through most of the two-day seminar?

That person I've met. At conferences. That person is what I call an accidental scam artist.

And now a bunch of you are asking yourselves, "How can you be an accidental scam artist?"

I go back to intentions. If I told this person that they were a scam artist, they'd be appalled. This person is really and truly trying to help people get published. This person's intentions are very, very good. The advice given at the seminars is probably excellent when it comes to believing in yourself, and awful on the nuts and bolts of publishing in 2010.

The problem is within my industry itself. So many peripheral parts of the publishing industry are unregulated. People can call themselves editors just because they know how to pick up a pen; people can call themselves agents just because they want to; and people can call themselves book doctors because they have opinions on what a novel should be, not because they actually know. Only two states in the nation regulate agents—California and New York—and those regulations only apply to the agents' fiduciary responsibility.

My business isn't the only one with unregulated "experts." The financial services markets are filled with them. And even if they are in a regulated industry, that doesn't mean that they're good at their jobs. I know of one very famous speaker in a regulated industry who is so successful at speaking that he now holds seminars all on his own. My friends in that industry point out that this man cannot hold a job in the industry ("He's been fired from all the best places," said one), but he is making his living teaching seminars geared to beginners in that industry. I have a hunch this sort of thing goes on more often that we like to think.

My friend came to me through traditional and nontraditional networking means. He asked the only person he knew well who worked in the writing field about the credentials of the folks putting on the seminar. He would have called me (old-fashioned networking) if Facebook hadn't provided a quick and easy way to contact me.

If the web didn't exist, I would have had to ask my friends about the unintentional scam artist, and after a few queries, I would have remembered that I had met this person. My recommendation would have been the same—don't waste your money on that seminar—but it would have taken me longer to find answers.

All I did after receiving his message was use Google, and I found more than enough to jog my memory. I also found the brochure for the seminar that my friend was thinking of attending, and I saw how the classes broke down among the instructors.

Had, for example, the two people with actual credentials in the hyphenate thriller category been doing most of the speaking, I would have told my friend to go and avoid the accidental scam artist. But the other two speakers were incidental; the main focus was the one person who really didn't know the industry.

I wrote back to my friend, told him to avoid this seminar, and suggested other seminars for him to attend. I also mentioned conferences and organizations in his area that would be worth his while if he wants to learn how to write a thriller set in his professional world.

Then I paused, and realized that he would be just as vulnerable (if not more vulnerable) to scam artists, bad advice, and wrong turns at those conferences and in those organizations as he would have been at that continuing education seminar.

And therein lies the problem of networking.

It's only as good for you as your bullshit meter allows. If you have a faulty bullshit meter, you're in trouble as a freelancer, my friend.

Let me give you a case in point. Dean has been writing a series on his blog (deanwesleysmith.com) called *Killing the Sacred Cows of Publishing*. Parts of that series have focused on the worth of agents to the writer. Dean believes in having an agent, but he also believes that writers who hire one should know what the agent's job is before hiring any old person.

A number of successful freelance writers visit Dean's blog and discuss their experiences with agents at length. No one blogs anonymously. Everyone gives credentials and opinions, and uses experience and statistics to back up their point of view.

Recently, Dean got some rather hateful mail in his comments section on the first agent post. He let the least egregious of the comments (the ones that didn't use foul language and call him horrible names) through to the site. But it wasn't until he got a few of them that he realized where they were coming from.

They were coming from a blog by someone who claims to be an editor, someone who blogs anonymously. Now, I've only read the unbelievably nasty post about my husband that this anonymous person has put on its (his? her? I dunno) blog, so I can't tell you if this person's advice is sound or not. And after that attack on my husband, I'm likely not the best judge of the anonymous blog.

However, I can tell you this: that is a blog—regardless of the attack on my husband—that I would never read. Why? Because it is anonymous. I cannot check the credentials of the person writing the blog. Whereas, in the case of the accidental scam artist, I could easily check credentials. That person was up front in on the website that this person now makes a living giving seminars about how to get published. The accidental scam artist even mentions that their experience is thirty years old (as an editor) and more than fifteen years old (as a writer).

The accidental scammer's blog and seminars look positive, upbeat, and cheerful, helpful in a believe-in-yourself kinda way. If that was what my friend needed, I'd tell him to go and ignore all the nuts and bolts publishing advice. Because the accidental scammer isn't hiding anything for the person who knows how to look.

But the anonymous blogger is hiding something. And when Dean pointed this out in his return e-mails to the people whose posts he declined to put on his site, they wrote back to him *telling him they would trust someone who blogged anonymously over someone with his credentials, because the anonymous blogger is taking a risk and could possibly lose their job by being honest about the industry.*

Okay, that might be true for whistle-blowers and some political bloggers (a columnist in Madison, WI in the 1980s comes to mind, who wrote for *Isthmus* under the name the Capitol Eye), but it's not true in publishing. There is no reason to be anonymous in this business. Lots of editors blog as a way of helping writers, yes, and as a way of promoting their book lines.

The poor naïve writers attacking my husband through his site have faulty bullshit meters, and until they get those meters fixed, they're not going to survive in the big, international world of publishing.

Unlike my friend. Who took one look at that seminar and contacted someone who could verify credentials. My friend has a mighty fine bullshit meter, and knows some of the basics about life: find out whom you're taking advice from. Figure out if that person is worth listening to.

And figure out if the advice is worth following. Not all advice is. Not all advice—even from the best people (like me, she says with an evil grin)—is worth following all the time. What might be right for me might be wrong for you. Think it through before doing it.

Especially advice that comes through anonymous sources.

Recently, I read a post by comic book writer Kurt Busiek about breaking into the comics business. (busiek.com/site/2009/06/ breaking_in_without_rules.php) In my opinion, his advice applies to all freelancers. He says, "If you need to have someone lay out a set of instructions for you, you probably don't have the skills or imagination to be a freelance writer." He goes through the long arduous up-and-down path it took him to get to his place in his freelance career. It's an excellent analysis of the ups and downs of freelancing. It's also an example of someone who knows who he is and what he can do as a freelancer in order to survive.

On an episode of 2010's *American Idol*, Ryan Seacrest pointed out to Crystal Bowersox that she received contradictory advice from two of the judges, Kara Dioguardi and Simon Cowell. Dioguardi told Bowersox to lose her guitar for her next performance. Cowell told her to keep the guitar.

"Who're you going to listen to?" Seacrest asked.

Without missing a beat, maybe without taking a breath, Bowersox said, "Me."

Both Dioguardi and Cowell applauded, because Bowersox was right.

If you're going to survive as a freelancer, the only person you can trust to do the right thing is yourself.

As I realized in the middle of a negotiation last week, if I screw it up, no one is going to give me a failing grade. Three years from now, I'll probably not even remember that I was negotiating, let alone that I had made a minor mistake. I'm not going to get slapped; no one will yell at me. The worst that can happen is that I can make a bad deal or do something *I* don't like. Oh, well.

The advice side of this is pretty simple: listen with your bullshit meter on. Realize that good advice for the person next to you might be terrible advice for you. Figure out what you need and then go after it, through networking, education, and of course, good hard work.

I have no idea, as I write this, if my friend will go to the seminar. For all I know, he'll still sign up. It might be worth his time to listen to the two legitimate writers at the seminar. He might need a trip to Los Angeles and an excuse for some downtime. He might think he can get something out of the seminar, especially now that he knows that one of the speakers cannot help him get published as promised.

Or he might take my advice and go to other conferences. Of course, at those conferences, there will be scammers and frauds, people who set themselves up as experts when they know little about the industry, and people who have incredible credentials, people who know quite well how to do something.

My friend will survive whatever he does, because he knows how to filter information. I don't know how to teach you how to do that, except to research experts before you take their advice. And even then: once you've taken their advice, that becomes *your* decision. You have taken the action; it's not their fault if something goes awry. It's yours.

I can't tell you how important a good bullshit meter is. Without one, you're drowning in the deep end, unable to know where to turn for help. Start training yourself now; it'll save you a lot of grief later.

Chapter Thirty-two
Personality Types

Shortly after posting the chapter on groups, the chapter briefly went viral. People who worked on conventions in science fiction, mystery, and romance shared the chapter with each other. So did some SCA people, gamers, and lawyers. Each retweet and post with a link mentioned a group experience that had something to do with the group dynamics that I had described. Several folks used the chapter as a cautionary tale for groups that were just starting up.

In that chapter, I discussed the group as a group, and the freelancer as an individual. But we all know that groups are composed of individuals, all with different needs and different focuses.

In this chapter, I'm going to discuss two different kinds of individuals you might find in a group. They are:

1. The master networker who has no work to stand on.
2. The excellent craftsperson who can't network to save her life.

I'm going to discuss both of these individuals from two different perspectives—first as if they were someone you, the freelancer, might meet, and second as if they are you, which they very well could be.

First, the master networker.

I love people who talk a good game. I married two of them. One of my closest friends is a third. I really enjoy watching a good salesman, and I love listening to a sales pitch and/or hustle. I'm attracted to self-confidence, and I adore highly verbal people. I was a theater geek in high school (among other things), and actors in particular catch my attention. I love how flashy and showy and downright entertaining they are.

Master networkers talk a good game. Like actors, they're flashy and showy and entertaining. They're highly verbal, and they're excellent salespeople. And the product they're selling is themselves.

The problem is that they aren't a commodity. With the exception of actors, comedians, and the occasional public speaker (or radio talk show host), most people can't get by on hyping themselves alone. They need to have a real product or a real business behind them.

My first husband sometimes had a business behind his talk, but not always. (Although, to his credit, he tried to back up his words.) My husband Dean has always had a business to promote. In fact, he was so paranoid about being perceived as just a talker when we started up Pulphouse Publishing that he insisted we do an Issue Zero of our hardback magazine—a hardcopy blank book to show that we knew as much about *publishing* as we did about editing.

In fact, Issue Zero was the reason our first issue had great writers. I solicited my favorite writers to write for the publication, and to prove we were serious, I enclosed an Issue Zero. Later, more than half of the writers told me that they wouldn't have written for us without the Issue Zero. Harlan Ellison told me that it was Issue Zero which convinced him that we were legit.

What I didn't know at the time—and what Dean did know, because he studied the history of the field—was that so many other publications started with a great editor and a bit of money, solicited writers and maybe even paid them, but never got the first issue off the ground. He was proving to everyone he talked to that we would get our first, second, third, and fourth issue off the ground—and we did.

My good friend Kevin J. Anderson has always talked a good game. He can promote himself better than anyone I know. But, like Dean, Kevin has always had the work behind him. In fact, I learned that on the first day I met Kevin, in a college creative writing class. Kevin challenged the instructor on some issue (I can't remember what), and the instructor shot back that he had been published, so he knew what he was talking about.

Kevin snapped that he had been published too—over 100 times in the small and specialty press. In that instance, I went from ignoring the loud young guy with opinions I (mostly) agreed with to deciding that this was someone I needed to pay attention to.

My habit of looking for credentials, however, comes from my love of the hype. Too many times, I've been bitten by someone who talks a good game but never has anything to back it up. Most of those disasters happened when I was in my teens and twenties. I was a gullible person who believed that if someone said she would do something, she would do it. After all, I did what I said I would do. Didn't everyone?

Well, as this sadder but wiser girl (to quote *The Music Man*, which is an entire musical about the hype) now knows, not everyone who claims she'll do something will do it. Worse, not everyone who *says* she's done something has actually done so.

These people thrive in networking situations, particularly conventions and out-of-town continuing education events. They're new to the other participants, and get a lot of attention. They do better with people who don't know them, because people who do, know that they haven't (yet) done the work.

I put the "yet" in parenthesis because sometimes the master networkers do become established professionals. At some point, they realize they're not producing, and they learn how.

How do you, the freelancer, deal with the master networker?

Mostly you don't. If you're just an attendee at the conference, make sure you're sitting at another table during the group lunch or that you are in a different panel than they are. The problem with master networkers is that they often take resources and energy from folks who are already doing the work, and that can be both difficult and frustrating.

A side note: Master networkers often graduate to presenters at some conferences, and then they use those credentials to run their own conferences. These are often the accidental scammers that I was talking about above. They might know a lot about a little, but they have almost no hands-on experience. What experience they do have comes from listening to others.

If you're a presenter at the conference, how do you tell a master networker from an outgoing professional with a lot of questions? You can't. You answer everyone's questions with equal sincerity. For all you know, you might provide the spark that takes the

master networker from all talk to production, leading them to become
the outgoing professional at the very next conference.

If you teach continuing education classes, as Dean and I do,
you'll need to do some extra work to weed out the master networker.
You will have to research them. Because we teach established pros,
we ask about work ethic (in some very pointed questions), publication
credits, and workshop history. (Often, too many workshops and very
few [or no] publishing credentials shows someone who is addicted to
workshops, but not to the craft of writing itself.)

But, as I promised, I'd look at these personality types from the
outside and the inside.

How do you know if you're a master networker?

You probably already know. You've probably winced a bit as
you read the above chapter. And, I'm sure, there are a handful of you
who *think* you're master networkers, when you're not even close;
you're outgoing working professionals who worry that you talk too
much.

What's the difference?

That's pretty simple, actually.

The working professional has a body of work behind her.
Or an active and thriving business. Lawyers who have clients are
working professionals, just like bookstores that keep their doors open
from 9 to 5. Writers who write for publication every day—even if
they haven't yet been published—are working professionals. (Of
course, those writers need to mail their work to someone who might
buy it or they're not really working professionals. Real writers need
an audience, just like real artists and real actors and real musicians.)

Of course, we were all beginners at one point, and when we
began, we didn't have any work behind us. We went to conferences,
and some of us asked a lot of questions. (Right, Kev? Dean?)
That's good and healthy. But once you've reached your fifth year of
conference attendance without doing the work, then you are a master
networker. You can talk a good game, but you can't deliver.

The only way out of that trap is to figure out what's stopping
you from actually following your dream. I can guarantee that
whatever is stopping you—fear, or a lack of discipline, or a lack
of time—has deep roots somewhere. I can also guarantee that the
problem is solvable if you but try.

What conferences do for you, in this instance, is substitute for
the work. At a conference or continuing education event, you can be

taken seriously without having to actually make an effort. And while that's good for the ego in the short term, it's not going to help you in the long term. Next time you go to a conference or class, go to the sessions on getting started or overcoming your fears. And then go home and apply what you've learned.

Once you actually get to work, you'll have something most professionals are never able to do well (or comfortably): the ability to promote yourself. You've got the self-promotion part down. It's the work part you have trouble with.

So the other personality type we're going to discuss is the exact opposite of the master networker: **the excellent craftsperson who can't network to save her life.**

I feel your pain, sister, because I've been there. When I graduated from college, I received a membership in the Wisconsin State Historical Society as a graduation gift. It was a gift I treasured. (Once a geek, always a geek.) Along with the gift came a free membership to the group's conference that year.

I drove by myself to a small Wisconsin town I'd never been to before. (And since, at that point, I'd lived in the state for most of my life and traveled all over, that was saying something.) I went to the conference, excited to hear some of my favorite historians speak. I got up early, went to panels, listened, and took notes—

—and didn't talk to anyone, except for the nice people at my lunch table during the sponsored luncheon, after which a world-famous historian gave his (riveting and still memorable) speech. The people at my table forced me to tell them why someone so young was there (most attendees were either professional historians or retired), and they asked me (politely) what historical areas interested me the most. I spoke for maybe five minutes total during that entire weekend.

I even went (briefly) to the reception on the second night. I walked through the group, drink in hand, dressed to the nines, stood in a corner for a few minutes, then went timidly back to my hotel room and watched *Bye, Bye Birdie* on the small color TV, feeling like I was missing something, but having no idea at all how to participate.

I felt out of my depth and lost, and I'm sure no one who attended that conference remembers me, although I remember them. I certainly did not network.

Nor did I network at my first science fiction convention, although my buddy Kevin did his best to get me to do so. He was the one who dragged me there—a Wiscon around 1980 or so. In those days, most attendees wore Tom Baker Dr. Who scarves, and if Kev had had one, I'd have taken the end and tied it to my wrist so that I never, ever, lost sight of him. Kev took me to panels where he asked good and pointed questions (working professional, that boy), and tried to introduce me to some of my favorite writers. (Which did not work; I went into fan-girl-stammer mode or [more often] refused to meet them at all.) I did learn a lot, but I missed a lot, too.

It wasn't until my first romance convention, which was held at the University of Wisconsin, that I figured out how I could survive. I went as a reporter, doing a story for *Isthmus* and for WORT Radio. I had my press badge with me, and I played Reporter Girl the entire weekend. No one was fooled. They all knew I wanted to write fiction. But as Reporter Girl, I could ask questions without embarrassing myself (too much). I could even talk to my favorite writers, so long as I clutched a microphone.

I know, I know. Most of you competent introverts don't have that option. You go to conventions, skip the socializing, and spend too much time in your rooms. I'll get to a solution for that for you in a minute. But first, let me talk to the extroverts out there.

How do you know who the introverted professional is? (The person I'd called the excellent craftsperson who can't network to save her life. I'm changing that here, because that phrase is too long to type over and over, and besides, a lot of excellent craftspeople can network. So, we'll go with introverted professional from now on.)

How do you know? Look around. There's an overdressed, tense person in the back of the room, hunched over her laptop or notepad, not making eye contact unless something inspires or surprises her. She's taking copious notes. She'll bolt from the room the moment the panel is over, lurk in the back of the cocktail reception looking horribly out of place, and concentrate on her food during the networking lunch.

If you're another participant, you won't be able to draw her out with pointed questions. Better to smile, nod, and acknowledge. Maybe a quiet hello or a comment on a panel you both attended. That should start a discussion, which might actually lead to a contact that will benefit you both.

If you're a presenter, make sure everyone at your panel has a chance to ask questions. Limit everyone to two questions. That'll control the talkers and the extroverts. If the panel is small enough, start in the back, and ask each person what question they most want to ask. You'll get the introvert to ask her question—which will probably be a good one. Then check with her after the panel to see if you answered it. If you talk to her, you'll open the door for others to talk to her as well, and her networking will have begun.

Of course, as a presenter, it's not your responsibility to make sure everyone has a good convention, just as it's not your responsibility to separate the never-gonna-do-it types from the real future professionals. But networking is a two-way street, and often those silent types are valuable friends, allies, and resources down the road.

If you are an introverted professional, there is hope.

If I could learn how to survive the convention circuit, you can too—and you don't even need a personality transplant. Here's how:

1. Remember you're there to network as well as learn.

So make a point of getting a few business cards or introducing yourself to a few people.

2. Ask questions.

Give yourself an assignment. Ask one question in the morning session and one question in the afternoon session. Yes, your voice will quiver. Yes, your heart will pound. No, you won't die. And most people won't even notice how nervous you are.

3. Ask more questions.

Instead of sitting quietly at the scheduled networking events like the cocktail reception and the sit-down lunch, ask someone a question. At the reception, find another person who looks as lost as you do, and ask what they're looking forward to at the conference or if they heard a particularly good speaker that day or if someone's upcoming session is worthwhile. At lunch, ask what people enjoyed in the morning session. Then…

4. Listen.

People love to talk about themselves. So if you ask them a question, they'll answer—sometimes at length. Don't then ask the next person a similar question. Listen to the first answer, and use it to ask another question, possibly related. *Since you liked his morning session so much, are you going to his afternoon session?*

5. Sit next to someone you talked to.

If you spoke to someone at the reception the night before, and they're in your panel the following day, then sit near them. Ask another question—as simple as "enjoying the conference?"

6. But don't sit near them all the time.

Make sure you talk to a handful of people, so that you don't seem like a silent stalker. One or two sentences, a few questions, sitting near them in a panel, and you've made a connection. If it's one you want to keep up, that's when you ask the personal question, such as "Where are you from?" and "What do you do?" But don't start with those.

7. Celebrate that you've spoken to more than one person.

Eventually, over time, you'll be more comfortable at conferences. You'll still need the conversational tricks—I do, when I don't know anyone—but you'll be used to using them and won't feel so awkward.

And, over time, you'll make some friends who'll be at other conferences. You'll slowly build your network. You don't have to do it in one conference or one continuing education session. Build on your successes. Eventually, you'll be one of those people greeting old friends and having loud enjoyable conversations at the reception. No one will remember that you were the introverted professional a few years back. (Except, of course, the friend who kept trying to introduce you to all your favorite authors when you refused. [Sorry, Kev.])

Conferences and continuing education are useful for both learning and networking. The master networker uses them for networking, but hasn't mastered the learning part. The introverted professional knows how to learn, but misses all the networking opportunities. Try not to be either person at a conference. Network a little, learn a little, be quiet for a while, and talk a little.

You'll get a lot more out of your conferences if you do.

Chapter Thirty-three
Groups

Ah, groups. This is the topic that I was surprised I missed, and yet when Carolyn Nicita proposed it, I realized the topic itself was a large one. In her e-mail, Carolyn combined online groups with in-person groups. Under the group topic, however, I'm only going to deal with in-person groups, saving online discussions for the social media and internet chapters of networking.

As for groups themselves, let me share Carolyn's list with you just because it's so nice to have insights other than my own. Then I'll discuss group dynamics, behavior, and the pros and cons of groups.

She wrote, "I wonder if the pros and cons of organizations and other support systems would be helpful. These would include the workshop groups, of course."

Then she listed some other possibilities, including:
- **Mentors, unions, medieval craft guilds, farmers' co-ops, dental offices that share resources among doctors.**
- **Professional think tanks.**
- **Professional organizations (such as Science Fiction Writers of America).**
- **Babysitting coops for working mothers.**
- **NHEA for tutors/homeschoolers/educational-materials authors.**
- **Clubhouses.**

"What I mean by clubhouses," she wrote, (is) "in Provo (UT)'s comic store, Dragon's Keep, Howard Tayler inks his webcomic *Schlock Mercenary* for four hours a day while talking to fans. Other authors have meetings, RPG groups in the basement, using their tables and comfy couches for hanging out purposes.

Dragon's Keep hosts book and comic signings, and charity events. Utah NaNoWriMo holds events there in November, and people can post messages on the Keep's large bulletin board."

Fascinating stuff. For those of you who don't know some of the lingo in that last paragraph, RPG is short for role-playing games. NaNoWriMo stands for National Novel Writing Month, in which writers spend the month of November challenging themselves to write at least 50,000 words of a novel. Last year, for example, many of my friends, including one of my editors, participated in NaNoWriMo. NaNoWriMo functions as both an online group—the contest is international and people post their results, sometimes daily—and an in-person group, as participants assemble daily or weekly at local coffee shops (and, apparently, comic book stores) to encourage each other.

In-person groups can be extremely encouraging. They can also be highly toxic. Sometimes they're both, depending on who you are and how you react to the various personalities involved. Often they start as encouragement and become quite toxic over time.

First, let's discuss whether or not you need a group. Freelancers, who often work alone, generally benefit from membership in at least one group. It gets the freelancer out of the house and out in public. Often, the best group, when you're using it as a tool to leave the house, is a group that has nothing to do with your work.

My husband is a professional poker player, although he hasn't played seriously for some time now since he's concentrating on his writing at the moment. He belongs to a local group of poker players who get together once a week and pass around the same $400. (One week, one player wins; the next week, another player does. They have financial limits, and no one ever wins more than $200. The net effect is that they're just passing the same amount of cash back and forth.)

The group knows that Dean plays professionally, and invited him anyway. But they don't play Texas Hold 'Em. They play weird table games which sometimes flummox Dean. For his part, he never puts on his full shark when he's there—it's a for-fun game, not a for-profit game.

What does he get out of the evening besides a needed escape from the place where he lives and works? A lot of contacts. The other players are a hotelier (who also owns an international computer business), a retired military man who also worked in Hollywood among other things, a local contractor, and a utility worker. The amount of local gossip that Dean brings home is astounding. Plus the insights from people outside our usual social circle—writers, writers, editors, and more writers—are crucial.

The guys aren't really there to exchange information; they get together to relax. But in their relaxation, they discuss work, they discuss our little town, they discuss politics, and they discuss anything else that crosses their minds. It has turned into a valuable evening in more ways than one.

Dean could easily have ruined it, however. He could've played in those early games as if he were in Vegas. He could've turned on the skill and played cutthroat poker, making it unpleasant to be in the same room with him. This game has gone on, in various incarnations, for nearly 30 years, and other players have been kicked out. Dean could've been evicted if he hadn't meshed with the group.

He understood the value of that group, and didn't do anything to jeopardize his position there. He's been part of it now for years—sometimes when he's playing professionally, and sometimes when he's not. He's not in the group for poker. There are local groups that would probably be better for him as a professional player—groups of other professionals who meet in the various casinos and card rooms in the area. This group is for relaxation, and that's how all of the men (yes, men only) in the group use it.

That group started informally and has no real rules—although it has a few unwritten ones. Since I'm not part of it, I'm not privy to those, but I do know one—if you're unpleasant week after week, someone will let you know that you really don't belong.

Sounds fair to me.

So many groups start informally. Sometimes they become bigger and then have to build a real structure around the informal one (which can lead to turmoil). Sometimes they stay small and continue to function just fine that way. Other groups begin big and get bigger, and some struggle to survive.

When you decide you want to be part of a group, figure out what you'll get from that group. I believe a night of relaxation among friends, in which no real work is discussed, is highly valuable—particularly for freelancers who often do not take a day off. For a while, I was part of a local singing group—until it took too much of my time. I was also part of a Masters swim group, until one of our members got elected mayor and kept wanting to co-opt me to join various local committees or to run for city council. I knew that would take too much time, and it grew harder and harder to say no to her. So when she's no longer mayor, I'll probably rejoin the swim group. I don't want to worry about turning down volunteer political assignments each and every week.

The group worked, and then it didn't, and it might work again. If I didn't have trouble staying out of public affairs, I'd still be in the swim group.

What groups do I currently belong to? Informally, a group of writers who meet at a local restaurant every Sunday. I am part of the science fiction community as well—which mostly entails going to the occasional convention. I am peripherally involved in the mystery and romance communities. I also have a toe in several writers groups, although I don't really belong to any of them.

Formally, I belong to one writer's organization (down from my high of two). I'm not much of a joiner, partly because I'm such a troublemaker. I either get angry at the organization or I become its president, neither of which serves me or the group very well in the end.

I'm much more active in the online communities, because they suit me more. I can visit them—or not—at any hour of the day or night. I can lurk (for those of you not on lists, it means read but not participate), which is not an option for me in person. No matter how many groups I join, I always get noticed and almost always become one of the group's leaders, whether I want to or not. (This even happened to me on jury duty. They voted me foreperson—this group of 11 people I didn't know. My only act as foreperson of that jury was to appoint someone else. ["You all agree she'd be better, right?"] and then step down.)

I also do very well at conventions because I have no desire to run them, and they only last for a weekend or so. I can be social that long, and charming, and quiet (if need be), and I learn a lot in those circumstances.

Every time I join a local group, however, I end up leaving within the year—for the reasons I cited above.

I have learned how I am as a group member and what I need, as a freelance writer. My needs would differ if I ran a local business. If I still had a storefront, I'd be a member of the local chamber of commerce. If I were a psychologist, I'd go to the meetings of the local psychological association. I can get a lot of what I need as a writer at conventions and online, and I can't get much locally unless I run it myself. (Which is one of the reasons Dean and I put on workshops—

so that we have new writerly blood come in and out of town on a regular basis.) I have no need, as a freelance writer, to do a lot of group work locally.

However, the conventions and seminars are a real godsend for me.

I have learned who I am as a group member. I'm loud and opinionated; people tend to defer to me (probably because it's easier than arguing with me), which often puts me in leadership positions I do not want. I cannot relax in a formal group, and function best in an informal one, like our Sunday meeting.

I have also learned, however, that I don't need a lot of out-of-the-house group time, provided I get my occasional convention or workshop. I'm a more effective writer if I stay home and stay in my routine.

Dean, on the other hand, needs to leave the house every day. He needs the contact more than I do, and he belongs to more groups—more informal groups—than I do. It works for him. We have another friend who also likes the group contact, but so much that we've actually had to have interventions to stop her from volunteering one more time.

You need to figure out what kind of group you need (if any). Do you need one affiliated with your work? Do you need one that takes your mind off work? Do you need a hobby? (I almost joined the local softball team until I realized that it met nearly every day in the summer, and I didn't have the time for that. Dammit.)

Then you need to figure out how many groups you can be in and still get your work done. Because we live in a tourist town, a lot of writers and publishing professionals show up while on vacation. For a while, we took every visitor to dinner. I finally put an end to my involvement in that. I lost about six days per month to socializing, days I needed in my writing. Often, I'd see those vacationing writers on Sunday anyway. So I have (mostly) limited my involvement in the informal writerly gatherings to one day per week.

Recognize the difference between formal and informal groups. In informal groups, you can get away with showing up every once in a while. In a formal group, attendance at each meeting might be mandatory. (Like it would have been on that softball team.) If you miss, you jeopardize your standing with the group.

Time is your most valuable commodity. You can't let outside organizations eat up too much of it. You need to balance the time with the things you get from the group itself.

You also need to recognize if you're part of an informal group that doesn't call itself a group. Some families, for example, operate as an informal group. They have weekly gatherings, and attendance might (or might not) be mandatory.

Figure out how many groups—formal and informal—you belong to, and make sure they are all valuable to you. By valuable, I don't just mean in a crass commercial way. The group may be valuable because it helps you relax or take your mind off your work. It might be valuable because you have fun while you're part of it. (In the U.S., I think, we don't always put enough value on fun.) In fact, you might opt to keep one of your fun groups and get rid of one of the professional organizations you belong to. I've known people who have felt guilty about those choices because (theoretically) the professional organization will help their business.

Sometimes the structured night off will help more.

In fact, a structured night off is very valuable to the freelancer. It helps you keep track of the days (which is a problem for those of us who have no other real structure in our lives), and it also ensures that you will take a night off weekly. So many freelancers would work seven days a week without a break without some kind of reminder to take a few hours to yourself. And everyone needs that break.

Besides, you don't know how valuable a non-related (or relaxation) group can be. Dean has made contacts through his poker group that have come in handy as we're planning an upcoming remodel. He also knows (too much) gossip about our little town. We do our workshops at the hotel owned by his poker buddy. We both have benefited a great deal from his structured night off, in ways we never would have predicted otherwise.

So, as you can tell, I am pro-group, with reservations. I think we, as freelancers, need the contact. I think we, as human beings, are better off when we remember that we are social creatures.

I am an inveterate group builder. I can't help myself. (My dictionary, consulted because I can't spell inveterate to save my life [you should have seen my first attempt], tells me that inveterate means fixed in habit and practice, particularly a bad one. Yep. That fits.) I build groups wherever I go.

Dean told me once that we needed to move somewhere where we didn't know anyone, and we needed to remain anonymous after we did. I told him it wouldn't work and added, "Wherever we go, we colonize."

And we do. We bring other writers with us. We built a writing community in Eugene, Oregon. We've built another here in Lincoln City, Oregon. And we've built two international writing communities, one of which died a rather ugly death, the other of which is still ongoing. In fact, our Eugene writing community continues as well, even though we left the community fifteen years ago. We have no involvement in the writing community in Eugene, yet people still ask me about it all the time, thinking I still go to meetings.

Amazing. Groups do live long after their founders. Dean started a writing community in Moscow, Idaho, when he lived there, and was one of the three founders of the Moscon Science Fiction convention, all of which lived for decades past his residence in the town. My writing community in Madison didn't live beyond my move, but I had just started it when I left. My radio community, however, is still alive and well (and we're all now Facebook friends).

I have been a part of so many groups that I've learned they all follow the same general pattern: Groups form among like-minded people who gather in a fit of enthusiasm. Sometimes those groups have rules. More often than not, they don't.

The group then has some kind of success—however that group measures success, whether it's in a large membership or in putting on a successful convention or successfully arguing for someone else's rights. The success reverberates through the group, giving it confidence and helping it grow.

Growth is a group's friend and a group's enemy. Groups with a lot of members gain clout, but those groups also gain strife.

The group's founders usually run the group until they get tired—usually both physically and emotionally. Then they hand leadership to someone else, someone less or more qualified, but (and this is important) someone who usually has a different vision for the group.

In the last stages of the group's founders phase, several things can happen: the founders realize they're not up to the task of running a large group; the founders no longer have time to run the group; the founders aren't capable of running anything—they're starters, not managers; the founders are no longer all that interested in the group; or the founders hold on to power with everything that they have to the detriment of the group.

At the last stages of the founders phase, the founders are usually in the way of good group growth. Someone will point that out. There will be bickering and strife, bad feelings and nastiness all around. The fighting can (and probably will) get ugly.

The group will probably splinter if the founders are still interested in running it. If the founders aren't interested, they'll leave the group. If the founders are interested but aren't very politic, they'll get kicked out of the very group they started. Or, if the founders are smart, they'll find their own replacements before all of this happens *and they'll let the replacements run the group with no interference.*

This is the phase at which many groups implode and disappear. The enthusiasm can't carry the group through all the strife.

But if people are smart and the group is still valuable to a large number of members, it will survive. (Or a new group, with the same membership minus a few troublemakers, will start under a new name.) If the group does survive this phase, it will often grow and become more professional. It'll develop written rules, maybe even rent a meeting place, and elect officers—sometimes paying them.

Eventually, these groups become established parts of the landscape, their beginnings lost in the mists of time. People can't imagine life without that particular group. Or a profession without a particular professional organization.

Eventually, the group gains power of its own. It will survive without any of the founding members. It will become an entity in and of itself, one that can hire and fire employees, one that can admit or discharge members, one that can make statements about its beliefs with the weight of history behind it.

Because I love history and politics and group dynamics, I read about group beginnings all the time. And every group goes through these phases. (There are more, but these are the general ones.)

For a few examples: The Science Fiction Writers of America began around the dining room table at Damon Knight and Kate Wilhelm's house. Damon became the organization's first president; Kate designed the Nebula award. I don't know much about the early years, but I do know that the infighting among the early members became so extreme that two decades later when I met all of the founding members, half of them hadn't spoken to each other in fifteen years or more.

Most members of the Science Fiction Writers of America can't tell you a thing about those early years. Nor can they tell you who the past presidents were, what the infighting was about in the 1970s, or why the organization even got founded. But the current members can tell you about the current infighting, the good things that the organization is attempting to do, and why they joined this particular group. (For many sf writers, joining the Science Fiction Writers of America is a goal—from childhood.)

Romance Writers of America had a similar start. I don't even recall who started the organization. I do recall going to some early RWA meetings in 1979 and 1980. Everything was mimeo-ed, meetings were on the fly, and the organization's bulletin was photocopied and stapled.

Then RWA wanted the publishing industry to acknowledge that romance novels sold more copies than most other genres combined. The early mission of RWA was to gain respect for its members. The organization achieved that better than any organization I've ever seen because somewhere along the way—in the years I was solely in science fiction and not romance—someone decided to follow the feminist model: *Don't demand respect; earn it.* The women of RWA became experts at the business of writing. They used statistics, knowledge, negotiation, and guts to take on the publishing industry. Even now, when I teach new writers, I tell them to get a membership in RWA *whether they write romance or not.* They'll learn the business, and how important it is. Only one other writer's organization teaches business, and that's Sisters in Crime, who followed the same model for the same reason.

Has RWA had infighting and strife? Oh, yeah. I missed most of it, either by joining too late the first time or by being in science fiction for the tough middle years. But just a few years ago, there was another major battle, one that led to the tightening of the organization's rules.

Unlike the early battles, though, later battles in a group rarely lead to the group's demise. The early battles can kill a group.

This trajectory I'm discussing doesn't just happen in writers' groups. It happens in all groups. Recently, I talked with someone who used to run the local chamber of commerce in our small town. Our town was so tiny that it didn't have a chamber for many years. When it formed a chamber, it did so with enthusiasm and joy. Then came the problems, the strife, and the splintering. Now, in our town of 7,000 people, there are several business organizations, some of which seem very chamber of commerce-like. And of course, the chamber still exists.

I'm discussing all of this in a very rational, cold-blooded fashion. But my cold-blooded rationality is hard-earned. I've been kicked out of groups that I've started. (Remember my comment about not being politic? That's…um…me.) I've been kicked out of groups that I didn't have much invested in, including one group that threw out a block of members because the group didn't approve of our day jobs. (We were writers and editors; it was a writing organization, and it felt that editors were the enemy—even if some of the editors were writing more books per year than the so-called writers.)

I've been the hatchet man for more than one organization—or, if you prefer a different analogy, the canary in the coal mine. I get annoyed at bad behavior faster than most, so people expect me to blow first—and are relieved when I do so. I have learned that I don't play well with others, so now, when I join a group, I don't get involved with the day-to-day politics of that group. I remain a rank-and-file member.

And the groups I start? I run them—or we do, Dean and I—with an iron fist. I've told more than one group member that if they don't like the way we run the group, they have two choices: they can suck it up and get used to our method, or they can leave. Most stay. Over the past five years in more than one group, only two people have left.

What does all of this mean for you, the freelancer? Quite a bit, actually. Once you've figured out that you need or want to belong to a certain group, then you must decide how you will fit into that group. Because I have a strong personality, I tend to lead groups, whether I want to or not. So I have to figure out how to mute my personality to remain rank and file. Often that means avoiding any policy at all and staying away from mass meetings.

So how does the group benefit me?

I generally join groups for knowledge. I want to learn something. So I become part of an organization. In those groups, I remain quiet and I stay as uninvolved as possible.

In the groups that I start, I remain in control, and the groups stay relatively small. They also have strict rules that everyone in the group knows about, and those rules are enforced.

Mostly, though, I don't join many groups. It's safer that way, for me and for the group.

But you've chosen to join a few groups. What can you do with the knowledge of the pattern that I gave you above?

1. Know that the pattern exists.

Figure out where the group is in its trajectory, and stay out of the infighting. Realize that groups, like individuals, change. The things you joined for may disappear. Or they may grow stronger. Or the group might improve in ways you hadn't expected at all.

2. Keep your involvement to a minimum.

Remember that you're in the group to help your business, not to help the group. If you keep that rule firmly in mind, you'll stay out of 90% of the problems that come up inside the group.

3. Remember that infighting is *normal*.

Wait for the fights to pass. Remain silent. If you can't remain silent, then drop out of the group. You can always rejoin later. Remember that you joined the group to make connections, not to make enemies. If you keep that as your golden rule, you'll gain a lot from the groups you join. If you forget that one piece of advice, you'll lose half your life to battles that, on the scheme of things, mean nothing at all.

4. Reevaluate your memberships in all of your groups once a year.

Figure out if you're getting anything from the group. (And remember that structured time off has worth.) Figure out how to maximize the benefits while avoiding the problems. If you can't avoid the problems and they're taking over your life, then quit.

5. Evaluate the groups themselves.

Some groups become toxic. They started with noble purpose, but got hijacked by the worst personalities inside the organization. Sometimes those people tarnish or destroy the group's reputation. You don't want to be painted with that same brush. If your group is known for terrible behavior and has an awful reputation, then you need to leave the group—even if it had a great reputation once upon a time.

6. Remember that loyalty has a price, and is sometimes misplaced.

Your first loyalty should be to yourself, your family, your business and your beliefs. The groups you join may have your loyalty only if those groups do not, in any way, interfere with those four things. The moment those groups do interfere, then you need to leave the group.

7. Limit the number of groups you belong to and/or the number of hours per week you spend in your various groups.

For example, I know a lot of writers who belong to a dozen writers' organizations and who never miss a meeting, but haven't written a word in years. Those writers have their priorities in the wrong place.

I suspect the same thing happens in other organizations. I do know that a few organizations I belonged to when I had other professions used those types of people mercilessly, running them ragged because they were the only ones who had time to work for the organization. Every other member of the organization did paying work that took time away from the organization—which is as it should be.

8. If you joined a group to network, then network.

Talk to the other members of the group. Find out who they are, what their interests are, what they do in their own businesses, what their spouses do, and what their hobbies are. If you want them to do you a favor, make sure you do favors in return. Be nice, be polite, and be reliable.

9. Remember that a group is only as good as its members.

If you don't like the other people who belong to the group, ask yourself why you belong. If you think highly of them, then stay and try to be worthy of their respect.

Groups can be extremely beneficial to your freelance career. They can also destroy it. The key is to find the balance. Figure out which groups will benefit you, and which groups will harm you—and realize that next year, some of the groups that benefited you might harm you and vice versa.

Be smart and (this part is a do-as-I-say, not-as-I-do) be politic. If you're all of these things, then you should have pretty smooth sailing in any group that you choose to join.

Chapter Thirty-four
Networking Online

I would have missed the topic of networking entirely if I hadn't decided to write this non-fiction how-to on my blog. Even if I had hit upon the topic somehow, I wouldn't have added much of the wonderful advice found in the comments section, particularly the advice from people who actually know how to network. (You can still find the comments at kristinekathrynrusch.com.)

One of my favorite comments came from Kevin J. Anderson in reference to that science fiction convention he dragged me to in 1980. He thought I had it together back when we were beginning writers; I *knew* he had. Both of us were doing the best we could and putting our best faces to the world. Even though we were best friends, we managed to keep our anxieties to ourselves, and use each other's presence to help us through our difficult first conventions.

I think we stumbled on an excellent formula that I'm sure most other convention-goers have stumbled upon as well.

I saved the most difficult networking topic for last because I feel insecure about my abilities to write about it. Even though I have had an e-mail address for more than fifteen years, and even though I was online as early as 1990, I still feel like a newbie in the field of social media. In preparation for becoming active online, I started observing others who I thought had an effective online presence. There's a lot to online networking, some of which I'm just beginning to understand.

While we all understand how to network in person—whether or not we're capable of doing it—networking online is a new and different animal. And yet, in some ways, it has some of the same rules as networking in person.

Networking online requires observation, just as it does in person. So to network well, you need to know what works.

Since I feel so new to this topic, I figured I'd better get some assistance. I knew there would be areas I would miss. So back in February, as I started on the networking topic, I asked anyone reading this blog to tell me how they use social media. Writer Ryan Viergutz responded immediately, and I'm going to share his insights first because they'll put everyone else's comments in context.

Ryan is just beginning his freelance career. He's still in the early phase, so he's gathering information—and he's using the internet to do so. Initially he wrote, "I don't know firsthand, but I do see a swarm of musicians on MySpace all the time. They show tracks and it probably helps. Facebook I don't get at all, but Twitter is bizarre and unique. It's a great source of news if you're wary who you follow!"

Before I go on, let me second Ryan's Twitter enthusiasm. As a former journalist, used to taking in news from a hundred different sources and distilling it into something I can use, I adore Twitter. It replicates that feeling of being in a newsroom for me—part gossip, part fact, part lunacy. I leave TweetDeck, a Twitter filtering program, open as I do my e-mail and constantly go back and forth between one and the other. Because of Twitter, I'm often ahead of the major news outlets on the news of the day (I love that feeling) and I'm keeping track of friends as if we live in the same town. I use Twitter to make announcements, sure, but I also use it to forward information I find interesting or to comment on a friend's good news. Twitter, more than the other social media programs, truly feels social to me.

Ryan's experience as a social media consumer, however, is much more vast than mine. He writes, "Web forums are astounding, too. The really huge ones, like RPGnet, can be completely overwhelming. You can get sucked in like people who play World of Warcraft. For that matter, WoW and almost any page online is social media, even your blog, and my mind was blown when I realized that. Anything allowing comments can act as one!"

I hadn't really put that together either, although I know that each blog can develop its own community. Every now and then, the combined intimacy and vastness of the internet boggles my mind, and makes me miss the obvious. I'm glad that Ryan pointed that out.

After he had sent me the initial comment, I asked for clarification on the way he uses web forums, and how he follows musicians online.

He wrote, "I'm not sure how much traffic the musicians get through their Myspaces, but they do load tracks and link to other places and build exposure. For a different site, I originally heard one of my favorites, Nightwish, thanks to an AMV on YouTube. People load entire albums up on there, which is funky, but I've found several I would never have heard of any other way. So that says something!"

I too have found a lot of musicians on the internet that I wouldn't have found any other way. In fact, I have an appointment each week with iTunes to check the free material. I don't download all the free music, but I have found a lot of musicians I would never have found otherwise. I particularly like Canción de la Semana, which has introduced me to a lot of music in Spanish I might otherwise have missed. I have also noted that a lot of the songs I downloaded for free, even from unknowns, later climbed the music charts and got a lot of airplay.

I like free on the internet, for a short period of time. I like the way that folks who keep up get freebies which will inspire them to buy other works. When Audible.com asked me if I "minded" giving away *The Disappeared*, the first novel in my Retrieval Artist series, for one week for free, I said, "do it" without hesitation. I got a relieved response. It seems other authors got angry at the request.

Maybe I understood because I consume free materials on the web—when they are legal. (Please don't steal my copyrighted material, folks.) But I never completely understood how important it is to be web-accessible until a few months ago.

I wanted to buy a song by one of my favorite 1970s musicians. I searched iTunes. I searched Amazon. I searched other *legal* download sites. I knew I had some of this guy's songs on my iPod, but I also knew I hadn't bought any of his CDs. (Had some albums back in the day; sold them in a move.)

So I searched for his website. Even though he's a name you'd recognize, he had no website. Nor did his band members. He's mentioned on his label's website, but no downloads available at all, not free and not for purchase.

After all that searching, I went to see where I had gotten his songs for my iPod. I got them from some movie soundtracks I'd purchased and put on the iPod.

I found myself getting angry—*at the musician*—as my odyssey to find his music went on. Which is not what you want your fans to be.

Now, as an artist myself, I know that this may not be his choice. It all depends on the contracts he signed and the agreements he had with his record label.

Many of my novels are not available as e-books yet, and many of them will take years to become available because I sold the e-book rights to my New York publishers more than ten years ago. Those publishers refuse to exercise the e-rights (in other words, make an e-book), and they refuse to return the rights to me so that I can do so.

Imagine my frustration. I want to provide the books to my readers and can't.

But I'm not so sure about the musician. His lack of web presence makes me think he doesn't understand the importance of the new market, and how shopping and information has changed.

I now have an app on my iPhone that will allow me to get the name of any song I hear on the radio and immediately order that song if it's available for download—even if I hear that song at 2:37 a.m. Brick and mortar stores are closed, yet I can have a piece of music that I enjoy with the flick of a button.

Or I can buy a novel.

Or a short story.

The key is finding out about them, which comes back to networking. Which comes back to Ryan's letter.

The last thing he discusses is one of the areas of the internet I don't participate in: web forums.

He writes, "I use web forums maniacally. You can usually surf them without being a member, but a few have private boards like RPGnet's Tangency or administrator boards, where only specific people can go. I found Greg Rucka, one of my favorites, from a thread about spy books. I found Dresden there, too, and Jim Butcher gets insane amounts of love on the place. Word of mouth no fooling! People even post history books there. Roleplayers like unique settings."

Other groups form over different connections. I had the good fortune to watch one of my articles go viral a few months back. A reader pointed out that my article had suddenly become a trending topic on several listserves. The article, one of many I've written for BenBella Books' SmartPop Series, had just gone up on their site as the essay of the week.

I followed as much of the viral trail as I could, learning as I went. Many readers had no idea who I was. Because the article was somewhat political (which is why I'm not giving the title here), many readers assumed I was a journalist or a political blogger, never reading my bio which was attached to the article. But quite a few people posted my sf credentials.

Had I been prepared, had I been savvy at that point, I'd've had one of my novels featured on my website. The article is about comic books as well, and I wrote a romance novel about comic books. If I had been thinking, I could have gotten quite a few readers at that point.

But I hadn't been thinking. It was a live-and-learn situation—as is much of networking.

I'm just starting to get ideas on how to network effectively online. I know what I like: I follow people who are informative and interesting as well as people whose work (in the arts or in the public realm) I admire and/or love.

Because I'm so new at online networking, I asked my readers for assistance on this part of the Guide, and several of you responded. I also asked people who I think are good at networking for their assistance. I asked them two questions:

1. How do you network on the internet?
2. How has it helped/hurt your business?

I got wonderful answers—so many, in fact, that I have probably 10,000 words of material from folks, and that's without any comments from chatty old me.

As I made up my list of people to ask about online networking, I noticed that most of them were either writers or bloggers. That's partly my bent: I don't follow musicians' blogs or artists' blogs, although I do visit their websites. Another reason is that it's easy to make the transition to online networking when you're already writing, as writers do every day. So my list of effective networkers is writer-heavy.

I also noted that politicians and journalists (writers, again) were also very good at online networking, but I decided not to ask them about their online networking habits. As I've mentioned before, I have a strict no-religion and no-politics rule on my blog, just as I do at most social gatherings. Much as I love a good political discussion (as my good friends will attest), I am also savvy enough to realize that not everyone shares my views. I would rather keep you reading my work even though we disagree about health care or financial reform or the party in power rather than lose you to one of my political diatribes.

So I didn't ask journalists from my favorite publications/ stations/programs (some of which might come from a particular political persuasion) to comment. Nor did I ask any politicians to comment either, even though I know a lot of very effective networkers among them. I didn't want you to think I was endorsing them in any way, while I don't mind if you think I'm endorsing the writers/bloggers mentioned below.

The one thing I did notice about everyone I contacted—and I do mean everyone—is that they all responded to me. Most responded faster than I expected; I had 90% of my answers within six hours of sending out the questions. That's impressive. It's even more impressive because I sent out the questions on Sunday afternoon, hoping to get in line for everyone's Monday morning work response. Instead, I had my answers by Sunday night.

The handful of people who took longer to respond e-mailed me, and asked for more time or asked when my deadline was. And a few took longer to respond because of me: I had to contact them via Facebook or Twitter rather than via their preferred e-mail account because I didn't have that account.

Still, I've been writing non-fiction for more than 30 years, and I've never had a 100% response rate before to interview questions. And in the decade-plus that I've been sending questions by e-mail, I've never had such a rapid response. I could have written my article that Sunday night.

That instant response tells me right there why these people are effective networkers. They *responded*, first and foremost, and to a person, they answered my questions.

Part of this chapter initially appeared as a stand-alone post on the blog. After I posted the initial chapter, a few readers expressed concern in private e-mails that I was confusing networking with marketing. But I didn't: as you'll see below, online networking and marketing go hand-in-hand.

I think this is best summed up by Sarah Wendell who, along with Candy Tan, writes a marvelous blog about romance novels called *Smart Bitches, Trashy Books*. Smart Bitch Sarah, as she signed her letter to me, also has her own blog, sbsarah.com.

She wrote, "I network on the internet by talking to people who share my interest or by answering questions from those who are curious. It helps my business, but then, my business is creating a space for conversations about romance novels."

I found her via Twitter, but I found her blog because of a review of a book she and Candy Tan wrote called *Beyond Heaving Bosoms: The Smart Bitches' Guide to Romance Novels*. What I like about Sarah's Tweets are the fact that they maintain the same attitude as her blog, but they also provide a link to the romance community online, since she forwards other people's tweets (called retweeting, for those of you not on Twitter) and she often has links to good blog posts elsewhere.

In other words, her networking isn't just me, me, me. It's useful and fascinating and opens doors to other worlds.

As does the networking of everyone else I talked to for this piece. As writer Patrick Alan (patrick-alan.com) mentioned, "Networking online is the same as off. It's about engaging and being engaged. First you have to be present. Then you have to engage. Eventually, someone will engage back."

"I like to think of the social networks as one big ongoing party where there are lots of conversations ebbing and flowing," writes Brenda Cooper, who is a writer, futurist, technology geek, and public speaker (brenda-cooper.com and brenda-cooper.blogspot.com). "Some [conversations] are small talk, some are business, some are deep questions. And just like at a party, I try not to commit social errors—not walk up to strangers and say, 'Buy my book,' or 'Book me for a speech.'"

"The most important things are personality and a point of view—like your mom always said, it's what makes you unique," writes Glenn Hauman, who publishes comicmix.com. "And since it's been reported that 70% of the content read online by under-40-year-olds was written by someone they know—be someone that your readers know, or at least feel like they know."

"The key to doing it well is you have to enjoy it," writes technology journalist and internet marketing consultant Mitch Wagner (copperrobot.com). "You have to appear natural. Nobody's going to listen to what you have to say if you *only* use it as a platform to promote your work, any more than anyone is going to want to listen to you if you go to a party and all you try to do is drum up business.

But if you go to a party and behave pleasantly and people know that you're in business, a couple of them might remember you when they have a need for services like the one you provide."

"I'm not sure if any [of what I do online] is networking," writes bestselling author Neil Gaiman (neilgaiman.com). "I mean, if it is, I never did it to Network. I did it because it was fun, and because writing can be a very lonely profession. It's fun to have people to talk to, fun to have people who talk to you, and great to have people who will answer your questions (even if they're wrong). I also feel that it levels the playing field, which I like."

"I don't specifically set out to 'network,' which sounds like something you'd do for immediate personal gain," writes John DeNardo, who blogs at SFSignal.com. "My goal is simply to connect with like-minded people who also love genre fiction. Ask me what the best part of blogging is and I'll tell you it's the variety of good people you meet. Sure, it's networking on one level, but the motive is—and always has been—about having fun and connecting with others."

Note the theme? The emphasis on socializing, the repetition of the idea of a party—which is one I also floated just this weekend, during our weekly professional writers' lunch. Writer J. Steven York (yorkwriters.com) and I were trying to explain how to use Twitter, and we both mentioned how you discuss things you'd talk about at a party.

That's how social networks feel to me: they're one big party. Although they're parties that you can choose to attend when you feel like going to them, as opposed to scheduled social events that are often connected to a business conference or a family gathering. Then you're on someone else's schedule. With social networking, you set your own schedule.

"Most conversations occur through e-mail these days—you can do that and multitask," writes Lou Anders (louanders.com, louanders.blogspot.com), writer and editorial director at Pyr Books. "Whereas if I have to talk on the phone, all other activity must stop, and what could be a five-minute exchange takes 20 to 30 minutes minimum."

John DeNardo mentions the same multitasking benefit. "In those in-between time-slices (queuing up in a long line, waiting for a movie to start, etc.) is when I find some time to visit social networking sites like Facebook and Twitter."

"I'm pretty disciplined," writes Brenda Cooper. "I check in on the tweet stream regularly, I un-follow people I don't get any value out of (which might just mean they're talking about things I'm not interested in), but I don't immerse myself except for about a half hour in the morning and about a half hour at night. Now that's an hour I could be writing in, and I do think that costs me some output—but writing is like any other business and being good is not enough. It's also being connected."

"Pick one or two services you're most at home with and focus your attention on that," advises Mitch Wagner. "I'm most at home on Twitter, where I'm @MitchWagner. I post there all day, mostly links to articles I find interesting and the occasional dumb joke or observation. People seem to find what I tweet interesting. I have 3,500 followers on Twitter, which isn't a lot, but which seems like a lot to me."

It seems like a lot to me as well, but then, my Twitter follower list hovers around 900 these days. I have more followers on Facebook. But I'm just learning this stuff—and I'm having fun.

Mitch focuses more, and he's good at linking. In fact, when I sent my e-mail, he asked if I minded if he answered the question on his blog, and link to my freelancer's guide. I'll be excerpting from everything he wrote, but if you want to see his answer in its entirety (and in the order in which he wrote it), go to blogs.computerworld.com/wagner.

Mitch writes, "The key to networking on social media is just like networking at a conference or meeting of a professional association: spend a lot of time talking with people, not at that them, and listen and respond to what they have to say."

Bestselling writer Michael A. Stackpole (stormwolf.com) agrees. "A chunk of networking boils down to listening and responding. For example, if I see friends on Facebook are having a birthday, I wish them Happy Birthday. I don't get to respond to everything, but I respond to significant things. I especially respond to questions asked directly which result from a discussion or a post, furthering dialogue."

Or as Brenda Cooper says, "What I try to do is add value to my friends and followers—to tweet out interesting links, to maybe make someone smile. To be honest. To reply or retweet or recommend at least as often as I post."

Michael Stackpole does that as well. "On Twitter and in other social media, redistributing contributions by friends also helps, since friends notice and others get the benefit of their wisdom."

Or as Mitch Wagner says, "Think more about how you can help other people than about how they can help you. You'll get more from your networking efforts if you think about helping others than if you think about helping yourself. It's a Zen thing."

My study of these fine folks' networking ability continued after some of the above appeared as its own post. I posted the *Freelancer's Guide* late on Wednesday night—about midnight or so Pacific Time. It was too late to tweet that the *Guide* was up (no offense to the Australian readers) and the wrong time to post on Facebook or on my various listserves. So I waited to announce the new Guide until I got online the following morning.

By the time I logged on the next day, I found that half of the people I had quoted in the *Guide* had not only figured out the *Guide* was up, they had also tweeted about their participation *and* in most cases, they had also written a small post on their own blogs about the *Guide*.

Whoa. That's impressive. And impressively fast. The internet—not bound by time or tides—allowed them to respond when they saw the post, long before I had contacted them. In the case of the regular bloggers (who were the ones who responded quickly), I have a hunch they have their blogs set up to accept pingbacks, which are notifications that someone has linked to their blogs (for lack of a better definition), followed the pingback, and saw the post.

But still, impressive. I often follow pingbacks to my blog, but I usually don't have the time to write a short post about them. (Or maybe I don't make the time. Hmmm. More learning here.)

When it comes to internet networking, everything does move at light speed—rather like a real time conversation. But unlike a real time conversation, the back-and-forth remains on the internet for a long, long time. (I hesitate to say "forever" because I am a science fiction writer, and therefore am quite aware that nothing lasts forever.)

Writing about online networking has helped me in some respects. I realized that I automatically do a few things right. I also realized that I'm more experienced at online networking than I thought. Like everyone else, I tumbled into the online community (several of them, in fact) and accidentally used it to build a platform. While I've come late to some parts of the game (blogging, Twitter,

Facebook), I've had a website for nearly fifteen years and I've been on listserves and e-mail networking lists since the early 1990s.

Many of the people I interviewed for this part of the Guide have similar experiences.

Neil Gaiman (who, when asked for a description of what he does, wrote, "I write books and stories and things") says he got his online start on CompuServe in the late 1980s when he still lived in the United Kingdom.

"I was on the comics, SF, and writing boards," he writes. "Then when I moved to the U.S. in 92 I started using GEnie, which I used until it died a few years later. In the late 90s I used the Well as a forum/platform, then started my own blog in 2001. I started twittering about 14 months ago, after resisting it for a while, and a couple of months ago I got tired of explaining that I had nothing to do with the Neil Gaiman Facebook page, and took over the Neil Gaiman Facebook page too."

Mitch Wagner started his online presence in much the same way as Neil.

"I very much enjoy conversation over Internet text," Mitch writes. "I find it gratifying. I became active on Usenet and the Genie online service in 1989 and just stuck with it, until sometime in this century someone slapped a label 'social media' on the activity and it became mainstream, with participation from politicians and TV and movies stars as well as just us nerds."

After I tweeted about the online part of the *Guide*, writer and editor Cat Rambo (kittywumpus.net) sent me a link to her excellent article called "The Networks Around Us." (sfwa.org/2010/01/social-media/) In that article, she gives a history of the rise of social media. Even though she has given me permission to quote from the article (excellent networking, folks), you are better off using your mouse and clicking on the link. She does a much better job of explaining the rise of social media that both Neil and Mitch refer to above than I ever could.

For those of you too lazy to click, however, let me give you a few salient points: She found a Consumer Research Center study that says 43% of online users visited social networking sites in 2009, up 16% from 2008. I'm sure in the time since her article was published, that number has increased even more.

Cat believes—and I think she's right—that cell phones are what has made the difference. Now that you can access the internet on your phone, you can check e-mail, search social media sites, Tweet, or easily post a newly taken photo on Facebook.

Still, the internet is full of something I call "the noise." So much is happening online that no one can keep track of it all. Rising above "the noise" takes a special project or a confluence of events or maybe just a cute cat playing the piano. (You know who you are, YouTube.) Justin Bieber and Susan Boyle both became international celebrities because of the internet—YouTube in particular—but I'll wager there are a few of you reading this who have not heard of one or the other of them.

The internet makes it possible to specialize, and to spend your entire online life in one particular area, ignoring all others. Programs and apps facilitate this. For example, I use TweetDeck on both my iPhone and on my laptop to access Twitter. Without TweetDeck, Twitter would be impossible for me. But TweetDeck lets me separate the people I follow into various categories—friends, publishing, writers, news, etc. I still don't see everything in my own categories, but I see more than I would if I just followed the stream.

I'm sure that over time, more and more programs and apps will become available that will streamline things even more. Just today, I noticed that there's an iPhone app which will organize everything that I experience on a trip so that I can easily blog about it or send it to my friends via e-mail. And I mean *everything*, from my GPS locations (you really want to know where I walked on my journey?) to my hotels and meals to my photographs. And honestly, if I decide to blog about an upcoming trip, I might download the app to keep everything organized in one place.

But while that organizes information for *me*, it doesn't help you thread your way through the various social media. Again, let me point you to Cat's article, because she separates out the various online sources, from LinkedIn to MySpace, and discusses what they are used for. Remember Mitch's advice: pick the sites that you're most comfortable with, and use them.

Everyone I asked seems to use the various sites differently. Some do it haphazardly, doing whatever works for them without a lot of analysis, while others figure out what's best given their limited time resources.

Brenda Cooper is quite organized about her social networking. "I have a blog (associated with my website), three Twitter accounts (I am a technology professional in government, so I have one account for that personality, I have my own personal Twitter account with my real name, and I am one of many futurists who Twitter occasionally on the joint account 'futurefeed.'), a LinkedIn account, and a regular Facebook page (no fan page so far). I have some things I'm not really using well yet like a YouTube channel."

But she admits that she uses some technologies more than others.

"I spend more time on Twitter than anywhere else, followed by Facebook," she writes. "I pretty freely mix the science fiction writer and the technology geek and the futurist and the dog lover. I figure what I'm marketing is me, and that's me—a pretty wide-ranging person with eclectic interests."

Patrick Alan isn't quite as technical about his approach, although he's very aware of the networking potential.

"I have a blog solely for internet networking," he writes. "I'm not promoting anything because I have nothing to promote. The thing is, it's me online. I comment on forums and blogs. I Twitter. It's an opportunity for people who my comments have amused or annoyed to go find out who I claim to be. The most important page on my website is the 'About' page."

John DeNardo is quite creative about how he uses the internet to network.

"The problem for me (as blogging is not my day job) is finding the *time* to network after the all-consuming task of feeding the blog is done," he writes. "What has evolved over time is a mixture of networking while providing content. For example, our Mind Meld roundtable interviews provide our most consistently popular content, and they are also a great excuse for me to contact folks (authors, fans, actors, producers, scientists) out of the blue. Also, folks will contact me out of the blue with a tidbit suggestion or to say thanks for an unsolicited plug. The connections made in these cases are nice side-effects to the main task of providing content."

Carolyn, who runs the blog Bookchickcity.com, says, "I network by using Twitter and Facebook mostly. I use Twitter for publicising posts on my blog as well as communicating with other book bloggers."

And in the lovely charm that is the internet, the only way you can tell that Carolyn's blog is based in England is that she spells things differently than I do (but still correctly, I might add).

Glenn Hauman runs an e-mail list that includes a ton of professionals in various entertainment industries from all over the world. (It has been running since the early 1990s, and in the beginning, most everyone was just starting in their industries.) But he does a lot more, even though he writes,

"I don't do as much as I'd like to; too many things get in the way. But I always try to get in a few tweets in a day, at least one blog post a day if not five."

Which sounds like a lot to me. Five posts in one day? I can barely manage a few a week.

He adds, "For me, it's a blog with an RSS feed, Twitter, and some Facebook. And a widget from Widgetbox.com. And posting on other web sites, being part of the community."

Community is also important to Michael Stackpole, although he doesn't use the word. He writes,

"I network on the internet in several ways. First, I maintain a website and blog regularly about fiction, entertainment, writing, life and I use the blog to provide samples of stories. The idea is to establish myself as being entertaining, since entertainment is what I do. Second, I use Twitter, Facebook and Myspace (which are all linked) to get my blog further out there, and to interact with my various constituencies."

But that isn't all Mike does.

"I participate in a few listserves," he adds, "and have organized some projects among peers. Being the motive force on a project that helps others earns a lot of good will. Folks return favors, which is always useful."

So far, so familiar to me. But Mike has ventured into an area that I'm not technologically able to follow in at the moment. (I have to upgrade a computer before I can do so—and honestly, I can hardly wait.)

"Finally," Mike writes, "I use podcasting and Second Life as audio vectors to reach folks. Podcasts can go into MP3 players, so folks can hear me even when they're not at their computers. Second Life allows me to do live readings and classes for an international audience. All of these opportunities allow folks to become invested in my success, which is rather critical if one is to succeed."

Mike isn't alone in using secondlife.com. Mitch Wagner uses it as well.

He writes, "Second Life is where I do interviews for my podcast Copper Robot. I like the community there, and the crazy 3D visual effects. We have a good bunch of people who come to the show regularly and make smart comments and ask intelligent questions. Copper Robot is also available as a podcast."

He's also active on Twitter, which he says he prefers. But, he adds, "Facebook is a close second for me. I try to keep my friends list on Facebook to people I know and like, either in real life or by reputation. I use Yakket, a Facebook app that echoes my Twitter updates to Facebook. I have Yakket set to exclude any update that contains a URL. I found Facebook users aren't as tolerant of the constant stream of links as people on Twitter are."

As Cat Rambo points out in her article, each social media site is different, and Mitch seems to understand what he wants from each.

"I use my personal blog," he writes, "mostly as a feed of articles I've published elsewhere, as well as the occasional professional announcement or—very rarely—a personal post. I'm finding it more rewarding to post on other people's sites rather than try to build an audience for my own blog."

And finally, he uses a network I'm just beginning to understand: LinkedIn. He writes, "I use LinkedIn as an extended business card or resume. I've never found the kind of community on LinkedIn that I get from other social media."

If you take anything from this series of advice from good networkers, take this: Do what feels right for you. Doing it because you feel you have to or because you heard that everyone else is doing it will seem phony. Do what you enjoy.

Because the key to effective networking is to have fun. The first word for online networking is "party"—social media is like a big cocktail party and it's the amusing person who gets remembered. But the second word is "community." If you're there and interesting and enjoying yourself, even if you're relatively quiet or not the most noticeable raconteur, you'll find a group of like-minded people to spend time with.

Now to the all-important question: Is online networking worthwhile for the freelancer?

You'd think, since I devoted so much space to it, that online networking is important. And it is. You should understand what it is and how it functions before making the decision for your business. But the decision as to whether or not to use online networking should be *yours*, and not anyone else's.

One of the questions I asked my panel of online networking experts was this:

1. How has online networking helped/hurt your business?

Because I asked it as a binary question, most everyone answered it that way. The most succinct answer to this question came from writer and Pyr editor, Lou Anders.

He writes, "I'd say the internet is more than essential. Since I'm located in Alabama and my employers are in upstate New York, there is no business without the net. Beyond that, my writers are all over the country and the world. But really, if you're asking about networking, it's the same. The internet allows for close relationships with contacts in other countries that never would have been possible ten years ago. I'm pretty (in)famous at work for doing most of my job via an iPhone. Not sure I'm answering this except to say—internet, positive."

I've had similar experiences. As someone who started her freelance writing career thirty years ago, I find the internet and the quick access invaluable. Let me give you a few examples. The first is this chapter. In the 1980s when I wrote non-fiction full time, I spent much of my time on the telephone. My long distance bills were ugly. The only communication I had with my out-of-town editors was by snail mail, unless they picked up the phone to call me. The interviews I did for this chapter would simply not have been possible thirty years ago—especially not on a project that might or might not pay me this week.

Secondly, I made my first international sales twenty years ago. All of my communication with my foreign editors was via fax and snail mail. There was no talk of having me promote my British books because I would have had to go to England to do so.

In June, the British edition of my novel, *Hitler's Angel*, appeared from John Blake Publishers in their Max Crime line. It'll also be the first paperback appearance of the novel in English. I talked to British bloggers and did quite a bit of promotion on my site— something inconceivable at the start of my fiction career.

Will it get me more sales? Absolutely. In Great Britain? I don't know. But here in the States, I know of many readers who have asked about the book and are happy to hear that a new edition is coming out.

Neil Gaiman uses the internet as I do (only more effectively). He writes, "I think having an online presence is great for an author, mostly because you can tell people when you have something new coming out. You aren't at the mercy of advertising or luck. You can tell millions of people yourself."

But he adds a warning.

"Like anything that happens online," he writes, "it can be a time sink."

It can be and is. And that's part of the analysis that you, the freelancer, have to make. You'll need to do a cost-benefit analysis about your time.

Freelancer writer Dave Creek (davecreek.net/blog), who supplements his fiction writing by working as a web producer for a TV station in Louisville, Kentucky, e-mailed me with some great advice for promoting my blog. Since I was familiar with his writing from *Analog*, I asked him what he did to promote his own writing.

He answered, "I'm afraid my experience in online networking isn't much help. I have a website, a professional Facebook site, I'm on Twitter, and I have a blog. But nothing much comes of them."

The reason? Time.

He writes, "A problem as a part-timer is that I spend 40+ hours, plus commute, at a 'real' job every week. I have maybe an hour or so a day to write. A day spent writing a blog posting or tweeting or anything else is often a day I don't spend on a new story. I'd rather write the story."

This is precisely the kind of cost-benefit analysis that I mentioned above. Given Dave's limited time, he's better off *doing the work* instead of networking. It seems like good old common sense, but not everyone understands this.

Still, Dave isn't about to give up his blog.

"All the same," he writes, "I'm glad I have those presences in place, and I have to take it on faith that continuing to reach out may let me 'make my own luck' sometime."

Exactly. As mentioned so many times in the networking chapters—not just by me, but by others as well—you never know which casual contact will turn into a profitable business relationship.

Everyone who networks does some form of the time cost-benefit analysis—or should. What works for one individual might not work for another.

Different businesses have different needs as well. I think writers can survive without much of a web presence. What matters is the story itself. Retail stores who cater locally might benefit from a web presence, but it's not necessary. And too much information from an attorney online would be counterproductive to a business that has confidentiality at its core.

Glenn Hauman noted that his time is limited. However, he writes, "The Internet *is* my business. We publish electronically at comicmix.com, so we have to be here."

Being online is part of his job. But that's not all that factors into his online networking calculations.

"More to the point," he adds, "[the Internet] is where the readers are heading. Wishing for newsstand sales to come back—well, first you have to wish for newsstands to come back. The good news is the barrier to entry is lower, so you can get out there. The bad news is the barrier to entry is lower, so you're competing with everyone else on the Internet for attention."

While his second point might—and has—discouraged some people, it doesn't discourage Glenn.

"You don't need the world's attention," he writes. "Heck, having the attention of 5,000 dedicated people can be far, far more than enough."

I've noticed that with the *Freelancer's Guide*. My readership has grown steadily and it's more constant than a readership I would get from a non-fiction title, thrown into the mix of thousands of other non-fiction titles, with a month of shelf life. Another positive? A large number of my *Guide* readers picked up my fiction for the first time, which is an unexpected perk. And finally, I've made a lot of contacts and revived the part of my non-fiction career that I enjoyed. I'm doing more articles than I was, about topics that I love. All unexpected, and all quite fun.

Online networking has benefited Carolyn at BookChickCity as well. She writes, "I think both Twitter and Facebook have helped my blog in so much as it lets others know I have a new post up, etc. It's also a great way to let my readers and followers know if I have any author guests. I don't think as a fairly new blogger that my blog would have been as successful as quickly if it wasn't for the use of these other online mediums."

John DeNardo says that online networking helps bloggers.

"Professional bloggers will tell you that Networking is essential to building a successful blog—and they're right," he writes. "That's a big part of the story, immediately on the heels of the even-more-important Providing Valuable Content. Blog networking consists of visiting similarly themed sites, leaving comments, making yourself known, etc. It also means joining social networks like Facebook and Twitter.

"Is there a negative to networking? Only if you are disrespectful or otherwise troublesome to those you interface with. Because then instead of making contacts, you're making enemies. And who wants to do that?"

Politeness has been a theme throughout the networking chapters. In fact, I think it might be the Golden Rule of Networking, based on all the comments I've gotten from others. It's very easy to get the reputation as an unreasonable hothead online, primarily because things you can say with a smile in person often sound nasty online. (That was my biggest worry when I increased my online presence; I'm blunt and sarcastic by nature, and I was afraid of alienating my readers simply by being myself. I don't know if it's happened, but I've strived to avoid it as much as I can.)

For example, on a private listserve that I share with other professionals in the business, I mentioned a positive comment another professional had received from an editor of an online publication. I wanted to point out the compliment to my friend. She responded with shock, and said that the online editor had never said a kind word about her before and had, in fact, been actively nasty to her (something I hadn't known). Others responded as well with the same experience. I'd had a similar experience with the online editor—he'd made a comment on one of my articles elsewhere online that dripped with venom, and I had wondered what I had done to offend him. Turned out that was his main online persona—one that alienated instead of helped him grow his online business.

If I were advising him, I'd tell him to ease back on the networking, since it was having the opposite effect than desired. But I'm not advising him (and am actually not sure I want to meet him in person).

So you should also be aware in online networking, as in personal interactions, how you come across to others, and whether or not you're going to be an effective networker.

Because I asked people I thought were effective at networking to help me with this topic, I received a lot of positive comments about online networking. Some of the benefits people listed were a bit of a surprise, but made sense after I thought about them.

Brenda Cooper writes that online networking gives her four general and ongoing benefits:

"1. I meet new people.

"2. I stay in touch with my friends—for example, I like to hear what you and Dean are up to—it makes me feel like we're still friends even though we don't have much face-to-face interaction at all.

"3. I learn stuff. Other people are out there adding value, too, and I benefit from that. I find new markets, I get pointed to interesting new articles, and I've even sold a few stories because of interactions started on Twitter. My monthly column at Futurismic started because I was introduced to Jeremiah Tolbert who introduced me to Paul Graham Raven—all online. I've not ever met either of them. I love Starship Sofa, and I've been a guest on the associated podcast Sofanauts for the same reason—through an introduction from Jeremy and ongoing Twitter interactions with Tony C. Smith.

"4. I also follow people who I think are good at this and try to learn from them. I follow Neil Gaiman, and Jay Lake, and Tobias Bucknell and others. Most of these people are also my friends (I don't know Neil), but they're good at this in their own ways and have more followers than I do."

She concludes with, "I don't think it has ever hurt me."

So far as I can tell, she's right.

Like Brenda, Mitch Wagner has had some tangible benefits from online networking.

"When I was laid off in December of 2009," he writes, "I announced it on Twitter and my blog (making sure it was OK with my soon-to-be former employers, who I expected would soon be clients). Within a day or so of announcing my availability, I had several offers of work, and within a month I had lined up two really sweet jobs, blogging at Computerworld where I write the Tool Talk blog as well as occasional features, and as Internet marketing director at Palisade Systems which makes an Internet security solution for business. I believe both of those clients found out about my availability over social networks. One of them contacted me; I think the other one is someone I called first, but he'd already been planning to reach me because he heard I was available."

That's how we all dream online networking should work. We make our presence known and we get a positive response, one that will help our business in good ways. Often, however, we have no idea whether or not the networking helped at all.

As writer Patrick Alan writes, "That's the thing about networking. Sometimes you use it, but have no idea if it does anything. It's like pressing the sidewalk button. You press it, but then wait. And you don't know if it's still on the same cycle and would have turned to 'walk' anyway or if pushing the button sped anything up."

Networking is networking is networking, whether it happens online or in person. You need to do it occasionally, but do it too much and you're not tending to the actual work of your business. Ultimately the best use of networking is the one that benefits *you*. And only you can determine what that is.

Chapter Thirty-five
Professional Jealousy

Over the course of writing the *Guide* on my blog, I asked people to submit topics I needed to cover. Only once did I get a request that I wasn't sure I'd write about. And that was on professional jealousy.

I wrote back to the woman who made the suggestion and said I wasn't sure I had anything useful to say on the subject. But I did put it on my subject list, and surprise, surprise (at least to me) the topic has risen to the forefront of my brain.

One reason, I think, is the entertainment news: I've been following the Jay Leno/Conan O'Brien *Tonight Show* mess with rather too much interest. I like to tell myself it's because I'm curious about the contracts and the negotiations—and I am—but I also think there's a bit of gossip-girl, train-wreck-watching going on as well. I predicted Conan's failure in the 11:30 p.m. slot to anyone who would listen, but I had no opinion on Leno's move to 10:00 p.m. except a slight feeling of disappointment, since I like scripted material.

Other than that, I have no personal involvement. I am watching the negotiations, and honestly, I think Conan is one of the best negotiators in the biz. He got *The Tonight Show* on a negotiation several years ago when Leno wasn't even considering retiring, and now Conan's done what I've told you all to do in negotiation if you can: he's holding firm to his position. If he doesn't get what he wants, he'll walk. (Note who delivered Conan's demands to NBC? It wasn't his people. Oh, they might have sent it. But he's the one who handwrote it, so everyone knew this was Conan talking and not his representatives. Savvy, savvy stuff.) (Added later: Conan held firm to his position, but he ended up walking. The jury's still out on whether

355

his new show will do well, but the ratings went back up on *The Tonight Show* with Leno back at the helm.)

Anyway, as I thought about this whole mess, I realized that professional jealousy may have had something to do with it. Leno got *The Tonight Show* after Carson retired. Conan wanted the berth, and realized he probably wouldn't get it, since he and Leno are closer in age than, say, Leno and Carson. So Conan, who had a successful talk show at 12:30 a.m., looked at *The Tonight Show* and made a play for it.

Which is now biting him in the ass.

Do I know that professional jealousy was involved? No. I'm not that into the gossip rags. But I have a hunch. So let's talk professional jealousy and its uses, if any.

First, let me be clear about the reasons I initially declined to cover this topic. I think jealousy is one of the most destructive emotions in the world. I think you can attribute more horrible things to jealousy than you can to most other emotions, including anger. I see nothing positive about jealousy. I've watched it ruin friendships, marriages, and professional relationships. I've watched it destroy careers. I know of cases where jealousy has led to actual physical harm, including murder.

I also know that certain schools of thought encourage jealousy in professional situations, thinking that jealousy makes someone more ambitious or more effective. I know of a few university programs—including a few in law and medicine—that thrive on pitting the students against each other, inflaming jealous reactions in the hopes of making the students rise higher.

I can't think of any process more dysfunctional than that.

Yet…

Jealousy happens. For some people, especially the insecure, jealousy happens a lot. They have developed a jealous mindset, one that minimizes their responsibility in any situation. People who can't take responsibility for their own mistakes and shortcomings are often among the most jealous people we all know.

But, like all emotions, jealousy strikes every single one of us, from the most controlled to the most emotionally secure. It surprises us, overtakes us, and makes us petty.

And it can, if it goes unchecked, become the most destructive thing in our lives.

So how do we avoid being jealous? We can't, not really. But we can avoid letting it take over our lives.

First we need to know what it is that's making us jealous. Is it a friend's natural beauty? Is it someone else's excellent relationship? Has someone else "taken" the person that we love?

All of those are personal jealousies, ones that we're familiar with. But professional jealousy happens as well—someone else has a better timeslot or a more prestigious gig; they have more customers; they're *New York Times* bestsellers; their business constantly makes money; they have better offices…on and on and on.

But jealousy isn't about "them." It's about you. What you want. What you're missing. And it's also about your attitude.

We'll get to the attitude in a minute. You can find the key to what you want and what you're missing once you figure out what's making you jealous. You might think you're jealous of your friend's lovely store, when really, you're jealous of your friend's thriving business—the one that allowed her to remodel her store in such a gorgeous fashion.

Figure out what it is that you are truly jealous of, and you have the key to your own heart.

Then, *figure out how the person you're jealous of got that thing that makes you jealous.* Here are the unacceptable answers in this category: Oh, she's more talented than I am. Oh, she's prettier than I am. Oh, she's luckier than I am. Oh, she's more devious than I am.

Those comparisons do no one any good. You have to step out of your emotional framework which is (sorry) "I want what you have and I can't have it. Waaa!" and become a full-fledged professional. You have to calm down and look at the other person's situation dispassionately.

Did your friend get her lovely store (and the money to remodel it) from hard work? Did she have an inheritance? Did she overspend? What is she doing that you're not doing?

You need to see the reality of the situation before you can go any farther in your analysis. It might look like your friend's lovely store is successful, but in reality, she spent too much money and she may hasten the store's decline. A truly jealous person would think that's just desserts, but that's taking the wrong lesson from someone else's mistake.

The lesson you should take from that is to spend within your means.

If someone truly has achieved success, and you have not, then you have to analyze what that person did right. You have to be fair and open-minded about it.

A dear friend of mine can talk his way into any circumstance. He says he's the luckiest person in the world because he creates his own luck—and he does. He comes up with ideas, approaches people with a full-fledged business plan, and convinces them to let him do the bulk of the work for a hefty fee.

I'm not really the jealous type—I can count the number of times I've been jealous on one hand—but I am insecure. And his aggressive business practices made me feel extremely inadequate for years. I didn't do those things, and my career went in a different direction because of it.

Only when I reached my thirties did I realize that I didn't want to have his kind of career. Being aggressive is difficult for me and—here's the key part—when I am aggressive, I don't value the result. I want to get jobs or work based on merit, not on my ability to talk my way into a situation.

With that realization came another: if my friend's work lacked merit, it didn't matter how aggressive he was; no one would have hired him. If I were a different person, that realization would have allowed me to become more aggressive in my business dealings. But I am who I am. I like my career as it is, and I have trouble tooting my own horn (as my mother would have said). I do as much as I need to and no more.

All of those realizations have been important to my career. I realized I don't have to be uncomfortable to be successful. I also realized I can define success on my own terms.

But I wouldn't have been able to do that without my own discomfort at my friend's highly successful methods.

Fair and open-minded is the key. If you can't be open-minded about someone else's success, then you need help. Usually the help is minor—you can ask for help assessing what the successful person did right.

For example, when Dean and I teach professional writers who have stalled in their careers, we often run into professional jealousy. Not against us (although, believe me, we've been victims of other people's jealousy in the past), but against *New York Times* bestsellers.

My favorite comment—and I hear it each workshop—is this one: "I don't read Stephen King (or Nora Roberts or Clive Cussler or J.K. Rowling) because they write crap."

"How do you know they write crap if you don't read them?" I'll ask.

"Because they're on the bestseller list," comes the response.

This, usually, from someone who wants a successful writing career—one they often define as being on the bestseller list.

Sometimes this prejudice against bestselling authors comes from a writer's schooling. Often, though, this prejudice against bestsellers *from someone who wants to be one* is pure professional jealousy.

My job as a teacher, then, is to break down the jealous response, force the writer to look at the bestseller's work and see what that bestseller is doing right. One-time bestsellers, people who only have one book on the list and never repeat, may be accidental bestsellers, because of marketing, timing, or the popularity of the topic. But repeat bestsellers are on the bestseller list because readers like their work. And for writers, the only way to measure success is in how many readers like our work.

There are a lot of writers on the bestseller list whose work I don't like. That's personal taste. But if you ask me what they're doing right, I can tell you. And I'll be honest here: I won't say they're on the list because they're lucky or they got a good advertising budget or because readers are stupid. Chances are, writers are on the list because they tell stories that readers want to read.

If I can't figure out what makes a bestseller work, then I ask the fans of that writer. Fans will always tell you what they like about a book, with great enthusiasm and a desire to share.

Asking what successful people are doing right, asking not the successful person, but their fans or readers or clients, is the best way you can understand what's working.

If you do all that, and you still have trouble understanding why that person is successful—(yeah, they sure duped a lot of people), then the problem is deeper. You have other, personal issues that are causing the jealousy. You'll need to get professional help resolving the negative emotion.

Because jealousy will eat you alive.

Let me say from experience that it's unpleasant in the extreme to be on the other side of someone else's jealousy. I used the phrase "victims of someone's jealousy" on purpose, above. Because jealousy is irrational and harmful and—to the object of the jealousy—something that seems to come out of the blue.

Often the jealous person does everything she can to tear down the person she's jealous of. And if the jealous person simply puts all her energy into her own life and her own career instead of going after someone's livelihood and career, she'd be a lot more successful.

Jealousy is a warning sign that something is seriously wrong in your own life. You can't change the person you're jealous of. You can learn from them. You can try to understand them.

In other words, you can focus on improving yourself.

If you take responsibility for your own situation, your jealousy will decrease—maybe even go away.

When you're feeling jealous of someone else, realize that you're experiencing one of the most destructive emotions humans have. You need to resolve that jealousy.

You need to resolve it. You need to step beyond it, learn from it, and improve your own life.

Never use professional jealousy to tear down someone else.

Or you might end up in the kind of mess NBC is in at the moment. If Conan O'Brien had seen how successful he really was back in 2004 when he negotiated the disastrous contract that started this mess, he wouldn't be about to lose his dream right now. If he had waited until Leno retired, he might have gotten offered the gig.

Or he might have realized, as I did with my friend, that he was already doing what he did best.

You can't live someone else's life. You can't have someone else's career. You'll only have yours, and it will never be exactly what you expect or even dreamed of.

Learn to accept where you're at. If you're not happy there, figure out how *you* have to change to improve your situation. Not what others need to do for you or how others have cheated you. Figure out what you can do.

Take responsibility, and you will have fewer moments of jealousy.

I promise.

Chapter Thirty-six
Surviving Someone Else's Jealousy

About five minutes after I posted the chapter on professional jealousy, I got back-to-back e-mails from regular readers of the *Guide*, asking me how to deal with being a victim of professional jealousy. Both letters had poignant stories of betrayal and utter nastiness on the part of the jealous person, and sadly, both e-mails were familiar because I've been through that, and worse.

I got more e-mails like that throughout the week, as well as some good comments in the comments section. On Twitter, someone asked me if jealousy was wrong, but envy was okay because envy wasn't as personal. That tinged me a bit, but I wasn't sure why, so I asked him to explain. (He did, kinda, but honestly, it's hard in 140 characters.)

He was wrestling with the idea that sometimes someone else's success spurs you on. Sometimes it's because that other person seems like a regular person to you (not a Writer or a Superstar, but a wannabe made good), and that serves as inspiration. And I have to admit, I've experienced that. I've looked at someone else's success as inspiration, partly because I believed I was as good at the chosen task or better than that other person.

The difference has always been that the other person tried to succeed in their chosen field, and I hadn't. That other person led me to try when I hadn't had the courage to try before. I still think envy is the wrong word here—and I'll expand on that in a moment—but I have a few other points to make first.

A few people wrote on their blogs that envy is necessary. One person told me that jealousy is hardwired and we shouldn't fight it, and I should (basically) stop telling people to avoid it.

He needed to read the chapter again. I recognized that we'll all feel jealous. We just need to put that jealousy to use—and the use should *not* be tearing the object of our jealousy down.

But to the handful of people who flatly said in their blogs or in response to other people's blogs and tweets that jealousy is necessary and that we need to tear down others to build ourselves up, let me say directly: you folks have a serious problem. You need to solve it or it will eat you alive. It's not okay to destroy others in order to succeed.

Oh, you might have some success for a while, but it won't last. And when it ends, you'll be stunned at the amount of hatred that comes your way—hatred that you've earned by destroying (or trying to destroy) the people around you.

I'm going to talk about being on the receiving end of that nastiness in a moment. But first, let's talk about the inspiration thing, because it's subtle and difficult.

I think all of us have looked at someone who has achieved success and said, "If you can do that, I can do that." This is, I think, a healthy reaction if kept private. It's also healthy if you use that person as inspiration.

I do this all the time with exercise. If you read my recommended reading lists on my website, kristinekathrynrusch.com, you know that I read *Runner's World*, and in every issue, *Runner's World* has inspirational stories of people who've overcome great odds to run a marathon or even a 5K. Some of these people have suffered horrible trauma. Others have prosthetics. One recent article was about a blind woman who ran races.

I look at the folks overcoming illness like cancer who run every day, and I think, *if they can run while having chemo and weakness and tremors and surgery, I can run with a headache or when I'm feeling a little cranky or when it's raining*. I'm not trying to tear them down. I'm using them to *inspire* me.

I think that's what a lot of you envy folks meant. I think you're talking about looking at someone who wouldn't logically be someone you'd think would become successful in a certain field and yet who is, and examining what it is that person has done that you haven't done.

That's not envy. That's inspiration. And yes, I agree. It's a good thing.

It's sometimes hard to separate out from the negative emotion. Because that inspiration might have started after a burst of jealousy. Again, see the previous chapter about how to turn jealousy around. The key question is: *what is that person doing that I'm not doing?* And if your answer is always negative—that person is pandering; that person has no talent, just luck; that person bribed her way into that position—then you're jealous. But if you can find what that person has done right, you've found the way from jealousy to inspiration.

When I was twenty and still in college, I met a man who wrote part time for the same organization I wrote for. He was also a non-fiction freelancer. He paid for his apartment, his food, his car, and his clothing out of his non-fiction income. I saw his product at work. He had a great voice and a lot of talent, but he couldn't spell his own name and his manuscripts were almost unreadably sloppy.

I figured if he could succeed in the cutthroat non-fiction world with those messy manuscripts, then I could with my clean manuscripts. I wasn't the wordsmith he was, but I was more professional.

My analysis of his work got me started. I wrote for some of the same places he did, and began to wonder how he funded his lifestyle. I wasn't getting paid enough per article to pay for my apartment and my expenses. Eventually, I moved to larger and larger publications, publications that paid me a month's worth of expenses per article. It wasn't until later that I found out that he had supplemented his income writing term papers for students, and (ahem) dealing cocaine. (It was 1980, after all.)

I didn't take the negative view—that you can never make a living at writing; that you need to deal drugs to make any money at all. Instead, I saw that he was succeeding as a freelancer, getting work published *even when he wasn't trying hard*. And that inspired me even more.

Because I hadn't been trying *at all*.

I had misunderstood how he made the bulk of his income, but my misunderstanding had gotten me off my butt and into my first writing career. And I am very grateful for that.

So yes, use others as inspiration, but don't envy them. Don't tear them down, and don't belittle them or their accomplishments.

It will do neither of you any good.

Every year, Dean and I do a short weekend workshop on becoming a full-time professional writer. We do it for very little money, but we do it because we have knowledge that needs to be shared with the folks out there, from two successful writers, not burned out and bitter ones.

One thing we always, always talk about is this: when you achieve your dream, when you start having success in your chosen field, you will lose friends.

What causes the loss? Jealousy, bitterness, and anger on the friend's part. These people can't be happy for you and your success. Instead, they're upset that they haven't achieved the same level of success at the same time.

It's especially bad for couples. We advise couples who are in the same field to prepare for this long before it happens. Because you'll never have the same degree of success. Someone will always be better off, and that success will go back and forth (provided you're both working to succeed; if only one person works, then only one person will succeed). You have to prepare for that or your relationship will end.

You can prepare for the different degrees of success by talking about all aspects of it, including the pie-in-the-sky aspect—the dream of dreams. What happens if one of you achieves that and the other doesn't? If you've talked about it, you have probably worked out the worst of the problems in advance.

If you think there won't be any problems or if you think you'll deal with it if (when) the time comes, you're in for a heap of trouble.

Once we've warned people that this possibility exists, they do go home and talk to their spouses, their family, and their close friends. That should cover the problem areas, right?

Oh, no. Because you never know where this toxic jealousy will come from.

Let me give you a few personal examples.

1. I interviewed for a prestigious job at the request of the business owner. He interviewed two other people as well. One of those people, a man who had been in the field for thirty years at that point, came away from the interview telling all his friends that he had nailed it, and that he would have the job. The business owner told me (in my interview!) how badly the other man had blown the interview, telling the business owner how his business sucked and how only the other man could save it. (Oops. Don't ever do that, folks.)

Anyway, a month later, when the announcement came that I—a relative newcomer—had gotten the job, the other interviewee was shocked. Then mortified. And then he proceeded to do everything he could to trash me and my work for the entire time I held that job. He actively, hatefully, and spitefully badmouthed me to everyone in our mutual business.

I was appalled. I'd only met him once or twice casually, and the things he said about me were among the worst things anyone had ever said about me in my life. I didn't know what to do, so I consulted some longtime friends, who told me not to do anything.

One of those friends is known for suing people. I was stunned to get that advice from that person.

But my friend turned out to be right.

Because here's the thing: in that other interviewee's thirty-year career, he had done this countless times before. He had actively destroyed the careers of others—successfully, in his early years, and unsuccessfully later on. Why wasn't he successful later on? Because he became known as a spiteful, mean-spirited man who deliberately badmouthed anyone who was more successful than he was. And as time went on, that became most everyone else. He stalled his once-promising career with his nasty mouth.

2. When I quit editing the *Magazine of Fantasy and Science Fiction*, I had a terrible year in public. Because I was no longer perceived to be in a position of power, people felt they could tell me exactly what they thought of me to my face with no reprisals.

Mostly, people made snide comments on panels. But on one particularly memorable afternoon, a woman came up to me after a panel and screamed at me for ten minutes, calling me every single name in the book. I figured it had something to do with my editing. Nope. Turns out she believed she was a better writer than I was, and she deserved "fame" more than I did.

Finally one of the convention security people pulled her out of the room. My other panelists were shaken. I was surprised that the screaming had nothing to do with my editorship (as it had other times, mostly because I rejected someone's story), but with my writing.

I had never met this woman before, although I've seen her since. (She's still unpublished, by the way.) She hates me for my success. I avoid her…for obvious reasons.

With the rise of the internet, you get to see more and more of this bile. Once you have name recognition, people will hate you for something *they perceive* that you've done. Not necessarily something you've done at all. And you will never have met this person (nor will you ever want to).

Sadly, it's one of the prices you pay for success. People will have opinions about you. And sometimes, those opinions are rooted in jealousy.

Honestly, all of these things and the hundred or so more examples that I have (I am not exaggerating) are relatively easy to deal with. They're expected. If you follow the careers of successful people, you know that they deal with stalkers, the unhinged, and the unbelievably jealous. You will get that, even on a local level, especially in a small town. (A friend of mine is dealing with that at the moment; her business is successful and a former friend of hers is going bankrupt. He's attacking her in public because he can't look at her success without seeing his own failure.)

All of that is occasionally frightening, often worrisome, and sometimes laughable. (Another friend of mine overheard himself being described as the floating turd of literature—no matter how many times he got flushed, he still rose to the surface—and he thought that the funniest thing he'd ever heard. I've heard a few gems like that about myself, although none quite as colorful.) But none of it is as painful as the loss of a friend to jealousy.

The worst case that I can write about publicly, without revealing any identities except my own, happened in my last year editing *F&SF* and in the first two years after that. My writing career was really taking off. Dean and I were both making a great deal of money writing and we were being published everywhere.

I had to quit *F&SF* because I no longer had time to do the work. I needed to spend 24/7 on writing. I had to choose between the two careers—editing and writing—and I chose writing.

I was clear about that with my friends and with the field. When I gave my notice to the publisher, I told him that argument and an increase in salary wouldn't help. I made nearly 10 times more as a writer than I made editing, but I spent 30 hours of my 40-hour weeks editing. It was no longer cost effective for me to edit, and he couldn't pay me enough to keep me.

Around that point, six months before my last issue as editor appeared, rumors started about me in New York. I was unreliable. I was crazy. I was impossible to work with. At the same time, casual acquaintances called me to ask about my health or some personal problems that I had confided with only a few very close friends. These acquaintances were concerned for me, and they were kind enough to tell me who had told them of my personal problems. They also added that they didn't think that person was my friend, because that person also started the rumors that were spread around New York.

I had worked in the field long enough that I'd worked with a lot of people in the business. They knew the rumors weren't true. But they were worried that I'd be damaged anyway, particularly since the rumors came from my hometown. They were afraid that others would think the "friend" was in the position to know.

I gathered information, including e-mails and letters. Then I talked to my so-called friend, who told me that I had become too big for my britches (seriously! He used that cliché) and I needed to be taken down a peg. He felt he had to do it *for my own good*.

Needless to say, that was our last conversation. Ever. I was heartbroken. I had liked and trusted this person, and believed us to be very good friends. He had spent three years of our ten-year friendship quietly trying to destroy my reputation.

Why? Because when we met, he was more successful than I was. With several short story sales and one novel sale, he was the expert on publishing. I surpassed him, selling eight novels in one year while editing, and then I won awards. He continued to write, but at his slower pace. And he apparently couldn't deal with my success.

I needed to be taken down a peg.

He was doing it for my own good.

All he managed to do was destroy a friendship and harm his own career. People who had worked with me, people to whom he had badmouthed me, told me years later that from that moment forward, they considered him untrustworthy. They decided they'd do business with him only when he had something so good that it was worth suffering his destructive personality.

To date, most of these people have never, ever, worked with him—and probably will not.

I'm not the only person he has done this to. His behavior hasn't changed over the years. Recently, he did this to an entire science fiction convention because he didn't like its chairman.

As far as I'm concerned, this is the behavior of someone who has gone off the rails. But he continues to function in the real world, making a small living and paying his bills. But that promise of success he had back in the late 1980s? It's gone now—primarily because he has put more energy into destroying others for the past twenty years than he has in improving his craft.

So, how do you handle all of this?

Oh, jeez. If only I had a simple solution for you.

But I'll give you what I know.

If the jealousy is minor or distant, as in those first two instances I described:

1. Have a sense of humor.

You could get mad at being described as a floating turd, but really, seriously, that's just wasting energy. Have a good belly laugh at the stupidity of the commentator, *whom you don't know and probably will never meet,* and move on.

2. Have a good attitude.

It's about them, not you. They just happened to choose you that day to be the target of their own self-loathing. As long as you remember that, you'll be fine.

3. Have someone else read your hate mail.

I stopped having Dean do it when I became editor of *F&SF* because he got angrier than I did. Then I realized that I would've gotten angry if someone had described my husband the way people were describing me. So I had my assistant open the hate mail. However—here's a key point—keep that hate mail. You might need it if things escalate.

4. Don't engage.

Don't answer the hate mail. Don't write a comment on the stupid person's blog. Don't tweet about it. Don't give this person the attention he so obviously craves. And don't let him know that he's gotten to you (if, indeed, he has). Just make a note of his name, add it to your nutball file, and move on.

As a sidebar, the more successful you get, the more you'll need a nutball file and a hate mail file. Keep the stuff, but don't focus on it. I've never had to use mine for anything, but a friend who ended up with a stalker used his to show how the stalker escalated the horrid behavior over time.

And if you don't think jealous people and stalkers have anything in common, then you're quite naïve. Sadly.

5. Move on.

You can't do anything about these people. They exist, they have troubled lives, they're probably miserable. Don't let them make you miserable. Enjoy your life and *invest no energy in them.* None. Take your hands off the keyboard. Now….

But—

If you're suffering from attack from someone you know, someone who is jealous of your success, then you might have to take some serious action.

First you need to protect your heart. Most often— · unfortunately—the people who start these attacks are (were) friends. Or you thought they were friends.

I've only had one friend acknowledge jealousy and get help to overcome it. That friend said some pretty awful things for a while, didn't like the person she'd become, apologized, and then became a true friend.

But out of the dozens of incidences I've gone through since I've had some success, I've only had one friend remain a friend after all of that bile. (And hers wasn't very bad, on the scale of nastiness.)

So take my experience as a cautionary tale. You will lose friends as you become successful. You might not get them back. And that'll be on them, not on you.

Here's what you do when someone you know actively tries to demolish your success.

1. Discuss the problem with them, sometimes using a mediator.

Not another friend, but a therapist or some kind of helping professional (minister, rabbi, counselor). Sometimes people don't realize how toxic they're being. They might quit. Chances are they won't. But they might. Give your friend the chance to step back from her behavior and apologize.

2. If the friend continues to attack, walk away.

Don't actively end the friendship. Just stop calling, stop socializing, and stop interacting. If the friend then asks why you've left, you can tell him about how uncomfortable his behavior has made you.

Most of the time, these people don't ask. Your presence inflames their jealousy. They see you and your success, and it angers them because they haven't got that success. (Usually, they haven't worked for it and don't want to work for it.) So they attack you. If you're not there, they'll find a new target. And they'll be more comfortable with you gone.

3. Take legal action.

I've had a few people actively try to destroy one of my many careers. One person was so active in his attempt to destroy me that a high-powered attorney friend begged me to let him file several lawsuits—one for restraint of trade, one for libel, and a couple others that I no longer remember. Since I didn't want to pursue that career, I didn't want to pursue lawsuits either. But had I stayed in that career, I would have had to defend my career and my reputation in court.

Remember that lawsuits take years, and can be as or more toxic than the behavior that starts the suit. Don't go to the legal option lightly. It will take over your life—and who wants to spend years on that kind of unpleasantness?

Number 2 is your very best option. Walk away. Don't engage.

It's also the hardest option, because you want to fight back. The worst thing you can do is retaliate. Suddenly you're on par with the jealous person and you're giving them more ammunition.

I have not engaged in dozens of these things, and eventually the jealous person gives up. They move on to new targets or they quietly slink into the background. Let them.

It's hard. It's very hard. As I wrote this chapter tonight, I walked away from the computer four separate times. I had chocolate. I ordered some books. Then I ordered some music. I watched news. I had to force myself to come back.

I'm still furious at some of these people, particularly the ones I can't mention here because you'll know who they are. With the exception of the person I mentioned during my *F&SF* days, I've left out most of the people who've tried to hurt me since my writing became well known.

Did they hurt me? Not the people I didn't know. I find them amusing. But my former friends? Oh, yes. I feel betrayed and sad. I still want to retaliate. I want to write a long essay about each and every one of them, by name, telling you how awful they are.

But I won't. Probably not ever.

I have learned that dealing with other people's jealousy is one of the downsides to success. So I breathe. I take long walks. I throw rocks in the garden. But I never, ever, engage.

Because that way lies madness.

So to answer all those questions about what you do? Be sad. Be angry. Take care of yourself. And move on.

That's all you can do.

Chapter Thirty-seven
Professional Courtesy

When I posted the previous chapter on my blog, the chapter went viral. I got more e-mail than I've ever gotten on a single *Freelancer's Guide* post, and more people tweeted, blogged, or commented on various social networking sites than ever had before.

I had no idea how many of you had suffered from someone else's toxic emotions in the pursuit of your dreams. I suggest you look at the comments on the blog posts associated with these chapters on my website, kristinekathrynrusch.com. Lots of good stuff there.

Mixed among the e-mails were several sympathetic e-mails—virtual hugs—for which I thank you very much. But honestly, folks, I'm okay. The examples I wrote about, while disturbing to remember, are long in the past. Yes, occasionally, I have more trouble with toxic personalities, but as I learned, we all have that kind of problem if we're doing something that we love. Which is just sad—not for us, because we're living fully—but for those jealous, rage-filled people out there, who don't understand that they need to take care of themselves first.

Chapters like the previous one make me nervous when I write them because they talk about the negative sides of the business. More than one e-mail writer confessed that they had no idea how difficult things could get with friends, family, and even strangers. A few of those e-mail writers wondered if the price of freelancing—of succeeding at what you love—is worth it.

Absolutely. I don't want to do anything else. In fact, I can't imagine doing anything else. At the end of this *Guide* is a chapter on the benefits of freelancing. And believe me, there are a lot of benefits. One of them is the ability to do something like this *Guide* just because I felt the time was right, not because someone told me to or I had to or because someone thought I was the person for the job. Nope. I got the idea and did it when I felt like it, working at all hours of the day, as I could fit it in—sometimes in the early morning (bleh), sometimes late at night, and sometimes pushing up against my own personal deadline. You guys—and the recession—have gotten me to write a book I'd been thinking about for years, but had never committed to. And I'm quite happy with the interactivity because without it, I wouldn't have completed the *Guide*.

Nor would I have some of the topics I've covered. Like this chapter's topic, Professional Courtesy. I got several letters complaining about the boorish behavior of professionals. All of the professionals discussed in the e-mails were professional writers, and at first, I thought of starting a new book when this one was done, called *Etiquette for Writers*. (Although I'm not sure I should be the Miss Manners of the Literary Set, particularly when I emitted an involuntary "fuck you!" at a friend this weekend in response to a comment about my age. [Granted, he is a friend, so he's used to me. He said humbly, "Well, you know I mean it," in the tone someone else would use to say, "Well, you know I *didn't* mean it," and we all laughed and the conversation went on from there.])

As I pondered this *Etiquette for Writers* idea, I got more and more e-mails about terrible behavior by professionals. (All writers.) I had experienced some awful behavior by musicians and actors, so for a while I wondered if the bad behavior belonged only to people who make their living as artists.

Then, on Dean's blog, deanwesleysmith.com, writers started discussing the way that agents—people they hired!—had treated them, and that's when I remembered grumping a few years back about sending gifts to friends and never receiving an acknowledgement or a thank-you. (One friend actually criticized the gift!) It took a four-year-old whose father had to dial the phone to remind me what courtesy was like; she was so thrilled with her gift that she had to tell me *now*, and her response pleased me to no end.

Dean teases me about being too polite (despite the occasional involuntary "fuck you"), especially when dealing with people I don't know. I'm "yes-sir-ing" and "no-ma'am-ing" and "please" and "thank you" and "would you mind?" and "excuse me" and smiling politely even when I want to rip someone's head off. When I'm startled, I revert to polite.

Which is a good response, considering my potty mouth. (I was startled this weekend, but relaxed and among friends, hence the blue outburst.)

We all know we should be polite to others, particularly in a business situation. But let me share with you some of the bad behavior I've heard about this past week, as well as some things I've experienced. I'll start with writers, then move to other professions. Then we'll talk a bit about obligations.

1. An unpublished writer bought a published novel written by a friend. The unpublished writer was excited to buy the friend's book, complimented her on it, and had her sign it. The friend proceeded *to badmouth her own book*—talking about the problems she still had with it, the things she should have done, the things her editor should have done, the problems with the sales department, and more. The unpublished writer thinks of that every time she looks at the book, and probably will not buy any more books by the friend because the experience so soured her.

2. I was signing books with a *New York Times* bestselling author. A fan, clearly excited to meet NYT author, brought in her entire collection of said author's work. The author signed the books, but loudly demanded to know why anyone would want her books defaced like that. "What's the point?" NYT author demanded. "Proof that you met me so you can show off to your little friends?" The author continued along those lines—not in a humorous way, but in a very mean way—and the fan left. In tears.

3. I got five e-mails—five!—in which the e-mail writers recounted stories like the ones above. Each e-mail mentioned that the fan had told the published writer how much the fan had liked the work; each time the published writer had criticized the work or the publishing company or the bookstore where the event was being held. And each e-mail letter complained that the published writer had never once said thank you. Not once.

4. My favorite bookstore pet peeve: I get to the checkout counter with my half dozen books (try to get me out of a bookstore with fewer than six—I dare you), and the employee behind the cash register—or worse!—the bookstore's owner tells me that the books I'm buying aren't any good. Usually the employee/owner hasn't read the books. Often the employee/owner sniffs and says something like, "Since you're buying so many, maybe you'd like a really good

book" (in a tone that suggests my choices were substandard). This, by the way, is different from "Do you like that author? I want to try his books," which just shows interest.

5. My second bookstore pet peeve, which used to be a general retail pet peeve until the rise of online ordering (especially for music): Being told in the same snobby tone as the examples above that "we don't carry *that* product." Now I'm okay with a place not carrying everything, but in bookstores you'll hear this as, "We don't carry <sniff> romance or <snarf> science fiction." I recently encountered this attitude at a pet store, when I went to buy cat food because my usual venue was closed. I was told in no uncertain terms that I do not love my cats because of the food I feed them (recommended by my vet, btw—capitalist dog that he is). I ran from that pet store, and have not entered it since. (Since this was the store's owner who uttered that "you clearly don't love your cats" line, I also actively discourage friends from going there as well.)

6. I was accompanying a friend as her eyes and ears while she prepared for major surgery. When she started questioning her surgeon about the procedure, he told her she wasn't smart enough to understand everything he had to do. I stopped him, asked a few more clarifying questions, and he got angry with me for questioning him. We had other problems with this man as the days progressed. I urged her to get a second opinion—and to find another surgeon. She didn't. She came out just fine (thank heavens). But no degree of expertise should allow anyone to treat a patient/client/customer as he treated her. (And we'll not discuss the things he said to me while she was being anesthetized.)

I could go on and on and on. I'd like to say that this is an American problem only—and honestly, our culture has become very, very coarse in the past twenty years. But I've encountered rude behavior from professionals everywhere except (dare I say it?) Canada. Although, come to think of it, the first rude writer I ever met was a famous Canadian literary writer (who has also been on the *New York Times* list) who spoke to my college creative writing class. We spent a week preparing for her visit, reading her work, and preparing questions. Then she arrived, gave a short talk, and proceeded to insult us all by saying that since none of us would ever be published, we weren't worth her time. Since we weren't worth her time, she wasn't going to take questions. I haven't bought her little books now for 30 years because of that rude and condescending afternoon.

So…am I saying to be polite at all times?

No. That would be hypocritical of me. Generally speaking, I'm not polite. I'm blunt and foul-mouthed, particularly among people who know me. I don't suffer fools very well (and certainly not gladly), and I have been known to take someone apart piece by tiny piece when I get irritated.

But I try to be polite most of the time, partly because I have been on the other side of the bad behavior. When people tell me they like a book I've written, I thank them. When they have a question about my work, I try my best to answer it. When they scream at me in public (see the previous chapter), I do my best not to scream back.

Let's talk about fans/readers/clients/patients for a moment.

Without them—oh, freelancer—you are nothing. If you do not have a readership, then you won't last long as a professional writer. If you don't have clients, then you won't make it as a lawyer. If you don't have patients, you're not a doctor.

Granted, that surgeon I mentioned above never got his patients directly, as a family practice doctor does. If you see that surgeon, you usually see him once or maybe twice, and always at the recommendation of another doctor. Believe me when I tell you that I reported that surgeon to all the doctors I know who recommended him, and all of them were shocked at his behavior. I don't know if I had a negative impact on his recommendation rate, but I like to think I did.

Be as courteous as you can. I've had fans go through my books line by line, telling me what's wrong with them, and then buy another book and have me sign it. If I had gotten defensive at those critiques (and trust me, I was feeling defensive, I just didn't express it), the readers wouldn't have purchased another book. Do I want fans like that? Of course I do. *I'm* a fan like that. I won't tell a favorite writer why I think she went wrong in her most recent book, but I will tell another fan and we'll discuss the problems. And then I'll go out and buy the next book. I'll wager a lot of you are the same way.

Most of us just wouldn't tell the writer how much we hated one of her efforts. And that's the only difference.

I can be very forgiving of fans, just as I can be forgiving of customers. I went out of my way as a waitress and as a retail clerk to make sure that the customers were happy, even if the customers were drunk or rude or wrong. That old adage, the customer is always right, is a good one to remember when you're in public.

Of course, there are times to toss the adage. The customer should not be abusive or violent. Certain types of behavior should not get a pass, ever.

But mostly, what does it hurt you—the professional—to bite your lip? To be polite or just not say anything at all? Writers, say thank you when someone compliments your work. Bookstore owners, be thankful someone is buying your stock. Lawyers and doctors, expect your clients to be a bit emotional, for most are seeing you at a tough time in their lives. A little empathy goes a long way.

Remember, though, that everyone has a bad day, and not everyone has social skills. I think the reason so many of my examples this week were about writers is not just because I am a writer, but because writers usually don't need social skills. We sit in a room and make things up. We interact with ourselves, our families, our friends, and our imaginary friends. Sometimes we forget how to survive in the real world.

I think everyone should get a pass for the occasional rude remark. If the behavior is continual, though, like that surgeon's, then don't go to that professional again.

If you're a person who has poor social skills, figure out how to ameliorate the problem. There are actual classes to shore up your public behavior, should you want to take them. Community colleges offer them, as do regular colleges. In my small town, our chamber of commerce has a once-a-year course in public relations. Taking something like that might be worth your time.

If you're like me—a person who can be polite some of the time, but not all of the time—figure out a way around the problem. In most instances, I'm just fine. But when I'm teaching a one- or two-week workshop, with long hours, I know I'll relax and then my potty mouth will get the best of me. So I warn my students ahead of time, and I apologize in advance. Then I try my best to be on my best behavior.

A lot of people can't be polite when they're busy. Politeness is the first thing out the window. In that instance, I'd recommend hiring a receptionist, a secretary, or a clerk—someone to handle the public while you're handling the actual business. (See the chapter on employees first.) And if you can't afford the help, then take classes. Make an effort. Learn how to put your best foot forward.

Here are a few tips to help you be courteous.

1. Never take your fan/reader/client/customer for granted.
Treat them with respect and maybe just a bit of awe. After all, they've deemed you worthy of their time, trust, and/or hard-earned dollars. Honor that.

2. Say please and thank you.
I know, I sound like your mother. Well, take those lessons to heart. In response to a compliment, a simple thank you means a lot more than a critique of the work at hand. Show some appreciation for the person who came into your store, ordered food off the menu you designed, or bought a book you wrote. They didn't have to do that, you know. You're not entitled to customers or nice comments. You have to earn them, like everyone else.

3. Dress up.
This goes for anyone who interacts with the public. It's better to be overdressed than underdressed. As I mentioned in an earlier chapter, I watch *American Idol*, and I use it as a learning tool. One thing that continually shocks me is how many people claim that being a professional musician is their lifelong dream, yet these people show up to their auditions in sloppy sweats, ratty blue jeans, and ill-fitting t-shirts. One girl in 2010—who was chosen from the auditions to go to Hollywood Week—was incredibly poor (I mean horribly, awfully poor). She managed to scrounge up $4 to buy a dress at the Dollar Store—and you could tell that purchase meant she went without food or gas or something else important. She worked hard to look her best. Yet people with a lot more money looked like they had just gotten out of bed. Most of these folks weren't wearing their punk rocker costume. They just hadn't bothered to clean up for this big opportunity.

If you work at home and don't normally dress up, your "public" clothes will become a costume. I have my jeans and ratty sweaters for at home, and my business attire for book signings or conventions, and my black-tie outfits for banquets. When I wear the business attire or my black-tie outfits, I'm wearing something slightly unusual—and it serves as a reminder that I am out in public. My costume, if you will, helps me be just a bit more formal than I would usually be.

4. If you have trouble being polite, smile and say very little.

The smile is important so that folks don't think you're surly. But put on your company face, and do the best you can.

5. Be respectful.

I think half the writer examples I read this week wouldn't have occurred if the writer had taken a moment to view the person they were talking to with respect. Success doesn't give you a license to be rude.

6. Enlist a Rescuer.

This may sound silly, but it's important, especially if you have fans. You'll need someone to grab your arm and pull you out of a crowd. I've done that for some famous writers back when I was editing. Dean does it for me at my signings, and I do it for him at his. Sometimes fans don't know when to stop hogging your time. A bookstore clerk will often hustle the fan along, but at conventions, no one will do that. Your rescuer can get you out of a tight situation without insulting the well-intentioned person who has backed you into a corner.

The other thing your rescuer can do is stop you from making a fool of yourself. I have a look that I get when someone has crossed over this mental line that I have that goes from "nice" to "fool." (Usually that line gets crossed by some unforgivable [often bigoted] political remark.) I've had half a dozen friends save the poor person who crossed my mental line by recognizing my look and getting me away from the person quickly.

Once I was at a dinner with a famous person whose politics are—shall we say politely—the opposite of mine. We had a business relationship that I carefully kept out of the political arena for years. But, as luck would have it, our dinner fell two days after a particularly hard-fought election. And he launched into some horrible, unbearable diatribe filled with n-words and other such things. My assistant, who was having dinner with us, grabbed my knee in the middle of that diatribe, and while I thought of going for the steak knife and disemboweling this famous person, my assistant held me down and dug his fingers into my thigh until I was black-and-blue. But I didn't destroy a lucrative business relationship with my potty mouth and my politics—only because I had a rescuer at that table. (Or rather the famous person had a rescuer. Because, had we been alone at that dinner, I might be in prison now.)

I guess I shouldn't be surprised that my chapter on surviving other people's jealousy brought out this dark side of professionalism. I think most of you who are being rude—and believe me, some of you are reading this blog—don't realize that you are. Figure out how to gain some self-awareness in this area. Maybe even practice the things you'll say when you go out in public.

It's important.

Remember this: *Professional courtesy brings repeat business.* Rudeness will often destroy the relationship. Granted, there are times when you don't want to do business with that person ever again. But usually, you do. Be nice. Be polite. Be respectful.

Really, it's not that hard.

Section Six:
Risks, Setbacks, and Emergencies

Chapter Thirty-eight
Risks

My initial post on risk happened in the middle of a long string of posts on other topics. I wrote out of order because of things that happened in the week before the post appeared. First, I read a couple of articles, one a couple of months old. Then, I watched the Oscars, as I do every year. And finally, I've been dealing with some major risk-takers in my business, negotiating with them, and finding my own footing.

As I've said in the negotiation section, I can negotiate quite well on paper and via e-mail, but I have trouble in person. Or, I should say, I *had* trouble in person. I'd been avoiding in-person negotiation for so long that I hadn't done it in nearly 15 years. Not only did I realize this time that I wasn't nervous, I was downright easy-going about the whole thing, quite willing to walk away where I wouldn't have been years ago. I did everything I said Dean does in the negotiation posts, and more. And I did well. I didn't get everything I wanted, but neither did the other side.

How that fits into this whole topic is the in-person negotiation was quite a risk for me. I could have passed this off to a third party—an agent, a lawyer, Dean himself—and I didn't. I decided that, in this particular instance, I knew better than anyone else what I wanted and didn't want. Since the situation was extremely fluid, it was easier for me to handle it than to guide someone else through the ups and downs.

The risk paid off, and I learned something about myself in the bargain. I learned that I am not the person I was twenty years ago. I have a lot more knowledge and self-confidence. More than that, though, I have a longer view. I know that if I screw up on this one thing, my life is not over. I won't die of embarrassment. I won't even die from the botched negotiation. I'd simply not have everything I wanted.

The next thing that happened to me this past week was that I watched the Oscars. I have watched the Oscars every year since I can remember—even scrounging around to find the telecast when I didn't own a television set and the internet did not exist so that I could watch highlights on YouTube. (Yes, I'm old.) I love the Oscars for a variety of reasons, most of them personal, and some of them to do with my history. (The Oscars [as well as television itself] was one of the few places where I saw artists talking about their art, even if it was in the artificial environment of an awards show.)

In 2010, as every year, award-winners talked inspiringly of being true to yourself, becoming an artist, and taking risks. Three things caught my attention. First, the mention by someone— Mo'Nique? Oprah? Geoffrey Fletcher (the screenwriter)?—about the difficulties they had bringing a hard-hitting movie like *Precious, Based on the Novel "Push" by Sapphire* to the screen. The movie is about a topic that most people prefer not to think about. Yet several someones decided to make the movie, to finance it, to distribute it; and even more someones decided to see it, and slowly people realized just how special the film was.

Had the filmmakers listened to conventional wisdom, *Precious* would not have been made. No one would have considered *Push* a novel that could become a major motion picture, and Gabourey Sidibe would be attending college somewhere in the Midwest instead of embarking on an already stellar acting career.

The second speech that caught my attention was Mo'Nique's acceptance speech. She took several risks, not just the risk of portraying a deeply unsympathetic character in a difficult movie. She also decided not to play the political award-nominee game. Nominees go from event to event, campaigning for votes without really ever mentioning their films. The conventional wisdom is that if the nominee wants to win, the nominee must charm the establishment. Mo'Nique refused, saying her performance was on the screen, and she should be judged by that.

Her refusal paid off.

The other interesting aspect to her speech was her phrase "doing what's right." Her husband supported her as she decided to portray this character, to go outside of the Mo'Nique brand—and she has quite a brand as a comedian, and as a talk show host on BET—and try something new. She could have flopped. Instead, she became known as a serious actress, one who can go places that more famous actresses refused to travel to.

The final speech that caught me was Sandra Bullock's. It wasn't this speech so much as her Screen Actor's Guild speech for the same role. But she reiterated part of it in her Oscar speech.

She said she wasn't happy with her work. So she took time away from it, to reassess, and decide what kinds of roles she wanted. Then she took roles that challenged her. Again, other actresses had turned down the role in *The Blind Side* that gave Sandra Bullock her Oscar. Would they have won for the same part? Hard to know. Probably not: she owned it.

Again, she had support. And while she credits the support with enabling her to make the changes, she might have made them anyway. She did so before, after the disastrous film *Speed Two*. She took more control over her career—producing more films, and making sure she had a lot more creative input.

Risk-taking. Very important to those of us in the arts. Important in other ways as well.

But risk-taking in the form of making a knowledgeable choice, one that assesses the pros and cons, not in the form of a flyer or a gamble.

I've been accused of being quite fiscally conservative—and I am, when it comes to money I already have. I used to think that the way I earned money was risky too, until this economy proved to me as well as to everyone else that my way—as a freelancer—might actually be fiscally conservative as well.

Like Sandra Bullock, I prefer to control my career. I can't do that when I work for someone else. I can work *with* someone else. But working *for* them is a greater risk for me than working *with* them.

I think freelancers must identify the one risk they want to take—starting a business, for example, or becoming an actress instead of a 9-5 worker at whatever job will take them, or stepping outside their comfort zone to attempt something that gives them the greater benefit. Once the freelancers have identified the risk that they want to take, then they research that risk to death. They figure out how to take it in a manner that isn't risky at all, or that minimizes risk, or that takes the risk into account and compensates for it in another area of the business.

An article that I read recently delves into this aspect of freelance risk-taking in great depth. Malcolm Gladwell wrote an article for *The New Yorker*'s January 18, 2010, issue called "The Sure Thing: How Entrepreneurs Really Succeed."

The article discusses the high-level entrepreneurs, the Ted Turners of the world, the guys who have tried something seemingly impossible and who have reaped big rewards.

But Gladwell uses his article, quoting many sources, to disprove the idea of entrepreneur as gambling risk-taker. Instead, he discusses how the successful entrepreneur finds a way to make the risk into a sure thing—often at the expense of the entrepreneur's reputation. (He calls these men—and his examples here are all men—predators. I'm not sure that's accurate either, because the entrepreneurs aren't out to kill their opponents. They're out to achieve some sort of success, often by taking advantage of something someone else missed.)

In the middle of this article, he paraphrases the economist Scott Shane, from Shane's book *The Illusions of Entrepreneurship* (which, full disclosure, I have not read).

Gladwell writes, "[Shane] says many entrepreneurs take plenty of risks—but those are generally the *failed* entrepreneurs, not the success stories. The failures violate all kinds of established principles of new-business formulation."

He then goes on to list these things that the failed entrepreneurs did wrong. Those things are:

- **They undercapitalized the business.**
- **They didn't form corporations (which, Shane says, gives a better chance of success).**
- **They didn't have a business plan.**
- **They underemphasized marketing.**
- **They didn't understand financial controls.**
- **They tried to compete on price**.

Shane (and Gladwell) list several other factors, too complex to explain here, then Gladwell writes this:

"Shane concedes that some of these risks are unavoidable: would-be entrepreneurs take them because they have no choice. *But a good many of these risks reflect a lack of preparation or foresight.*" (Emphasis mine.)

I wrote *The Freelancer's Guide* for precisely this reason: I want you all to be prepared before you leap into the freelance lifestyle. I want you to know—as best you can—what you're getting into.

I'm not saying that you should become a freelancer, and I'm not saying that you shouldn't. I'm simply saying that you should educate yourself before you make that choice.

Then I came across this article in the *Washington Post* of March 10, 2010. Written by Steve Pearlstein, the article, "News Flash for Wall St.: Money Isn't Everything," also cites Gladwell's book, but focuses mostly on a book by Daniel Pink called *Drive.* (Again, I haven't yet read this book either.)

The Pink book uses decades of research from various sources to show the limits of money as a motivating tool for employees. (Which is why you can find this article in the business section—and why it's aimed at Wall Street, with its high bonuses and ridiculously overpriced compensation packages.)

"The conclusion Pink draws from all this research," Pearlstein writes, "is that once people achieve a reasonable level of economic comfort and security, they are likely to be less easily motivated by monetary carrots and sticks than they are by more emotional factors. And in modern workplaces, Pink argues that the most powerful emotional motivators are the desire for autonomy, the satisfaction that comes from mastering a skill or a task, and the need to serve some larger social purpose."

In his *New Yorker* article, Gladwell also addresses the emotional side of work, only he discusses the emotional satisfaction the entrepreneur gets from his work. (Substitute "successful freelancer" for "entrepreneur.")

He writes, "…people who work for themselves are far happier than the rest of us. Shane (the economist) says that the average person would have to earn two and a half times as much to be as happy working for someone else as he would be working for himself."

This all dovetails with my other experience during that week. I turned down a high-paying writing gig that was mine if I but said I wanted it. It would have paid all of my living expenses for six months, with more income off and on for years.

I didn't even have to think about my choice. Once I heard what the project was, I said no. When the editor offering the project pushed, offering more incentives, I still said no.

Why? Because I knew that this project wasn't worth the price. Essentially, for that huge paycheck, I was going to have to be in someone else's employ until the project ended, and I was unwilling to do that.

The "no" was so automatic, and cost me so little emotionally, that I didn't even remember the conversation until Dean asked me later why the editor had called me. When he heard the price tag, he asked why I hadn't dropped his name into the mix. Then I told him the conditions of the project, and he recanted. "Good thing you didn't mention me," he said.

This interaction fit into one more aspect mentioned in Gladwell's article. He writes, "People who like what they do are profoundly conservative."

He then cites a study by sociologists Hongwei Xu and Martin Ruef. They asked a large sample of entrepreneurs and non-entrepreneurs which of these three scenarios they'd choose:

1. **A business with a potential profit of five million dollars.**
2. **A business with a potential profit of two million dollars.**
3. **A business with a potential profit of 1.25 million dollars.**

Business Number One—with the possible profit of five million dollars—has a 20% chance of success. Business Number Two has a 50% chance of success. Business Number Three has an 80% chance of success.

The successful entrepreneurs generally went with Business Number Three, "the safe choice."

He continues, "[The entrepreneurs] weren't dazzled by the chance of making five million dollars. They were drawn to the eighty-per-cent chance of getting to do what they love doing. The [entrepreneur] is a supremely rational actor. But, deep down, he is also a romantic, motivated by the simple joy he finds in his work."

What Gladwell misses—or perhaps ignores—is that there is still a 20% chance of failure in that third scenario. A 20% chance that the entrepreneur—the freelancer—will not make that $1.25 million dollars, no matter what he does.

That 20% chance is too much of a risk for most people. Most people want the completely sure thing—the paycheck at the end of the week, the schedule imposed by someone else, the benefits paid for by the company. Most people don't like to be on a 5% ledge, let alone a 20% ledge. These are the people who got caught flat-footed by the Great Recession. People who thought they had a guaranteed income for the rest of their lives, people who believed their jobs were secure because they were good employees who worked for stable companies.

As I mentioned in the Day Job chapter, no job is secure. But the illusion of security is often more important to people than the reality of risk.

It's because of this 20% risk that more people don't become freelancers. And it's because of the lure of big money (that $5 million Number One choice) that too many people give up their day jobs—and then fail big time.

Those of us who have worked for ourselves for a long time have figured out what makes us happy. We balance our income with our taste for risk. We know what we need to survive, and we do that. Then we figure out how much risk we can tolerate—and what we're putting at risk.

Are we risking our homes? Our families? Then, in my opinion, we're taking too much risk. Are we risking a $750,000 profit instead of a $1.25 million profit? Is that part of the 20% failure rate? And in what world does a $750,000 purely profit paycheck constitute a failure?

Assessing risk is one of the most important parts of a freelancer's business. Risk-assessment is a constant undercurrent to everything.

Time to do some risk assessment of your own. Figure out what you need as a freelancer and what you want for yourself and your career. What are you risking when you step out of your comfort zone, as Mo'Nique did? A few days of work? An emotional upset? A flop? And if you are risking a giant flop, will it have an impact on your everyday work? In Mo'Nique's case, I doubt that it would have. She would have continued her careers as a comedian and as a talk show host.

If *The Blind Side* had flopped, would it have damaged Sandra Bullock's career? *All About Steve* flopped so badly that Bullock earned a Razzie for the Worst Actress of the Year on the same weekend that she won her Oscar. Not all of her risks have paid off. And yet, she is taking them.

I don't know the calculations she made in accepting the roles in these two films. Since Bullock has proven herself to be a smart businesswoman over and over again, I'm sure she went into both projects with a lot of analysis, looking at the potential upside versus the potential downside.

As freelancers, that's our job. We might not earn six-months' living expenses with one project, but we also don't have to work for anyone else. I wasn't willing to trade three months of misery for six months of money. Other people make different choices.

But I might miss the brass ring on occasion as well, because I wouldn't have gone for that $5 million/80% chance of failure choice. I have never taken a flyer like that, although I have failed at businesses for precisely the reasons listed in the Gladwell article. I've learned my lesson in that beloved school of hard knocks.

Dean and I have been discussing risks a lot this week, partly because we're planning a class in money management for freelancers which we're holding this weekend. We've also been discussing the risks some friends are taking in different careers in the arts, as well as some risks we're considering in our own careers. Risk seems to be in the air. I think some of that is due to the Great Recession. People have already lost their jobs and their security, so they believe that now is the time to take a risk.

I think so too. But each person assesses risk differently.

I did some discussion of risk above, but I didn't give a definition. So I'm going to haul out the handy-dandy dictionary again, and give it a go.

(Why do I define words we already know? To make sure there are no assumptions here.)

Risk, according to my lovely *Encarta World English Dictionary*, is complicated. I did not expect five different definitions—and that's just for the noun. The verb form has a few of its own. Here are all seven definitions—noun first, then verb:

Noun

1. *The danger that injury, damage, or loss will occur.*
2. *Somebody or something likely to cause injury, damage, or loss.*
3. *The probability, amount, or type of possible loss incurred and covered by an insurer.*
4. *The possibility of loss in an investment or speculation.*
5. *The statistical chance of danger from something, especially from the failure of an engineered system.*

Verb
1. To place something valued in a position or situation where it could be damaged or lost, or exposed to damage or loss.
2. To incur the chance of harm or loss by taking an action.

Wow. Look at those loaded words defining risk: injury; damage; loss; harm; danger. *Danger.* Jeez. The only time you see a word that's positive is in the verb form, and even that's not good—"to place something valued in a position or situation where it could be damaged or lost."

Yikes. With definitions like that, it's amazing anyone ever takes a risk. Even the synonyms are scary: danger; jeopardy; peril; hazard; menace; threat. The antonym is a word that makes us all feel better: safety.

Safety is the opposite of risk.

Yet if you're freelancing, playing it safe is a risk.

Huh?

To freelance in this culture is to go against cultural norms. We're all raised to get a good job with job security, work our way up in that job, and eventually make manager or executive vice president or even president of the company/corporation. Let the company pay for our vacations, our retirement, our 401Ks, and our insurance. If possible, get a job with longevity, so you can stay at the same corporation all of your life.

Those myths were myths back when my father spouted them. My father—a professor with tenure who had jobs at five different colleges and universities (more if you count the summer school classes and semesters away that he taught). Five different employers in three different states. Even while he was telling my siblings and me to get a good job with a long-term employer, he wasn't living that life.

Neither were our neighbors, although the neighborhood looked very *Father Knows Best*, with the husbands leaving for their corporate jobs and the wives staying home to tend the kids. Peel back the surface, and you'd see that the family next door had only lived in the house for five years because the husband kept getting promoted and moved to a new area. Or the family two doors down who kept moving from state to state like we did, following the professor husband from one tenure track position to another. Or the family across the street with the outspoken wife who didn't believe women should stay home, and had never, ever, gone without a job, not even when she was raising three boys. (Her husband was gainfully and happily employed—the only one who had been in the same job in the same place for more than twenty years.)

I could go house by house, memory by memory, in a time when the myth of the lifetime job got engrained into the culture—the middle of the twentieth century—and show you anecdotally that I knew no one who lived that exact lifestyle.

Yet we all believed it to be a goal. And that goal continued to be the pinnacle of achievement until the Great Recession began in September of 2008. Recently, one of the national newscasts revisited the Class of 2009—the first college class of the Great Recession—to see how those kids were getting along in "the real world." None of them had gotten the job they wanted. All of them had learned that life was harder than their parents, teachers, and older siblings had made it out to be. The world had changed, and that prescribed path—the one that said if you walked this way, you'll have a job for life—had vanished.

These changes provide opportunities. I saw a statistic a few weeks ago which, of course, I can't find in my internet search this evening. The statistic stated that the number of new small businesses had grown exponentially in the past two years. So many people decided that if they couldn't get a job, they'd create one for themselves.

They took a risk, which may not have been much of a risk at all. In fact, continuing to search for a job in a tight market might have been more of a risk.

But for everyone who tried, dozens of others did not. They were risk averse—and really, who in their right mind wouldn't be risk averse with words like danger, jeopardy, and peril hanging over them? Why would anyone take a risk at all?

Some people had no choice. But that's not a good way to start a business—to do it because there's nothing else to do.

Why do sane people start businesses? Why do sane people take risks?

Or better yet, how do you correlate all those risk-takers who start businesses with successful entrepreneurs who are essentially conservative people? How can you be conservative in your business practices and take a lot of risk?

Ah—here's where the definition of risk fails. Risk is not absolute. It's relative. Something that's risky for me isn't risky for you at all.

If I decided tomorrow that I was going to become a math professor like my father, I'd be taking a huge risk. I'm dyslexic, and my dyslexia manifests itself worse in numbers. I'm not sure I can operate with the precision needed to do higher math. I learned in school that I can understand the concepts, but I can't translate them accurately into numerical form. At some point, I dropped out of higher math, so I have no idea if my understanding would have continued through Advanced Calculus.

However, the invention of the spell-check has allowed me to write, despite the dyslexia. No one dies if I misspell a word—and writing isn't about spelling anyway. It's about storytelling, which you can do with or without dyslexia.

Yet there are people out there—my husband is one—for whom math is a gift. He can do everything from arithmetic to calculus with ease. He was a professional golfer and an architect, so thinking in three dimensions—which baffles me—comes easily to him.

Going to school to major in math wasn't a risk for him. It would have been laughable for me.

Innate ability, however, is just one example of different way risk spreads out among the population. In fact, ability is probably the most worthless measure of whether or not someone will succeed. I'm sure I could have found ways around my mathematical challenges if I were motivated enough. After all, I overcame the dyslexia to write (yep, before spell-check). I survived my math classes with straight As, but I had to work harder than I wanted to because I didn't enjoy the subject.

If I had wanted to, I could have learned how to turn that numerical dyslexia into an annoyance rather than an excuse.

So how do you accurately assess risk—for you?

1. Know who you are.
Know what you like and dislike. Figure out how much work you're willing to put into something. If you constantly skate by in a particular area, doing just enough to be "good enough," then that's not an area for you. But if you're willing to buckle down and work harder than anyone else in an area—even if you have no obvious ability—then that area is a place where you could succeed. Enjoyment, for the freelancer, is the heart of the business. It's what keeps you at your desk for long hours. It's what makes all the hard work worthwhile.

Enjoyment is different for each of us. Tasks that would drive me crazy please a lot of other people. And thank heaven for that. Otherwise, there'd be a lot of jobs that no one would want to do, and we'd all be poorer for it.

2. Understand the economic principles at play.

If you're going to freelance, make sure you understand the business you're entering before you go into it. Or at least, understand it as best you can. Learn the ups and downs. Find out who is successful and who isn't, and look deep to understand why. Figure out the business part of your business before you jump into it.

3. Use your imagination.

That's why we're given one, so that we can imagine scenarios before they occur. Look at the upside and the downside of any potential business. Imagine yourself working hard in that business—doing the dirty work, the nitty gritty details, pulling the long hard hours. If you can see yourself happily working away, then maybe that job is for you. But if you hear yourself saying, "I'll hire someone to do that task," then rethink your decision to work in that particular area. Because early on, as a freelancer, you'll be doing *every* job in your business.

You also need to know how to do every job, so that you know how to assess any potential employee you hire. If you can't imagine yourself doing the hard work of the business—whatever it is—for a long period of time (more than five years), then this business is not for you.

4. Enjoy the learning.

If you don't like studying for this business, then you're not going to like the business. And if you think that doesn't matter, then you're in deep trouble.

Because any business you go into will grow and change over time. People who keep up with the changes become successful *and remain successful*. Everyone else falls by the wayside.

5. Learn how to assess risk versus reward.

Would you take something with a high reward that also has a high risk? (Most successful business owners would not.) You want the greatest reward for the lowest risk. And that risk must be a risk *to you*. We all have different levels of risk tolerance. Too much risk tolerance and you become a gambler. Too little and you will never achieve your dreams. Figure out the balance, and then find ways to maintain it.

6. Don't just assess the financial cost; look at the personal cost.

Starting a business—any business—takes time. It also takes dedication. Do you have the time? Can you work ten- and twelve-hour days? Can you focus on that business at the expense of most other things in your life?

Maybe you already have a job that takes a lot of your time, and you would simply be trading working for someone else with working for yourself. You still need to look at the personal cost. You might not be taking risks just for yourself, but for others as well. Can your relationships survive a failure of this business? Or worse, can they survive its success?

7. Learn to walk away.

We've all heard the expression "throwing good money after bad." But most of us don't apply that to time as well. Sometimes you invest time into something, realize that it's not working, and try harder. When you try harder with little chance of success, you're wasting time better spent on a different endeavor.

Many people cling to a job or a business or a failing relationship because they have already invested so much time and effort into it. You need to assess whether or not that struggling business or failing relationship can *realistically* improve. If the answer is no, extricate yourself from the situation.

Sometimes it's better to spend a few months or a year winding something down than it is to spend five years trying to save it. If you'll end up in the same circumstance in either situation, do the one that will take the least time out of your life.

8. Learn from your mistakes.

Because, as I've said before, you will make a lot of them. Just don't make the same mistake twice. Learn from your mistake and do something different next time.

9. Realize that *nothing* is inherently risky or inherently secure.

This used to be a hard one for people to understand—back when corporations seemed monolithic and strong. The past two years have taught people that anyone with a "secure" job can lose it overnight. Just like people who have "taken risks" can succeed "against all odds."

You need to question who is making the odds, and whether or not they know as much about the risky situation as the people involved do. Just because something looks secure from the outside doesn't mean that it is. And the same thing applies to something that's seemingly risky.

10. Bet on yourself.

Which goes back to #1. If you know yourself, then you can make the best choices for you. If your choice is between relying on someone else to take care of you or doing it yourself, do it yourself.

Invest in yourself. Believe in yourself. Work harder than anyone else. Work smarter than anyone else. Learn from your mistakes. Do what you love.

If you apply those six principles to your work, then you'll mitigate risk no matter what endeavor you try.

But be honest with yourself. Any time you leap without enough preparation, without enough study, and without understanding what awaits you, you're taking a risk. A real risk, with all of those scary words behind it.

If you're not ready, and you leap anyway, you're going to hurt someone. And that someone will probably be you.

Being seriously risk averse is as harmful as having too much risk tolerance. If you're seriously risk averse, you'll never try anything. You see risk everywhere.

If your risk tolerance is too high, you'll take stupid chances.

You need to learn how to mitigate risk in everything you do. Accept that some risk will always exist—that's life, y'all. We take risks when we do anything—from crossing the street to cooking lunch.

Accept the risks, try to minimize them, and then follow your heart.

Chapter Thirty-nine
Insurance

Before I get into the topic proper, I have to issue a disclaimer. I am not an insurance expert. I'm not an accountant. I'm not a lawyer. The advice given below is simply my opinion. It's an opinion based on decades of freelancing, and based on watching others freelance as well.

Here's what I've observed. Most failed freelance careers fail for four reasons. Let's do this like a *Late Show Top Ten List*— backwards.

The fourth reason freelance careers fail: a lack of discipline on the part of the freelancer.

The third reason freelance careers fail: a lack of business savvy on the part of the freelancer.

The second reason freelance careers fail: a lack of money management skills on the part of the freelancer.

And the main reason freelance careers fail: a lack of insurance.

Now I know I have your attention, and I also know that most of you don't believe me. I don't have statistics to back up these observations, although I'm sure I can find them.

What I do have are countless years of watching friends and other freelancers fall by the wayside. I've also failed in a few freelance ventures myself, although never for lack of insurance. Lack of money management skills—check: that was the first time I tried to go freelance with my writing. Lack of business savvy—check: that would be the art gallery I owned with my ex-husband. Lack of discipline—oh, well, never mind. I've never lacked for discipline. Discipline is the one thing I've always had…when it comes to something I love. If I hate something, I have no discipline at all. But why start a business of any kind if you hate the work?

How does a lack of insurance tank a freelancer's business? Easy. All it takes is one catastrophe. Just one. And most people don't make it through life without at least one catastrophe.

My husband Dean Wesley Smith had a house fire, as have several of our friends, including writer Len Wein and his wife, photographer Christine Valada, who lost their home to fire in 2009. A lot of writers, artists, and musicians—all people I know—lost everything in Hurricane Katrina. That doesn't count the hundreds I didn't know, including small business owners, who lost not just their homes, but their storefronts as well.

Several years ago, the brush fires in Oakland threatened many in the Bay Area's science fiction community. After the Northridge Earthquake, I flew to L.A. to help writer Harlan Ellison clean up his ruined home. I heard firsthand from several other writer/artist/bookstore owners about their ruined businesses as well.

Then there are the lawsuits. As my husband Dean—the guy who went to law school and quit during the last week of his third year so that he wouldn't become an Idaho attorney—says every time some idiot files a suit for something dumb: *anyone can sue anybody about anything.*

The suit doesn't have to be legitimate. The filing of the suit will still equal legal fees for you, even if the judge throws the case out on day one. Not to mention time lost and everything else.

There are other legal problems you can face, from liability issues to stalking issues (if you become famous). Right now, a well-known friend is trying to block someone who is posing as him on Twitter and posting egregious things.

Liability issues happen whether you're famous or not. At a restaurant where I waitressed in high school, a little old lady slipped on a wet floor and broke her arm, then sued the restaurant for *years* for neglect and other things, even though the wet floor was clearly marked as wet (with a big yellow CAUTION sign), and despite the fact that the restaurant's insurance paid for her medical care.

Insurance is for the unexpected, the catastrophic, and the extremely expensive events life throws at you. Even if you weren't considering the freelance life, I'd urge you to get insurance.

I learned early how few people actually get the insurance they need and how much lack of insurance costs them. I rented apartments to students and low-income folk, most of whom told me they couldn't afford the $8 per month (then) renters' insurance. The gamble that nothing will happen to you is huge.

Something will happen: the key is surviving it. And guaranteed, you'll survive it better with a little money from insurance payments than you will with no money at all.

So here are the insurance items every freelancer needs:

Health Insurance

I know, I know. In the U.S., the government has passed a health care law. As I started to revise this chapter, I went to the web to look up the law's provisions. It's September of 2010, and I couldn't find any clear guideline as to when something will kick in and what that something will be. It will vary state to state, and most of the provisions (if I'm reading this right) won't be fully active until 2014.

So I'm skipping the revision of this section (for now), and leaving what I wrote in spring of 2009:

You have no safety net if you don't have health insurance. Your business depends on you. If you're incapacitated, then your business doesn't run *at all*. Money stops coming in, and the savings you've built up will disappear.

It's amazing how fast money disappears when you aren't getting paid and you have to pay medical bills. I had emergency gall bladder surgery five years ago, and my insurance paid about $30,000—much of it they had negotiated down from the sticker price. I paid the deductible—$5000—and was happy to do so.

That surgery, which required tests, an ambulance ride to a bigger hospital (I live in a small town), and an overnight stay in that hospital, is considered bread-and-butter surgery—not all that hard, and not all that expensive.

I guided a friend through her breast cancer from diagnosis to reconstructive surgery, acting as her hospital partner. I have no idea what that experience cost her and her insurance company, but I do know that $30,000 would have seemed like a drop in the bucket compared to her bill for days in the hospital, two major surgeries, three different surgeons, and tests, tests, tests.

Think you're relatively healthy? Good for you. Exercise a lot? Eat right? Take vitamins? Even better. Never been sick a day in your life? Wonderful.

Get the damn insurance.

Why?

Runner's World ran an article on Matt Long, a New York fire fighter and Ironman triathlete who was in top physical condition… the day a bus hit him and dragged him (and his bike) along its undercarriage. His excellent physical condition allowed him to survive the accident, but essentially every system in his body failed that day, not to mention the multiple broken bones, etc. It's been years, and he's just recovering. (*Runner's World* profiled him for a variety of reasons, not the least being he just ran in the New York City marathon. This guy is nothing if not determined. You can find the article online at runnersworld.com.)

All he had done was ride his bike to work that day. The bus driver, who was at fault, hit Matt Long while going around a corner.

And in that instant, Long's life was changed forever.

I'm sure you all know stories like that. And stories like that are what insurance is for. I don't care if you're twenty and just starting out, feeling marvelous, or if you're sixty and have a mountain of pre-existing conditions.

Get health insurance.

Before you quit your day job, research health insurance. If you have a spouse who can include you on her plan, then get added in. Make sure the entire family is covered. If you're single or your spouse isn't insured, then investigate every option.

By law, most employers are required to keep you on their group health plan for at least 18 months after you quit/get laid off/ are fired. That law, the Consolidated Omnibus Budget Reconciliation Act or COBRA, passed in 1985. It was designed to make sure that no one lost coverage because he lost his job. However, the moment you're no longer employed, you must *pay* for that coverage, and it's often hugely expensive. (I'm told that there's a provision in the stimulus bill that changes this for some people. The information isn't on COBRA's public website, but it might be on the private part of the site. Since I'm not in need of COBRA, I didn't research this part.) (This may be one of those things covered by the new health care law. Again, research for your own situation.)

It's based on the premium your employer paid. As I wrote this article, I asked folks who've had experience with COBRA to let me know how much they paid per month, so I could give you a range. The responses I got ranged from $400 for a healthy, single thirty-year-old to $2000 for a family of five. These numbers are *per month*, not per year.

COBRA is designed as temporary insurance—a bridge insurance to carry you from one job to another—not as a lifelong insurance. If you can get health insurance through another group like AARP or an organization affiliated with your freelance business, then investigate those.

Most insurance that you buy on your own will be much cheaper than COBRA. The key is to get the best price for the best coverage. And that can be tricky.

And look at my tips on shopping for insurance below.

But don't make the jump to full-time freelancing without health insurance.

Homeowners or Renters Insurance

You should have this regardless of whether you have a day job or not. House fires happen. Trees fall through walls. In my small town a few years ago, some doofus drove his car off an overpass and the car landed on another guy's house.

Weird stuff happens. Be prepared.

But when you work at home, a house fire or similar disaster means you'll lose your place of residence *and* your place of business. Make sure you're covered.

Homeowners or renters insurance covers your place of residence. Your stuff, essentially, everything you use for leisure and for living. It does not cover business in the home. We'll get to that in a minute.

But here are a few tips:

Get a high deductible, and pay for minor repairs yourself. Insurance companies often jack rates on frequent users of the homeowner's policy. So if a tree branch cracks a window, pay for the repair out of your own pocket and don't make a claim.

Take pictures or make a video of everything in the house at least once per year, and keep those pictures and/or that video off premise. You'll be glad you did, because you'll never remember what you owned after the crisis happens. The pictures are a great guide for doing an inventory, which the insurance company requires when you make a claim.

Get the appropriate insurance rider. If you live in earthquake country, get earthquake insurance. Yes, it's expensive. But it's better than losing everything—and the insurance company will deny your claim if your house is destroyed in an earthquake and you don't have that earthquake rider.

The same goes for flood insurance. If you live in a flood plain (and so many people do), then spring for the very expensive flood insurance. If flooding is a distinct possibility in your area—if you live near a river, near a beach, or in a place with severe wet storms—then get flood insurance. Insurance companies hate to pay for water damage and will often deny anything they can pretend is water damage. (See what happened after any of the hurricanes in the south, but particularly after Katrina.)

If you don't know whether or not you live in a flood plain, research it. Go to your county assessor's office and ask. Look at historical flood maps. Plan that the 100-year-flood will happen next year. To you.

Yes, you're gambling some money that you will need the coverage. Better to have coverage when the disaster hits than to say you wished you'd gotten that coverage.

Business Rider

You'll need a business rider on your homeowners or rental policy to cover office equipment and your home business. For example, the computer that your kids use for games and homework gets covered in a disaster, but your work computer, the one that keeps the family in video games, won't be covered at all without the business rider.

Unlike (say) flood insurance, a business rider is relatively inexpensive and is an essential part of a freelancer's insurance package.

Liability Insurance

If you're running a home business that requires clients to come to you—like a law office out of your garage or a photography studio in your basement—get liability insurance. That way, when the innocent-looking old lady who slips on the stairs and cracks her rib decides to sue you for negligence, your insurance company will handle the claim. All you have to do is file the forms.

Umbrella Policy

Get an overall umbrella policy to cover all sorts of disasters. Have it start at a million dollars, or five million, or whatever is the limit on your other policies. That way, you're covered for catastrophic events, major lawsuits that run on and on for years, and other disasters that I can't even foresee as I write this.

Business-Specific Policies

I've listed the policies that a freelance writer needs because I am one and I'm familiar with what's needed. I added the liability insurance when we taught workshops at our home. (We don't teach at home any longer, having graduated to a marvelous old hotel in the same town. Now the hotel handles the liability claims.)

Each business has specific needs, most of which I know nothing about. Find out what your business needs as far as insurance is concerned, and buy it.

Here's the main rule on insurance: *never skimp. Buy exactly what you need or more. Preferably more. It's better to be over-insured than under-insured.*

Finally, here are a few tips on shopping for insurance.

First, don't do it alone. The Internet has provided a variety of tools for buying insurance without an agent. Use those tools to research coverage.

Then talk to a series of insurance agents—not just one. Ask a lot of questions. Find out what kind of coverage you need and how much it will cost.

Remember that many insurance agents work on commission, so they're often just trying to sell you product. Weed out the agents who are in the business only for the sale.

A lot of insurance agents love what they do and love the challenge of providing the best insurance possible for their clients. This is the kind of agent you want. You might end up with different agents for different kinds of insurance. If that's what you need, then that's what you do.

You need the best coverage *for you,* not the best coverage for their commission.

The most expensive insurance isn't always the best, so make sure you do your research.

And know what you want. Figure out how you want to live if disaster strikes. If you suffer as Matt Long did, do you want long-term care, or do you want to stay in your home? Can your insurance cover the multimillions it took to care for him? His could. But a lot of health policies limit the insurance company's liability to $1,000,000. Often you need riders or umbrella coverage to handle more than that.

Buy policies with the highest deductible that you can reasonably afford. That way, your monthly bill will be cheaper. But make sure you can afford that deductible.

Remember that you're buying insurance for the occasion *when* disaster happens, not *if* disaster happens. So one year, you'll have to pay that deductible, as we did that year of my emergency gall bladder surgery. It was a stretch, but we managed.

Reassess your insurance coverage annually. Things change. You get older, your health gets worse (or better). You change your business (like we did, moving our teaching outside the home). You get new equipment that needs better coverage. Your youngest kid graduates from college and has a full-time job with his own health insurance, so you no longer have to pay for his coverage. And on and on and on.

Insurance protects you in tough times—if you have the right coverage. So make sure your coverage is the best you can afford.

And remember: You must be able to afford insurance. If you don't have it, you're gambling with your career, your family's safety, and in some cases, their very lives.

Chapter Forty

Emergencies

I am writing this in a hotel room in Boise, Idaho. I'm not really on a vacation, but I did sorta plan for this trip. I knew I'd be away, planned projects I could do on the road, and brought a lot of electronic hardware with me. I feel a bit odd traveling with laptop, Kindle, iPhone, and iPod, but now that I'm here, I'm happy to have it.

Especially the laptop. This morning, I answered e-mail, shipped materials to editors in New York and Italy, and answered a few queries. I also put a few things off because I forgot to update my laptop calendar, so I'm clueless about the year ahead. And I didn't want to spend the few work hours I did have on things that would be better suited to do at home.

Even though I planned for this trip, however, it put me in mind of the last trip I took to Idaho which I did not plan for. Four years ago, my mother-in-law called. Dean's stepfather had died an hour before. The authorities had left, and she was informing everyone.

The death was not a surprise. Bill had been ill for the twenty years that I'd known him. But he was a strong man, determined, and a force of nature. That he had left the planet was shocking nonetheless.

Within six hours, Dean and I gathered our finances, paid bills, juggled work schedules, called our house sitter who was miraculously free on such short notice, packed, and headed out of town. We spent nearly a week in Boise, doing all that terrible work one does with a funeral, and then we made it home, exhausted, grieving, and re-entered our lives.

Although much of our work was at a standstill for that entire week, we lost only time. Our businesses were fine, our finances remained healthy, and I doubt any of our editors/readers noticed we had dropped everything for a week to deal with a family emergency. I don't even remember if we informed anyone we were working with that we had left town.

We were able to do that for a variety of reasons. The first is simply that we're organized. We know where everything is and how to deal with it quickly. The second is that we're good at juggling schedules. We figured out on the drive how to make up for the lost time. The third is the advent of electronic communication. We were able to stay in touch, even though we weren't at home. The fourth is the nature of our business. Much of what we do does not rely on face-to-face contact. We stayed in touch by cell phone, our house sitter monitors the home phone, and we made certain we had internet access wherever we went.

Even though we worked like crazy to prepare to leave town, we were able to do so in six hours. Even though we were tired and disoriented when we got home, we didn't screw up any projects or any possible jobs while we were away.

If this emergency—or one like it—had occurred fifteen years earlier, we would not have been so lucky. Cell phones weren't common. Business did not occur on the internet. We owned a business with 19 employees, and we supervised them. We had a great manager, but she couldn't do everything.

Whenever we traveled on planned trips, Dean found the nearest phone and spent an hour on it per call, giving orders, updating information, and running the business from the road. I recall many times when we nearly missed our connecting flights because he was giving important information on a nearby payphone and couldn't leave until he finished the conversation.

Emergencies happen. We've dealt with one aspect of them in the insurance chapter. Insurance is extremely important to a small business. In fact, I was just scanning a book called *Killing Sacred Cows: Overcoming the Financial Myths That Are Destroying Your Prosperity* by Garrett B. Gunderson to help Dean prepare for a class he was teaching on Money Management for Writers. Gunderson says that lack of insurance is one of the biggest reasons that small businesses fail. (He says a lot of interesting things in that book. I recommend it. You don't need to do all the stuff on his website, etc., but do read the book. It will change your attitude toward money, which will help you as a freelancer.)

Insurance can't help you with the hidden costs of an emergency, however. As the poor small businesses are learning during this horrible Gulf Coast oil spill, one of the most difficult aspects of an on-going emergency is predicting when it will end. Not every emergency is finite and quantifiable. Some go on for months—and in the case of the Gulf Coast—years.

Beyond having insurance, you must plan for all types of emergencies, and plan in ways you might not have considered.

First, let's deal with finite emergencies.

Finite emergencies are things that happen and end quickly. Things as dramatic as tornados are finite emergencies. But so are things like broken arms or a car accident.

Finite emergencies can be devastating, but they end relatively quickly, and you can usually measure their impact in both time and dollars. If a tornado destroys your business, the destruction itself will take seconds. You will then be able to assess the damage, figure out how long it will take to repair that damage, and whether or not you can afford to do so. Uncertainties include things like whether or not your insurance company will pay for all of the damage or only some of it, whether or not you'll be compensated for time lost, and whether or not you can accurately predict how much the weeks or months of rebuilding will cost you.

Finite emergencies often give you time to reassess whether or not your business is working as it should be. Many businesses rebuild in a different location or use the opportunity to redesign their office/ shop into something more efficient. They upgrade computer systems, make the building more comfortable, or put in the state-of-the art equipment they'd always planned to buy but never had the time to install.

Freelancers who work for themselves can also use finite emergencies to reassess. I broke my elbow ten years ago. For some business owners, a broken arm is an inconvenience. I'm a touch typist who thinks faster than my fingers can move. I tried to write with pen and paper; I also tried to type one-handed. If I never had use of the arm again, I would have been able to relearn how to write. But I knew I'd be able to type again in a few weeks, so I used the time to plan projects, research, and do things I normally didn't have time to do.

A broken elbow, for me, actually caused work stoppage. A broken elbow for someone who owns a retail store would be an inconvenience. I broke my foot five years later, and didn't stop work at all. In fact, with a broken foot, I had more time to write because I had to stop exercise for a few weeks. I wasn't even allowed to use the swimming pool for two weeks because the doctor feared I'd damage the foot permanently getting in and out.

Planning for a finite emergency is relatively easy.

First, you need insurance for as many things as you can possibly insure.

Health insurance, disability insurance, fire insurance, flood insurance, business insurance—you name it, you should have the coverage. Again, look at the insurance chapter to understand why.

Second, you need an emergency fund

—and it should *not* be credit cards. You need cash in the bank to handle the unexpected occurrence. Experts recommend that your emergency fund should be able to cover anywhere from three- to twelve-month's expenses. Not every freelancer or every business can handle this. But if you have at least one-month's worth of expenses, you should be able to handle many of the finite emergencies that come your way. Of course, in this case, more is always better.

Third, you need an emergency plan.

The plan should cover all types of finite emergencies. If you live in tornado country, as I used to, then you need a plan for the various types of damage that a tornado can do. I live on the Oregon Coast, where we have category one hurricane-type storms every winter. (They're not called hurricanes on the Pacific; I don't know why.) We can expect at least two or three days of power outages per winter. We can also expect some wind damage, usually in the form of downed trees or torn shingles off a roof.

Every ten years or so, we have storms that would be classified as category two or three hurricanes if they occurred in the Gulf or the Atlantic. The last time we had one (in 2007), we were without power for a week. In fact, a fiber optic cable to our small town got severed in the mountains nearby, and we didn't have cell phone service either. Everything was down. We went from the 21st century to the 19th in a matter of hours.

We struggled during the aftermath of that storm. The advantage I mentioned above—the fact that most of our business occurs on the phone or the internet—became a disadvantage. After they cleared the roads, we had to drive forty miles to find civilization. We went to restaurants, hauled out our laptops and phones, and informed the world that we were unavailable for the duration. It cost time, and since Dean also has an eBay business, it nearly cost him some customers. (It was December; people needed items by Christmas. He managed to get them their items, but only because we recovered by December 12. Had we been down another week, his eBay business might have been seriously harmed.)

We've lived through these storms for the past fifteen years. We'd never had one that shut down cell services from *all* providers before. But we now have contingency plans for that happening. We've also had internet outages without power outages during our winter storms, so we bought smart phones after that horrible December, figuring we could use a cell connection to get online if we absolutely had to.

Those are strange contingencies, brought on by where we live. I've also stopped doing exercises that could hurt my arms. I realized during that spring of the broken elbow that my arms are important to my business. I need to treat them the way an athlete would treat his body—as part of my income capacity.

When you're a sole proprietor, or if you're the only person in your small business who can do certain tasks, then you need to figure out what will happen to that business when you're incapacitated. Your finite emergency plans should address what happens on those occasions when you're too sick to work, when you're injured and unable to work, or when you're incommunicado for long periods of time.

Do an accurate assessment. It rarely hurts my business if I'm down for a few days, but my entire schedule gets screwed up if I'm out of commission for a week. If I'm working on a tight deadline, I might hurt my business if I'm sick for a few days and miss that deadline. I was very lucky I didn't get ill at the end of April, first of May because everything had piled up, and I would have missed four deadlines if I had gotten food poisoning or a serious flu.

I try not to allow my deadlines to get so close to the actual deadline for that very reason. I plan in emergency time, sick time, downtime—and the occasional impromptu trip. I try to have my work done a month or more before the actual deadline. Sometimes I turn a book or story in early. Sometimes I'm struggling to meet the actual deadline because illness or power outages put me "behind."

The emergency plan becomes even more important if you're the only one who can do the job. What happens if you're unavailable? Ill? Out of communication range? Have a back-up for the two-day emergency, the week-long emergency, and the month-long emergency. And remember: sometimes it's just better to close the business for a few days to solve the problem than it is to have someone who is unfamiliar with the tasks attempt them.

The emergency plan should cover as many finite emergencies as you can think of. Write the plan down—and make sure that the people upon whom the plan relies know where to find it. Also, make sure they understand it. A note like *If I'm gone, Suzy's in charge*, probably won't help in most cases. Write out the plan point by point. That's even more critical if you're a sole proprietor and the only one who can do the job. Instruct the person who is answering the phone or dealing with the e-mail on how to tell clients that you're unavailable.

In some businesses, telling a client that you're gone for weeks having cancer treatments might make the client flee the business because they'll fear that the business is in trouble. Telling them that you're dealing with a prolonged family emergency on the other hand will be easy to understand and doesn't give out any unnecessary particulars.

Finite emergencies are awful and sometimes difficult to handle, but they are measurable.

The worst situation you can find your business in is an ongoing emergency.

Right now, small businesses all over the Gulf are in a state of ongoing emergency. No one knows how long this crisis will last, what communities it will affect long-term, and what the area will look like when the last drop of oil gets contained. That doesn't count the environmental impact or the PR nightmare that many tourist-oriented businesses are facing.

I live in a tourist town. When our nearby big city's weather reporters say that we'll have torrential rains or cloudy days (in the summer), the tourists don't show up. After that major storm I mentioned above, the local Portland news reported repeatedly on the "devastation" on the coast. The devastation was limited to one town up north, but the rest of us saw no tourist business in all of December, even though local businesses were fine.

The Gulf Coast is facing this same problem on an infinitely larger scale. Tourists didn't show up this summer. But what about next summer? Or the summer after? It depends on what happens there, and the PR that comes out of the area. If no one says that such-and-so beach is fine, then the tourists will not come back to that beach no matter how pristine the sands are, devastating all the tourist-related businesses in the area.

And that doesn't count the businesses that rely on a clean and healthy ocean. In 1999, an oil tanker called the M/V *New Carissa* spilled oil along the Oregon Coast. We suffered a very tiny version of what's happening in the Gulf. The *Oregonian* newspaper published an article this week on one oyster-harvesting business, and the impact that oil spill had upon it. The business, Clausen Oysters, did amazingly well, considering. They still have a business. Most people wouldn't.

It took Clausen Oysters ten years to recover from the New Carissa spill. For four years after the spill, the company had no income. I suppose you could save that kind of money and try to ride it through, but that's unrealistic for most small businesses. (oregonlive. com/news/index.ssf/2010/06/clausen_oysters_of_north_bend.html)

Here's how you have to think about ongoing emergencies.

First, realize that there are a variety of ongoing emergencies.

If the owner of a business suddenly gets ill—and the illness will take a long time to recover from, if recovery is even possible—then the business needs to have a plan for someone else to take charge. That plan needs to have an implementation clause. Meaning—who decides when it's right to install the new boss? The incapacitated owner? (And what happens if that person is in a coma?) The board of directors, if there are any? The employees? The owner's family?

Decide these things before the emergency, and have a plan in writing to deal with whatever you can foresee.

The same goes for physical emergencies. For example, not all disasters are finite. A tornado may wipe out a block or even a small community, but generally not a region. A hurricane, on the other hand, can wipe out an entire state or area, as we learned during Katrina. And as we learned, the Gulf Coast region hadn't yet fully recovered when the oil spill hit. What does not fully recovered mean?

In human terms, it means that people hadn't finished rebuilding their lives yet. The population is still down in New

Orleans. Entire neighborhoods in Mississippi are still shut down and boarded off. Businesses are still fighting insurance claims from 2005. And the tourists hadn't completely come back yet.

Disasters sometimes come in waves, just as the Gulf is suffering now. A community in rural Eastern Oregon suffered devastating fires three years in a row due to the annual fires we have in the mountains here. The community hadn't had any fires near the city limits for decades before that.

Sometimes your business might recover, but the area around you does not. If you have a job like mine, which doesn't depend on foot traffic, you can survive that neighborhood shift. But if you own a restaurant or a retail store, you might have to move or shut your doors because no one comes to that neighborhood any more.

In the midst of an ongoing emergency, one discussion you have to have is whether or not to shut down the business. Sometimes it's better to walk away than it is to continue in a terrible environment.

It's better for a sole proprietor to have a list, written concurrently with the emergency plan, of times when the business should be abandoned due to crisis. That way, you're not making the decision in the middle of the crisis.

The worst thing about an ongoing emergency is the unpredictability of it. If you're an optimist—and deep down, you have to be to own your own business—then you're going to want to believe the best-case scenarios. Often, in an ongoing emergency, the best-case scenario is wrong. Believing it might prevent you from walking away from a situation at the wrong time.

What happens if you wait too long in an ongoing emergency to walk away? You can't cap damages. You can't put a financial value on what you've lost. Worse than that, the waiting and the fight to survive will damage your own personal finances, as well as your ability to get other work. They'll damage your relationships, and they'll damage your health as well.

Rarely does anyone talk about the effect of stress on business owners in any sort of emergency situation. In a finite emergency, the stress is there, but survivable—partly because we know roughly when the end will occur. However, in an ongoing emergency, the stress can last for a year or ten years. Stress raises blood pressure, causes illness, and leads to heart attack and stroke. You might want to wait out the ongoing emergency, but the toll it will take on your health might prevent you from ever reopening your business again.

When you sit down to make your emergency plans, look at every scenario you can think of. Imagine every single worst-case disaster, and then take a good hard look at your own health and your stamina. Could you survive the last ten years like the owners of Clausen Oysters? Or would you (or your family) fall apart?

Be as honest as you can. Figure it out. Make plans. Revise those plans every few years as your business grows and changes. What you decide today might not apply five years from now.

Realize too that some emergencies will have elements of the finite and the ongoing. When my father died in 1990, I expected to return to work after a short mourning period. Had I waited tables, I could have done so within the week. But my grief for my father, for some reason, robbed me of the ability to read and write. I simply couldn't concentrate. For six months, I couldn't practice my business, no matter what I did.

I managed to survive that, but I made a mental note of it. When my mother became very ill, I added a six-month grieving period to my emergency plan. However, when she died, my grief didn't take the same form, so I didn't need to use that plan. But it was in place, just in case.

For people who live through tornados or other natural disasters, the finite emergency might become ongoing because the finite emergency triggered health problems or financial issues that will take years to resolve.

When it comes to emergencies, follow the old cliché: Plan for the worst and hope for the best. Your life will be much easier if you do.

Chapter Forty-one
Setbacks

Let's start by being completely honest: Setbacks hurt. And I don't simply mean that they hurt your business. They hurt personally. They're embarrassing, difficult, infuriating, and terrifying. They make us feel as if this hasn't happened to anyone else before, ever, and yet they happen to all of us.

They happen in successful businesses as well as unsuccessful ones. They happen in start-ups and they happen in long-term businesses.

The real key with setbacks isn't preventing them; it's surviving them when they happen. Over the years, I've become a connoisseur of setbacks. I'm not interested in other people's misfortunes (except as a grist for my own fiction), but I am interested in how other people survive those misfortunes.

In other words, I am an inveterate studier of setback recovery. And believe it or not, that's a hard thing to study, since most people hide their misfortunes, and do so very well. They pretend that nothing has gone wrong, and most of us remain fooled, partly because we can't see deeply into other people's lives unless they let us, and partly because we really don't pay attention to anything outside of our circle, unless we're forced to.

I spend a lot of my time imagining "what would happen if." In fact, that's my job. I must imagine what would happen if, because that phrase is at the heart of all fiction. So it's only inevitable that sometimes I turn "what would happen if" from "what would happen if Godzilla suddenly appeared on the Oregon Coast" to "what would happen if I suddenly lost every dime I ever had."

They're not just good exercises for fiction writing; they're good exercises for future planning. Fortunately, my husband has the same bent, so he doesn't think I'm ghoulish when I start a "what would happen if" conversation.

In my studies of setbacks and recoveries, I've deduced this: there are four categories and probably a million subcategories of setbacks.

The four major categories are:

1. Financial
2. Mechanical/technical/production
3. Physical
4. Emotional

So let's look at them in depth.

Financial Setbacks

The name speaks for itself. For some reason, something happens in the financial side of the business that hurts the business. Did the business undercapitalize? (What the hell does undercapitalize mean, anyway?) Is the business underperforming? Does it pay its bills? (What the hell does paying the bills mean, exactly?)

Those are the practical aspects of finances, things that you and your accountant or you and your bookkeeper, or you and the math expert in your family should be able to figure out with a calculator, the invoices, the checkbooks, the bills, and a stack of receipts.

But I'm not referring to that here. In some ways, figuring out the profitability (or lack of profitability) in your business is the easy part.

The hard part is simpler—and much more terrifying.

Something financial that you planned on went horribly awry. Financial setbacks are always a surprise. Maybe not in hindsight, but as they happen, you're usually caught flatfooted. This doesn't mean you can't plan for them, but you'll never know when one is going to strike.

If you've been paying attention to the business news since the fall of 2008, you have heard about setbacks.

Some are extreme. For example, people who invested with Bernie Madoff and the swindlers of his ilk (well, of a lesser ilk, since he seemed to be the master swindler) lost everything. Or the bulk of their savings. Or the money they were going to use to survive their retirement.

In this case, people went from affluent to poverty-stricken in the space of an afternoon. Or at least it seemed that way from their perspective. In reality, they went broke the moment they handed Madoff a check.

As an aside: I have little sympathy for people who dealt with Madoff directly. Those people didn't do their due diligence in hiring an outside investor for their funds. Madoff didn't respond well to questions, which is a large red flag. But so many people had invested with a marketing fund or an investment group who then put the money into Madoff as part of a package deal. I feel for those people. I know what it's like to be embezzled from. It's happened to me twice—once a relatively small amount, and once a larger amount. That larger amount had never been in my pocket, however. The embezzler (a book agent) skimmed the money off the top and I didn't even know that money existed. So I didn't miss it when I learned it was gone.

What happened to Madoff's investors is an extreme case. Most people never suffer through that, but they do go through very tough times. The news in the first week of September 2009 reported that more than one million people lost their jobs since the beginning of 2009. That's more than 125,000 per month—all of whom had just received a financial setback.

That setback is worse for some than others. Some had warning. Others planned ahead and had savings. But for each person who lost a job, the setback is severe. Immediately, the calculations begin: How long until I can't pay my bills? How long before I lose my house?

I've gone through several financial setbacks in my life—from the first (and only) job I've ever been fired from when I was twenty (seems I had an attitude problem [go figure]) to the crash of our publishing company, Pulphouse Publishing, in the early 1990s to some business setbacks that started around 9/11. I honestly don't want to count how many financial setbacks I've survived; just thinking about them makes my stomach twist. I know just how close I was to falling off some kind of horrible precipice, and how each day was a struggle.

But I've never fallen off that precipice. I've always found a way to make money, and I've always had a home. Which is more than my husband can say. He was homeless for a while in his twenties, and he talks about that with understatement. The difficulty of those days, the moment-by-moment panic, must have been agonizing.

Financial setbacks hit businesses as well. From the embezzling employee (as I mentioned above) to the loan that doesn't come through to the big client who goes bankrupt, financial setbacks in a business can be as devastating as the ones in your personal life. In fact, they can lead to financial setbacks in your personal life, if you're not careful.

And often, the financial setbacks are related to other setbacks, which I'll talk about later.

How can you protect yourself against financial setbacks?

1. Plan for them.

I know. I just said they're always a surprise. But I also said that they hit every single business—and they hit every single person at one time or another in life. So have a reserve fund. Have a game plan for tough times. Have contingency plans. Try not to overextend credit to one client. Make sure you have more than one client. Know how much you can afford to lose in one year, so that when a problem does hit, you can assess whether that problem is minor, major, or devastating.

2. Assess the damage immediately.

When a financial setback occurs, don't think things will get better. Assess where you are now in the new reality, and then plan for things to get worse. Sometimes one financial setback is a precursor to others. (Think of the banks denying all commercial credit in late 2008, and then cutting credit lines. That destroyed a lot of businesses that use those lines to order stock and stay afloat in the off-season.) Figure out immediately how bad the loss is and how bad it could become.

3. Cut your losses immediately.

If you lose a major client, don't expect another to take his place. Cut your expenses, cut your salary to the bone, lay off workers if you have to, move to cheaper digs—do whatever you need to in order to compensate for that huge financial loss. The faster you do this, the more likely you are to save your business in the long run.

4. Search for a way to replace that income.

This, of course, depends on your business. Get another big client, take out a loan from a different organization, sell off some inventory at lower than usual prices. Do what you can. If you do 3 &

4 in conjunction, you might just turn a financial setback into a blip on the balance sheet.

5. Be realistic.

If the financial setback damages your business so badly that you are bailing water out of a bottomless boat, then shut the business down. Again, the faster you take action, the better off you'll be. Too many business owners incur tens of thousands of dollars in needless debt by hanging on to a business that will die anyway.

Financial setbacks are often the easiest setbacks to see. Numbers rarely lie. In that way, they're the easiest ones to deal with. You know what's happening—it's all there in black and white. Doing something, however, is harder.

Add to that the feeling of failure that inevitably comes with being unable to meet your obligations or pay your bills, and that's a recipe for disaster.

Talk to the people closest to you. Have a plan. And expect the worst. You'll go through it and come out the other side if you do.

Mechanical/Technical/Production Setbacks

These are often product-related setbacks, or setbacks that in some way involve the center of your business. For example, grocery stores went through this a few years ago when the government discovered e-coli in spinach. Thousands of dollars worth of produce got tossed, and even more didn't get purchased. Even now, spinach sales are down from their peak before the e-coli debacle.

And imagine what that did to farmers who produced the spinach and the processing plants that packaged the wash-and-eat spinach. Some of those businesses got wiped out, just because some spinach somewhere (and I can't remember where) got contaminated *as it grew*, and so the e-coli was entwined in the actual plant, and not on its surface. Who could have planned for that?

A writer I know got a million dollar book contract, paid out over years and several books. One editor bought those books, then left the company. By the time the writer turned in the first book in the contract (on time, mind you), she had been orphaned three times (meaning three other editors had presided over the project). The new editor who got the book wasn't even familiar with the genre the book was in. My friend rewrote that book to the editor's specifications for another year plus, before the editor decided the book was unacceptable, and asked my friend to repay every dime paid out in the contract thus far.

Think on this: the advance had been paid, the author had done the work—in fact, she'd done three times the normal amount of work—and she still had to repay the money. (She eventually negotiated this down to repayment when she resold the book, which she did—the original version, not the thrice-rewritten thing.)

For two and a half years, this writer made no money; and at the end of that period of time, she was told she had to repay money she'd spent three years before. *That's* a setback.

Sometimes mechanical/technical setbacks are the fault of the business owner. My friend could have written a bad book. (In this case, she hadn't, but if she had, then the fault would have been hers.) Some of the e-coli cases in the news lately have been the product of filthy processing plants and uncaring business owners. They're criminally negligent, and deserve the punishment they'll be getting.

In some cases, though, setbacks are part of the business. Contractors who remodel houses, for example, never know what they'll find behind ancient walls or underneath a rotted floorboard. And some businesses—like oil drilling—are by nature speculative, with many more failures than successes. Setbacks are planned things in those businesses.

How do you survive a technical/mechanical/production setback?

1. Have insurance.
Most businesses have insurance for just this sort of thing. If something goes wrong in the manufacture of clothing, for example, then insurance should cover the losses.

A business rider on your insurance policy will help with some of the smaller problems. But not every business can be insured. Writers can't, for example. We have to cope with the occasional failed manuscript, bad agent, or new editor. So the next best thing is—

2. Make sure you have more than one client or more than one product.
Buggy whip manufacturers never recovered from the switch over to the automobile a century ago, but bicycle repairmen suddenly had a whole new business if they wanted it, because no one knew

where to take their car to be repaired, so they went to the bicycle guy, whom they saw as the next best thing to a car repairman. Writers should work for more than one publisher (and in more than one form or genre); stores should carry more than one product.

The more you diversify your business, the better off you are.

3. Have a contingency plan.

Nothing ever goes entirely as planned. Assess what'll happen to your business if the main product line has serious problems *before* those serious problems occur. You might be able to turn what could be a setback into a minor problem.

4. Cut your losses.

Sometimes you try a new product and it doesn't work, for whatever reason. Pull out of that area as soon as possible, and reassess. Make sure you haven't overextended or jumped into an area you didn't fully understand.

5. Be realistic.

If something went wrong with your machine, or your product, or your timetable, it was probably your fault. Find out where the mistakes were and change that behavior immediately. If the problem wasn't yours, note that. It still had an impact on you, however, and you need to be realistic about whether or not that impact was minor, bad, or severe.

If you're not realistic, you won't be able to solve the problem. Worse, you won't be able to prevent future, similar problems.

6. Take responsibility.

If you're at fault, say so. Offer the client some kind of recompense for the problem. Act swiftly, and the client will usually respond well. (This works, except in cases where the problem caused some kind of legal hassle. Then talk to a lawyer [preferably more than one lawyer] and take his advice.) The faster you own up to a mistake, the more the client is likely to trust you in the future. Especially if you do good work from that point forward.

Physical Setbacks

Physical setbacks find many forms, but they're always caused by something outside your freelance business acting upon your freelance business.

Some are things the insurance companies call "Acts of God." Fires, earthquakes, floods, tornados, hurricanes are all "Acts of God." You can insure for most of them—you need special insurance for floods, for example—but insurance doesn't stop the setback. It only ameliorates the damage.

Let me explain what I mean. Before I met him, Dean lost his house to a fire. The fire started in a control panel, and had he been home that day, he could have stopped the damage. But he was out of town, and arrived at the house in time to see the fire department hosing off his collectible books in the front yard.

Dean has always been a big believer in insurance, and he was fully covered for the damages that occurred that day. He got reimbursed for all the lost items, including the collectibles, but some problems that occurred from the fire couldn't be fixed.

In those days, Dean wrote on a typewriter. He lost dozens of manuscripts, many single copies of his publications, and some works in progress. He was too traumatized to go back to the works in progress, even though he could have reconstructed them from scratch, but the lost manuscripts were another matter entirely.

You see, after writing for some time, we writers don't remember our early works very well. Just the other day, I found a story I had forgotten I had written. At Worldcon in 2008, a publisher asked to reprint a story I hadn't thought of in nearly 20 years. I reread the story, realized that now I would write it differently, and looked at it as an artifact of another, younger version of Kris. Just as valid, but very, very different.

Most businesses would have some of the same problems. If the collectibles store that we sold a few years ago burned down tomorrow (God forbid), many rare items would be lost. The owner is insured, but the hard-to-find items would be impossible to replace.

Events like this take an emotional toll, just like financial and mechanical/technical/production setbacks do. Even now, reminders of the fire make Dean take a deep breath. We cleared our house of unwanted possessions as we moved our offices, and we found the dishes that Dean had managed to save after the fire. He waved a hand, said, "Get rid of them," and then, not an hour later, changed his mind. He couldn't bear to part with something he had worked so hard to save.

Here's the thing about physical setbacks: there's the event, and then there's the aftermath.

The fire took place in a single day. Dean can still tell you the exact date. But the aftermath took years.

For a larger example, look at Hurricane Katrina. People all over the Gulf Coast lost homes, but they also lost businesses. Areas remained closed for months. Some of those businesses—although insured—never reopened. Some are still being rebuilt.

Imagine losing four years of your life to rebuilding your home and business. It takes a special kind of person to dive in all over again. You have to rebuild your life, of course, but you don't always have to rebuild it in exactly the same way.

Sometimes the physical setbacks don't even have to happen to you or near you. When the planes struck the Twin Towers on 9/11, Dean and I were at home in Oregon. Yet that single event caused a huge ripple through publishing, which is based in New York.

My main publisher at the time was located in an area near Ground Zero, an area that was shut down by the city for more than a month. My secondary publisher lost a number of people in accounting, including the main person who signed the checks. Dean has similar stories.

We did not receive any of the monies owed to us from New York for more than six months after 9/11. We didn't get paid on our contracts—money due to us that September—until March of 2002.

That was a financial setback for us, but it was caused by a physical setback, and my brilliant husband saw it coming. (If you're ever in a disaster, you want Dean at your side. He can see all the implications immediately.)

While I watched television, horrified by the events, and worked the phones and the internet to see if our friends and colleagues were still alive, Dean piled a bunch of collectible books into our van and drove two hours to Portland. He went to Powell's Bookstore and traded those books for cash. Good thing he did: Powell's shut down its trading arm the next day for some time (a month, I think) and as I said, we didn't get paid for six months.

We didn't need that thousand dollars on 9/11, but we sure needed it in the weeks that followed. I would never have thought of that, but Dean did, and he acted swiftly.

It's tough to act swiftly in a physical crisis. If the crisis is happening near you or to you, you often can't act swiftly. You're involved in the event, and then you're surviving the aftermath.

Sometimes the very nature of the physical setback—such as

Katrina—will cause the aftermath to seem very much like the event. The trauma will continue for some time before recovery can even start.

There's another kind of physical setback, one that can be as bad or worse. You get hurt. If you're the sole proprietor of your business and have no employees, you suddenly have no ability to work either. Even those businesses with employees might not be able to go on for very long without you, because you might be the only one with check-writing ability or the ability to find the jobs or the vision to keep the business on track.

Recently, I was talking with our gardener. He's a strong and able man, who gets more work done in an afternoon than I can imagine. He has at least three employees.

The week before, he was cutting down a holly tree with a chain saw on one of his many job sites. He inspected the tree before cutting it down, looked at the area around the tree, and saw nothing amiss. Then he fired up the chain saw and started cutting.

The sound of the saw awoke yellow jackets, which had nested in an underground hollow. He said, "I looked up and saw at least 600 of them heading right toward me."

He jumped, with the chainsaw still going, off the incline he was working on and ran for his truck. Halfway there, he realized the yellow jackets were going for his green shirt, so he pulled the shirt off. Many of the yellow jackets stayed behind, stinging the shirt.

The rest came after him.

He was stung at least 35 times.

To make matters worse, he's allergic to the stings. His assistants drove him from the job site to the nearby hospital, a drive of less than five minutes, and he could barely breathe by the time he got inside the emergency room.

So what did he do?

He took the weekend off. But he was back to work on Monday. He's still puffy, and he says he's downing Benedril like crazy, but he's working.

The man should be at home. He should be recovering. He should be resting and taking care of himself. But it was summer, his busiest season. He can rest when the rains start in November.

Until then, he's moving through the pain.

His assistant, who helped him get to the hospital and who is at least twenty years younger, is astonished by this. But his assistant doesn't own the business. He doesn't know how important it is to keep working. The assistant—like so many employees—would have the luxury of taking the time off.

Sometimes you can't keep working. Sometimes you have to rest. Sometimes you have to recover. I often say—only half joking—that I could get hit by a bus tomorrow. But I could. And depending on the damage, I might not be back to work for months, if ever.

One more story, and then I'll quit and get to the bullet points. At the age of nine, I fell off my bicycle and landed on my face. I have a lot of physical scarring. Most people don't notice it, but the scarring is severe enough that most plastic surgeons, when they meet me, wave a hand around their face and say, "I can fix that for you if you want."

(I don't want. What I do want is for plastic surgeons to leave me alone.)

I have never fixed the scars, but the teeth needed repair. I had knocked out my front teeth which were, unfortunately, my permanent teeth. First I had them capped, then they got recapped twice in my twenties. All of these procedures were supposed to be permanent. In my late thirties, the dentists just replaced the front teeth entirely. (That cost money, since I can't get dental insurance because of my pre-existing condition.)

After the first surgery to replace the teeth, I spent a day or so on my back. I'd had dental surgery before, and I planned for those two days off. The third day rolled around, and I stumbled to my desk. Then, I began to cry. I couldn't remember how write. I thought something in my brain got damaged in the surgery.

Turns out that certain extremely strong pain pills block parts of the brain from communicating with each other. I could want to write, but I couldn't quite figure out how.

I stopped taking the pills. I'd rather hurt than not write. I'm a person with a very high pain tolerance. I can go without pain pills for things that knock most people over.

Most folks wouldn't have been able to forego the medication, and what should have been a few days off might have become weeks.

So how do you handle physical setbacks?

1. Plan for them.
I know, I know. How do you foresee a disaster like Hurricane

Katrina? You don't, exactly. (No one could have predicted the bungling that made the results of that storm even worse.)

But you do know the Acts of God that threaten your part of the world. If you live in Southern California, for God's sake, get earthquake insurance. If you live on an historical flood plain, pony up the extra money and buy flood insurance.

Make sure you're insured for fire, and make sure you have a business rider on your homeowners policy.

Insurance isn't enough, however. Most of us, no matter what business we're in, do some work on computer. Store your back-ups off site. I keep one current back-up of everything in the car and older back-ups in our storage unit, far from our house.

I'm putting my publications in order as well, and when I have enough, I store the extra copies in the storage unit. That way, if something happens to our house, I can reconstruct most of my published material. I won't get all of it, but I'll get some of it.

Store financial records off-site (in a secure location) and store other important things off site as well. For example, I had a computer meltdown earlier this year. The one thing I didn't back-up was my e-mail addresses. I'm still reconstructing those.

2. Assess the damage as quickly as you can.

If you're lucky, you have a mind like Dean's, and can foresee future problems on the day the event occurs. Most of us don't think that way. But as soon as you can, dust yourself off and take stock. Look at the extent of the damage and figure out what it will take to fix everything.

Don't just look at the financial impact. Look at the physical one. Must you rebuild your office? Can you rent an office suite? Are you living out of a hotel? Did the doctor find additional problems in that exploratory surgery?

Get estimates from contractors, talk to your physicians, and then take their timelines and double them. Assume that as the rebuilding happens, something else will go wrong. If you plan for a long setback (like Dean did on 9/11), you and your business will survive the crisis.

You also need to figure out if you'll be able to work during the rebuild. Can you supervise construction and continue your legal practice? Are you clearheaded enough to continue offering therapy to your clients?

These are important questions, not just for your future, but also for the future of your business.

3. Expect a long aftermath.

Yes, I just dealt with the length of the physical aftermath above, but there's also an emotional aftermath. Dean was still having trouble working when I met him a year after the house fire. The loss of his manuscripts had devastated him. He got work done, but he had trouble believing it would last.

Severe physical events cause emotional trauma. Expect it, be kind to yourself when it happens, and if need be, get some professional help to overcome the most serious effects. You'll be glad you did—and so will the people around you.

4. Be honest with yourself.

Physical setbacks are often opportunities in disguise. Maybe you felt trapped by your at-home business. Maybe you actually hated going to the store every day. Maybe you aren't really fond of plumbing after all.

If that's the case, use this loss as a chance to start over.

If you still love your work, you might have developed bad habits or overspending. This setback might be the time to rebuild the way you should have built the business in the first place.

Be honest about the business's flaws and try to fix them as you rebuild the business.

5. Be realistic.

Will the insurance money be enough to rebuild the business? Will your savings cover you while you're recuperating from major surgery? Make sure your assessment of these crucial things is honest and straightforward, and a bit on the pessimistic side.

It's always better to plan for the worse case scenario. That way, when things aren't as bad as expected, you're actually ahead.

6. Find a way to replace the lost income.

During the rebuilding period, you might have to get a day job to tide you over. Do so as quickly as you reasonably can, so that your basic expenses are covered. This is not a failure. Instead, it's another forward step toward getting yourself and your business back on your feet.

Physical setbacks are a lot more powerful than we give them credit for. They last longer and are often harder to overcome than anyone expects.

Emotional Setbacks

In some ways, emotional setbacks are the most difficult setbacks of all. You can blame outside forces for each of the previous three setbacks. For example, you ran into trouble because the economy collapsed. Or because your biggest client didn't pay you. Or because someone sold you tainted spinach to sell to your grocery store customers.

And whose fault was Hurricane Katrina? Even if the government had responded quickly, the hurricane would have still hit the Gulf Coast, ruining countless businesses.

Sometimes someone else truly is responsible for what happens to you—whether it's an Act of God or whether it's someone else's incompetence.

And sometimes, setbacks are your fault.

Face it. We all make mistakes. Sometimes we make doozies. The mistakes might be the result of ignorance or overconfidence, arrogance or inexperience. Whatever the reason, the best thing we can do is own up to our mistakes, and not make the same mistake again.

The problem, however, is that you will have an emotional response to any setback that happens to you. Sometimes that response will be relief, which means that you shouldn't rebuild your business in the way that it was before. (Or you shouldn't rebuild it at all.)

But other problems lead to other reactions.

In addition to the physical crisis caused by Hurricane Katrina, that disaster also created emotional setbacks. The survivors grieved. They lost their homes, their businesses, their communities. In many cases, they lost relatives as well.

Grief is a real, powerful, and sometimes crippling emotion. The grief books (and there are many) recommend going easy on yourself and understanding what you're going through. Survive it, the books say, and eventually you'll feel better.

Which is all well and good when you have a day job that allows you to take personal time, or a job that doesn't require your attention every minute of every day. But imagine what it took for these folks to rebuild their businesses and their lives while grieving. They didn't have time to go easy on themselves. They had to work through the grief.

Many people who suffer physical setbacks actually postpone the emotional reaction to it. For some reason (and I'm not a psychologist, so I'm not sure what the reason is), some people can hold back their emotional reaction until a more appropriate time. Soldiers, police officers, and firefighters do this routinely.

The problem is that when the actual physical crisis ends, the emotional reaction begins. And it's a powerful reaction—all the more powerful because it waited to come out.

That's when you'll hear people apologize for "unnecessary" tears, for "emotional" outbursts, for "inappropriate" anger. The emotional reaction is part of the physical setback, and needs to be treated that way. If you skip it—and people do—then the emotion will come out in other ways. Many sufferers of post-traumatic stress disorder never had time to deal with the emotions during the crisis, and so have to deal with them when the crisis is over or face a crippling unpredictable reaction.

If you go through something severe—a fire, a flood, the loss of everything, complete financial collapse—get some counseling as well. You'll need some kind of support to get through the emotional aftermath, whether that support is through your faith, your friends, or your therapist.

But what of emotional setbacks that have no relationship to the first three setbacks? In some ways, these are the most difficult of all. Because, as much as we like to think we're an understanding culture, Americans prefer to ignore deep emotions. We don't want to hear how sad someone is or how angry he became. We might listen sympathetically the first time the story gets told, but if the teller doesn't recover quickly (and we each have a different definition of quickly), then we avoid the topic, or worse, avoid the teller altogether.

We have a pick-yourself-up-by-the-bootstraps mentality, and that often means that the people around you expect you to recover right away. The flip side of this are the people who allow one setback to destroy their lives. They find like-minded individuals who never get past whatever it was that destroyed their lives, and they spend the rest of their lives reliving it.

Most people in that second group don't have the physical or emotional stamina to own their own businesses. But most people don't fall into that category. Most people can recover, given time and support. Both of those things are difficult to give, which is why I recommend that people in crisis get professional help whenever possible.

Generally, the negative emotions cause the most setbacks—although not always. I'll end on a positive emotion that can cause the most trouble of all.

Here's the problem with emotional setbacks, however. Unlike fire that destroys a business or financial meltdown that destroys nest eggs, emotional setbacks aren't always obvious problems. Something emotional that will destroy me won't even bother you, and vice versa. Something in our individual make-up causes one type of emotion to hook itself into one person, and not bother another person at all.

Take anger. Some people can't abide anger. They fear it. They avoid it in themselves. I've known people who quit jobs because their boss had a quick temper. I used to work for a man who broke phones when he hung up. I worked for a woman who threw dishes while screaming at the top of her lungs. That bothered me, sure, but not enough to quit.

But liars, backstabbers, and manipulators? Whenever they appeared at any job I worked, I quit in an instant. I can't abide people like that, and the smallest incident involving me will make me run from that person forever—paycheck or no paycheck.

Why did I call this difference between people a problem? Simple. Something that might bring you to your knees might strike your best friend as hilarious. It's not that your friend is insensitive. In fact, your friend might be the first on the scene with money and a place to stay if your home and office were leveled in a tornado. But have an emotional tornado, and that friend might not understand what you're going through at all.

When the people around you don't understand, you start questioning your own reaction. Are you overreacting? Are you too sensitive? Are you, in fact, being silly?

Probably not. You're having an emotional setback, and unless you figure out a way around that setback, it might devastate you and your business.

Signs of a severe emotional reaction: inability or lack of desire to go to work, crying jags, extreme (and seemingly unprovoked) anger, and/or something the psychologists call emotional lability—excessive emotional reactions and frequent mood changes.

If these things are happening to you, you'll need to figure out the underlying cause, and find a way to release that emotion or to deal with it or (worst case) to block it.

Sometimes, as in the case of grief, you'll just need to endure until the emotional reaction lessens. Time really does heal, although it's hard to realize when you're in the middle of it all.

Often, in the case of emotional setbacks, you're experiencing a problem, but you don't know why. You're less enthusiastic about work. Your habits have changed and you don't know why. You have no joy in something you used to love.

In fact, you may find yourself looking for a way out.

Sometimes that's a legitimate response to a business you thought you'd like, but you didn't understand or you don't like as much as you thought. Maybe there's more drudgery than you were prepared for or maybe you're not suited to the day-to-day tasks of the business. That's a different issue.

What I'm dealing with here is something more subtle. You've been working at your business for a long while now, and up until lately, you've enjoyed it. Then something changed.

Usually what changed is an event that precipitated an emotional response. So let's look at some of the more common negative emotions and the way they can manifest in your business.

1. Fear.

Fear is insidious. It paralyzes, quite literally. If you can't get anything done when you used to get a lot done, you might be suffering from excessive fear.

Some of us were raised to be fearful, so this is a natural state. My parents suffered some extreme financial reversals when I was a little girl, and they taught me (through their actions) to quit when the going gets rough. I'll give you one example:

At twelve, I was the best swimmer in my age group at the YMCA, where the local pool was. I won every race among our group. So I represented our group in an actual race against other groups and as I was swimming, I realized I was half a length behind some other girl. Instead of pushing harder, I climbed out of the pool, claiming I didn't feel well. My parents let me. They took me home, and we never spoke of that race again.

As an adult, I now realize that my coach had the proper response: *"Get back in the pool! You're not sick! Keep swimming!"* But to me, losing was worse that quitting, so I quit.

I often wonder how different my life would have been if I'd continued. But my parents, because of their own reversal of fortune (and their reaction to it), told me later I clearly wasn't a swimmer or an athlete. I shouldn't try any longer.

I remained paralyzed with fear over athletics until my late 30s, when I realized that I could finish swim races. Sounds like a minor thing, but it was pretty major for me. Overcoming that fear led to all kinds of other activities, and gave me strength in my writing business.

A lot of us were raised to be perfect, to make no mistakes, so we live in fear of mistakes. We make a single mistake and we freeze, afraid to make another. Instead of charging ahead, we don't do anything.

That's why fear is insidious. You'll lose your opportunity or your advantage or your business because you're taking no action at all. And it's always better to take action, even the wrong action, than it is to remain motionless.

So if you suddenly can't get anything done, ask yourself what you're afraid of. You might be surprised at the result.

2. Anger.

My favorite emotion. Really. I get a lot done when I'm angry. In fact, anger breaks me out of fear (usually anger at myself). While anger is a driving force for me, it's a paralyzing force for others. Some people—especially women of a certain age—were raised to suppress their anger. Anger was an unacceptable emotion, so they weren't allowed to express it.

If you can't express anger, it comes out sideways—either in snide comments or passive/aggressive behavior. Better to figure out who—or what—you're angry at and confront that person in a non-threatening manner, than to continually punish them with verbal asides or hurtful behavior. Particularly if that person is a client.

Here's the problem with anger, though. It can easily turn into uncontrollable rage. I had to learn how to control my anger and turn it into a positive force. My ex-husband gave me a metal garbage can and told me to kick it every time I got angry over a rejection. Believe it or not, that worked. I loved that can. It dented easily, so I could see the damage. And then I could calm down and write another story or deal in a dignified manner with the person who made me angry. A therapist told me once that she has her clients punch pillows when they're angry. *"It gets the violent part of the emotion out,"* she said, *"and leaves the constructive part."*

It's really not good to own a business with employees, and be a shrieker or a person who smashes phones. Extreme anger directed at employees can get you in trouble with the law these days. Better to find a constructive way to deal with it, and then move on.

Sometimes that constructive manner is to get the emotion out, and then fire the employee. Or tell the client you don't want their business any more.

Getting rid of the object of your anger will often make the anger go away.

3. Betrayal.

This one's hard. Betrayal happens in all kinds of ways. A trusted employee goes to the press with lies. A client badmouths you to other clients. A friend tells your confidences to others who really shouldn't know.

If the person who betrayed you works with you, then often you don't want to go to work even if you own the place. It's easier to avoid that person than it is to confront them about their behavior. And it's easier to avoid work than it is to get rid of the person who hurt you.

Often the best thing to do in the case of betrayal is to take the person who caused the hurt out of a position to hurt you again. Don't confide in that friend any more. Fire the employee who went to the press. Refuse new projects with the client who badmouthed you.

And, otherwise, don't engage. Let the incident fade into the past. That might seem hard—and it is, initially—but after a while, it gets easier. And then it becomes unimportant.

I wouldn't have believed that last, twenty years ago. But I've · experienced it. And I learned something else.

People forget.

So often we worry about our reputation. We worry that people will misjudge us or damage our reputation. (Or maybe we damaged it.) Here's the funny thing: most people never notice. If the harm to the reputation is severe, repair what damage you can and then go on. Over time, it'll be a small part of your résumé, if it's there at all.

I haven't edited for 12 years. Recently, a friend of mine interviewed me for a short profile that will appear in a science fiction magazine in a few months. This friend is a student of the field and has known me for at least fifteen years.

He asked me about my writing, about the various genres I publish in, and then asked if I thought we needed to cover anything else. Since the interview was going to go into an sf magazine, I said, "You'll probably want to mention that I won a Hugo for editing *The*

Magazine of Fantasy & Science Fiction, and that I used to own (with Dean) Pulphouse Publishing." He laughed, and asked (rhetorically) how he could have forgotten.

He forgot because I haven't done it for so long.

When I was editing, people used to forget that I was also a writer. They see what they want to see—or what you present to them.

Recently, Dean and I asked various writers with long publishing careers how many crashes they had. All of them answered with at least three. Now, these folks were close enough friends that we could even broach the question without apology, and with the exception of one friend, we hadn't seen any of those crashes. And we try to stay current with other people's careers.

Things you think might have an impact on your reputation probably won't harm it at all.

Betrayals that have an impact on reputation probably aren't as severe as you think. Betrayals that are personal will probably make you angry or upset for the rest of your life. But you can't let them make you bitter. Take *constructive* action against the person who hurt you, and then move on.

4. Failure.

I have a longer chapter on failure in this section, but failure deserves some mention here. Often we feel like failures when we're not failing at all. What's going on?

Usually you've failed in a personal dream or goal. Or you've perceived a failure where there is none. Sometimes it's a simple as attitude.

A friend of mine says that his wife can see a black cloud in every silver lining. I can be that way as well. If twenty-five good things happen today and one bad thing happens, I'll focus on the bad thing. Many people are like that.

When we do workshops, I make the students write down the good things we say about their work as well as the bad things. In fact, I harangue them until they do so.

That's because we often don't hear the compliments. We're looking so hard to improve that we never see what we're doing well.

If you take an attitude of "one mistake is failure" into your business, you won't survive. You really do need to think positively, even if you have to make lists to keep yourself on track. I write down every good thing that happens in my business in my calendar, so when I get into a failure funk, I look back and see the good things. It helps. It really does.

5. Success.

As with failure, success can sometimes cause an emotional setback.

I know, I know. You're all shaking your heads.

But here's what happens.

You have a goal which you thought was unattainable. That goal is what drives you, deep down. You are striving to meet that goal, thinking it'll keep you going for the rest of your career and then, suddenly, you attain it.

You'll stop working. You won't know why. But you've just lost your driving force.

I've seen this happen countless times. With writers, the goal is usually publishing related. Some writers quit when they sell their first story because they met their goal. Others can't go on after their first (and therefore only) *New York Times* bestseller.

What you have to do in this circumstance is reset your goals. That's not easy, and if you need an unattainable goal, you're going to really have to reach for the stars.

I can't tell you how many people I know have quit because they attained their driving goal. So if you're having trouble working and you just had a major success, it's time to re-evaluate where you are and what you want from your career.

Emotional setbacks are as real as any other kind of setback. They're sometimes harder to identify, and often harder to overcome. But you can do it.

My philosophy about any kind of setback is simple: It doesn't matter how many times you fall down. Nor does it matter how long you remain sprawled on the floor. The only thing that matters is how many times you get back up.

The key to setbacks is twofold: expect that you'll have some over the years, and figure out how to survive them.

And if you really want something, you can survive anything.

Chapter Forty-two
Flexibility

The *Washington Post* on November 18, 2009, inspired this chapter. Well, it didn't so much inspire me as it reminded me of something I had forgotten—a hard lesson Dean and I learned when we ran Pulphouse, one I've acted upon ever since.

Your business has to be flexible.

What does that mean, exactly?

Well, let's let the inspiration speak first. A front-page article titled "Of The Signs of The Recovery, Few Say 'Help Wanted,'" focused on businessman Tom Hudson, president and CEO of a company called Nth/works. Nth/works makes parts for small appliances, things like dishwasher doors and oven brackets. As the housing market boomed, so did the small appliance business. New houses needed new stoves and refrigerators. Companies like GE and Whirlpool hired Hudson's company to make parts for their small appliances—and everyone made money.

Then, according to Hudson, "the orders just stopped."

They stopped. Hudson cut back, and cut back some more. He called the effect "devastating," and he's hoping for a turnaround. But he knows that the good old days are long gone.

I scan my newspapers and I scanned over the part in the body of the text about the decline in sales for his business. The writer, Dana Hedgpeth, did a nice job of leading the reader through the collapse, but I had lived through this kind of thing and read tons of these articles. I swear as I read, some part of my brain added "yada, yada, yada."

Until I got to those two sentences: *It was devastating. The orders just stopped.*

Suddenly, I was catapulted back to the offices of Pulphouse Publishing in Eugene, Oregon, right after the start of the first Gulf War. And that war—the first TV war, everyone was calling it (even

though that wasn't true; it was the first 24/7 TV war)—devastated the
book industry. No one went into bookstores. No one read for pleasure.
Bookstore after bookstore had no customers day after day.

So the bookstores called us, the supplier, and asked us
for forbearance on their usual payments. Then the stores stopped
ordering. So did our regular book customers, people who shopped
mail order.

Quite literally one day, the orders stopped. And you know
what? It was devastating.

This isn't like the buggy whip example I've used countless
times. We at Pulphouse had no idea that the spigot would get turned
off. I'm sure Tom Hudson at Nth/works didn't know, either. Had
I been in his shoes, I would have known that the sustained growth
wouldn't happen year after year after year at that pace—there aren't
enough people to buy houses for that—but I wouldn't have expected
the orders to stop.

Every now and then the culture takes a sharp right turn. One
day something works, and the next it doesn't. That's frightening
and impossible to predict. On December 6, 1941, the U.S. economy
was still trying to recover from the Depression. It was a peacetime
economy with an interior focus. Then on December 7, 1941, the
Japanese bombed Pearl Harbor. On December 8, 1941, we went from
a peacetime economy to a wartime economy. By January 1, 1942, we
had mobilized an army. Thousands of people had left the work force.
Production changed from peacetime things to wartime things. The
culture had taken a hard right turn and we never looked back.

World events have a significant impact on businesses. All
through the month of November, the news media has reminded
us that, twenty years ago, the Berlin Wall came down. An entire
generation has grown up without the Soviet Union or the Eastern
Bloc. The economic changes have been staggering. I don't think the
definitive books on the business changes from that one event have
been written yet.

But I can tell you what that hard right turn did to some writers
in my business. It put them out of business, overnight. The bestselling
authors of Cold War spy thrillers lost their readership immediately.
I know of one author whose book was in the works. He had a
significant six-figure advance. The book came out and died—selling
less than his mid-list books—and nearly destroyed his career. Only a
few writers survived—John Le Carré being one of them. But if you

look at Le Carré's post-Wall books, they don't focus on Europe. They deal with places like Panama.

In July of 1989, Cold War spy novels were bestsellers. By December of 1989, no one wanted to buy those books. An entire corner of an entire industry vanished overnight. (It's been slowly creeping back, twenty years later, because Cold War thrillers are now historical novels. Go figure.)

Some writers who weren't flexible and couldn't switch categories never sold another book. Others managed to rebuild their careers, but it took years.

At Pulphouse, we made all the wrong decisions. As I've said many times in this *Guide*, people who run their own businesses are, by nature, optimists. We may recognize that things are bad, but we're convinced they'll eventually get better.

And that was the approach we took at Pulphouse. We figured the precipitous drop in sales (actually, the complete lack of sales) would end within a month. Within two months. Within three months. It took us nearly one quarter of a year to begin our response, and that was three months too long.

We should have cut costs the week sales stopped. We should have laid off employees, slashed expenses, and cut production. Instead, we borrowed, figuring things would turn around.

We went from a completely debt-free corporation to $250,000 in debt in three months—with no hope of recovery. We weren't flexible enough.

What advice can I give businesses who find themselves in the same situation? Cut fast and hard. Reassess immediately. Plan for the crisis to be a long one (instead of some kind of one-month blip).

Expect things to get worse before they get better.

And ask yourself, "What will happen if things don't get better?" Will you have a business? Will you be able to survive? If the answer is no, then cut your losses now. Sadly, it's better to shut down your business quickly than it is to extend the pain. Because extending the pain means extending the depth of your (or your business's) indebtedness.

The problem, though, isn't what to do during a hard right turn. If we could anticipate these kinds of cultural disasters, we'd all be rich. From the perspective of my lifetime, they seem to happen once every 15-20 years or so (once a generation). But of course, that's unscientific. We could have another hard right turn tomorrow, followed by a different one the next day. We just have to live through them.

But if you look at the history of businesses, some survive these disasters and others don't. What's the difference? Foresight and flexibility.

Sometimes you can have foresight. A lot of us knew that this housing bubble would end. If I were in the appliance business, I would have been socking away half my profits for the years after the housing bubble burst. I probably wouldn't have expanded quite as much as some of my competitors did. But I saw this bubble very clearly—I used to work in real estate, and I learned my trade in a down market, so I knew that what was happening was unusual.

Sometimes I do think businesses are lucky enough to be forewarned—and I do mean lucky. Because you need someone in your business prescient enough to understand the information that comes your way, and strong enough to know what to do with it. Take the end of the Cold War. There had been rumblings for months that it was on its last legs. No one knew the Berlin Wall would come down in one dramatic night, but they knew that something was up. And I know of some writers who moved out of Cold War fiction before the Wall came down, which seemed like a dumb move at the time, but seems smart in hindsight.

In his fascinating autobiography, *The Way the Future Was*, Frederik Pohl describes the same kind of circumstance, which saved *Galaxy Magazine*, once one of the premiere science fiction magazines. In the late 1950s, the American News Company vanished quite literally overnight. American News distributed magazines all over the United States. For reasons too complex to detail here (but all of them having to do with business and stocks and takeovers), American News disappeared. And when it vanished, it took hundreds, maybe thousands of magazines with it.

Old-time science fiction writers still talk about the effect on the sf field. One day, there were dozens of markets for sf. The next day, only a handful. And *Galaxy* was in the handful.

How did *Galaxy* survive? According to Fred, *Galaxy's* editor heard "rumblings" about the upcoming problems and warned the publisher "only a matter of months [before the collapse] that it was time to move. So [the publisher] took his business from ANC to one of the Independents just before [the problems] began and in the panic that followed, [the publisher] could look on with compassion and complacency because he already had his contracts for distribution signed." [Pohl, Ballantine Books, 1978, P. 234]

In other words, *Galaxy* heard the rumors and acted on them quickly. By acting quickly, *Galaxy* survived one of the biggest collapses to hit publishing.

But some of that was luck. Hearing the rumors, having the foresight to act, and the ability to act. Somehow, *Galaxy* either got out of its distribution contract with ANC or it was ready to renegotiate its contract at the exact right moment.

You, as a small business owner, can't rely on luck. And you can't assume you'll have the foresight to act when you hear rumors of an upcoming problem.

So what can you do?

Prepare in advance.

Of course, I just told you that you can't foresee a lot of these hard right turns. So how do you prepare?

You learn flexibility.

So many writers lost their entire careers to the collapse of Cold War fiction because they didn't know how to write anything else. And even if they did, they had no track record in other forms of fiction. They weren't nimble enough to move to another area of publishing when their area collapsed.

At Pulphouse, we didn't move quickly enough. Our operation couldn't survive without 19 employees and a lot of product. Cutting back didn't seem like a viable option, so we didn't do it. We probably could have survived with some judicious planning, long before the First Gulf War ever hit.

I'm not saying here that guys like Tom Hudson need to add another product line to their business. Nor am I saying that he should suddenly go into the business of building truck parts or making yarn.

What I am saying is that you need to have contingency plans. If you can't do anything except sell widgets, then when the widget market collapses, you'll have to shut down your business. But if you can move from widgets to books or farm out your manufacturing team to another business for the duration, you'll survive.

In other words, you need to plan for a crisis. And you need to ask yourself what would you do if the market for your wares dries up entirely? Can you still run your business? Can you move to another product line fast enough to keep your business viable? Can you—should you—add a different product line to protect yourself against an incoming disaster?

At Pulphouse, we thought we had enough product to weather any disaster. What we didn't have was the right kind of distribution. We had a lot of product going to the same clients. If we wanted to expand correctly, we should have considered product going through other supply chains. But we were already stretched to our limit. Our best bet would have been to cut expenses quickly, and then retool the business to the new era.

We didn't do that. Our business failed.

Ever since, however, I have developed flexibility into my writing career. I write novels and short stories, which go to different markets and distribution chains. I have always kept my hand in the non-fiction market, just in case I need to go back to work in that field (which is very different from fiction). I write under a variety of names, in case one gets caught in some kind of collapse like the kind that happened to the poor Cold War writers. My books sell here and overseas. I'm learning about the new media—websites, e-books, podcasts—just in case publishing moves exclusively online.

I am always learning. I will still make mistakes, of course, and I probably won't see the next hard right turn, but I believe I will survive it precisely because I am flexible.

So let me see if I can boil down what I mean by flexibility:

1. Know the strengths and weaknesses of your business.

2. Keep track of the news.

Sorry, I know. You're busy. But read the newspaper, watch the national news, go to online news sites. And don't just listen to the people of your political persuasion, whatever that may be. If you're liberal, watch Fox on occasion. If you're conservative, listen to NPR now and then. Follow the business news. Follow the international news. And don't believe the analysts. They tend to miss these hard right turns I've been talking about. Analyze things yourself. If it feels wrong to you—like the housing bubble did to me—figure out why. See if your gut is on to something. It probably is.

If you keep track of the news, you won't be surprised when the Japanese attack Pearl Harbor. You'll already know about the war in the Pacific, and the rumblings that President Roosevelt wants to get involved in the war in Europe. You'll be preparing for a war economy as your worst-case.

3. Figure out the worst-case scenario.

What happens if the market for your product (whatever that is) goes away overnight? What will you do? What can you do?

4. Look for opportunities.

Some businesses prosper in a crisis. Sometimes it's because the business is the last one standing (see *Galaxy*). Sometimes it's because the business is the right business for the new economy. When the housing bubble burst, some cleaning and repair businesses grew. Those businesses specialized in cleaning "empties," places that someone had moved out of. They worked for the banks or the lenders and prepared houses for resale. Opportunities exist. You have to see them and figure out if you can reposition your business to take advantage of them in the new economy.

5. Make sure you have economic flexibility.

Make sure you can shut down quickly if you need to, or trim your workforce and still be productive, or trim your expenses and still make a profit. Or maybe you need the money to reposition your business to take advantage of the new opportunities that become available. Repositioning takes capital, and in a crisis, capital dries up. So you might have to provide that money yourself. If possible, have enough money set aside to buy time in a chaotic market. Often, waiting a few months before you retool your business is the best strategy. Most businesses can't wait, however, because they're operating on such a thin margin (or paycheck-to-paycheck in 9-5 parlance). In that case, trim, trim, trim and hope you can ride out the problem.

6. Vary your product line and your distribution system.

I watched a local retail store with a very loyal clientele go out of business because the owner refused to have a website. She sold a specialized product. Before web stores, people from all over the country would visit her brick-and-mortar store once a year or so, and buy the specialized items. As the internet became ubiquitous, her shoppers didn't have to leave home to get their favorite items, so her national clientele dropped off. Her shop, in a town of 7,000 people, died.

She was aware of the internet factor, but she refused to start her own website. She badmouthed the Internet all the way to the bankruptcy of her business. If she had only spent the cash to set up a site and learned how to maintain it, she would be in business today. Her old clients would have ordered from her *off the internet*. She had a built-in market base, and she never realized it.

7. Expect change.

If you think things will be the same next year as they are this year, you're heading for a world of trouble. Just because something has worked year after year doesn't mean that it will work in the future. Plan for the change, be ahead of it if possible, and figure out how to use it to your advantage.

Flexible businesses survive. It doesn't take foresight and forewarning as much as it takes an ability to remain nimble. Keep your options open. Remember that the more static your business, the greater danger it's in.

Then go learn something new, something that might benefit you. Have fun with it. Because there's no reason to own your own business if you're not having fun. Imho.

Chapter Forty-three
Failure

Since I've been dealing with setbacks, I suppose I should go all the way, and talk about failure. Failure isn't something I'm fond of, but not for the reason that you think.

I happen to believe in failure. I think that we learn by failing. Watch any child learn how to walk, and you realize that it's all about failure. No child gets up and walks the first time he is set on his feet. Children pull themselves to their feet, then fall on their butts. Then they pull themselves up, take a tentative step, and fall.

We as adults know that it's only a matter of time before the child starts scurrying across the living room toward the collectible books (better move them to a higher shelf *now*), but the child doesn't know that. Still, he tries, and tries, and tries.

I've watched my siblings and my friends raise their children. I've seen a lot of kids in this stage, and I've noticed something. The parents who comfort the child when he falls, *especially if he's not crying,* actually impede his development.

One afternoon in the early 1980s, I was at my grandmother's house with my mother and a cousin who had a year-old boy. (I think it was my cousin; it might have been a neighbor. I'm hazy about whose child I actually was watching that day.) The boy was pulling himself up and then falling, and he was making his way around the dining room, standing, taking a step, falling; standing, taking a step, falling.

My grandmother had a non-intervention policy with her children and her children's children. She gave her opinion when asked, but didn't volunteer much. Or maybe she did, but certainly not in front of others. When I got married the first time, she supported me. When I got my divorce, she was there for me (even though she was getting frail). When I met Dean, she pulled me aside and said, "This is a good one. You keep him."

Not only was that the best advice she ever gave me on my personal life, it was one of the only direct pieces of advice she ever gave.

So what I'm about to tell you remains clear in my memory because of my mother and my grandmother, not because of that little boy trying to walk.

We four women were talking and keeping an eye on the boy, when suddenly he pulled one of the chairs over. It knocked him down, but didn't hit him. He sat in the middle of the floor, unhurt but startled, with that lovely expression startled toddlers get: *Do I cry? Should I cry? Did this really bother me?*

He had already decided it didn't bother him and had reached for the next chair to help him stand up as my mother ran to his side, checking in a great panic to see if he was all right. The boy's mother, seeing my mother react, hurried to the boy too.

The boy started to cry. He didn't just cry. He wailed and sobbed and it took them nearly fifteen minutes to calm him down.

When the drama was over, my grandmother looked at my mother. "Marian," my grandmother said, "if you had left that boy alone, he wouldn't have even noticed that he had fallen."

"But he might have been hurt," my mother said.

"He wouldn't have noticed that either," my grandmother said, and then changed the subject.

I was startled at two things. First, that my grandmother had spoken up. As I said, she had a non-intervention policy. But second, her insight from (by that point) almost seventy years of child-rearing and child-watching struck me as true.

Children, raised in loving homes with parents less nervous than my own, fail easily and rarely notice. They take spills, and then they get up. They drop a ball, miss a catch, or trip over a crack in the sidewalk, and they laugh as they try again.

We let toddlers do this. In fact, we let children do this up to the age of three or so. We know that the try-and-fail method works, and that the child will eventually speak and walk. We gently guide our children by telling them no when they get near a hot stove, by steering them away from an aunt's favorite glass vase, by holding their hand as they cross the street.

But we accept the try-and-fail model.

And then the child goes to school.

I don't know when this happened, but it happened after I graduated from college but before my friends started sending their children to school in the 1990s. Suddenly, everyone got gold stars and encouragement. Kids didn't fail classes and rarely got Ds.

College professors I know started complaining about this, because these kids often got their first D in college. Or, God forbid, their first F. And you'd think the world had ended.

My sister, a professor, visited me in Oregon shortly after her semester ended. A few nights into the trip, she was still dealing with a student who was protesting his less-than-stellar grade, a grade she said he deserved. (And I believe her. She's the tough but tender teacher who taught me how to read and gave me some of my most favorite novels.)

Why am I going on about this? Because failure is something we need to practice. Handled well, failure leads to success. In fact, I know of no long-term successful business person who lacks a failure in her background.

Don't believe me? Think about this: Henry Ford went bankrupt five times before starting Ford Motor Company. Walt Disney's first cartoon studio went bankrupt.

Read the biographies of successful people. Some of these biographies will focus on the failures, and show them for the learning experiences that they were. The show *Biography* on A&E skips over the failures by mentioning them and then saying, "Five years later…" or placing a commercial break between the failure and the next success. Your job, as someone who studies how successful people do things, is to find out what happened in those intervening five years and figure out how that person who is famous enough for A&E to waste an hour of air time on him turned that failure into a success.

That's why I was initially reluctant to title this post "failure." I don't believe in failure. Not really. I know it happens. I know that it's part of life. But I also know that failures are opportunities.

Opportunities to start over. Opportunities to make changes. Opportunities to learn.

And that's the key. Like the toddler who has fallen on his butt, you could sit there and cry and wait for someone to pick you up. Or you can reach for the next chair, haul yourself to your feet, and stagger forward.

A few weeks ago, a friend asked me if I made a mistake

when I married the first time. I startled him by saying I didn't make a mistake at all.

Now, knowing that my first marriage ended in divorce, you'd think that I would acknowledge the failure and say that I shouldn't have married my first husband at all.

But I would have lost so much. I would have lost several good years of a friendship I valued. I would have lost lots of learning experiences, and I would never have walked the road that led me to this moment, to this part of my life.

Joyce Carol Oates writes in her essay "Nighthawk" about her failure to qualify as a PhD candidate at the University of Wisconsin. The essay is a rumination on failure and its importance, but also on the opportunities that it brings.

Most things that people identify as failures aren't failures at all. They're setbacks, which I dealt with in the previous essay. Setbacks turn into failures when you let them defeat you. When they crush you and keep you from achieving your dreams.

That said, I have failed many times in my life. I've been failing for the past month. I've been trying to write a novella that I have had to restart four times. That's right. I've failed at writing this damn thing four separate times.

But is that going to stop me? No. I'll keep trying until I get it right.

That's a small failure. But I've had larger ones. I've gotten divorced, and in the process hurt the man I loved enough to marry. I've been fired. I've had two businesses fail. I've had two separate people embezzle from me. I've had two people who I thought were close friends actively try to destroy my business.

I count all of those things as failures. I've responded well to some of them, and terribly to others. I've survived them all. I'm sure I'll survive many more.

Because that's the key to failure. Unless the mistake(s) you make actually kill you, you will survive. Whether or not you live with those mistakes is your choice. Whether or not you use them to better your life is also your choice.

In her essay, "Nighthawk," Joyce Carol Oates says that had she gotten that PhD, she wouldn't have written the work that has made her one of our most distinguished artists.

If I hadn't gotten the divorce, I wouldn't have started Pulphouse Publishing, edited *The Magazine of Fantasy & Science*

Fiction, or written one-tenth of the stories I've written. Because Dean has been beside me in all of those ventures, and sometimes he's the one who has dragged my very best work out of my closed fists and given me the courage to mail it.

Did that toddler fail when he pulled the chair down all those years ago? No. He learned that chairs aren't as stable as he thought and that they could be dangerous. (He also learned that if he gives women of a certain age a watery startled look, he'll get hugged [whether he wants the hug or not].)

As tough as it is, we all have to learn how to accept failure in our lives. For some of us, we have to bring it back into our lives.

How do you deal with failure? Honestly, that was what the essay on setbacks is all about. At the time it occurs, a setback is a potential failure. It becomes a failure if you never move forward.

As I prepared to write this section of the guide, I looked up the word "failure" in the indices of my business books. Most avoid the topic altogether, which is a shame. Only one deals with it at all.

That single book is, believe it or not, *The Complete Idiot's Guide to Getting Rich* by Larry Watchka, published in 1996. Watchka has one paragraph on failure.

He writes, "Fear of failure will kill your business. You should always ask yourself, 'What is the worst thing that can happen?' Next, you should ask yourself, 'Can I handle the worst thing?' If the answer is yes, then don't worry about it any more. Make plans to handle the worst thing, and then eliminate the fear."

It sounds so easy, but it's hard. Most of us had the fear of failure pounded into us. We're supposed to "get it right the first time." We should "avoid mistakes at all costs." We're supposed to be perfect.

As if perfection is even possible. It's not. We all know it—at least when we're watching toddlers. We know that they'll try and fail. Just as we know that they'll eventually succeed. Because, unless they have serious health problems, all toddlers learn how to walk eventually. You just have to give them the time and the breathing space to do so.

You have to do that for yourself as well. You have to expect the mistakes and expect the failures. Plan for them.

Then change your attitude. You could focus on the failures. I didn't have to marry again. I could call myself a loser because my first marriage failed. Or leave publishing because my first publishing company failed. Or quit writing because my first novel got rejected (many, many times).

Instead, I deal with the failure, call it a setback, and move on. That's why I hate the word failure. It has such finality to it. A failure is only a failure if you let it become one. Otherwise, it is an opportunity.

Or, as Winston Churchill once said (Churchill, who lost most of his fortune in the Crash of 1929 and had to go back to work), "Success is the ability to go from failure to failure without losing your enthusiasm."

Yep. And if you do lose your enthusiasm, you struggle to regain it. I've had that happen, too.

That's why I insist you should only freelance at something you love. Because there will be times when the only thing that gets you through the day is the fact that you love the work. Not that you love the fame or the money or your co-workers. But that you love the work itself.

This essay is deliberately short because I don't like to dwell on failure. I like to figure out what went wrong, and then move right past the difficulty, heading to the good stuff. I reach up to grab the next chair so that I can toddle on my merry way.

So toddle on, my friends. If you keep that in mind, you will become a success.

Chapter Forty-four
When to Return to Your Day Job

I know, I know. Many of you don't have day jobs to return to. Perhaps I should have called this section "When to Return to *A* Day Job," because there are always day jobs lurking out there, especially bad day jobs, the kind that work you to death and don't pay the rent, let alone benefits or vacation days.

Most freelancers bounce back and forth between a day job and no day job for years.

Let's talk about why.

First, freelance work is unreliable. I've discussed this in previous sections. (I could go into a long diatribe about day jobs being unreliable as well, but you all get that now; you've lived through the last year just like the rest of us.) Freelance work is unreliable in a variety of ways: you don't get paid on time, or you don't get paid as much as you planned; you don't get as much work as you hoped, or the work takes longer than you expected; and you need to learn how to do the freelance work.

In short, the minute you quit your day job, you think you'll have more than enough time to get the work done. So you procrastinate. Without someone else to schedule your time, you allow entire days to go by without accomplishing anything. You have to learn how to manage yourself so that you can actually do your new job which is, after all, working for yourself.

But bad things happen. Sometimes those bad things are so severe, you have to go back to work.

For someone else.

Going back to a day job is tough.

First, you have to figure out if you should go back. Are you out of money? Has a physical disaster struck? Are you utterly demoralized due to some horrible business trauma?

Then maybe it's time to let someone else worry about keeping a business alive. You go and man a desk or tend bar or attach yourself to a university press as a copy editor. Report at nine, leave at five, and hope you get an hour for lunch.

Rest, recuperate. Save money.

Then plan your return to the freelancing business slowly and with forethought.

We'll get to that part in a minute as well, but let's concentrate on deciding to go back first. Because there are some major things you have to consider.

1. Are you running away?

Has the going gotten so tough in your freelance business that you're actually dreaming of working for a corporation again? Is this a temporary feeling, or have you discovered that you're not suited emotionally to being your own boss?

A lot of people aren't able to freelance. I know half a dozen local professional writers who actively shudder at the thought of doing without a day job. These writers actually make more money at their writing, but they like the security and structure of the paycheck, and they can't abide the idea of getting paid "whenever." Work outside the home gives them structure. A paycheck from an outside business, however small, gives them a base.

Yes, it limits how much work they can do on their freelance business, but it also saves them from the extreme lows that come with such work, those scary moments when you have no idea how to pay the rent or when the next check will actually show up.

But let's assume you're not one of those people. Let's assume you love freelancing—or you did, until something bad happened. That something bad could be a horrible occurrence, like a theft, or it could be prolonged stress from a series of late payments.

Whatever that something is, it has made you want to give up freelancing and get a "real" job.

(An aside: I really hate the idea expressed by "a real job." My job is real, and is damn hard. It's not brain surgery [thank heavens— you don't want a dyslexic woman with a short attention span operating on your brain], but it takes more time and effort than almost any other job I've ever held—including the full-time reporting/radio work. My job is real; it's just unconventional and hard to categorize. And that's the difference between a "real" job and freelance work. A real job is easy to define. Freelance work isn't.)

Before you quit freelancing, go through a thorough analysis. Will you be able to keep your current clients or meet your contracts while you have that day job? Can you shut down your freelance business with no harm to your reputation? Will you be able to collect on those back debts if you shut down? (Dean kept Pulphouse Publishing alive all by himself [from a staff of 19] in order to collect more than $100,000 of back debt so he could pay off the company's creditors. If he hadn't done that, the $100,000 would never have crossed our desk.)

Be brutal and honest with yourself. Ask yourself whether or not your desire to return to the day job is a legitimate response to your current crisis or if it's just you looking for the easy way out.

I've done it both ways. I've taken day jobs as a legitimate response to financial crisis, and I've run to day jobs because I didn't trust my freelancing ability. The ones I ran to because I didn't trust my own ability didn't last long, as I realized that I am both unsuited to corporate work and that, even in my twenties, I could earn more writing than I ever did at a salaried position. I just had to hustle more.

The jobs I went to as a response to a legitimate financial crisis lasted longer. I stayed until the crisis was well past. Each paycheck went to repaying debts or keeping a roof over my head. Those jobs I did gratefully (or as gratefully as I could, given who I am) and while I did them, I continued to freelance.

I stopped freelancing at the run-scared jobs, and then busted out of those quickly when I realized I was much happier working for myself.

I like to say I'm unemployable, but I still get job offers—two just last summer, for editing positions. I'm old enough now that I recognize the looming disaster. I doubt I'd have the patience of my youth. I'd probably bust out of those new jobs in less than a week. Once the novelty wore off, I'd be gone.

But if you've never gone full-time freelancing before, you have no idea what your response to that uncertain lifestyle will be. After you've tried it, you'll have some idea. That's where the honesty comes in.

My writer friends who need their day jobs get nervous whenever I talk about pushing back bills to cope with a $20,000 check that's overdue. They understand that a day job isn't secure, but they know that a day job often has the *illusion* of security, and for them, that's enough.

Freelance work has no illusion of security. You deal with uncertainty every single day. What will I work on next? Where will I be tomorrow? Who'll pay me next March?

In addition, there's the personal insecurity. Sure, people are buying my work now but will they buy it two years from now? Will tastes change? Will a new contractor (a better contractor) come into the area and steal my clients? Will people continue to value my work?

Not too long ago (a few years, maybe more [I'm being vague to protect the guilty]), I had a series of setbacks. Bad ones. Two publishing deals went south. I hired the world's most incompetent agent and didn't discover how bad this person was for 18 months. I lost a lot of money when a publisher went bankrupt. And I started getting the nastiest letters I'd ever gotten from editors—even nastier than when I started as a know-nothing beginner.

Eventually, I learned that the nasty letters weren't directed at me, but at the incompetent agent, who managed to screw up most everything (and anger people in the process). I managed to squeeze some money out of that bankrupt publisher, one of the few writers to do so. And slowly, I rebuilt from the publishing disasters that befell me at the same time.

I'd been through similar things before. I'd never had an agent who was that incompetent, but I'd had bad employees. I knew how to rebuild from that. It took a while to recover from the blows to my ego from those nasty letters, but once the agent/middleman was out of the equation, those editors were quite friendly with me.

I had two very bad years, years where I'd walk into my office with a "what's the point?" attitude. Dean got me through them. Dean, and the realization that the other two things I could do—edit and teach—were things I most decidedly did not want to do. (Besides, to teach and make money at it, unlike the workshops that we do which are mostly paying forward, I would have had to go back to college and get a Masters and a PhD, the thought of which gave me the shivers.) I'd edited before, and even though I'm good at it, I hate having someone else dictate what I read.

In those years, I even considered waitressing again. I liked waitressing. Eight hours of scramble, followed by rest. No mind work at all. Very good. I also investigated jobs at the local radio station, which I was overqualified for.

All of the other jobs I could do would pay less and have more aggravation than my writing at its lowest ebb. So I continued writing.

Had I been twenty years younger, I would have jumped. In my twenties, I did jump. Repeatedly. I became a full-time journalist because I thought it would be easier than full-time freelancing. (No.) I edited because I thought it was a good base for my freelancing work. (No.) The jobs that worked best—secretarial work and waitressing— were the emergency jobs I got to pay the bills. I still managed to freelance while doing those jobs, and I never ended up hating the work.

It's been a long hard slog to learn that I'm better suited to be a freelancer than someone's employee. I've learned to weather the setbacks and freelance my way out of them.

My friends who have kept their day jobs have learned the opposite lesson. And fortunately for most of them, they learned that lesson while they still had the excellent day job with the great benefits; they didn't quit and then realize what they'd lost.

So let's assume that you're not running away, that you actually need this job, and you plan to return to freelancing some day.

2. What kind of job should you get?

If you don't need the insurance or the high corporate salary (and honestly, where are you going to get that salary these days with so much talent already looking for that work?), then you should get what I have always called a shit job. Pardon my language here, but it's apt.

You want a job with no illusions, one that both you and your boss know is a job you're working because you need the money, not because it's your career or you hope to advance.

There are a million types of shit jobs out there. My favorite is waitressing. Dean's favorite is bartending. Other people work retail. Some writers prefer to work in bookstores so that they can keep up with everything that gets published (and have access to free books). Others work as many different kinds of jobs as they can find just to gain the experience for their later writings. I know a lot of people who've worked on cruise ships as staff—either in housekeeping or in the casinos or as waiters—just so that they can travel.

Take the best shit job you can find. The best shit jobs are the ones you'll enjoy while you're there, but you won't have any desire (or capability) for advancement. Make sure they're jobs you can do well (you don't want to get fired [trust me]), but make sure they're jobs you won't regret quitting.

If you get an actual shit job, one that you don't take home with you (except maybe as a pair of sore feet), then you'll be able to continue freelancing. When your bank account recovers, when your clients get too numerous to maintain with a full-time job, then you will quit—and quit quickly. You don't want loyalty or the promise of advancement to keep you in what some of my freelancing friends have called "golden shackles."

3. Benefits.

Some of you will have to return to a day job because you need insurance. The cost of health insurance has risen 120% in the past nine years. Some freelance businesses simply cannot afford that kind of increase. Rather than go without insurance, get a job with benefits. Many shit jobs, especially those in resorts or chain businesses, have benefits for employees who work more than 30 hours per week.

If you need health insurance and can no longer afford it on your freelance earnings, bite the bullet and get the day job. Then figure out what changes the new health reform law brings to your situation, and when those changes take place. Plan accordingly.

4. Remember who you are.

You're not a waitress or a bartender. You're not the guy who fixes copy machines. You're still that freelance businessperson. In my case, I'm a writer, whether I'm working as (the world's worst) secretary or not.

Keep your focus on the fact that this day job is to help you through a transition—either to get you on your feet financially or to help you rebuild your business the correct way.

Every single freelancer has to return to a day job at one point or another. That's part of the career.

And here's the most important point:

Returning to a day job is not a failure.

In fact, it's part of your success. You know your limits, manage your money and time well, and know when you need help. Only successful people know how to do that.

That said, it's hard to return to a day job, particularly if you had a particularly public crash or a very visible business. I've watched a lot of retail shops go down in our little resort town this past year, and all of the proprietors have different jobs locally. Some of these people are embarrassed. They won't meet my gaze, afraid I'll judge them poorly. Others shrug, blame the economy, and tell me about their eBay sales or their plans to reopen when the upturn begins.

Be part of the second category. You may think getting a day job is a setback, but don't ever call it a failure. Regroup, plan, and start all over again.

See the day job as an opportunity to rebuild your freelance business as something stronger, healthier, and more secure. Maybe build up your savings so that the next time you have a severe setback, you won't have to return to a day job. Figure out ways to keep expenses down. Analyze what went wrong—and what you did right.

Use the day job as a chance to take a breather from your freelance work. Figure out if you want to go back.

If you do, then realize that this day job is just a stepping stone to a better future. If you believe that the day job is just part of your transition, not a symbol of failure, you'll move forward; and eventually, your freelance business will be a success.

Chapter Forty-five
The Benefits of Hindsight

I don't know if we get wiser as we get older, but we certainly gain a lot more experience. The experience comes in handy, if we choose to use it. And sometimes that experience is just there, a part of our personal history and nothing more.

I had a discussion with someone recently about hindsight. We both discussed our fathers, both of whom discouraged us from our first marriages. The person I was talking to is going through a divorce right now. I went through mine 24 years ago.

We both agreed, in the course of our conversation, that our fathers had been right. We also agreed that if we had looked at those relationships now—from the outside (with someone not us) and with the benefit of another couple decades of living—we would see the upcoming problems as well.

Relationships follow patterns, and people often get attracted, particularly early on, to someone who might give us an opportunity to heal problems that currently exist in our own lives. Watching other people's relationships has given me insights into my own. But that all comes from experience (and an annoying tendency toward nosiness).

The conversation with my friend wasn't a bitter one, though. In fact, we both laughed about our poor fathers' inability to stop us, and we both expressed some empathy for our fathers in that situation. Because as clearly as our fathers could see the situation, their experience didn't extend to preventing it.

Then, of course, both of us contemplated what might have happened had we listened to our fathers. If I hadn't married the first time, I would probably never have met my current husband. If I hadn't met Dean, I certainly wouldn't be typing this now.

As I've said before, I don't regret that first marriage, despite the pain and anguish it caused me and my ex. Not only do I (we, I hope) have some good memories, but that relationship was a critical one in forming both of us. Fascinatingly to me is this: had my ex and I stayed together, his children would never have been born. Had we done things "right," he would have lost the family he has now, and probably not had a different one in its place. I never wanted children, which we discussed at the beginning. My ex, at nineteen, figured (without telling me) I'd change my mind.

I never did.

Most of us use hindsight the way I did here, to explore the various possibilities of our lives, the paths not taken. I actually looked at that very topic in a story I just published in *Analog*, called "Red Letter Day." The idea being if you could write a letter to your younger self, helping that person either change something in her life or not, what would you write? Would you write at all? (Still haven't entirely answered that one for me.)

But we can use hindsight for more than what-if exploration. We can use hindsight as we build our businesses. In fact, I believe hindsight is an essential tool of business building.

What changes a failure to a setback? Attitude. I know a number of people, several of them men, who have not remarried after their divorces. Most of those men never even dated again. They were so rocked by the failure of their marriages that they simply could not conceive of another relationship at all. They weren't willing to try again.

Sometimes this attitude is healthy. It comes from suffering physical pain. It's hardwired in. When we get hurt badly, we don't want to repeat the behavior that caused us that pain. This makes sense when it comes to touching a hot stovetop with your bare hand— you're not going to do that again if you can at all help it—but makes a lot less sense when applied to everything else in life.

If we avoided everything that hurt us, emotionally and physically, over the years, we'd eventually stop doing anything. I've turned my ankle crossing a room without tripping on anything; does that mean I shouldn't walk again?

Back in the failure chapter, I used the analogy of the child learning to walk. Toddlers don't give up. They want to move on their own too much to stop, even though they fall constantly and often hurt themselves.

But that's a simple analogy. I don't think (don't remember, honestly, and don't really know) whether or not toddlers analyze what made them fall. I suspect toddlers just get right back up and try again without any real thought except some version of *I'm going to conquer this thing; everyone else I know has.*

That bullheadedness serves us well in many areas of life. Sometimes you need to get right back on the horse, the bike, whatever cliché you prefer.

And sometimes you need to analyze what went wrong. You need to use hindsight.

Because I have a driving desire not to ever make the same mistake twice, I get really angry at myself when I do make a single mistake over and over again. I don't quit whatever it is I'm doing— I'm closer to that bullheaded toddler than I let on in public—but I do rethink it, and sometimes I take a vacation from it.

Case in point: Business. Business, unlike writing, is something I learned as an adult. I'm a very organic writer. I read, gather information, and eventually apply it. I can teach what I've learned— somewhat. But as I recently explained to a group of professional writers who had all come to study with me, if you delve too deeply into my ability to express my knowledge about writing, you'll learn that my ability to describe what I know is pretty shallow. At some point, I just shake my head and say, "Look, just do it. If you can't do it, then we'll see what else we can figure out." Not because I'm frustrated with the student, but because my own learning process in that area is so subconscious that I can't even articulate how I know what I know. And sometimes expressing what I know is equally hard.

On the other hand, I learned business in the school of hard knocks. And when I say hard knocks, I mean the kind that make little cartoon birdies and stars revolve around your head for years. I can point out each wound and scar, each dent to my thick skull, and every single slight that ever happened, my fault or not.

Why am I not bitter? Sometimes I am. I occasionally indulge in the pity party or the nasty analysis of someone who has hurt me years ago. But mostly, I learned relatively young that looking backwards and wallowing in regret does me no good whatsoever.

Life moves forward whether we want it to or not. Our choice is whether or not to move with it or to give situations the permission to batter us around.

Hindsight is the tool that allows us to move forward. It is also the tool that allows us to go near a stove again. We assess what went wrong, and then we see if it's even possible to move forward again without repeating the same mistake.

Once you put your hand on a hot stovetop, you realize that you have to approach that stove with caution. A toddler might stay away from the stove entirely, since a toddler can't see the top, and judges the entire thing harmful and can't yet understand a stove's benefits.

But an adult realizes that there are many ways to approach that stovetop, most of which will not hurt, if you're careful. One thing most of us do, however, is keep our bare hands away from any part of the stove that's on. Most of us never again put our hands on that top without looking at it first.

Simple caution, based on experience. It allows us to have a useful, if dangerous, item in our home.

But let's move hindsight away from the realm of the physical into the realm of the mental. Pain can be emotional. The emotion comes from severe stress and trauma.

I've owned many businesses, and I've failed at a lot of them. I've approached each one with the idea that I won't make those same mistakes again. Often, I decided not to go into the same kind of business again.

When Dean decided to open a collectibles store as a hobby, I wanted nothing to do with it. I had worked retail from the age of twenty forward, and my ex and I owned a frame shop and art gallery that was a retail shop.

I hated most of the aspects of owning a store. I hated the hours. I hated the stuff. I hated the cash outlay required to get inventory, to rent (or buy) a building, and most of all, I hated waiting for customers to come in.

But Dean had owned several shops, and had loved them. I was not about to stop him from doing something he loved. So I helped him plan, using the mistakes my ex and I had made in the past, combining those mistakes with the ones Dean made in his early stores.

That planning, and all of that hindsight, allowed us to build a successful business. I didn't ever stand behind the cash register, but I was part owner. Dean and I made the major decisions together.

Our experience paid off. Dean's expertise in collectibles made the store a destination stop within its first year. The inventory came from Dean's collections, and his judicious purchases of other people's collections.

Because Dean knows himself quite well, he also realized that the joy in any project for him is building that project. He literally built

this business from scratch, making a deal with an owner of a strip
mall that we would pay to fix up a dilapidated space inside that mall
in exchange for three years of rent.

The nice thing about that rent deal and the previously owned
inventory is that together, they gave us the opportunity to walk away
from the business if it didn't work. We had three years of free rent, so
we had three years to see if the business could sustain itself. We had
more than a year's worth of inventory, so we had relatively few start-
up costs.

The business became so successful so quickly (which we
did not expect) that Dean realized he was going to have to put more
time into it than he had planned. That realization, too, came from
experience. He had done this before, and he knew how to grow a
business. He did not want to become a collectibles mogul. This was
supposed to be his hobby, not his life.

Once he made that realization, he sold the business—for a
profit—six months after Oregon, already ahead of the curve, had
sunk into this deep recession. The new owner, who had worked at the
business from the start, maintained it, and it continues to grow even
now, doing extremely well in this tough economic climate.

Every single plan we made about that new business came from
hindsight. We knew, first of all, that Dean needs to build things. He
always has something going on besides his writing. Before he wrote,
he had two or three new things happening as well. He must create on
a variety of levels, and it's impossible to hold him back—although
he's great at analysis, and able to figure quickly if a new project is the
right project for him.

That ability to figure out if a new project is right also comes
from experience. In our lifetime together, he's started projects only to
abandon them within the week as it became clear that he wasn't suited
for them. Time has taught us to evaluate first, sink money in later.

Experience taught us to do the financial plan up front. We'd
both started businesses by the seat of our pants, with just a vague idea
that it would work out. Once or twice it did, but mostly it failed.

We also learned that we needed to spend as little on start-up
as possible because we were taking no outside investors. We needed
to be able to walk away from this business. Because of our years of
experience, we knew that the economy was headed downward (long
before the "smart guys" in Washington had it figured out), and we had
to make the business as recession-proof as possible. We'd both started

businesses in a recession, and we lost Pulphouse Publishing in part because of our response to the recession of 1992. So we knew how dangerous the overall economic climate could be to a business.

We planned for that.

We also knew the price we needed if we decided to sell the business, and we knew it up front. Mostly, we expected to shut it down if it didn't work. The fact that we found a buyer with little effort had more to do with Dean's planning abilities than with mine, but he doesn't like building things only to take them apart. So he worked hard to keep potential buyers interested, even while he started the business up.

All of this planning was extremely different from the planning we had done in our early businesses. Those, as I said, were done without enough planning at all. In fact, I didn't understand why places like the Small Business Administration wanted a business plan. How could we know how the business would operate when we hadn't operated a business?

I recently watched a business go through the same by-the-seat-of-their-pants start-up, and I haven't even talked to or met the owners. I recognize the signs from experience alone.

Down the hill from our house, a lovely Italian restaurant went out of business—but not because of financial mismanagement. The place was wildly successful. Instead, it closed because of what I think of as a weird Oregon Coast phenomenon. The owners got sick of tourists.

We went to this restaurant a lot, and in hindsight, the signs of the closure were obvious. It started when the owner decided that locals could make reservations, but tourists could not. Then it migrated to little signs on the table, telling people to control their children and not to use their cell phones. Then the hours got strange—staying open on Monday and Tuesday (traditionally days on the Oregon Coast when business are closed because there are no tourists) and closing on Sunday. In their last year, the owners closed for the summer (the high season) and reopened in the winter (when the town is empty). The reopening didn't last. In fact, the restaurant closed for good during, of all things, spring break.

The owners loved to cook. They loved to cook for people they liked. They hated dealing with rudeness, demands, and all the other things that come with owning a restaurant.

They had owned their building, and it sat empty for two years, waiting for a buyer or for someone to rent it.

This spring, someone rented it.

Because the restaurant is so close to us, we watched the newcomers build it. A small sign went up immediately, announcing the future home of the new restaurant. The front door sat open during the business day, as the new owner painted and did a slight remodel. The official sign went up in late May and with it, an announcement on the changeable sign below, that the restaurant would open on June 25.

Well, I could see the interior of that place, and it was clear to me that they would have to push to hit their June 25 deadline. On June 20, the furniture got delivered. On June 24, the sign changed to a July 2 opening. Fourth of July is the biggest weekend in our little tourist town, so it became clear that these new restaurateurs wanted to take advantage of that.

But both Dean and I have worked in restaurant start-ups, we know that a menu, a good chef, and a well-designed interior do not a restaurant make. Every single successful restaurant that we've worked at—and that Dean has managed—has given itself a month to work out the kinks. Mostly, the restaurant holds practice nights with the newly hired wait staff, without opening the restaurant at all. When I was a teenager in Superior, Wisconsin, one restaurant invited the relatives of every single person on the staff to come into the restaurant and *eat free* for Thursday, Friday, and Saturday night. That restaurant did so for two weeks.

By the time it opened, the staff knew the menu, knew the quirks of the kitchen, had made (and corrected) dozens of errors, learned where everything was kept, and learned how to pace themselves through a restaurant slammed with customers.

(Our local six-plex movie theater did the same thing, by the way, just to get the bugs out of their system.)

Dean worked varieties of the same practice session. Every restaurant that does this opens to acclaim, if not for the food, at least for the service.

On July 1, the restaurant below announced a July 5 opening date.

On July 4, the opening date was gone.

On July 17, the place held a stealth opening. They'd lost an entire month of revenue from their business plan (if indeed they had one), and they have so far gotten no word of mouth throughout the community. The stealth opening allowed them to practice a little, but they probably lost customers who expected a more polished staff/ restaurant.

I hope they'll survive, but the cold opening probably made things harder than they needed to be. And the cold opening is a clear sign of inexperience.

So how do you make hindsight work for you?

1. Do a fearless inventory of what went wrong in your previous business(es).

Make a list and *be honest*. If you're not honest, there's no point. If you did something wrong, or several somethings wrong, admit them. You need to understand where *all* of the mistakes are, not just some of them.

2. Evaluate whether the mistakes came from (a) the economy; (b) your response to the economy; (c) your inexperience; or (d) your personality.

If the mistakes came from the economy, then you better make sure you know how to weather the same economic climate.

If they came from your response to the economy, then you better learn how to be more flexible in response to a crisis.

If the mistakes came from your inexperience, don't get overconfident. Just because you have experience now doesn't mean you're all-wise. Plan to make more errors.

If the mistakes came from your personality, you better find a way to negate that part of you that has the tendency to do things wrong *for the type of business you're opening*. I'm great at publishing and editing, but I'll never edit again. I'm good at it, but not suited to it. No amount of "change" will make me and editing suit. I might be able to do a small project or two, but I won't make a career out of it—not without a personality transplant. Been there, done that, spent enough to buy a factory's worth of t-shirts.

If the mistakes came from your personality, you might need to hire someone to take that part of your personality out of play. I could own a publishing company (in partnership with Dean) again, if I don't edit. But I would have to remain hands-off with the new editor. I would have to trust that person—which is a tall order. As I said, I'm very good at editing, and I'd see mistakes right off. I'd probably drive that person out of the business if I weren't careful.

Hiring a person to do the part of the job you're not suited for has all the pitfalls of hiring an employee for other aspects of your life. Employees often create problems instead of solving them.

If your previous business failed due to your personality, then you might want to reconsider stepping back into that same kind of business at all. Sometimes it's better to say that you don't suit than it is to keep pounding your head against the same brick wall.

3. Use other people's hindsight.

Ask them about the mistakes they made in the same type of business. Do this even if you've owned a business before. You'll learn something, guaranteed.

However, make sure you listen to their advice. At least three start-up publishers interviewed me and Dean about what went wrong at Pulphouse Publishing. We were very honest with them, told them about various warning signs, and told them to call us if things got dicey.

All three of those start-ups failed, one spectacularly. All three of them followed the exact same path that Pulphouse followed, and all three responded to the problems the same way we did—which is to say, the wrong way.

They were forewarned. Of course, they took no notes during our meetings, never contacted us when things got dicey, and only one remembered our advice at all. He later admitted to us that he was in the hospital (the failure caused a physical collapse that put him in the hospital for weeks) and he kept hearing our voices, telling him what, exactly, would go wrong if he didn't take our advice. He says we haunted him, and he apologized for not listening.

He didn't owe us an apology. He owed himself one.

5. Let hindsight help you in all aspects of your business.

Because I know how a failing business behaves, I often will not work with a business that is exhibiting the symptoms of a business on the edge. Because we had a publishing house collapse, I particularly know the signs of that, so I won't approach a company that even whispers of trouble. The trouble is often obvious to those of us who have been through something similar years in advance.

In fact, when Dean and I talked with one of those start-ups all those years ago, the owner told us in the middle of the meal he was buying us that he "would never, ever, make such dumb mistakes." We immediately decided never to work with him—not because he insulted us, but because his ego was so large that he believed he was immune to our stupidity.

He compounded our stupidity, and his failure was so spectacular that people within publishing still discuss it as an example of what not to do when running a business.

6. Remember the most important lesson of hindsight: *you are fallible.*

Sorry, kiddo. You'll make mistakes just like the rest of us. In fact, you'll make mistakes every single time you start a new business. You'll make mistakes after owning that business for ten years, fifteen, twenty. Face it: You'll make mistakes.

This is where I get my mantra. The key is to avoid making the same mistake *twice*. You'll always make new mistakes. Be creative about them. Make new mistakes in the pursuit of the perfect, mistake-free business. Then learn from those new mistakes.

That's what hindsight is for. Toss out the regrets and the "I wish I hads." Stop fantasizing about going back in time and fixing things.

Move forward with the right attitude—after you've fearlessly looked backwards, of course—and you'll have success.

Section Seven:
Success

Chapter Forty-six

Success

Success. Why, you ask, should we discuss success? Success is success is success, right?

I wish it were that simple.

We need to discuss success because success is more complicated than failure.

Infinitely more complicated.

And sadly, success can cause your freelance business to fail. I don't have any statistics, but I do know from anecdotal evidence that success has caused a lot more freelancers I know personally to fail than their repeated setbacks did.

Huh? Most of you don't believe me. But it's true. Success derails people, partly because it's unexpected.

First, let's define success. Even that's not easy. It takes my handy dandy *Macmillan Contemporary Dictionary* (which isn't contemporary any longer, since I bought it while in college in 1979) three different bullet points to define the word. It takes my handy dandy *Encarta World English Dictionary* (which is a bit more contemporary, since it came with the four-year-old Macintosh that I write on) four bullet points to define the word. Neither dictionary put the bullet points in the same order.

So, combining the dictionary definitions and putting them in my own words (since dictionary definitions are copyrighted), with my own numerical bullet points (more than four), here are the dictionary definitions of success:

1. **Achieving something planned.**
2. **Achieving something attempted.**
3. **A favorable result.**

4. **Attaining a goal.**
5. **An impressive achievement, especially (as both dictionaries note) fame, wealth, power, or social status.**
6. **A person who has a record of achievement, especially (as one dictionary notes) in gaining fame, wealth, power, or social status.**
7. **A person who is successful (says the other dictionary, thereby defining a word with the same root word, which has always irritated me. So let's break down successful from the same dictionary which defines it as…attaining success. Grrrr).**
8. **A person who succeeds (says the other dictionary, doing the same damn thing. What does "succeeds" mean? Having the desired result; obtaining a desired object or outcome; coming next in line…um, say what?—oh, as in the prince succeeded his father, the king, who died last week in a horrible dictionary accident. Grumph).**

Since I'm dissatisfied with these definitions, I'm going to look in one more dictionary. (Yes, I have a million of them. Or maybe only a thousand.) [Writer walks her library, reads half a dozen dictionary definitions, invades her husband's office, reads three more dictionary definitions, gives up, makes herself a cup of tea, grabs some pretzels, and returns to her computer where she types…]

Okay, that was lame. All of these dictionaries are obsessed with wealth and social standing. One says that success is the gaining (the gaining—what a construction) of wealth, fame, or power and/or (get this) the extent of that gain.

That snobby dictionary not only measures success in wealth, power, and fame, but also in expanding that wealth, power and fame—and no, this was not the *Oxford English Dictionary*. It was some paltry American wannabe.

Look at this: I've just spent four hundred words attempting to define success—and here's the really sad thing. While most of us would agree with those definitions in principle, they're wrong in particular.

In other words, each one of you—each one of several thousand people—has a completely different definition of success.

For Reader A, success might be writing an entire novel. For

Reader B, success might be earning a million dollars. For Reader C, success might mean buying a house. And so on and so on.

Most of us can describe what we believe success to be. Sometimes success is small—selling a short story, for example, or cooking your first soufflé. Sometimes the success is large—hitting *The New York Times* Bestseller List with not one, not two, but eight books in the same week as Charlaine Harris just did, or running your own well-reviewed restaurant in Paris.

But here's the thing. Sometimes success means nothing to the successful. Nothing at all.

Because, as I said, we all define success differently. Joyce Carol Oates examines this phenomenon in her excellent personal essay, "Nighthawk." In a parenthetical aside, she mentions something about the well-known writer Henry James, something I did not know:

"…Henry James's most passionate wish was to have been a successful playwright, not a practioner of the highest Jamesian ideals in prose fiction. Writing the great novels of his mature career had been, for Henry James, a second-best alternative."

In other words, had you asked Henry James, the revered novelist whose work is still read nearly a hundred years after his death, whether or not he was a success, *he would have said no*.

Got that? *He would have said no*.

There are so many examples from the world of writing, which is the world I'm familiar with. I'm a person who studies success and failure, and I do so primarily within my own profession, that of professional writer.

So I know of Frederick Faust who labored over his poems each and every afternoon, sometimes writing only one or two words as he crafted each piece. He published a few poems in his lifetime—and none of you have heard of Frederick Faust.

At least, not under that name. But all of you have seen his most famous pen name on the bookstore shelves, as well as on the credits of television shows and countless movies. For Frederick Faust became Max Brand so that he could pay the bills. He wrote Max Brand stories and novels in the morning to fund his poetry.

Poetry which, by the way, was so bad that almost no one bought it. One editor who wanted another Max Brand story agreed, as part of the contract, to publish a Frederick Faust poem as well.

Was Frederick Faust a success? He would have said no.

Yet by the dictionary definition—wealth, fame, power—Max Brand had more success than he could have dreamed of.

Milos Forman and Peter Shaffer produced an entire movie about this phenomenon. 1984's *Amadeus* is a (clearly fictionalized) account of Antonio Salieri, the most acclaimed, successful musician of his day, who was jealous of Wolfgang Amadeus Mozart—not for his wealth or fame or power (Mozart did have fame, but no wealth or power)—but for his talent, a talent the fictional Salieri believed he did not have. (I emphasize fictional here because there is no evidence in the historical record that Salieri believed himself inferior to Mozart.)

Most people see the movie as a story about professional jealousy, but if you go beyond that, you'll see that it's a film about a man whom the world perceives as successful, a man who does not see himself as a success *because he has not achieved his own dreams* and, sadly, for this character, who believes he is not capable of achieving those dreams.

So defining success is hard. The definitions are individual, and, generally, they come from somewhere deep. If you ask each and every one of us, we'll all have a glib answer about what we believe success to be.

When asked what he wanted—by anyone: acquaintance, waitress, stranger—a friend of mine would say, "I want to be rich and never have to work again." He meant it, but he also had other dreams, other measures of success. He certainly would never have attained that kind of wealth by robbing people or scamming people or lying to people. He had specific dreams of ways to make himself that wealthy.

But within that glib answer are some traps. What's "rich"? Could my friend have gotten by on one million dollars? Five million? Two trillion? What does "never have to work again" mean? Does it mean not having a day job where you work for someone else? Or does it mean sitting on your ass all day, having people take care of your every need?

I don't know. I'm not even sure my friend knows, deep down.

Sometimes your own definitions of success surprise you. In 2000, my novel *Dangerous Road* (written under my Kris Nelscott pen name) got nominated for the Edgar Award for Best Mystery Novel of that year. When I got the call (and they do call you—which is a great courtesy), my knees literally buckled. I fell into a nearby chair. I always thought buckling knees were literary hype, but they're not. I've experienced it.

At that point in my career, I had been nominated for many awards—Hugos, Nebulas, World Fantasy Awards. I'd won quite a few as well, including the *Ellery Queen Mystery Magazine* Readers' Choice Award for Best Short Story of the Year, which is a hell of an honor. But the Edgar was something else *to me*.

It took me a while to figure out the difference. From childhood on, I went out of my way to read novels marked "Edgar nominee." I hadn't done that with any other award, not even the Hugo. (Although I did buy *Dune* because it mentioned the Hugo on the cover.) Edgar nominee was, in my mind, the rubber-stamp of approval, a sign of high quality. I never even dreamed of being nominated for an Edgar—I thought it was so far beyond my skills that I couldn't even look at that achievement as possible.

So when it happened—and, that same year, my short story "Spinning" was also nominated under my Rusch name—I just about came undone.

I had achieved the impossible. The mystery field had branded me a success—in terms I understood. I felt…honored. But I also felt like a fraud. I was a science fiction writer who just "dabbled" in mystery. I knew nothing about the field. But the two nominations in the same year under two different names made the success hard (impossible) to discount.

Why would I want to discount success?

Good question, *mes amis*, which I shall leave for a later section. (What I have just done is what some writers call suspense, but we experts call it withholding information to create false tension. Yep. Guilty. I don't want to get sidetracked from definitions here.)

The point of my Edgar story is twofold. First, I had achieved success as I defined it, but second, I hadn't even realized that definition lurked within me until the success happened.

Success can ambush you that way. It's happened to me a few other times as well. My first full-page review in *The New York Times* made me feel like a "real" writer, even though I'd been a full-time freelancer for twenty years at that point. What had I been before? A fake writer?

I had the same response to my first ad in *The New Yorker*—there was my name in an ideal spot up front, along with reviews of my book and all kinds of laudatory quotes. Never mind that the ad had no measurable effect on the book's sales. Never mind that the ad wasn't a favorable review, or even a short story published in their pages. It was the sight of my name in *The New Yorker*.

Obviously, within me, lurks a writer with vast literary pretensions. I mostly ignore her because I don't think of myself as vast or literary or pretentious. But that person is clearly there.

Yet if you catch me off-guard and ask me what success is *for me*, I'll tell you that I believe a successful writer makes a good living, year in and year out, writing fiction.

I do believe that. It is success. In fact, I'm living that success, and have been for nearly two decades now.

But do I feel successful? No. Because I haven't achieved half of my writing goals. Or if I have, I cheapen the achievement. I've made *The New York Times* Bestseller List more than once, but only with tie-in novels. I've had bestsellers all around the world with my own novels, but never in the United States. I have not had a movie or television show made from one of my stories, although Hollywood has knocked several times and optioned my work. I am not a household name like Nora Roberts or Stephen King.

In fact, the older I get, the more I realize how lucky I am that I didn't become a brand name like Nora Roberts when I was young. Not because I'd be arrogant (I already am; there's no changing that fact), but because so many bestsellers get pigeonholed into writing the same thing over and over again. Some enjoy doing that. Others don't.

I don't want to be pigeonholed at all, but as a younger person, I would have given it my all, and that success—the brand name, the money, the vast readership—would have hurt me.

Oops, and there we go into another part of the topic, which I won't deal with until later. Because we're still on definitions.

Here's the fascinating thing about personal definitions of success: We often formulate them before we understand what success really means.

Twenty years ago, if you had asked me how I defined success, I would have given you my standard "making a good living" answer. If you had pressed me, and asked me what my biggest dream is, I would have told you that it would be to have a career like Stephen King's or like Nora Roberts' (she was still in the early stages of her bestsellerdom, not the phenom she is now).

At the time, I didn't know all the pros and cons of that kind of career. I only knew what I saw from the outside—lots of books on the shelves, books adored by the fans, books that climbed the bestseller lists. The movies didn't thrill me as much as the books did, although a movie deal or two would be nice. And so would the money which, in those days, was "I want to be rich and never have to work again" money.

In those days, I did not know that vast sums of money required vast amounts of money management. I did not know the downside to fame (like the struggle to maintain some kind—any kind—of privacy). I didn't know that writers like Stephen King (back then) or Dan Brown (right now) can cause entire publishing houses to have a good or a bad year just by releasing a book.

I didn't understand the pressure.

I simply thought that a brand-name bestseller had a damn cushy life of writing whatever she wanted and getting it published and then sitting on top of her pile of money. And I thought I wanted that.

Yet I heard myself questioning things. Like the "never have to work again" part of my old friend's quip. Um…but I like writing. I want to continue working. So what would happen if I became rich and never "had" to work again? Would I quit? Would I feel required to quit?

Would I be greedy if I continued to work while being filthy rich?

Such questions. Questions that I did not then have the answers to.

I do now. I've researched those early dreams and discovered that I don't want some of them. Money, yes, of course. Brand name status? <shrug> If it happens, it happens. It's no longer a goal. *The New York Times* Bestseller List? Yes, at least once with my own book before I die. And so on.

I have worked very hard to not only define what success means to me, but to understand what it is I'm hoping for. And even then, I know I've missed a few things.

For example, in 2009, Neil Gaiman accepted the Newberry Award for his wonderful novel *Graveyard Book*. On Twitter, he posted a picture of the ceremony where he got the medal and where he had to give a speech.

The picture (from Neil's place on the dais) was of a typical hotel ballroom, filled with earnest-looking faces looking up at him over plates of rubber chicken.

Mercy me, I'd always pictured the Newberry Award Ceremony at the Dorothy Chandler Pavilion, filled with lots of beautiful people in spectacular designer gowns. I was actually disappointed to see that hotel ballroom filled with well-dressed but non-glam people.

It took me a day or so to figure out where I had gotten that impression. My sister Sandy gave me books every year for Christmas and my birthday. As I grew up, I got Newberry Award winners at least once, sometimes twice a year.

The only awards ceremony I had ever seen as a child was the Academy Awards, which my mother watched faithfully each March. The only school night that I was allowed to stay up until midnight was Oscar Night.

So, to child-me, all awards ceremonies took place in pavilions with lots of cameras and lots of pretty, well-dressed people. And my subconscious had held on to that image of the Newberry awards (which was the only book award my child-self had ever heard of) for more than forty years.

See how the definitions of success get corrupted? Had it been me, getting that award before I came to my adult senses and remembered what an extreme honor it is, I would have been momentarily disappointed by that ballroom. Note that I did not expect the Edgars to be in the Dorothy Chandler Pavilion. Nor did I expect it of the Hugos or the Ritas. Just the Newberry, because that definition got set long before I understood the way the world really works.

Let's look at the toughest three definitions of success. They are:

1. The world's definition of success.
2. Other people's definition of success.
3. Your definition of success.

And those three things are all different.

Why is this important? Because you might seem successful to "the world," but not to you. Consider Henry James and Frederick Faust, and you're starting to catch my point.

1. The world's definition of success.
Let's define "the world" before we go any further.

The world is, for purposes of this section, *your* world. That includes the culture in which you live, the friends and family that you have, the things that you read, everything and everyone around you who have meaning.

So if you come from an athletic world where your father played college football, your brother played baseball in the minors,

478

and your sister has a shot at making the Olympic Swim Team in 2012, you're probably going to define success in win-and-lose terms. You might even feel pressure to perform well athletically yourself.

Success in your world might mean a starting position in a professional basketball team or a coaching position at a Pac-10 school. If you, the tall budding athlete, lead your college team but never make it to the bigs, by your family's standards, you've failed.

If you end up coaching high school, your family might also think you've failed. Or even if you end up coaching a Big Sky team, your family might think you've failed.

Think of it: the pinnacle of success for so many people might be, because of the culture/world/family you came from, a failure.

This works in reverse as well.

Thanks to the handy dandy dictionaries I combed through, we now know that success includes fame, wealth, status, and power. If you're missing any of those, by real world dictionary standards, you're not a success.

We can all accept that. We know how harsh the real world can be.

But what about the flip side?

What if you have fame, wealth, status, and power, but it comes from the catering business you started in the off-season when you weren't playing ball? The catering business grew enough so that people wanted your recipes. You wrote a cookbook, got on a local talk show and demonstrated your cooking, and then the cookbook started to sell. Or you opened a restaurant that quickly became a franchise. That franchise made you famous, wealthy, and powerful—in the world of cooking.

Basketball has never heard of you. When people talk about your athletic family, they mention your sister first, because she's almost to the bigs in swimming; your brother second, because he has a shot at the majors if he plays lights-out minor league baseball; and your father, who had a legendary college football career. If you get mentioned at all, it's in one line: their sibling is well-known chef So N So. Mostly, though, you won't get mentioned.

I noticed this phenomenon when Eunice Kennedy Shriver died. For those of you who don't know, Eunice Kennedy Shriver was the younger sister of President John F. Kennedy. Her grandfather Fitzgerald (Honey Fitz) was the legendary mayor of Boston. Her father was Ambassador to England in the late 1930s. Her brother

John became President of the United States, her brother Robert was Attorney General of the United States and then became the senator from New York, and her younger brother Ted became one of the most powerful members of the United States Senate (ever). Her husband, Sargent Shriver, headed and ran the Peace Corps. Her daughter, Maria Shriver, was a well-known journalist who married movie star Arnold Schwarzenegger, who went on to become the Governor of California.

You probably heard some, if not all, of that when Eunice Kennedy Shriver died. A woman defined by her more-famous family. Mentioned in passing was the fact that she started the Special Olympics. The Special Olympics, played year in and year out by three million differently-abled people, was such a revolution in its day that it proved that people with disabilities weren't *disabled*, they were, in fact, more able than the rest of us—in courage, in strength, and in stick-to-itiveness.

Not only did the Special Olympics change the way that differently-abled children and adults saw themselves, it changed the way that the world saw them as well. And it directly led to changes: from better care for institutionalized patients to things such as the Americans with Disabilities Act and other anti-discrimination lawsuits.

Only one of the major network news anchors pointed out that, in terms of lives touched by the Kennedy family, the person who touched the most lives (and in the best possible way, by *improving* those lives) was Eunice Kennedy Shriver, someone who held no public office at all. She wasn't president or senator or governor or mayor. She was a woman who got angry at her father for the way he had treated her sister Rosemary, who was considered, at the time, "retarded;" a word we don't use any longer, thanks to Eunice Kennedy Shriver. Rosemary had a frontal lobotomy to "control" her behavior, and went from a functional human being with a future to someone who could not function and had to be institutionalized for the rest of her long life.

Eunice Kennedy Shriver couldn't change what happened to her sister, but she could change what happened to other people just like Rosemary. And she did.

Most obituaries mentioned this in passing. Mostly they noted her death as another death in JFK's generation of Kennedys.

The obituaries also slighted her children. The only one who got mentioned much was Maria Shriver, who has continued her mother's work in many areas, and has done much as First Lady of California to work with all kinds of charities. But Maria Shriver is not the most impressive one of her siblings. Every one of Eunice Kennedy Shriver's children work in public service in one way or another. Bobby Shriver has co-founded three organizations to "help eliminate the financial and health emergencies threatening the people of Africa." Timothy Shriver now heads the Special Olympics. Mark Shriver is the vice president and managing director of Save the Children USA. And Anthony Shriver founded and chairs Best Buddies International, which "fosters one-to-one relationships between people with and without intellectual disabilities."

It seems to me—from my perspective and attitude toward success—that the Shriver family is infinitely more successful than any other branch of the Kennedy family. Eunice and Sargent Shriver helped millions of people by, for example, guaranteeing good treatment for the differently-abled, educating the poor in the Third World, and feeding hungry children here at home. What a legacy of service.

And in our fame/wealth/status/power-obsessed American culture, what did our fame/wealth/status/power-obsessed media focus on? Son-in-law, movie star governator Arnold Schwarzenegger, famous-daughter-former-journalist Maria, the brothers—president, senator, and senator, and of course, their famous and manipulative father who made the Kennedy family—all of them—into multimillionaires during the Great Depression.

I found the focus on what the other members of her generation did, rather than on Eunice herself and the amazing children she and Sargeant Shriver raised, disheartening at best.

But it is a prime example of the way the world—the world I see, the American culture and media—the way that world defines success.

You all live in different worlds. *The Freelancer's Guide* has had support from people all over the world, from Norway and Germany and England and Canada. And you all are somewhat familiar with the American culture. (How can you not be? We export it obnoxiously—I couldn't get away from CNN or David Letterman the last time I was in Europe.) But you all live in your own cultures, as well. With different definitions of success.

Even within the United States, the definitions of success differ. I grew up in a middle-class professor's family. Success in my nuclear family was about academics. We were expected to get a bachelors degree, the way that most families expect their kids to finish high school. We weren't successful until we got our PhDs.

I don't have one. In fact, I am the only one of my siblings who doesn't even have at least a few credits toward a master's degree. One of my sisters never got her master's, and she is the wealthiest of all of us through her savvy business choices over the years.

But money, past its ability to sustain a middle-class life, had no value in my immediate family. My parents weren't even envious of their wealthier friends, so far as I could tell. We didn't discuss money much.

We discussed education all the time.

When I gave up my full scholarship to get married, the only thing that saved me from my father's wrath was the fact that I left my "little Ivy" school and went to his alma mater, the University of Wisconsin-Madison. I think he figured I'd go on from there and get my advanced degrees. I thought about it, and decided against it. As I said at the time, I'd spent 22 years in college. I needed a break.

By the academic standards of my family in the world I grew up in, I am not a success. Yet by the other standards of my family, a family of readers, I am an amazing success. My brother has published books. So has my brother-in-law. (In fact, in his field—history—he's a much more successful writer than I am.) But I'm the only one who has published fiction. And I know of at least four close family members who also wanted to publish fiction and have not yet done so. (My father, who was one of them, can't, since he died in 1990.)

I am currently reading the biography of Ted Kennedy, *The Last Lion*, and have thought, repeatedly, of the pressure of growing up in that family. The oldest son, Joe Jr., was expected—*expected*—to become President of the United States. Not to try. But to succeed at it. When he died in World War II, that expectation fell to Jack. When he was assassinated, it fell to Bobby. And when *he* was assassinated, it fell to Ted.

Imagine that: Ted Kennedy's success in the Senate (whether you like his political points of view or not) would not have impressed his father, had he lived to see them. Ted never achieved the presidency, so Ted was not successful by his father's definition. Ouch.

But by the definition in *all* of my dictionaries, Ted Kennedy was a success. He was wealthy, powerful, famous, and he had a lot of status. I have no idea—and will never know—if he considered himself a success.

Are you beginning to see how tricky success can be?

As I've discussed this first point—the world—I've slid between the culture, the environment around you, and your family.

I mention your family because, as a child, your family is the world. In fact, growing up is a continual process of expanding your world. First it grows to include your family, then your school, then your community, then other communities, and so on. Some people never understand the worldviews of others; some live in them.

Only you know what your world/environment/culture is. Strive to understand it, and the expectations it has put upon you from your earliest years. That world, that culture, gave you your earliest definitions of success. Maybe you have achieved those. Maybe, as our fictional tall businessperson example shows, you never will.

2. Other people's definitions of success.

For the sake of this section, other people are the people you encounter throughout your daily life. Friends, family, colleagues, acquaintances and, if you're at all well known in your field, people you've never met.

These people all have opinions about you and everything you have achieved. These people also have their own definitions of success.

For example, the day I told my writing workshop that I had just been hired as the new editor of *The Magazine of Fantasy & Science Fiction*, the man standing next to me moved away from me. Literally. He was a writer, a longtime friend and colleague, and my status change—a success, as far as he was concerned—altered our relationship forever. Suddenly I was "above" him, and closeness became impossible.

Other people judge success using different criteria. Let's go back to the Eunice Kennedy Shriver example. The news coverage of her death says more about the people covering her death than it does about her. Her true success, helping millions of people, mattered less to them than her personal wealth, her famous daughter and son-in-law, and her powerful relatives. How sad.

There are three really tough aspects to other people's definitions of success. First, you won't know what their definitions are until they tell you. Second, once you have achieved their definition of success, they believe you will remain a success. And, finally, they will have a reaction to that success.

Some will become jealous. They'll do everything they can to tear you down. Sometimes they'll go from being good friends to reacting out of jealousy. It's destructive and scary and there's nothing you can do about it—except to walk away from that toxic person. I have a lot of stories about this from my first novel sale through my editing days and beyond. All of those stories are painful to me, so painful that I rarely discuss them, and then only with trusted friends. I can't even write about them in general terms because I get too angry at the treatment I received from someone I once trusted.

Some people will be in awe of what you've done. Others will believe that you have been touched by good fortune or God or had some kind of lucky break when, really, you had the kind of lucky break that comes from extremely hard work.

A few people will ask you for your secret, and when you tell them that the secret is hard work, they won't believe you.

And many, many people, particularly those inside your field, will want to become your friend because of your success. You hear about this all the time with lottery winners—how relatives and "close" friends come out of the woodwork the day after the win. But it happens in business as well.

When I became editor of *F&SF*, dozens of people assumed they were on a first name basis with me. One writer, who shall remain nameless, put his arm around me at the next convention I went to and introduced me as his friend Kathy to everyone he saw. My close friends call me Kris, not Kathy. People who really knew me found that moment exceedingly funny. I was astonishingly uncomfortable—and remained wary of my new "friends" from the beginning.

Most of those friends vanished when I retired from editing seven years later. They ran after Gordon Van Gelder, the new editor of *F&SF*, and I was happy to see them go.

But…I've seen a lot of people achieve success and become happy with their new-found popularity, not realizing that the "friends" aren't friends at all, but opportunists. Those opportunists leave when the successful person's status declines or some new hot young thing shows up.

Most people, however, don't pay much attention to your success. It doesn't have much to do with them, so they have little or no opinion about it. They also think that success is a static condition. They believe that once you have become a success, you will remain a success.

And that isn't always true. Just look at what happened to hundreds of thousands of wealthy successful people in this economic meltdown.

They lost everything. There are stories all over the press about families who drive to the food bank in a Lexus SUV, people who earned $500,000 per year, saved none of it, and now can't find work and can't sustain their lifestyle.

The sad thing about this, I think, is not just the situation, but the lack of sympathy these people receive. Others say these newly impoverished people "deserve" to be brought down to size. They "deserve" to suffer like everyone else. They "deserve" what happened to them.

Unless they were greedy and helped cause the meltdown, they don't deserve it at all. They might have made some bad decisions, but they don't deserve the lack of sympathy coming their way.

The Germans have a word for this. It's "schadenfreude," which means pleasure derived from the misfortune of others. And as much as we love success in America, success as defined by our dictionaries, we often love the comeuppance more.

I think that's quite sad, and again, it reflects more on the person who revels in the pain of someone who has lost the success. But tell that to the person who can't get food at the food bank because she "clearly doesn't need it" since she's driving an expensive car (that she might no longer be able to fill with gas).

We intellectually know that the successful fall, and we enjoy that downfall, but if their downfall isn't public—or if they don't have a downfall—then we assume that their success never changes. We assume that famous people remain famous. But they don't.

Anyone reading this ever hear of Beverly Garland, Julie Newmar, or Sheree North? All were major television actresses in the 1960s, all were famous and successful (although not superstar successful). Garland and North were also movie starlets in the 1950s. In 1970, had you said any of their names, most people would have known who they are. Now, only film/tv geeks and some of us with a memory for names remember them at all.

They're still successes if you look at what they achieved. But in terms of fame, that success has faded.

Which it usually does. Edward Bulwer-Lytton was the most famous writer of his day. He had a style that suited Victorian era. Victorians loved his books.

Now we use the poor man's name for a contest to find the year's worst sentence. Because his prose style went out of fashion nearly a hundred years ago. People still read Dickens. They still read Mark Twain. They don't read Bulwer-Lytton.

Fame, success, power are not static things. Fortunes rise and fall with taste and memory. Over time, wealth, the only real measurable sign of success, becomes "inherited" wealth.

These are public examples. There are many private examples—people in your community, former mayors or local celebrities now out of the public eye, maybe even the guy with the mansion who used to live on the biggest hill in town. Is he still a success? Or has the bank foreclosed on that house in the past year?

But in this subheading, I've been discussing people's reaction to a clear success *as they define it*.

There's a flip side to this, which I mentioned above. Sometimes you can be extremely successful and your friends and family won't recognize that success.

My husband Dean Wesley Smith's family is made up of very practical people. Readers, yes, but not involved in academia or publishing or any form of the entertainment industry except as consumers. For years, after Dean had achieved *international* success as a writer and publisher, his family kept asking him when he would get a "real" job.

I've seen that sort of thing happen many times. Sometimes, something that is so important to you means nothing to everyone around you. Explaining the success doesn't make it understandable. Often, all you're doing is making the people around you uncomfortable.

Personal achievements are just that—they're personal. They're unique to you.

I wrote the middle part of this piece during the Master Class. Dean and I teach a Master Class for professional writers who have plateaued in their careers. It's a two-week boot camp that's as hard on the three main instructors (me, Dean, and Loren Coleman) as it is on the students. I knew I wouldn't have a long, dedicated period of time to write during the class. Fortunately, I'm finding half an hour here and half an hour there to work ahead. This section will go live during my catatonic week (after the Master Class and Bouchercon and the jetlag of going to the East Coast and catching a flight home at 6:00 a.m. Indiana time), so I knew I didn't have to finish it before I left; but I also knew it would be better to write it while I still thought in English instead of in Kris's version of English While Exhausted— which isn't even readable to me, most of the time.

During these weeks of hard work and little sleep, I'm also carving out time to exercise (a needed stress reliever). Yesterday (as I write this), I got on the elliptical because I only had twenty minutes and, as I exercised, watched a section of *The Beatles Anthology* Part One.

And guess what this section was about?

It was about success.

The Beatles Anthology, for those of you who haven't seen it, is a 1995 documentary about the Beatles using their own words. The words come from some live interviews from 1995 and some old interviews from various time periods. It's a fascinating study of a musical phenomenon, and I recommend that you watch it.

I'm watching whenever I have to exercise indoors. The segment I watched yesterday was about 1963, as the Beatles were becoming superstars and Beatlemania was sweeping through England. (They hadn't become a phenomenon in the United States yet.) In that section, the four members of the Beatles started discussing success. They mentioned how sudden it is, how surreal it is, how hard it is, and how they coped (or didn't).

In a 1963 interview, George Harrison actually said that he didn't believe the "George Harrison" in the newspapers was him. He was coping, at the time, by distancing himself from the entire event. Two other Beatles mentioned how difficult it had suddenly become to walk down the street in London or in Liverpool.

John Lennon, in that same interview, said this, "It all sounds complaining [but] we're not....It affects your home world more than it does yourself because you know what to expect but your parents and family, they don't know what's happening."

I've never heard the phenomenon of becoming extremely successful described so accurately. What he said in a few words is what I've been trying to express here.

I'll get back to this inside/outside approach to success in a moment, but let me continue with *The Beatles Anthology* for a minute.

In some ways, George Harrison's 1995 take on the entire phenomenon that he and the other Beatles lived through in 1963 was the most interesting. Harrison, speaking from a distance of 32 years, as an older man instead of the 20-something he had been when superstardom got thrust upon him, clearly had had a lot of time to reflect on that period of his life.

In his interview for the *Anthology*, he said, "I always felt sorry, later, for Elvis because he was on his own. He had his guys with him, but there was only one Elvis. Nobody else knew what he felt like. But for us, we all shared the experience."

Let me repeat. *Harrison felt sorry for Elvis*. Elvis Presley, also a superstar, a man who had achieved his dreams. Most people would never feel sorry for Elvis, not in the way Harrison had felt sorry for him, because most people would have told Elvis how lucky he had been to be in that situation.

Everyone who has incredible success understands that he is fortunate to be in that situation. (Note I didn't say lucky. As my very successful friend, Kevin J. Anderson, repeatedly says, "The harder I work, the luckier I am." Successful people may have had luck, but they are where they are because they knew how to use that luck in their favor. Usually, successful people are where they are because they work harder than everyone else they know.)

Like Elvis, the Beatles were small-town boys thrust into an international limelight. Like Elvis, they had a rapid early success. Like Elvis, they had no idea how to handle the pressures, the money, or the fame. Both Elvis and the Beatles signed terrible contracts in their early years. Elvis hired Colonel Tom Parker as his manager. Parker managed to clean up Elvis's contracts (while signing him to some other bad contracts that helped Parker), but no one could clean up the mess the Beatles had created. Even now, they're paying for those early mistakes.

The Beatles signed away their musical copyrights in those years, and so now, they only get a percentage of the earnings of their music, instead of the full earnings. (You can see the difference in the income statements, mentioned in "How Rich Are the Beatles?" an *Entertainment Weekly* article published in the September 11, 2009 issue: Ringo Starr, John Lennon's estate, and George Harrison's estate are worth between $155 million and $228 million, but Paul McCartney is worth about $716 million. The reason for the difference is simple: McCartney continued to play on a superstar level (Wings) and record his own songs for the intervening decades. I believe that, had John Lennon lived, he would have had the same kind of career and a similar kind of wealth. George Harrison and Ringo Starr didn't write as many songs and didn't record very many solo albums, so their level of financial (and musical) success after the Beatles wasn't as great as Lennon's, and certainly not as impressive as McCartney's.)

In other words, success has levels. All of us would be happy to earn $9 million per year like Lennon's estate did in 2008, but how would we feel if we knew that had we negotiated a better contract forty years ago, we would be earning five to ten times as much? Someone else is earning the bulk of the money off the Beatles catalogue, a fact that still grates on Paul McCartney (and he says so).

Success is jolting and extremely unexpected, even if you've been preparing for it. What you have prepared for is never the same as what really hits you, which is what the Beatles were discussing in the quotes above.

So now, let's move to our third definition:

3. Your definition of success.
Of course, I don't know your real definition. I only know mine. So what I'm going to discuss is the personal definition of success that each freelancer has.

Our definitions of success are extremely personal. A benchmark for me would mean nothing to you. We discussed that from the outside earlier, but let's discuss it from the inside now.

I have learned through teaching the Master Class over the past decade that most people can't imagine success. Most people believe success will never happen. If it does happen, they think success will take care of itself. Or, if they do believe success will happen, their definition of that success is quite small.

For the Beatles in the early years, success was working continuously as musicians. They had become successful when they worked the clubs in Liverpool, even more successful when they went to Hamburg, and had achieved the pinnacle of success when their first record got played on the radio.

Had they imagined Beatlemania? Not in their wildest dreams. As a result, the Fab Four weren't prepared for the problems that came with that kind of success—some of which we can imagine (no privacy, getting mobbed in crowds, losing your anonymity) and some of which we can't imagine. (Hence Harrison's comment about Presley, from the point of view of someone who understands.)

When success hits, you have no idea what your reaction to it will be. Many people actually get depressed, because they have lost their goal or achieved their dream. They now have nothing to strive for. Or they feel like a fraud—especially if that success comes quickly. (You hear this a lot from people who became famous young. They have to prove themselves "worthy" of that success.)

But here's my favorite reaction: often the successful person discounts the success.

There are reasons for that. Sometimes the success is overwhelming, so the way the person copes is to deny it's happening. (That's in the 1963 Harrison quote; the person in the news articles is someone else.) That's an okay way to cope until it becomes impossible to deny. Then the successful person must in some way acknowledge the success.

But most often, the successful person discounts the success because to him, the achievement wasn't a success at all.

Again, we get back to definitions.

I'll use a personal one. In the early 1980s, I got three tentative job offers. They came from friends who had worked with me when I was in radio news. The first came from a colleague I respected greatly, a man who went on to behind-the-scenes success writing and researching for many broadcast news magazines. He told me that *60 Minutes* was hiring, and he'd already put my name in. He said he would help me put my demo tape together, and get me an interview with the head producer there. My colleague said the interview was a formality. They'd already heard my work on his demo tape (I had engineered parts of it) and wanted me there.

The second job offer came from a friend who had become one of the documentary producers at WGBH in Boston. He wanted me to work for him. No interview, no demo tape. I didn't have to do anything except get my butt to Boston to look for an apartment.

The third job offer came from a third friend. He had signed on with a start-up national television news channel called the Cable News Network, which was also called CNN. "They're looking for great writers and engineers, Kris," he said to me on the phone. "You have better credentials than I do and you'll look better on camera. Get here now."

I begged off the *60 Minutes* interview. I said no to WGBH. I never went to CNN. Later, I met a news cameraman from CNN, a man who had worked at the station from the same time period that I got recruited.

"Hell," he told me, "that's how CNN offered jobs in those

days. You would've been on-air talent. You'd be a household name by now."

That's when I realized that my work at the radio station in Madison, Wisconsin had been a success. I had—completely unsolicited—job offers or job solicitations from three of the best news organizations of the time. I had turned them all down—and I'm glad of it, even now.

Even back then, I knew that WGBH was a big deal. I figured being a researcher at *60 Minutes* was a foot in the door on the national level, but nothing more. I had never heard of CNN, but I had figured out that if I moved away from Madison for any of those jobs, my career as a journalist would be underway.

I just hadn't realized it was already underway, and that the offers themselves were a success.

Why hadn't I realized that? I usually say because I was young and stupid, but the truth of it is that I hadn't realized it because I didn't define work in journalism—particularly broadcast journalism—as a way to achieve success.

I wanted to be a *writer*. I didn't want to be an on-air personality or a researcher for someone else. I didn't want to produce documentaries (although I later did for both WHA in Madison and the Annenberg Foundation). I wanted to become an acclaimed writer, and I actually saw those job offers as roadblocks, not as stepping stones, to my success.

Honestly, for my goals then and now, those offers *were* roadblocks. Had I gone to New York or Boston or Atlanta, I would have become a different person. I never would have written fiction. I might be wealthier than I am now. I would certainly be more famous. I might even have a book or two under my belt—non-fiction, about some current event topic—and that book might have been a bestseller.

But it would have been a bestseller because of my on-air work, not because of my *writing*.

So, in reality, I wasn't stupid at all. I knew what I wanted and how to go after it.

Even now, however, when I tell someone about those opportunities, that person often can't understand why I turned down those chances. I could have become famous. I could have worked in TV. Why would I say no?

Over the years, I have watched a family member of mine do something similar. Since infancy, my relative was musical. He taught himself to play the piano quite young, learning to plink out songs by ear. He has an astonishingly beautiful singing voice. He composes stunning pieces of music. He's also extremely charismatic and has excellent stage presence.

Dean used to think I said these things about my relative because he was someone I loved. Then, at a family event, Dean heard this young man sing for the very first time, and realized I hadn't exaggerated. If anything, I had understated this young man's abilities.

In my heart of hearts, I always wanted to be on Broadway in a role in musical theater. I am musical, love to sing, and love musicals. But I'm also an extreme introvert whose stage fright goes up when faced with a script. (I can ad lib and talk without a script just fine. Go figure.) I didn't want to be a performer badly enough to find ways around my introversion and extreme stage fright.

But I dreamed…

Enter my young relative, whom I spent a lot of time with over the years. As he got older, he performed around the world with an international teen singing group. I went to New York to see him, and at the party afterwards, was there when he met some Broadway stars who had once been in the same international singing group. They offered to get him an audition.

He didn't take it seriously.

Nor did he take a then-girlfriend seriously when she went out to California and called with a job offer to play music for the movies. Or when another friend offered to help him launch a jazz career.

He never followed up.

Now, my thirty-something relative is a headhunter for a major corporation. He does not get paid for his music. He's happily married with a baby on the way, which, he tells me, achieves one of his biggest dreams.

I still want to see him on Broadway.

Note this: *I* want to see him on Broadway. He doesn't go. There's a small part of me that's disappointed that he didn't follow *my* dreams. Fortunately for him, I'm just a relative and not his mother or his wife. Imagine how that small sense of disappointment would gnaw at both of us—unfairly—for years.

I've known this young man his whole life. Never once did I hear him express a desire for a career in music or a life on the stage. If I had listened, I would have heard someone who wanted a happy family, a good job, and stability—things you will never, ever, have with an international musical career.

He's achieving his dreams. He has success, the success he wants. It's just not what I imagined for him. In other words, my disappointment in his choices has always been about me, not about him.

Over the years, I'm sure he had trouble talking to me about his goals and dreams, because not only did I not see the same things for him, I also place no value on stability or a good day job. So his dreams were difficult for me to understand and value.

When you are in the position that I put my relative in—a position where you have to explain what success is to you to the people who love you—it's an uncomfortable place to be. Most of us can't articulate the importance of our dreams to people who understand them. It becomes doubly impossible when the people around us don't understand them at all.

It's not as fun celebrating a milestone with someone who doesn't understand what that milestone means. It's harder to live day-to-day with someone who misunderstands your success (or your lack of it—according to your perception). Sometimes you have to celebrate on your own. Sometimes you simply nod and continue, never correcting the people around you.

But occasionally, these warring definitions—from the dictionary definition to the world's definition to other people's definition to your definition—cause serious trouble.

And we'll get to that in a minute.

The Washington Post's October 28, 2009, edition had an article that encapsulates much of what I've been discussing here. The article is about farmer, fish taxidermist, and wildlife artist, Robert Bealle.

Bealle has just won the Federal Duck Stamp Art Contest, which is the only art contest sponsored by the federal government. I'm quite familiar with the contest due to one of my past lives—when my ex-husband and I owned an art gallery, a regular customer bought the limited-edition lithographs from the contest every year. He had my ex frame them, along with the postage stamp featuring the art.

Over the years, I gained quite an appreciation for wildlife art and for duck art in particular. Even now, I can spout off the names of major duck artists and give you approximate years in which they won the competition—up to about 1985, when we closed the store.

So I read the article with great interest and found not just something about a bit of my own past (and past interests) but about success as well.

Bealle has entered the contest every year since 1982. He's been a finalist several times, even coming in second more than once. His work has won the Maryland Duck Stamp competition three times. But he never achieved his dream, which was to win the Federal Duck Stamp Art Contest. Until 2009.

He told the *Post*: "Now I'll always be referred to as a Federal Duck Stamp winner. It may not mean a lot to most people, but to me it means a hell of a lot."

And there, in a nutshell, is the definition of success I've been working toward.

It may not mean a lot to most people, but to me it means a hell of a lot.

Note how much work it told me to explain the contest to you. And I can't begin to express how much that contest art meant to the collector I knew twenty-five years ago. He waited for the announcement, put his order in for the first of the lithographs, always hoping to get one of the top ten signed-and-numbered pieces, and always brought the litho in with great pride the day it arrived. He wasn't an artist; he was a connoisseur. And if he's still alive today (I lost touch when the store closed), you can bet he ordered Bealle's work.

It may not mean a lot to most people, but to me it means a hell of a lot.

That definition sounds so simple, doesn't it? So easy, so perfect. You'd think, if you loved a person who can so clearly define what success is to him, that you'd understand when he achieved it. You'd be there, you'd be sympathetic, you'd celebrate.

But you might not.

Because life just isn't that simple—and everyone has their own definition of success. With that definition come expectations.

Let's take a fictional couple, Frieda and Ron. Ron defines success the way Bealle does—as winning the Federal Duck Stamp Contest. Frieda supports him in his art, year in and year out. She works at a corporate job, making a good salary that doesn't pay all of the bills, and certainly won't cover their two kids' college educations.

Ron works outside jobs to pay for his wildlife art. He's had showings in several galleries and has had some regional success. He has made some money, enough to supplement his part-time job, but never more than $15,000 per year before taxes.

Then he wins the contest.

Here's what Bob Dumaine, a Houston stamp dealer and founder of the National Duck Stamp Collectors Society, told the *Post* about the financial realities of the contest.

"The enterprising people make money at it. The ones sitting around waiting for the cash register to ring, they're still waiting."

So much to parse in those two sentences. First, clearly, the winner isn't guaranteed a fortune. The winner doesn't even get national recognition outside of wildlife art and duck stamp circles.

Then Dumaine goes on to say that the "enterprising people" make "money" at it. Which begs the question: how much money? What's his definition of "making money"? Does he mean that they make a couple of thousand dollars, or tens of thousands of dollars? Does he mean they make a fortune?

It's impossible to tell from that one quote.

The one thing you can tell from the quote is that even with the win, the artist hasn't been anointed with the brush of fame and wealth. The *enterprising* artist—in other words, the artist who works the business side—will earn more than the artist who thinks he's given a map to Easy Street.

After 27 years in the competition, I'm assuming Bealle knows this, and I'm pulling for him to be one of those enterprising artists, even though, before reading that article, I had no idea who he was.

But let's take our fictional guy, Ron. Let's say he doesn't know how hard it is to make money after winning the contest. Or let's say that success doesn't include money at all to him. He just wanted to have a federal duck stamp with his artwork on it. That's the extent of his dream.

If he and Frieda are like most couples, they discussed the win as success, but never discussed what that success meant. Ron's ecstatic because he's achieved his dream. Frieda's a bit peeved because she realizes—for the first time—that the winner gets no money at all. Just a framed pane of 20 duck stamps signed by the Interior Secretary (and the artwork on 3.1 million duck stamps).

Ron's happy with the win.

Frieda's furious.

Where's the money? Where's the instant riches? Where's the payoff for all those decades of hard work on her part, supporting her man in his dream?

What does she get, after all? Attendance at a ceremony. A few evenings at some gallery openings. Long conversations with other spouses about life with duck stamp artists.

And that's about it.

Except the joy of seeing her husband achieve one of his lifelong ambitions.

For some spouses, that's enough. But for many, it's not. And it doesn't have to be a duck stamp contest. It could be an athletic event—finishing a first ultra marathon for example (or a first marathon for that matter)—or a short story sale.

It could be a fan letter from someone you admire or a simple pat on the back from a mentor. For you, the freelancer, such things are so important that they can keep you going for days, months, sometimes years.

For the long-suffering spouse, they're just one more indication of your weird obsession with duck art or writing or building filing cabinets.

Those small indications are important, because they build. At some point, Frieda realizes that she'll always have to work her corporate job, that she'll never live in the manner to which she can become accustomed (unless she's the one who finds a new job, or a better way to earn money). At some point, she realizes that Ron will be content with his "little paintings" as she calls them, and could live in a hut in the woods, so long as he has food, electricity, and enough money at the end of the day to buy more painting supplies.

This, she will eventually say, is not what she signed on for, and she will leave. She will sound unreasonable to all of Ron's artist friends, but in reality, she's right.

Because she and Ron never discussed what success means to both of them. She signed on to support an artist who eventually becomes as rich as Owen J. Gromme. ("Who?" you ask…Only the most successful wildlife painter of his day—see how specialized success can be?) Ron signed on to have a partner in his work, one who celebrates the 20-panel framed stamps signed by the Interior Secretary of the United States with as much vigor as she would a fifty-thousand dollar commission from a local art collector.

Success is wonderful, but it can be a minefield. When you achieve a certain level of success, you will lose friends—some of whom can't deal with the fact that you achieved your dream before they achieved theirs. You will gain family members who believe that you owe them something, even though you had no idea that your Aunt Millie's second cousin's third wife had grown children. (Let alone that your Aunt Millie had a second cousin who had married three separate times.)

And you will run into some fascinating expectations, often from unexpected quarters.

After I quit editing *The Magazine of Fantasy & Science Fiction* in the late 1990s, I wrote a variety of novels under many pen names. I am a fast writer who loves to write. I also like the "security" of a contract, and I like the challenge of unrelated projects.

I was making a healthy living as a writer in those years and was beginning to make a name for myself in my various genres. Then my agent at the time got the idea that I should not take advances under $15,000. We did not discuss this. The agent simply informed companies who wanted to work with me that my bottom line price was $15,000 per project.

I don't know how long this went on before I stopped it. I have no idea how many projects I lost or how much goodwill that agent ruined for me. Because everyone who contacted the agent thought the agent was speaking for me—as agents are supposed to do.

When I confronted the agent as to the reason for this, it turns out we had a two-fold misunderstanding. First, I had said about one project and one particular company that I wouldn't work for them for under $15,000. That was a pain-in-the-ass tax. That company was horrible to work for. Second, the agent figured I was successful now, and needed to be "protected" from the "quick, easy, hack work" I had done before.

Never mind that I loved the "hack work" and didn't consider it hack work at all. Never mind that I never asked for protection.

Later, I learned that this agent saw it as part of the business to protect the client's reputation—as the agent saw the reputation. The reputation, according to the agent, was the only thing that constituted success.

My definition of success was completely different. I wanted steady, *challenging* work in a variety of fields so that my hummingbird brain wouldn't get bored. I didn't give a rat's farty behind about reputation. I figured (and still believe) that reputation happened to you after you died. The only reputation I didn't want was as a rude and difficult writer, someone perennially hard to work with.

Knowing that, a good friend of mine who was an editor at one of the publishing houses who had just been informed that I wouldn't work for less than $15,000 called me and asked what was up. Because she had a hunch that the edict hadn't come from me—and she was right.

But she made that leap because she'd had this problem with the agent before with other clients, and because she knew me really, really well.

It was that friend's action, that friend who understood how I worked and what I had repeatedly said constituted success *for me*, that stopped the weird little $15,000 downward spiral my career had slid into.

Such an edict might work well for other writers. It doesn't work well for me. Sometimes the most enjoyable projects I've ever worked on paid less up front. Often I got a huge return in royalties later. Or a better project from the same company. Or a hundred free research books. (That was lovely—worth another $2000 right there.) Or a great piece of art.

Late one night, I channel surfed to PBS and caught an episode of *Charlie Rose*. He was interviewing John Grisham at New York City's big Barnes and Noble store, just as *The Associate* was being released.

It's a fascinating interview, because Rose is a major reader with attitudes about art and artists that are diametrically opposed to Grisham's. Grisham writes to entertain. He makes no bones about that. He's doing his job when millions of people use his work as escape from their daily lives.

He stated one of his mantras to Rose, something I'd heard Grisham say countless times before. He said, and I'm paraphrasing here, *"If I get good reviews, I worry that I'm doing something wrong."*

Grisham's point is a simple one: critics often don't understand popular fiction. It's taken me a long time to understand this phenomenon and it wasn't until recently that it's made sense to me. Critics are required to read things they don't want to read. Worse, they're required to read a lot of stuff. And even worse, they're reading it *for their job*, not for enjoyment.

So if something breaks through the attitudes that the critic brings to the work [which are (1) I don't want to read this and (2) I hate this kind of fiction and (3) this better be worth the time I have to spend at it], then the critic likes the work.

That's a completely different attitude than the average reader brings to a book. The reader wants a few hours away from every day life, a few hours filled with entertainment, a few hours of escape.

Escape doesn't hold up well to critical analysis.

Grisham mentioned a variation of this in passing to Rose, but Rose still didn't understand. He values good reviews and critical opinion so much that he didn't seem able to envision a writer having success without it. In fact, he wondered aloud in the interview (more than once) how Grisham managed to have a career without critical approbation.

Grisham in turn wondered why anyone would want it.

If you want to see two competing versions of success, unable to talk to each other past a superficial level, watch that middle section of the interview.

So how does all of this apply to you, the newly successful freelancer?

1. Realize that some people will never understand your definition of success.

Then it's up to you whether or not to share your good news, or to even discuss your success with them.

2. Make sure that you know how the people closest to you define success.

Make sure they know how you define it. Make certain you discuss the future, not just achieving the success, but what that achievement means.

3. Remember that the world really doesn't care about your success.

The closest thing I've ever seen to the world celebrating a success was November of 2008, when Barack Obama was elected. People around the world danced in the streets. Yet millions of people in the United States and elsewhere were dismayed at the victory. What many saw as a huge success, others saw as a huge defeat. Days later, we all remembered that victory, but we all went back to our everyday lives. Many of us never spoke of it again. Yes, it was a big deal (and it was a very big deal for the Obama family [but I would have loved to have been a fly on the wall when the Obama girls realized they had to leave their school and friends for the next four years]), but it wasn't as important to most of us as our own jobs, our own families, and our own lives.

If you remember that no one cares as much about your successes (and your failures) as you do, then you'll keep a personal balance, one that will enable you to get through some of the treacheries that success can bring—some of those things George Harrison alluded to when he said he felt sorry for Elvis Presley.

I read a lot of biographies. Some are for my historical fiction—someone else's interpretation of lives long past—but many are autobiographies, written by writers.

I went on an excessive binge in the deep, dark days of this thing the press calls the Great Recession. During December of 2008 and January of 2009, I read the autobiographies of two Grand Masters of Science Fiction—Jack Williamson and Frederik Pohl. Jack's *Wonder's Child* helped me through that December, when the future looked particularly bleak. His chapters on writing during the Great Depression helped me over my fears of the future of publishing in this economic downturn. (I figured if publishing continued then, it would certainly continue now. And that turned out to be correct.)

Fred's autobiography *The Way the Future Was* served a more typical need for me. I was reading to see how a longtime writer coped with the ups and downs of a career. Fred's had spectacular ups and spectacular downs, and while he was candid about them, his analysis made them seem more intellectual than personal.

Right now, I'm reading the autobiography of another Grand Master, Robert Silverberg. Bob's book, *Other Spaces, Other Times*, unlike the other two books, is a compilation of autobiographical essays published throughout his career.

The net result is a very personal look at one writer's changing emotions about his life and his writing. I, of course, know how the field feels about Bob, and what has happened in the last 30 years of his career. I vaguely knew some of the early stuff.

What fascinates me the most about his autobiography, however, is its ever-changing view of success. The young Robert Silverberg—the boy who started mailing his stories to the pulp magazines in the 1940s—wanted to be published in those magazines. Then he wanted to be a science fiction writer. Then, while he was at Columbia University, he became one.

He even survived a distribution collapse in the late 1950s that killed most fiction writers' careers. But by the mid-1970s, he had retired from science fiction—and, in some ways, from writing entirely. He wrote a famous, bitter essay about why he left, which he included in this book.

I recognize that essay. I could have written something similar at one point in my career. Like Bob, I had a great feeling of being unappreciated by my chosen genre. Yet outsiders didn't understand this. Outsiders—meaning people who were not me.

Because, at the time I felt that way, I had a long career. I'd been published—and recognized—in every genre I tried to write. I had awards and bestselling books and acclaim. But I had hit a bump in the road—a big one—and I no longer saw those things.

In his famous essay, neither did Bob. He actually says at one point that the sf field has passed him by because, he writes, "though nominated every year, my books and stories have finished well behind more conservative, 'safer,' works." In other words, the nominations weren't enough; he was losing awards to works he didn't respect. He was selling novels and short stories as fast as he could write them, but once they were on the marketplace, they weren't performing to his expectations.

Eventually, he left the field, "retiring" until a novel practically wrote itself out of his subconscious. Then he embarked on another prolific and successful part of his career, before he "retired" again. By his count, he has retired twice from writing, and both times, he has returned.

At the end of a 1998 essay, he writes. "So my career, marked as it has been by triumph after triumph, has often seemed to me like nothing but a formidable struggle." I came across that quote just this morning, and it made me stop reading for two reasons. First, I've felt that way more times than I want to admit, and second, it echoes the Miley Cyrus song, "The Climb." If you haven't heard that song (and I have no idea how you missed it), go take a listen before finishing this short book.

I'll get to the Miley Cyrus song in a minute. But let's focus on the quote for a moment. I like this quote a lot. It shows two kinds of self-awareness.

First, Bob recognizes the triumphs for what they are. Actual successes—successes he didn't seem to value as a much younger man.

Second, he knows that the process—the internal process—is very different from the external one. That's what I've been getting at when I've discussed the differing definitions of success.

What I haven't explored in depth is that success itself is an ever-changing target. Last week, a former student of mine wrote me a panicked letter about the state of the publishing industry. Publishing news has been dismal of late, but as one pundit put it a few weeks ago, the book industry always reacts to any kind of change as if the world is going to end. Unfortunately, this writer either didn't know that or didn't remember it. She looked at the publishing industry, and decided that her recent sales were a fluke.

They weren't. All I did in my return e-mail was remind her that the woman I had met nearly a decade ago would look on her current career as an unmitigated success—which occurred in the middle of this awful downturn, making it even more of a success.

She took a virtual breath, laughed, and calmed down. Because I was right.

Bob deals with that in the same essay that has the great quote. It's hard to dismiss your own success when you're collaborating with one of your childhood heroes—as he had done, working with Isaac Asimov. I'm sure he had other undeniable benchmarks for success. I'm just not sure what they are.

After I finished last week's section on success, Dean asked me if I knew what his definition of success was. I told him I had known in the early 1990s, but didn't know now. He nodded, and then said he had thought it a trick question. It wasn't; we both know he's in the process of redefining success—again.

I seem to redefine success every year or so. Once you hit a milestone, it's done, it's gone, it's in the past. It is no longer something you strive for. It becomes part of your biography, not a goal to be achieved.

Success is something to strive for. If you look at it as something you've achieved, you rest on your laurels. There's nothing wrong with that. A lot of people stop striving after attaining a particular goal.

Because I live in the Pacific Northwest, I see one of those people on the news fairly often. Paul Allen, the co-founder of Microsoft, retired with his billions instead of working in the software field any longer. Bill Gates continued to strive in that field.

Paul Allen said he retired, but really, he just turned his attention to his other interests. One of them matches mine. We both want the Portland (Oregon) Trailblazers to win during every basketball season. Of course, I watch as a hobby, and he—as the owner of the Trailblazers—has an actual stake in the franchise's success.

I have never met Paul Allen. Nor have I read many interviews with him. I don't know how much his definition of success has changed. For all I know, he always wanted to retire early and pursue his hobbies with the same dedication he had once put into Microsoft. But I have a hunch his definition of success now is very different than it was in 1972.

I know mine is. I have always said that success, for me, is to continue making a living as a writer. I have done that for decades now. But, oddly enough, the definition of making a living has changed for me. I want to sustain the lifestyle I have now, not revert to the one I had the year I graduated from college.

Then I wasn't sure what I meant by "writer." I knew— knew!—that no one could make a living writing fiction, so that dream was out (even though I read books by professional fiction writers who had become rich off their writing every single day). So I figured I'd have to be a journalist. Then I realized that freelance non-fiction writers made money. Eventually I realized that fiction writers were the best paid of all writers.

My definitions kept changing.

I look around my office now and see hundreds of books and magazines that contain my work. I've been published in 13 languages. I've been an award-winner and a bestseller. I've traveled on someone else's dime because of my writing. I've gone places I never thought I'd go—like the United Nations. I've done things I couldn't imagine thirty years ago, all because of the profession I chose.

I value those things. I know they have made me successful in the eyes of other people—and in the eyes of my former self (if I could travel back in time and tell her about them).

But their bearing on my future success is minimal. I am in a different place as I define success now. I look at other things, things that I may not have valued then or may not have known about then.

This is what the Miley Cyrus song refers to. The writers (J. Alexander and J. Mabe) of the song envision success as a mountain range with differing peaks and valleys. If you've ever stood in the middle of a real mountain range, you realize that the mountain peaks disappear into the distance. Once you've climbed one, you see another ahead of you, and another and another. And at times, you have to climb down before you can reach the next peak.

The thing I didn't know about mountains when I was what my husband rudely calls a flatlander and the rest of the world calls a Midwesterner, is that often the valleys between mountain peaks are significantly higher than sea level. So if you're climbing and you've reached a plateau between the mountains, you're still higher than you were when you started.

It just doesn't seem that way.

My career, as Bob Silverberg writes, *marked as it has been by triumph after triumph, has often seemed to me like nothing but a formidable struggle.*

Exactly. Like climbing mountains. Up and down, down and up, achieving yet moving forward.

Because the people who accept their success and rest on their laurels—as the cliché goes—go no farther. Sometimes they don't want to go farther. Sometimes they vacate the field, as Paul Allen did in the field of software. Sometimes they retire, as Robert Silverberg did for a few years in the 1970s, and rest or read or travel.

But those people have decided, for whatever reason, to stop moving forward. Maybe they're happy with what they've done. Maybe (as one successful friend told me) they fear they can never do better.

I feel, however, if you're going to continue in your chosen field, you have to keep striving—even if you've had success. You have to acknowledge that success but—and this is an odd sentence— you can't let it limit you.

For example, Paul McCartney could have quit making music in 1969. After all, he would always be a member of the Beatles, a group of musicians who changed the music industry forever. He had co-written some of the bestselling songs of all time. Even with the bad contracts that the Beatles signed, McCartney had made enough money to last him the rest of his life—and he wasn't even thirty years old.

Instead, he has spent the last forty years making music, trying different things, learning new instruments and experimenting with new styles. In the 1980s, the joke was "Do you know who the Beatles are? They're the band Paul McCartney was in before Wings." Now that McCartney has gone solo for nearly two decades, a similar joke can be told about Wings.

His career has continued. I'm sure that his definition of success has changed mightily over the past sixty years.

I think if you want a lifelong career in your chosen field, your definition of success has to change. And if you have an ever-changing definition of success, you will eventually hear yourself utter a sentence similar to the one in Robert Silverberg's essay. Even though you've had triumph after triumph, your career will feel like a formidable struggle.

Because a long-term career *is* a struggle. It's a climb, as the song says. And that's the point. Not the success itself.

Success is good. Success is necessary to survival in business. Celebrate your successes when they happen. Then move on to something else. Some new project over the horizon. The next mountain. The next challenge—and conquer that.

If you do that, life will remain interesting. And on those few occasions when you look back, you'll realize you had more success than you thought, because while you were in the middle of them, you were struggling mightily.

Enjoy that moment. Then turn around and look forward. Face the next challenge.

Because that's really what it's all about.

Section Eight:
Goals and Dreams

Chapter Forty-seven
The Difference between Goals and Dreams

We use the words "goals" and "dreams" interchangeably. We achieve our goals, pursue our dreams. We pursue our goals, achieve our dreams. But goals and dreams are very different. A shorthand way of thinking about this comes from football.

That weird little H-shaped thingie sticking out of the end zone? It's called a *goal*post, not a *dream*post. I think football would be an entirely different game if it had a *dream*post. Hockey would be different too, if the players tried to get the puck past the dreamer.

In fact, the difference between a goalie and a dreamer are as illustrative as the difference between goalpost and dreampost. As I go on here, playing with words, you're starting to get an inkling of what I'm talking about.

Goals, simply put, are something you achieve. My *Encarta World English Dictionary* gives me five definitions of "goal." Four are connected to sports, including number five, which is "the end of a race." Number four is the only non-sports related definition of the word: "something that somebody wants to achieve."

Achieve. We achieve our goals. Goals are an end product. The other definitions include phrases like "a successful attempt at…" or "the score gained…"

There are no words like "successful" or "gained" in the definition of dream. Nor does the definition of dream include the word "achieve."

The same dictionary gives the noun "dream" six definitions, and most of them involve sleep or inattention or thoughts. First, of course, the dictionary discusses those visions our mind serves up when we're sleeping. It also discusses the daydream.

The two definitions that concern us are the third and the fourth. I'm going to start with the fourth: "an idea or hope that is impractical or unlikely to ever be realized." If that were the definition of goal, then every single sports team in the world would be in trouble. (Of course, I've known a few football teams bad enough to make a win an impractical hope.)

The third definition is a little more upbeat: "Something that somebody hopes, longs, or is ambitious for, usually something difficult to attain or far removed from the present circumstances."

Ah, now we're getting somewhere. And since I try to be very practical in the *Guide*, and you all seem to recognize that, you probably think I'm going to tell you to abandon your dreams and set goals.

Nope.

Both dreams and goals are necessary for success. You just have to understand the difference between them.

Deep down understand it.

I don't think a freelancer can survive long without a dream. I think the more impossible the dream, the better. If you don't set that impossible dream high enough, you'll reach your dream, and stop striving.

When students apply for the Master Class that my husband Dean Wesley Smith and I teach (along with four other established professional writers – find details at deanwesleysmith.com), we ask those students what their goals are and what their secret, most impossible dream is. The only students we take for the Master Class are those with either a professional career that has stalled (for some reason) or those with a strong work ethic who are having trouble breaking into publishing (and have excellent, professional-level skills).

We look at the goals and the secret dream more than any other part of the application. Because if the goals and the secret dream are nonexistent, we have learned that the writers often don't have the capability to survive the Master Class, let alone the business of writing itself.

What does an impossible dream add to a career? Purpose. Plain and simple. That dream is like the shining city on a hill, the one you can see in the distance, and you might never reach. But until your dying day, you'll head for that hill.

The other thing that the impossible dream adds is a sense of hope. As long as you have something grand to strive for, you also have something grand to hope for. Hope gets us through the dark times better than anything else.

When hope disappears, so too does drive.

Which is why it's so hard to succeed on a long-term level if you have easily-attained dreams. If you lack that one huge impossible dream. Because you might reach that city on the hill within the first few years of your professional career. And then what will you do What will you hope for? What will you daydream about?

I think the daydream part is also essential. You need something to entertain your imagination while you're working day to day. If you're an actor, you might spend time every day studying fancy gowns for your trip down the red carpet for your tenth Oscar nomination. Not your first, not your fifth, your tenth. Your impossible dream might be to have more Oscar nominations than Meryl Streep.

But if your impossible dream as an actor is to have a small part in a film—well, you might attain that dream the day you sign up as an extra in a large crowd scene. That's a dream you can attain in my tiny town on the Oregon Coast. Dozens of movies have filmed here since I've lived here, and lots of locals have had their mugs on the screen, if only for a few seconds. A few of the locals actually have had small speaking parts. Heck, my husband's best friend— an attorney—had a speaking role in a commercial filmed in Idaho. Because of those thirty seconds on the nation's television screens, our attorney friend is one of Idaho's members in the Screen Actors Guild.

Had his lifelong dream been to become an actor—someone who qualified for the Screen Actors Guild—then he did so in a single outing with a single commercial. But if his lifelong dream had been to become a famous star of stage and screen, someone who had not just an Oscar, but an Emmy and a Tony, someone who had a lead role on Broadway as well as starring roles in hit movies or hit TV shows— well, then he has a long, long way to go.

See the difference? Even those things I listed above might not be enough for that impossible dream. An actor might want to be considered the greatest actor of his generation. A writer might want to have the bestselling book of all time. A store owner might want to create the largest store franchise in the world.

Because these are dreams, not goals, it's okay to noodle on them, to see them as a shining light in the distance, as something to work toward, but not something to count on.

Goals, on the other hand, are stepping stones. Goals must be achievable. Goals should build on each other.

Go back to the football analogy. A football game in which a score is just a dream would be the dullest thing on the planet. In fact, football players wouldn't even have to face off. They could sit on the field, if they wanted, and imagine the score. Of course, no one would come to the game—because there wouldn't be a game. Just a dream of a game.

But football is a game of inches. It is built on phrases like "first and goal." The game itself sets up tiny goals that lead to a touchdown. And if the team fails in one tiny goal, then the ball goes to the other team, which then tries to achieve a series of small goals to get to the larger one.

The dream for football players isn't to win one game. A lot of players achieve that as early as the age of eight or ten, in a Pee-Wee Football League. Or they have the game-winning run (or the game-winning pass) as early as the first game of their high school career.

The dream for football players is to play in the Super Bowl. Or to win the Super Bowl. Or to be the Super Bowl's Most Valuable Player—not once, but several times throughout their career.

That's a dream that can't be reached without a lot of goals—small and large. From getting on the varsity team in high school, to playing well enough to stay, to winning game after game, to playing in college, to playing well enough to get drafted into the National Football League, to playing in the NFL (not sitting on the bench), to being a part of a very good team, to winning games inch by inch, yard by yard, year-in and year-out, to winning a division, and to going to the big game, and then, to winning it. More than once. Not-so-tiny goals, all leading to the big dream.

Not every professional football player makes the playoffs. A professional football player can have a successful—a highly successful—career without ever once playing in the Super Bowl. But if that player retires before he gets the chance to play in the biggest game of all, he will know he never did quite attain his dream. (I think this is why so many players try to become coaches. They might not get to the big game as a player, but they want to try as a coach.)

A goal is "something somebody wants to achieve." It's "the end of a race." Goals, in some ways, are the opposite of dreams. If you set your goals too high, you'll get discouraged and quit. If you set your dreams too low, you'll get discouraged and quit.

So how to do you set goals? You start with easily achievable ones. The best diet programs are set up this way. They don't put you on a starvation diet of 800 calories per day. If you've been eating 4,000 calories per day, the diet will reduce your intake to 3500 calories per day. Most people can easily cut 500 calories from their diet. That's one giant soda or one huge specialty coffee drink or one piece of pie with ice cream. As time goes on, the calorie count goes down incrementally. And the dieter achieves other goals—losing a pound here, fitting into her "skinny" jeans for the first time in years, getting compliments from friends on how good she looks.

However, you can't stop with the small goals. When you achieve a goal, another needs to take its place. Each goal should be a little more difficult than the last. It's like running a marathon: No one can walk out the front door and run 26.2 miles without training. No one, not even the best athletes in the world.

Most people have to walk before they run, and some people can't even walk an entire block without getting winded. Yet within two years, they're able to run 26.2 miles. They didn't increase their distance every day. They walked for a block until they weren't winded. Then they walked for two. Then three. Eventually, they walked for a few blocks and ran for 100 feet. And on and on.

The other key to following goals is to write them down. First you need to write down what the goal is. Then you need to keep a log, one that records your struggles to achieve that goal. You will fail. Be honest about those failures. Then get back up and try again, until you achieve the goal.

Sometimes the failures tell you that the early goals are too hard. If so, cut the effort in half, and try again.

The other thing you need is a timetable. Give yourself a realistic amount of time to achieve a goal. Once that goal is achieved, have the next goal ready to go, along with its timetable. This is why I tell you to have daily, weekly, monthly, and yearly goals.

Throw in five-year and ten-year goals as well.

Then, revamp them often. Preferably on a monthly basis. As you strive to achieve those goals, you will learn what is realistic *for you*. No excuses. You need to be one hundred percent honest about what you're trying to do.

If you're an underachiever, pay attention to how hard you work. Make sure you're putting in some real effort and not just slacking off.

If you're an overachiever, make sure you don't work too hard.

That last piece of advice comes from me, the woman who now runs about fifteen miles per week. When I started out, I didn't pay attention to my limits (yes, overachiever), and I achieved...a stress fracture in my foot. Which would have only been a sore foot if I hadn't been so focused on trying to keep up to the impossible goals I had set myself. It would have become a permanently damaged foot if my husband, the former professional athlete, hadn't had a long talk with me about knowing my own limitations (and who also dragged me to the doctor).

It's hard to find a balance between working too hard on your goals and not working hard enough. Which is why I tell you to reassess often. And to be honest with yourself. Because you're the only one who is going to know if you're trying too hard or not trying hard enough.

The goals are stepping stones to that impossible dream. They're the trail through the murk that will lead you to the city on the hill.

They're also the reality check. Because the farther you get down the road, the more you should reassess. You might not want to go to that city on the hill. You might want to jettison your impossible dream because it's not something you want to do any longer.

If that's the case, then you need to find a new dream, or you will stop striving.

I know, I know, I'm speaking in metaphor here. Let me be concrete. One of my early impossible writing goals was to have a career like that of Nora Roberts. But the deeper I got into the writing profession, the more I realized that Nora Roberts and I are very different writers. I would love to have that many bestsellers and all the perks that go with it.

But Nora, for the most part, has stayed within the same genre. She writes all aspects of that genre—romantic suspense, paranormal romance, contemporary romance, even science fiction mystery romance. But the books all center on a couple, either falling in love or striving to maintain their love.

I have a hummingbird brain. I can't even read one genre for longer than a week. Asking me to write in one genre for the rest of my life would actually be a hardship.

As soon as I realized that, I had to look for a new impossible dream. Which was harder than it sounds. Not many writers write in more than one genre. I had to refine the dream to be something that suited me. I've refined several times since then. I still have impossible dreams—but none of them entail writing in the same genre, book after book after book.

I reassessed.

If I had wanted a career similar to Nora Roberts's career, I would have had to change my goals. I would have had to write novels in only one genre (although I could've branched into all the subgenres), and I would have had to have small goals along the way—writing a contemporary, writing a paranormal (oh, I've done that), writing a romantic suspense novel (I've done that too!), writing a historical….

You get the picture. My imagination is too dark to sustain a happily-ever-after ending, book after book. My sense of whimsy is too powerful to write dark novels, book after book. My mind sees too many future possibilities to keep me out of science fiction for too long. But I love to dig deeply into the modern world as well.

I'm not suited for the first city on the hill that I headed toward. However, I've found others that suit me better.

If you think of goals as markers along the way toward your impossible dream, then you've got the right philosophy. If you confuse goals with dreams, then you're going to get stuck.

Imagine something grand for yourself.

Then figure out how to achieve it. If achieving it takes only hard work—if there isn't a little bit of luck and timing involved—then you haven't found your impossible dream yet. Because an impossible dream should have an element of the impossible to it. An element of being in the right place at the right time.

Know too, that you might never achieve that dream—and that's okay. Because you're going to be disappointed when you get to that city. It'll never, ever, measure up to your imagination. So as you're on the final road toward your dream, make sure there's a new one waiting in the wings.

And then plan those stepping stones that will get you to your next city on the hill. Set your goals.

Goals are the only thing that will lead to your dream. All of your dreams.

Even those that might never come true.

Chapter Forty-eight
Patience

Full disclosure time: I have no patience. Or very little patience. I do a good imitation of a person with patience in public, but in my everyday life, I have no idea why everything I want isn't here the moment I want it.

I do understand the irony of me writing a chapter of the *Guide* on patience, but as someone who lacks something but still desires it, I have made a study of patience.

Patience is essential to building a business, any business. You must do things methodically. You must do them in a particular order, and even then, you might not get an immediate response.

This last bit is a particularly difficult part of owning your own business. We believe that when we put our ads out there, launch our websites, mail our stories, or open our shop's door, people will flock in. We'll get an immediate response.

Often we get no response at all—at least initially. And sometimes, the only response we get is negative.

All of which we should expect—and plan for. But that doesn't make it easy. Nor does it become any easier with time.

Every year, my alma mater, Beloit College, puts out its freshman survey. Someone polls the incoming class about various things—mostly trends—and Beloit publishes the results.

The Class of 2009, born in 1991, is internet savvy, educated, and informed, but the one thing they lack, according to a former professor of mine, Tom McBride, is patience. This group of kids always got what they wanted when they wanted it. Not just things, but television programs, music, text—all at the touch of a finger.

They haven't learned how to delay gratification—and delayed gratification is what building a business is all about. (You can find 2009's results at msnbc.msn.com/id/32453204.)

I can handle some forms of delayed gratification. I learned, way back when, that the process is the important thing, not the result. So with that lesson came another: I learned that I had to enjoy the actual work. If I didn't enjoy the work, then I couldn't wait for the result.

This is where my lack of patience works against me. I can wait two weeks or a month or even three months for a check if I enjoyed the work I did to get that check. If I loathed the job, then I want the money immediately. If I don't get the money immediately, I don't do any more work. This is why I'm unemployable on the corporate level.

A business—any business—has good and bad days, fun and difficult work. Early in the life of the business, very little positive happens. You set up systems, establish an office or a storefront, hire a few employees (or not), take out ads (or not), make products, and hope they'll sell. You need to get the word out that you are there, wherever there is, and you're ready to do some work for someone.

Then when you do work for a few someones, you hope they like it enough to recommend you to someone else. In addition to building your office (or your store or your craft), you're building your reputation, good and bad.

You're also building your bank account. In the early days of the business, you're depleting the money you had saved to start the business. If you hadn't saved any money, you're depleting the loan someone (a friend or a financial institution) gave you. As I mentioned before, money goes out the door every single day, but early on, money rarely comes back in.

The early years of a business are all about patience, the early years of a freelance business even more so. You have to be patient as you learn your craft. You have to be patient as you save money to finance the start-up. You have to be patient as you work that day job while you're trying to build a nest egg. You have to be patient as you line up clients, expertise, product.

You have to be so patient that at times it feels like you are doing nothing but being patient.

It's tough, especially in our have-it-now society.

Personally—and this is a bit of an aside—I think one of the good things about the current recession is that people are relearning (or in the case of the 20-somethings learning) how to wait for something they want. Credit has become tougher to get, so you can't just charge whatever you want even if you can't afford it. Layaway is back. (I hadn't realized it had gone away.) Layaway teaches the value of paying for something without having that something until the money is all in.

In some ways, layaway is what happens as you start a business. You're laying away bits of money, bits of expertise, bits of knowledge, as you prepare for the entire product—which is the ultimate dream.

But patience isn't just essential as you start a business. It's essential to maintaining one.

I'm watching a friend do something fascinating. He has completely abandoned the regular publishing model because its difficulties and slowness drive him crazy, and is beginning to self-publish his work electronically. Unfortunately, he hasn't planned for the transition. He doesn't have money saved so that he can contribute to the household, nor does he know how much money he'll actually make on the self-published items.

It's a bold experiment, but he's doing it as a reaction to the things he doesn't like about the existing business he has chosen to participate in, not as a studied, planned expansion of the business he has freelanced in for decades.

If he's lucky, this experiment will work for him. But if the experiment goes as I think it will, he would have been better off working the system he already knew.

Part of the problem is that he's impatient to join the brave new world of electronic publishing. He's jumping in with both feet, without doing any of the due diligence that a wise business owner would do.

The world of electronic publishing is new, and it does require a certain amount of faith. But so does all small business, and there are ways to mitigate potential problems that come from the unknown. I've discussed some of that in previous chapters, and I'll discuss more in future chapters.

But for the moment, let's stay focused on the issue of patience. How do I, a person with no patience, thrive in a business that requires extreme patience?

I gave you a hint, above.

First, I enjoy the process. I love the work itself. If we got zapped back to the dark ages tomorrow and publishing as we know it disappeared, I'd still write stories on any scrap of paper I could find. I love to write, and that won't change.

(I seriously do not understand writers who say they hate to write but love to have written. That makes my brain hurt every time. If you don't like what you do, then why do it? There are easier ways to make a living than writing.)

In fact, for me, the process is why I'm in the writing business. I like everything about writing: I like telling stories. I like playing with words. I like research. I like being alone. I like spending my time in made-up worlds.

I also like the process of freelancing. I'm a bad employee. I hate rules and strictures. I prefer to do things my way in my time, which makes me the quintessential freelancer.

I like being in control of my own destiny. I like the fact that if I don't produce, I don't get paid. I actually hate the idea of going to a job, sitting at a desk, and twiddling my thumbs while I wait for someone to tell me what to do—all for the sake of a paycheck. If you look at my history, you'll realize that I lasted a grand total of three months in every job like that I took. (And I only made it three months because that's about as long as it took me to read every scrap of paper in a normal office.)

But there are many aspects of being my own boss that I don't like. Unfortunately, most of those aspects are essential to the business's survival. I have to mail my work. I have to pay the bills. I have to dun the occasional client for payment. I have to troll for new work. And I have to learn new methods of making money in new mediums or new venues.

How do I handle those things?

Several ways.

I plan. That sounds both silly and essential. Of course, I plan. Every business owner should plan. But as I pointed out above, with the example of my friend, most freelancers don't plan at all. They run after the newest, hottest, shiniest thing. Or they get rid of what's already working because it makes them uncomfortable, to try something new because it looks easier.

I research heavily, and then I lay out a potential schedule. I make educated guesses about how long it will take me to learn something or incorporate something or change something.

Then I write that plan down step by step in my calendar. As I complete each step, I check it off. If the step is particularly difficult, I reward myself with an afternoon off or an ice cream cone or a very noticeable pat on the back. After I've checked that step off, I make sure I'm still on track. If I've learned something that changes the schedule, I then make the changes before I move to the next step.

Again, I'm elevating the process into its own little returns-and-reward system. Dean does the same thing, only using his white boards. He makes his lists (charts, actually, for him) in erasable ink. Then as he completes a step, he either marks down the date or erases the step. He can monitor his progress in that way.

Rather than seeing the task—whatever it is—as one big, difficult, long torturous thing to complete, I make it a series of smaller tasks, all of them easy to complete. That helps with my impatience because I don't have to wait six months for results. I get results every week or sometimes every single day.

I only schedule things that I control. For example, when you open a store, you can't say with any certainty when the first customer will walk through the door. All you can do is plan for the moment the store is ready for business.

In publishing, I can't control when someone will buy something. I can only write to the best of my ability and have a lot of product in the mail to people who might buy it. There are three factors at work here: the product has to be good, there has to be a lot of it, and it has to be in front of someone who will consider it for publication. I can control all three of those things.

So I don't plan to have sold something by January 1. Instead, I plan to have five short stories done and mailed by that date. And then I move to the next date, and the date after that.

If I work on the things I can control, things that I know will improve my business, then the goodness will follow.

A note here: I have noticed that good things come in waves. In publishing, sales come in waves. As do good reviews or award nominations. This also happens in retail. A store will have several good days in a row, with a lot of customers and sales, followed by weeks of slow days or days with no customers at all. And the irritating thing about this is that the ups and downs are impossible to predict.

So if you're always waiting for someone else to do something, then you'll run out of patience quickly. But if you do the things that you can control, then you're going to be too busy to notice what that someone else is doing—and when they finally get to it, you'll be taken by surprise.

In this way, my friend's plan to self publish is a good one. He's taking control of his backlist and his front list.

What he's missing—at least from the outside—is this next thing.

I maintain my base. By this I mean I continue to do the things that allow my business to thrive. I write short stories, in part because I love them and in part because I have an audience for them. I resell things I've already published because that's income for very little work on my part. I am constantly looking for new markets so that when the old ones disappear, I still have work.

As I add in new things (such as slowly adding mystery writing to my science fiction writing), I don't abandon what has already worked for me. I research the new markets and slowly put a toe into the water, instead of jumping into the deep end, abandoning my safe spot on the shore.

In other businesses, that's keeping the regular clients while bringing in new clients. Just because one new client promises to give you more work than you can handle doesn't mean you should take on that client. Research first, see if the money is what is promised, see if the client will actually be someone you want to work with (or for), and then slowly bring that client into your business.

Don't let the untested new thing take over because you're impatient for results.

If you're anything like me, telling you to be patient is like waving a red flag in front of a bull. That's guaranteed to make me impatient. But if I have a plan, I can take all the time I need to get where I'm going.

Because I enjoy the journey.

And, ultimately, that's what freelancing is all about. Enjoying the process—and celebrating each positive result.

Chapter Forty-nine
Expectations

A short time ago, a young writer who did not know my history in the science fiction field mentioned in e-mail how much he hated certain editors. He felt those editors had mislead him, and were, therefore, unethical people.

Since those editors happened to be friends of mine of longstanding—I'd known both for more than twenty years—I knew they weren't unethical people. Nor would they deliberately mislead writers.

After a few back-and-forths, I found out what happened: those editors had met this young writer in a networking situation (one a convention, the other a guest lecture at a writer's workshop) and invited him to submit stories to their various projects.

The writer had submitted stories which were then kindly, but soundly, rejected. He was furious. He thought the editors had broken an implied promise. By inviting him to submit—he thought—the editors were committing to buy the stories.

Never mind that neither editor had ever seen his work before. Never mind that they had no idea whether he even wrote in the genre.

He hadn't thought the situation through. A little more probing uncovered something else: he had an improper understanding of the writing field.

Somehow, this young writer had gotten it into his head that most writers sold stories not because the stories were good, but because the writer had met the editor and the editor liked the writer. I have no idea where that idea had come from—it certainly isn't written down anywhere, even as a myth—but it had embedded itself firmly in this writer's brain.

(To clarify, in case any others out there have this notion in their minds: stories sell because the stories are good. There are other factors, such as what the publisher wants for the magazine/book line. For example, no matter how excellent a hardboiled mystery is, you won't sell it to a sweet romance book line. It just won't happen.)

Before you sit back smugly and think that you would never make a mistake like the one this young writer made, realize that everyone who is in business for himself—every single freelancer/business owner—has made this mistake at least once. Many make it every single day.

The mistake comes from unrealistic expectations.

I almost wrote that it comes from expectations (leaving out the word "unrealistic"), and while that may be true (we shouldn't have expectations; we should have plans), without some measure of expectation, we probably can't do what we do. I'll get to that in a bit. But first, let's deal with unrealistic expectations.

When my ex-husband and I opened our frame shop and art gallery twenty-mumble years ago, my ex was the realist (for once). He knew that he couldn't open the store without a customer base already in place. I was the unrealistic one: I thought that because we had a storefront and a sign above the door and lovely inventory and a talented framer, we would have customers on the very first day we opened. We did, but only because my ex ran his legs off. He planned a grand opening, sent out invitations (with maps), called people, and made sure everyone who needed to know about the store did know. And then he grew the business.

I had *Field of Dreams* in mind: somehow I believed if we built it, they would come.

Many retail store owners make that mistake. I just watched the same thing happen this last year. A woman opened a whatnot shop in the same local mall as the collectibles store Dean had started. The whatnot shop, which this poor woman had spent years saving items and money for, was no different than three similar stores that had not survived in that location, and sadly, her store wasn't as nice as the two other whatnot stores that already existed in the same mall.

Anyone with any business experience could have told her the store would fail. She had the wrong location, and she was undercapitalized. She couldn't wait long enough to build a customer base; she didn't even have enough money to join a group ad for the mall in the local paper. When the business went under after less than a year, none of her neighbors were surprised—and none were sympathetic. Everyone mentioned how unrealistic her expectations were, and one other store owner even mentioned the *Field of Dreams* analogy, albeit in reverse.

"Just because you build it," he said in his curmudgeonly way, "doesn't mean anyone will come."

He was right.

It made the loss no less painful for this poor woman. Her dream died in short order. But of all the things she did wrong—and she did quite a few (all first-time business owners and freelancers make horrible mistakes)—the worst thing was the devastation left by her unrealistic expectation.

How can you start a business without expectations? You can't. You have to have expectations of success or there really is no point in going out on your own. How many people do you know who start a business saying that they believe it will fail? I've never met anyone like that.

But your expectations have to be realistic. The woman shop owner hadn't done any research. She had planned and dreamed for her store, but she hadn't researched how to run a business or how much capital she would need. She had assumed these things would come to her.

I dealt with some of this in the section on Goals and Dreams, but expectations are subtler than either of those two things, and they blow up on you when you least expect it.

I had one of those expectation bombs blow up on me this year—and I didn't even see it coming.

My twenty-fourth birthday was terrible. I spent the day alone. My friends had moved out of town, my family forgot my birthday, and my ex-husband didn't even remember to get me a cake. (Yes, I know, the handwriting was on the wall at that point.)

I spent the day alone, stuck on the farm that we lived above without a car, so I couldn't even go into town to entertain myself. I read, watched a little television, and generally felt sorry for myself. I also—Scarlett O'Hara-like—vowed I would never have another crappy birthday again, even if I had to make sure the celebrations happened. I promised myself that when I got old and was rich and famous, I would give myself the party of a lifetime. I would pay for all of it—spending tens of thousands of dollars on caterers and airline tickets for all my friends and family—and it would last all weekend, and it would be very, very *Dynasty*, with designer clothes, rich food, and upscale swanky digs.

Fast forward to January 1, 2010. 2010—the year I turned fifty.

I had a complete and utter meltdown. Not because I turned fifty. But because— apparently—to the 24-year-old me, 50 is really, really old.

The expectation bomb went off. My 24-year old self had planted a huge landmine, and as the calendar turned to 2010, I stepped on that damn mine. I realized I don't have *Dynasty* level money. I couldn't afford to fly my friends and family in to some swanky resort somewhere and spend what would have been in 1984 dollars tens of thousands of dollars but what is in 2010 dollars hundreds of thousands of dollars on a party. I don't have hundreds of thousands of dollars lying around—and if I did, I'd pay off my house and add to my savings, not spend every last dime on designer duds for my shindig.

I knew that. Realistically, I should have shrugged and laughed at my 24-year-old self. But built into that party expectation were two other expectations. The first expectation was that fifty was really, really, really old. I became ancient—at least to that poor lonely girl I had once been. And second—I should be a multimillionaire, maybe even a billionaire, by now. I should have a household name like Stephen King or Nora Roberts or J.K. Rowling.

I don't.

So—by the lights of the expectation bomb I planted at the ripe old age of 24—I am both old *and* a failure.

Oh, and happy 50th birthday!

Ouch, ouch, ouch.

I've run into a million of those personal expectation bombs throughout my career. Some are pretty easy to see—if I sell my first short story, I'll have it made. If I sell my first novel, I'll be rich. But others aren't visible until you step on them (which is why I'm using the term landmine). When I got nominated for my first Edgar award (and typing that phrase is a trip, even now. My *first* Edgar), I almost declined it but I managed to stop myself just in time.

When Dean asked why I would do such a thing, I heard myself answer, "Because I'm not good enough to be nominated for an Edgar." It took some digging to find when I planted that particular landmine. I had planted it (we plant all these expectation landmines) during the summers of my childhood, then continued to grow the mine during my adulthood, by buying novels with Edgar-winner emblazoned on them. I had used "Edgar-winner" as a stamp of quality—and it is a tribute to that award that I was rarely if ever disappointed.

Instead of being flattered and honored at first, I was terrified that I had been nominated by accident.

Pieces of that landmine still exist, as you can tell from my parenthetical phrase about my first Edgar award, but now I have that particular bomb under control.

Not all of these landmines are about success. Some are about failure. A pragmatic friend of mine knew the statistics when he started his business. He knew that it took five years to establish most businesses, and since his was particularly tricky, he figured he might not be successful even five years in.

That was his expectation, and his mantra, and he recited it often.

Surprise, surprise: His business got established within two years. He started making a profit. About the time he should have grown the business or made a few changes dictated by his success, he didn't even notice. Instead, he continued to talk about the three more years he had before his business got established.

No amount of arguing could change his mind; he expected to have a rough first five years. He didn't notice the success and actively sabotaged it. By not seeing his situation realistically, he lost his business within six years, and declared himself unsurprised.

What surprised him was that, as he put the bankbooks into storage, he realized he had achieved his success four years previously. He was stunned. He saw his business through the prism of his unrealistic (negative) expectations, and as a result he made mistakes that caused his business to meet those expectations and fail.

How do you root out these unrealistic expectations?

I wish I knew. I'd do a deep personal inventory of my psyche right now and make all of my unrealistic expectations disappear. In fact, I would have done it years ago, so this past January 1 would have been a pleasant day instead of the nightmare it became, all because I tripped over a mental landmine.

In the 26 years since I planted that particular landmine, however, I have learned how to recognize some of those unrealistic expectations and how to prevent them from becoming time bombs.

1. Don't plant the unrealistic expectation in the first place.

Listen to yourself as you make casual and joking statements. An old friend of mine had a habit that he had to force himself to quit. When a waitress asked, "What would you like?" My friend would say, "I'd like to be rich and never have to work again."

That's a very funny statement—particularly in that context (and with the right waitress who also sees the humor)—but it has an unrealistic expectation built into the middle of the joke. "I'd like to be rich *and never have to work again.*" Most rich people work. The ones who lose their riches let someone else manage their money. Money management *is* work. So if my friend had become rich before he stopped saying this little bon mot, he would have stopped working too—and probably would have lost all or most of his money to an unscrupulous money manager.

2. Research your expectations.

Has anyone become rich and never had to work again? If so, how? And if not, why not? And really—this one was always the key for me when my friend made his little joke—do you want to stop working? I know a lot of fantastically wealthy people who still work. They work harder than everyone else *because they enjoy their jobs.*

I'm sure Steven Spielberg could have stopped working somewhere around 1980, but luckily for modern American film, he did not. Stephen King could have stopped writing about the same time. As a fan, I'm happy he didn't.

If I had *Dynasty*-level money and could have thrown myself that party this year, I would still be working. I love what I do. The money isn't the reward; it's a byproduct of being able to do what I love.

3. Research everything.

Before you go into business for yourself, research the industry. Then research money management. Then research business. Listen to the negatives and the positives. If you don't like what you hear, figure out how you can avoid those problems.

If someone tells you that no one succeeds in your industry (writers hear this all the time), investigate. See if that's true. See if you can find five people who succeeded in your industry. Then ten. Then twenty.

If someone tells you there's only one way to succeed, see if that's true. Usually it isn't. Ask questions. Find the answers. And don't take the first answer. Get a second, third, and fourth opinion.

4. Research continually.

Make sure you keep up with your industry. If your freelancing business is in trouble, figure out why. Make the necessary changes to save it. Then make sure you do enough research so that you won't make that same mistake again.

5. Listen to people who are already successful in your field.

Those people will often offer you advice, but that advice might be oblique. I can't tell you how many times, early in my writing career, a very successful writer would say in the middle of a conversation, "That attitude will get you in trouble."

I would be defensive or I would ignore the sentence. I'd rarely follow up. But years later, I would remember the comment when that attitude—in the form of an unrealistic expectation—*did* get me in trouble. And sometimes I was lucky enough to have the opportunity to go back to that writer and ask how to repair the damage caused by that expectation landmine.

Nowadays, however, I'm often the writer who says, "That attitude will get you in trouble," and I watch as writer after writer ignore me. Early on, a writer friend (and former student of mine) was making such an egregious error, based on an unrealistic expectation, that I actually told him point by point why he should not take that terrible action. He got angry and defensive and then told me I had no idea what I was talking about.

At that moment, I realized why the sentence "That attitude will get you into trouble," gets spoken, but no successful person ever follows up on it unless asked to. The newer professional has to want the information and has to be willing to hear the answer.

6. Pay attention to the questions you can't answer.

These are tough. They're the kind of questions that, if your parents had asked them when you were a kid, you probably would have answered like this: "*My friends are doing it.*" And if your parents were like mine, they'd haul out the old, "*If your friends were jumping off a cliff, would you follow?*"

You'll probably have elaborate justifications built up in your mind and you'll offer them as answers to the question. But listen to that whisper which happens just before you offer up the first justification.

For example (and I'm clearly making this up):

Question: Why do you need ten $250,000 cars?

Justification: I collect them.

The Whispered Thought: Rich people own dozens of outrageously expensive cars, and now that I'm rich, I need to *act* rich.

Each business has those same unrealistic expectations built in. A writer friend of mine rented an office outside the house because (justification) he "needed quiet to work." Real reason? He believed that people who worked at home were not working, even though he had made 50K a year while working at home. (The office ate up his profits, and he eventually moved back home to save money—and in the process had to ferret out the unreasonable expectation that had caused the problem in the first place.)

An acquaintance of mine graduated from law school in the middle of her class. The law school was the best in her state, and in the state's major city. However, that city was overrun with graduates from the law school, most of whom graduated with a better record than she had. When she couldn't get a job in any of the city's law firms (not a one) because her grades were not as good as other applicants, she didn't move to a different city. Nor did she do some volunteer lawyering or take a job at Legal Aid, like some of my other friends who had not graduated at the top of their class.

Instead, she hung out her own shingle in a town filled with lawyers. She got a few clients—not enough to pay the bills—and because she thought she only needed the law degree, not actually to do any hard work, she did a poor job.

Why would this bright woman believe that she could survive in the cutthroat legal atmosphere of the state's major city with just a law degree?

Her justification was that no law firm hired women like her— which was true in the year she was born. But in the 1990s, when she was trying to do this, law firms hired women all the time.

The whispered unrealistic expectation? Real lawyers worked for a law firm. If no firm would hire her, she had to set up her own firm. She didn't believe real lawyers worked for Legal Aid or as legislative counsel to a state senator or as in-house attorney at some corporation.

Her law firm—and eventually her dream of being a lawyer—disappeared under the weight of her unrealistic expectation.

7. If people tell you you're acting irrationally given the evidence around you or events around you, check to see if you're acting out of an unrealistic expectation.

Think back to my successful friend who refused to believe his business had become successful after two years (when he expected it to take five). From the moment he refused to believe his business was doing better than most, many of his actions were irrational—and people told him so. If he had analyzed the comments and done a little research, he might have saved that business.

But he attributed them all to jealousy or to other motives on the part of the other people. Granted, people will tell you things out of fear or jealousy. That's why I tell you to research their comments. See if their statements are true. If not, dismiss them. If so, pay attention—and maybe make some changes.

We all have unrealistic expectations about ourselves, our careers, and our birthdays. (Well, maybe I'm the only one with an unrealistic expectation about a birthday.) These unrealistic expectations can ruin our careers—either by giving us the wrong benchmarks (why does anyone need a *Dynasty*-style party at any age?) or by making us refuse to see what we really have.

You'll never find all of your unrealistic expectations. But you'll track down some of the important ones. And if you do, you'll stop tripping over landmines, and start walking forward—which, after all, is how every business progresses. One not-always-smooth step at a time.

Chapter Fifty
Giving Up On Yourself

Amazing the difference eighteen months make. I first wrote the posts entitled "Giving Up On Yourself (Parts One and Two)" in June of 2010. But as we head into 2012, I realize that some of what I wrote is out of date.

I've revised this section. The core information is the same but the outdated information is now gone. I initially wrote this section about giving up on yourself by focusing on publishing. But I no longer agree with those parts of the section. I am going to keep the overall structure, talking about artists first. So, the initial introduction is gone, but the important stuff remains.

KKR,
November 2011

First, a disclaimer. The *Freelancer's Survival Guide* is for freelancers of all stripes, not just writers, actors, musicians and people who work in the arts. The *Guide* is for anyone who works for herself.

This topic applies to all of us, but I'm going to start with artists—and by that I mean people who make their living in the arts—before I broaden the scope of the topic.

Artists occupy a rather unique place in the freelance firmament. Unlike most professionals, artists don't need a formal education. Artists don't need a license to hang out a shingle. Anyone can declare himself an artist, quit his day job, and try to make a living from his work.

While that's sometimes freeing, it's also a danger. Because unlike a doctor who can't get his license without years of formal training and a certain level of competency, an artist can start "working" the moment she sings her first note or draws her first straight line. In some professions (the securities trade comes to mind), this level of accepted incompetence gives rise to fraud. In the arts, however, the only person who gets cheated when an artist is inexperienced is the artist herself.

Most people who attempt a career in the arts suffer from a mixture of extreme ego and extreme insecurity. We need the extreme ego to attempt success on an international level. After all, what makes our voices different from everyone else's? There are billions of people on the Earth. Why do we believe that we will stand out?

Ego gives us that belief. But common sense tells us that we will fail at our goal. Worse, we take every mistake to heart. Most artists are sensitive souls, easily wounded by criticism. We believe in ourselves, but not all the time. That insecurity keeps us grounded. It also gives us an Achilles heel.

When the ego and the insecurity are out of balance, the artist tips in the wrong direction. Too much ego and the artist becomes insufferable. A mild-mannered bookstore owner once told me the story of the one and only time he kicked an author out of his store. The author was doing a book signing. A line of customers waited there to get their books autographed. The author was so abusive to his fans, he reduced even the most jaded of them to tears. The bookstore owner stepped in, stopped the signing, and when the author got more belligerent, asked the author to leave. The author refused, the owner threatened to call the police, and the author left in a storm of invective.

That author's ego was so out of control that he alienated everyone around him. In fact, when the bookstore owner told me who the author was, I was not surprised. I had heard through other sources what a mean, egotistical jerk this man was.

At the time of the signing debacle, the author had several books on the *New York Times* Bestseller List. Now, no major publishing house will touch him. Why? His ego. His writing is just as good as it always was, maybe better. But no one in a major publishing house—from the publisher to the editor to the sales force—wants to deal with the man. He has alienated everyone in the business.

An out-of-control ego is one side of the imbalance. The other side is rampant insecurity. I can tell you of writer after writer—many of them former students of mine—who write tremendous fiction and can't sell a word. Why? Because they refuse to let the work leave their offices, believing it no good. A single negative comment will get them to shelve not just that work, but also any other work that might be in the same genre or have the same tone.

I threaten a few of them occasionally, saying I'll go into their files and mail their stories for them, but, of course, I don't follow through. Because Dean and I have a philosophy that runs through all of our workshops:

You Are Responsible For Your Own Career

The egomaniacal writer I mentioned above is responsible for the downturn in his career. The insecure writers I mentioned right after him are responsible for the fact that most readers have never heard of them.

Artists must learn to balance that insecurity and ego so that they're not raving lunatics (except in the privacy of their own offices) and so that they're not so self-effacing that they refuse to let their brilliant work see the light of day.

Successful artists walk that line every single day. Push any of us hard enough in either direction and you'll hear a burst of ego or a whisper of insecurity. But neither will last long, and one (the ego) will often result in an immediate apology.

No successful artist has gotten where she is without paying her dues. Paying dues is a long, hard slog, often done in complete solitude. The end result is rather like the end result of going to medical school. You emerge exhausted, different, but with a working knowledge of your field and yourself. You must continue learning from that point on, constantly improving your craft, or you will destroy something (or someone—including, but not limited to, yourself).

When I started in the writing profession, paying dues took a certain amount of courage as well as ego. Most writers did not live anywhere near publishing central, which was (at least for Americans) New York City. We had to convince someone we'd never met to buy our work, and we had to do it via snail mail. Cold-calling an editor was a breach of etiquette. So was dropping into an editor's office if, indeed, you decided to fly yourself to New York. Writers' conferences were few and far between.

You had only yourself, your words, and your trusty (but somewhat inaccurate and out-of-date) *Writer's Market*. You had to take the flyer.

It took years to run that gauntlet, often with little or no feedback. The writers who survived the constant rejection, the writers who worked at improving each and every day, the writers who *persisted* against all odds, became the ones whose names you recognize now.

All of the arts had some form of this gauntlet: musicians made demo tapes that had to be mailed to various record studios; artists developed portfolios that had to be mailed to galleries or publishing houses; actors sent resumes and photographs before getting auditions. We didn't have the benefit of the Internet. We couldn't build websites that promoted our work, and we couldn't tell someone to look at our online résumé/portfolio/demo.

I'm excited about the changes digital media will bring to my industry. I already love the way that it has changed the other arts. I can now look at my favorite artists' portfolios online or listen to music from musicians who don't get Top 40 airplay. I watch made-for-internet-only video, and I spend too much time looking for the unknown on the web.

But I worry. I watch the Internet providing newer artists with an easy way to give up on themselves.

I see this most strongly in the publishing industry because that's where I'm tapped in. Instead of a writer enduring years of rejection to get a book published, learning craft, improving, figuring out how to entice a publisher to buy the work (learning the proper use of an agent—which is not as a publisher's first reader), learning the entire business as she gains experience, writers now make a few attempts and then give up.

Initially, when I wrote this piece, I said that new writers who didn't try the traditional publishing gauntlet were giving up on themselves. At the time—eighteen months ago—I was on the cusp of being wrong. I hadn't seen the changes in the industry or if I had seen them, I hadn't understood them.

Back then—and before—it was easy to see a writer who was giving up on herself. She tossed in the towel, didn't fight that gauntlet, and just defaulted with publishing online.

Now it could be argued—and I just might do it some day—that writers who refuse to learn how to publish their own work (particularly their backlist, if they're professional writers) are giving up on themselves. These writers don't have to do the work themselves, but they should learn how to hire the best help *for a flat fee*, and then get that work online.

Because, in just the eighteen months since I originally wrote this piece, e-books have become 25% of the book market (and they'll continue to grow), bookstores have all but vanished except in a few (lucky) places, and most books are ordered online. There is now little that a traditional publisher can do that a writer can't do herself—provided she's willing to learn how.

The learning is the key. Because the writer who gives up on himself is the writer who stops learning.

There are a variety of ways to see that unwillingness to learn.

Among professionals, it's a refusal to look at the changes in the industry and figure out how to apply those changes to the writer's advantage. The writer remains stuck in the old way of doing things and never even bothers to look at the new way.

Among newcomers, it's an unwillingness to admit that they still have learning to do in their craft. Maybe their self-published title isn't selling because it's unusual. But maybe it's not selling because readers have sampled it and found it lacking—either in storytelling, grammatical basics, or in just plain old good writing.

The publishing craft might be lacking, as well. The writer might have a great story buried in terrible formatting, hidden behind an awful cover, or hidden behind a bad cover blurb. All of these are skills that a writer can learn or, if he has the funds, he can hire someone to do the work for him *for a flat fee*.

I keep repeating that flat fee statement because yet another way for writers to give up on themselves is to fail to understand business. Right now, writers can post their work online or do the work to do a trade paper edition, and get up to 70% of the profits. But so many writers are refusing to learn the various ways to do this and retain that 70% profit. Writers can retain the profit either by learning to do the work themselves or paying someone *a flat fee* to do the work for them.

Too many writers—most of them, in fact—are paying some "professional" as much as 50% of that 70% to do the work for them. Work that will take the "professional" a few hours, and that professional will keep earning a profit on that work for years, maybe even decades.

The difference here is that the writer hasn't learned business, and refuses to. He's giving up on himself and in doing so is costing himself thousands, maybe hundreds of thousands, of dollars over decades.

That frustrates me to no end.

Musicians, who've been struggling with this ten years longer than writers, have learned to have multiple platforms. They make sure their music is available in vinyl, CD, and MP3. They license usage rights to radio stations as well as television shows and commercials. They do more concerts than they used to, just to get the music heard. The big recording studios still exist, but they are more selective than ever about the artists they back. The difference is that the artists who have a shot at the bigs and fail to achieve a studio's numbers now have something to fall back on, and a way to rebuild.

Actors no longer have to choose between stage, screen, and small screen. They work in short video, live-action films, YouTube stories. They work on basic cable and premium channel films. They take television shows, even though that would have been the kiss of death to a movie career twenty years ago, and they do a lot of international work. The markets, in all of the arts, are changing.

But the changing markets shouldn't be an excuse for failing to try hard. It's pretty easy to see why an actor isn't getting work if he posts his latest homemade video on YouTube and it's filled with too much emoting and not enough emotion. Anyone can spend days watching singers on YouTube attempting to become the next Justin Bieber. Most of those singers are out of tune and have no performance skills at all. It's hard to become a professional musician. You need a certain level of skill, not just a pleasant voice.

Sadly, it's the same for writers. You need a certain level of skill to succeed on an international level, and now, the only way to know if you have that skill is to trust the readers. The readers will find your work. If it's good, it'll sell—not at huge numbers per month, but a few copies here and there. If the sales remain consistent or grow, you're doing a good job. If you sell five copies in July of 2012 and only one copy in the next six months, then there might be something wrong with the product.

Should you figure out what that something is? Should you rewrite the book to death? Heck, no. You should practice—keep writing *new* material, and learn, learn, learn. After a few years, come back to the book that's not selling. You will see it differently. You will know if the cover is bad or the blurb fails. You'll know if there is no opening hook.

Provided you've been learning and growing and getting better.

All freelancers succeed because they persist. They try, they fail, they learn. They try again, they fail, they learn. They keep trying, keep learning, until they get a glimmer of success. Success rarely comes overnight. It comes after years of hard and often thankless work.

People who go into business for themselves expecting it to be easy are bound to fail, and fail in a spectacular way. Working for yourself is hard. You have a lot of decisions to make, a lot of assessing to do.

How does all of this publishing/artist talk apply to those of you who don't work in the arts? Simple, really. There are things that you can do for your business that look like get-rich-quick short cuts. You've probably tried them. You know that they don't work.

What works is learning the ropes and becoming the best at what you do.

Sometimes that means going out on a limb with a project no one else believes in. But if it's early in your career and no one has believed in you yet, then perhaps the problem isn't that the project is too new or too innovative or too different for other people to appreciate.

Maybe the problem is that you haven't learned your craft yet. You don't know how to run the most efficient business possible. You haven't learned the tricks of your trade.

When you always take the easy route, you're giving up on yourself. Take that ego of yours and remind it that you need to be the *best* at what you do. And the best never takes the easy route.

Then take that insecurity of yours and tell it that you need to work harder to get better. It'll take over from there. And it'll balance out the ego that seems to think it should be rewarded just for trying.

I know. I know. It's not always easy versus hard. The answers aren't always clear-cut. How do you know when you're giving up on yourself versus being innovative? What if there's no clear path?

I also know that it's different for other types of freelancers. The digital world isn't one-type-fits-all. For example, retail stores with unique inventories are actually hurting themselves if they don't have a significant online presence. Same with real estate agencies. Doctors are starting to investigate the benefits of e-mail "appointments" for minor matters. Every type of business is different.

So if they're all different, then how do you figure out where you stand? Are you working hard enough? Are you giving yourself enough credit? Are you hurting or helping yourself?

How do you know if you're giving up on yourself?

First, recognize that giving up on yourself isn't black and white. Just because something is easy doesn't make it wrong. Just because something is hard doesn't make it right. To know if you're giving up on yourself, you first have to figure out who you are.

Oh, yeah, that's simple. Take a lifelong task and figure it out in the next twenty minutes. Not.

What I mean by that is this:

Figure out what your dreams are. Write them down. Figure out what your goals are. Write them down.

Once you've figured out what your dreams and goals are *today*, *right now*, *this instant*, honestly assess if you're on the right road to attaining those dreams and goals. Only you know what your dreams and goals are and whether you're really on the right path to achieving those dreams and goals.

I stress that only you can figure out if you're on the right path because sometimes—to an outsider—it looks like you've given up on yourself when you really haven't.

For example, my husband has a degree in architecture and three years of law school. He quit in the last week of his last semester of law school because he realized he did not want to be a lawyer, and if he had graduated from the University of Idaho Law School, he would automatically have had most of the responsibilities of a lawyer, even if he never wanted to practice law.

So, one week before graduation, he became a full-time bartender and school bus driver. To anyone looking at him from the outside, it would seem like he had given up on himself.

Instead, he focused on his writing career. Becoming a full-time professional writer isn't something you can do overnight. It takes years, and he had just embarked on that career. But think about it from the point of view of his friends and family: he was a thirty-something former professional golfer and professional skier, who had given up "guaranteed" careers in architecture and the law, to what? Spend all his time in bars? Noodle on his computer?

It seemed like he had given up on himself when, for maybe the first time in his life, he had actually started to take himself seriously. Now he's a bestselling writer, with more than ninety novels published. In hindsight, he made the right—the obvious—decision. But only in hindsight.

What did Dean have that many people do not have? He had a firm belief in himself and a willingness to take risks to achieve his goals. Those risks often made him go against common wisdom, and to fight against the beliefs of others.

That's tough. But that's what people with non-traditional professions, freelancers in other words, have to do.

So, how do freelancers know when they're giving up on themselves?

Here's where it gets tough, because sometimes (often!) the act of giving up on yourself is by degrees. It's subtle. It's settling for a little less than you want. It's slowly moving off the path until one day you wake up and realize that not only have you left the path you wanted to walk but you're also not even going in the right direction any more. And you got there by varying your course by half-inches instead of making hard right turns. Sometimes you didn't even notice as you went off course.

To keep from giving up on yourself, you must:

1. Believe in yourself.

I know, I know. You're insecure. You're uncertain. We *all* are. And sometimes, articulating those big dreams out loud just sounds ridiculous, especially if you haven't had any achievements in your field yet.

So, how do you gain a belief in yourself when you really have none? I take a tip from the training that actors receive. Pretend. Pretend you have the belief. *Act* as if you do. Figure out how people who believe in themselves would act in that situation, and then mimic them. Eventually, it will become habit. And somewhere along the way, you will realize that you actually do believe in yourself. To be otherwise would feel odd.

2. Stop the negative self-talk.

If you hear yourself saying, "I'll never be able to do that," add "if I don't try." Give yourself little pep talks. Keep your focus on what you can control. Remember that your goal is a hard one and will take a lot of effort. So, reward yourself for the small steps.

A corollary to this is: stop talking to/listening to the negative people around you. For every person who thinks something will work, there are five who will tell you the flaws in your plan. First, look at the source. If the person who tells you the flaws hasn't done anything with his own life, realize that what he's telling you is what goes on in his head every single day. Those negative words are the ones he lives with and the ones that have prevented him from achieving his dreams. He thinks he's being helpful. And he is. He's giving you an example of where you'll be if you listen to him.

You can cut the negative people out of your life, but that isn't always productive. I have some marvelous friends who can be very negative about any dreams or goals. I just don't discuss my future plans with those people. (I often don't mention my successes to them, either.) I enjoy their company on a casual level, and I keep the relationship on that level.

3. Perform a daily gut check.

Make sure you're on the right path each and every day. Seriously. Your gut will twist slightly if you're making a poor decision. That feeling is different from the feeling you get when you make a risky-but-good decision.

Let's see if I can describe the difference. If you're making a risky-but-good decision, you'll feel a bit lightheaded, a bit breathless, and a little frightened. You know it can go wrong, but you're willing to risk it.

If you're making a mistake, veering ever so slightly off the road toward your dreams, you might feel lightheaded and frightened, but you'll also feel just a little sick. Often, if you're paying attention to that voice inside your head, the one that gives you advice (good and bad), you'll hear it say, *"That's okay. I'll be all right. I can live with that."*

4. Watch out for that evil phrase, "I can live with that."

"I can live with that," is often accompanied by "for a few weeks, for a year." But add "forever" to that phrase. Can you live with it now? Can you live with it forever, if you know it means you'll never achieve your dream?

Sometimes, you have to live with something. Several of my friends have been taking care of their elderly, very sick parents. My friends have volunteered to live with financial hardship and emotional difficulties so long as their parents are alive. My friends also know that this will lead to some deferred goals. But they're willing to make that choice—and they know, by the very nature of the task they're facing—that they won't have to live in this situation for the rest of their lives.

Dean has a great way of analyzing the "I can live with this" part of life. He asks—quite pointedly—"Do you want to be doing this in one year? In five years? In ten?"

If you answer those questions honestly, you'll know if you're making too many compromises. For example, I would hate to have to go back and wait tables to finance my writing. But I'd do it, if the writing stopped earning money for me. I'd do it for the rest of my life if it meant I could keep writing.

But I wouldn't take on another profession. I never could imagine myself being a news director forever or even a journalist forever. Nor could I imagine myself editing magazines and books for the rest of my life.

While those professions seem close to professional fiction writing, they *aren't* professional fiction writing. In fact, they get in the way of professional fiction writing.

For a while, I was better known as an editor in the field of science fiction and fantasy than I was as a writer. I was an acclaimed, award-winning editor, and if you look at the circulation figures, the years I edited *The Magazine of Fantasy & Science Fiction* were the years of its highest circulation *in its entire existence*. In other words, I was good at my job. Very good.

I liked the job at first, came to hate it by the end. If I had remained as an editor (and I had dozens of editing job offers after I quit; in fact, I still get editing job offers every now and then), I would have been remembered, acclaimed, famous—and I would have given up on myself. At that point in time, most people believed I was a better editor than writer, and that I was making a huge mistake giving up the editing career.

It was one of the best decisions of my life.

But editing was very seductive. It wasn't easier than writing for me. It was harder. I had to work for someone else. I had to fit myself into a mold that wasn't comfortable for me.

However, editing gave me great acclaim and respect. I had achieved, by the age of thirty-five, fame in my chosen genre (science fiction and fantasy) and I was at the pinnacle of my editing career. I could have stayed at that pinnacle for decades, if I had chosen to do so.

It would have been close to a writing career. In fact, it mimicked the writing career in all but the production of stories. I even wrote a lot of words—editorials, interstitial materials, essays. But I didn't write fiction.

I had been writing fiction since I was seven years old. Giving up on fiction for a career in sf would have been giving up on myself.

And yet, waiting tables—even now—wouldn't be. Waiting tables would enable me to concentrate on writing during my off hours. I would put in my time for my paycheck, come home, and do what I love. And that's extremely important to me—more important than being remembered or being the center of a certain genre or being a big shot.

I am a storyteller at heart. And I am happiest when I write down my stories and try to get them published. So long as I do that, I am staying true to myself.

5. Watch out for "good enough."

I hate that phrase, "Good enough." The thing that got me to work hardest on my fiction was a comment Frederick Pohl made about my writing at a writing workshop. He said he would have bought a story of mine—not because it was memorable or brilliant, but because he had a 3,000-word gap in his magazine and my 3,000-word story was *good enough.*

Ack. Kiss of death. I never want to be good enough. I want to be the best.

"Good enough" is settling. And I never want to settle. Not in my fiction ("Oh, my writing is good enough. I don't have to learn any more.") or in my life ("Oh, this job is good enough. I'll get by.") "Good enough" is as deadly as "I can live with that."

Only, "good enough" crops up in other ways. Like this:

- **I'm good enough to do something as a hobby, but not good enough to do it as a profession.**
- **This is good enough to get by.**
- **I'll never be good enough to achieve my dream.**

All three are deadly thoughts.

Let's take them one at a time. "I'm good enough to do something as a hobby, but not good enough to do it as a profession."

That sentence has a whole bunch of levels. First of all, who decides what "good enough" to do something professionally is? And let's say there are standards; who says you can't improve? Who says you can't get better?

Why are you afraid to try?

"This is good enough to get by." Why are you settling for "getting by"? Why aren't you striving to do your best?

"I'll never be good enough to achieve my dream." Here's a secret: people who achieve their dreams are never "good enough." They're always trying to get better. In fact, they never believe they have reached a plateau. "Good enough" suggests there is one.

And here's a final one. If you're constantly satisfied with "good enough" in your field of endeavor, ask yourself this: Are you in the right field? Because if you're not willing to constantly improve, if you're willing to settle, then you are not enjoying your work.

There are a bunch of reasons for failing to enjoy your work. You might be burned out. You might be overworked. Or you might not like the work itself.

Many of us have had dreams that have proven wrong for us. I love music, but when it comes to being a musician, I always settle. I never strive. I practice until I'm "good enough" to get by. And no matter what I do, I cannot break myself of this habit.

Which is why my career in the arts is as a writer, not as a musician. I never got to "good enough" as an editor, but I could feel it looming on the horizon. I moved on before "good enough" became part of my editing vocabulary.

This is why I tell you to do a gut check *daily*. Because you'll be able to chart the progress of what you do and how you're feeling. Honestly, it's okay to discover that a dream you've had is not for you.

But here's what's not okay: it's not okay to give up on yourself because you're not worthy, or someone else has told you the task facing you is impossible.

I have a quote on the bulletin board next to my desk. It's from Thomas Carlyle: "Every noble work is at first impossible."

And another from Judy Garland: "Always be a first-rate version of yourself, rather than a second-rate version of someone else."

That's what we're talking about here. You need to be a first-rate version of yourself, and only you know who that person is. You're living your life, not your mother's life or your best friend's life. Only you know what you're capable of.

Don't do what everyone thinks you should do. Do what *you* think you should do.

And don't give up because others tell you you're not capable of success. Prove them wrong.

6. Be tenacious.

Cling to your dream. Work for your goal. If you step off the path, climb back on the moment you realize you've veered in the wrong direction.

You will make mistakes. You will take the wrong path. The key is to come back to yourself, and come back to the right road *for you*.

I can't tell you if you're giving up on yourself. Only you can know that.

Dean has one other question, and it's a big one: when you're on your deathbed, what will you regret?

Will you regret not striving hard enough for your dream? Will you regret lost years while you were succeeding in a profession other than the one you love? Will you regret being "good enough?"

Only you can answer those questions.

And you should. Daily. To keep yourself on track.

To keep yourself from giving up.

Chapter Fifty-one
Staying Positive

I wrote chapters of the *Guide* every week. Mostly I answered questions or worked off a topic list. But the week I wrote this chapter, I had been dealing with some issues of my own, mostly to do with my office cat. She had lived alone in my office for more than a decade because she didn't play well with others (tried, in fact, to kill anything with fur, including raccoons). She had been quite ill, and the week I wrote this, we had finally decided it was time to end her misery.

My office will never be the same.

I took that opportunity to move my office to a new space, where I have three office kitties, and even more privacy than I had before. But it had been an emotional week for me, so I really didn't want to discuss money.

Instead, I thought I'd answer two questions, both on emotions and freelancing.

The first, from writer Michael Samerdyke, inspired the title of this chapter. He writes, "Will you include something on how to stay positive?"

Remaining positive sounds like such a minor thing. Yet it is the key to everything. Oddly enough, successful freelancers are the most cynical, hard-bitten optimists in the entire world.

We have to be. Who would believe in us if we didn't believe in ourselves?

No one discusses remaining positive at a day job, unless it is a requirement of that day job. When I worked as a waitress, I had to smile at the customers and be nice. It was in the job description. The same rules applied, perhaps more stringently, at my very first retail job. We had to be so incredibly nice at that store that we were required (again, as part of the job description) to wish each and every customer a very nice day.

This is not what I mean about positive.

You can grump around your home office for weeks if you want to. You can snarl at the cable news channels, as I often do (particularly during an election cycle). You declare a book useless and toss it across the room if you like, without worrying about hitting one of your co-workers, since you no longer have any.

You can be the surliest, nastiest person on earth because you work alone. If being surly and anti-social makes you happy, then by all means, have at it.

When you work alone, you don't need rules for office behavior. If you don't receive clients in your office, like most freelancers, then you can behave anyway you want to.

Most freelancers don't take this acting-out very far. Mostly they do a few cosmetic things they would never have done at the day job, like spend the entire day in sweats or in their pajamas. Some don't shower until they finish work.

Fine. Good. Whatever.

I do dress in Northwest casual to go to my office. I wear the clothes that I would wear to a restaurant or to the post office. My mother believed that appearances mattered, and that part of my upbringing rubbed off.

In fact, something she said (repeatedly) actually stuck. Dressing properly makes you feel better. And you know something? It does. I don't wear fancy clothes to the office because that feels ridiculous. But I always feel underdressed and vaguely unhappy when I wear my grubbiest clothes.

Clothing sounds like a side issue, but it's not. It's all a part of a greater whole.

A day job gives you structure. It structures your time—when you'll arrive, when you'll leave, and what you'll do while you're there. It structures your environment—someone else designs your workspace, and whether you get an office with a window or a cubicle with high-carpeted walls. It structures your appearance—you may have to wear a business suit or a uniform with the company logo. Some places have strict rules about grooming. Disneyland, for example, won't allow men to have facial hair. Many restaurants I worked in didn't allow the wait staff to wear perfume, cologne, or use scented soaps, because those odors would interfere with the food.

Each day job, whether it's acknowledged or not, structures the employee's attitudes. Some, like the retail shops I mentioned above, required positive attitudes at all times. But most emotional structures are subtler than that. Except for discussions of last night's episode of *Lost* or some (tame) discussions of this year's baseball season, personal conversation gets discouraged.

If someone asks, "How are you today?" they really don't want to know the answer. They don't want you to launch into a litany of your ills from your aching feet to the hangover that has lingered (been encouraged?) all weekend. In fact, too much personal discussion can lead to reprimand and ultimately dismissal for inappropriate behavior.

You don't have to be positive at these jobs, but you do have to maintain some sort of professional attitude. You know once you get out of the car in the parking lot that you have to be on your best behavior until it's time to drive home.

Now you work at home. Home, where you express every feeling, where you stay when you're sick, where you go for refuge. Home has suddenly become work as well, and the lines have blurred.

We allowed those lines to blur long before we went full-time freelance. Before we quit our day jobs, we did our freelance work when we "felt like it" or when we "found the time" or when the "muse showed up."

In the early days—for all of us—the freelance work was a side business or a hobby, something we did because we loved it or because it filled the time.

The day job, on the other hand, was something we did for the money.

Now we freelance for the money. We forget that we used to do this sort of thing for fun. Sometimes full-time freelancing takes all the joy out of the operation.

The key isn't so much recapturing that joy—remaining joyful day after day isn't something most humans are capable of—but remembering the joy. Remembering that you are doing the work that you love and you're lucky to be doing so.

One of the best pieces of advice I ever gave one of my writing students was accidental. He was so serious about his writing that every sentence had become torture. I told him to go play. The advice stuck. He made a sign that said *Go Play* and put it across from his desk where he could see it every single day.

It didn't put him in a good mood every day, but it did help him feel better about his freelancing.

Staying positive is tough for a variety of reasons. I mentioned one in the chapter on priorities. People who spend the majority of their time alone are prone to depression. Study after study has shown this.

The solutions are simple, but do take time away from the freelancing. Some are basic: Get enough rest, eat good food (not junk food), and exercise. In fact, a recent study showed that a half-hour run has the same effect on a person's mood that a single dose of Valium has. Plus the run is cheaper and has many other benefits.

You must also schedule time to be with other people, doing fun things. This sounds silly, but many freelancers spend their free time with other freelancers, discussing business. Take the time to see a movie or to go to the beach or take in a basketball game.

People whose freelancing requires little more than a computer and a wi-fi connection can go to restaurants, libraries, and other places to get some work done. One Christian writer I know spends every afternoon in a local restaurant, researching, writing, and going over his manuscripts. He eats lunch, pays a little extra for his coffee, and socializes just enough to keep his mood elevated.

It works for him. Sometimes that solution works for me too.

But the toughest part about staying positive has nothing to do with the lack of companionship or the right attitude. It takes focus to remain optimistic.

First, you need confidence in your work. Most of us don't have it. If pushed, we confess to all kinds of insecurities, problems, reasons why our work isn't as good as it could possibly be.

Yet we need to believe in ourselves to do a good job.

What do I recommend? Act as if you have the confidence. Eventually, you'll improve in this area. I learned this through theater training. Traditional acting schools teach that if you mimic an emotion, you can actually bring that emotion out in yourself.

Think about that for a moment: before you started freelancing full time, you probably described your emotional life as pretty balanced. It had to be. You had to maintain a professional decorum at your day job.

Then you quit that day job, spent all your time at home, and your emotions started running amuck. You didn't have to pretend any more. You could be yourself—and yourself, like the rest of ourselves, is an emotional rollercoaster.

That rollercoaster is fine—and often good for those of us in the arts—but you have to be aware you're riding it. You need to assume that mask of professional decorum when dealing with the outside world. You need to filter all the information from the outside world through the same professional mask.

If a new client doesn't return a phone call on time, it's not because the client hates you. It's because the client didn't have time to get to the phone that day, or forgot, or something equally silly. But we lose track of that when we work at home, for ourselves, with no one to balance us.

Work to retain your optimism. You quit your day job because you believed you could succeed as a freelancer. You need to remember that each and every day. If that means putting a sign up in your office that says *Believe in yourself!*, then do it. Who'll see the little aphorisms you post around your desk? You're not in someone else's building any more. Your office is private, so design it in a way that keeps you motivated and happy.

That includes things like music. Or an excellent view. Or a great screen saver. (I have one that makes me smile, no matter what.) I keep a cartoon-a-day calendar, and read it every day, which also helps, believe it or not.

But the most important part of staying positive is to remain realistic. If forty-five people say something nice to us and one person says something mean, we'll remember the something mean and discount the nice things.

As freelancers, we have to keep track of the good and the bad. And we have to give them the proper weight. Teaching reminds me how to weigh the things around me. As I explain things to my writing students, I realize the things I've overlooked in my own life.

However, I do work hard to remain realistic. My first and best tool for this is my calendar. I have a *New Yorker* desk calendar, encased in leather and embossed with my name, at my right hand, just past my computer's mouse.

I write every single good thing that happens to me in a day on that calendar. I keep track of fan mail, covers, publications, awards, and the amount of money I receive.

I think getting paid for my work is a good and positive thing. Rather than relegate it all to the accounting program, I also keep track in my calendar.

I also keep track of good comments, even from people who have rejected my work.

People who work for themselves have trouble keeping track of time. First-time freelancers soon learn that they can't tell Thursday from Tuesday without help. Even if you take the weekends off, the weekdays seem remarkably the same.

The good things that happen to you will seem far in the distance, even if they happened a week ago. The bad things, conversely, will seem like they happen every day, even if the last one happened a month before. Remember that we focus on the bad and often forget the good.

So on bad days, I go back through my calendar, and look at all the good things that have happened. It helps me maintain perspective.

I do realize that some professions don't have the regular positive feedback that my job does. Some people work for years on the same project, or they do healing work (like massage or psychotherapy) that often has no real end to it, or they work in professions with no real feedback at all.

How do you stay positive in jobs like that?

The same way you remain positive when you're just starting your business and have no real sticks to measure success with.

You have to learn how to measure success from within, not from the outside. In other words, set daily goals and reward yourself for achieving them.

The daily goals must be realistic. They can't be too easy or you'll finish in an hour and feel like you haven't worked. On the other hand, they can't be too hard or you'll never achieve them and will always feel discouraged. You must set a goal that makes you put in some effort and gives you a good result at the same time.

Writers generally set a word limit—writing so many words of new material each and every day. Musicians often set a time limit—practicing for so many hours each and every day. eBay sellers will often set a goal of making a certain number of listings each and every day.

The type of goal will vary from business to business, but it must be something that you can achieve *daily*. I also set weekly goals and monthly goals. Even though I'm very structured, I usually miss my monthly goals—something gets in the way or goes long or (as in this week) life intrudes a bit and puts me behind.

Sometimes I miss my weekly goals as well, due to illness or some other interruption. But I rarely miss my daily goals. But I still reward myself for achieving them. The rewards are small—an extra hour of television that night or a brand-new paperback book or just a simple pat on the back. I mark that success in my calendar, so that I can look back on bad days and say, "Well, at least I achieved my goals in the past week."

Sometimes that's all I need.

The other aspect to being realistic is to know your limitations. During the same week that Michael Samerdyke asked his question, Laura Ware asked something similar. Laura, a Florida columnist and freelance fiction writer, has had life intrude on her work in a very big way.

She has become the full-time caretaker for her very ill elderly in-laws. With the help of her family and an occasional visit from home health care services, she tends to her in-laws seven days per week. But Laura is determined to continue with her freelance work in the middle of all of this.

She asks, "When you're in the kind of place [that I'm in], how do you know what's slacking, what's too much, and what's appropriate?"

That's a very healthy question. Because if you set your goals too high, you'll feel bad. People whose lives have intruded on their work (not just freelancers, but everyone) suffer a lot of stress. Whether taking care of elderly parents or taking care of a newborn baby, things happen in all of our lives that cause stress and an additional burden (even if, in the case of the baby, it's a burden that we want).

What we have to do is, again, be realistic. If you're the sole breadwinner for your family, you can't drastically cut back your hours. You may have to hire outside help or work with other family members so that they can share some of the burden.

But if you're not yet a major breadwinner, if part of the condition that the family imposed on you quitting your day job was to be the stay-at-home parent or to take care of the elderly parents or, in the case of a friend of mine, to be the sole caretaker of a dying spouse, then you must shave your work goals accordingly.

You need to figure out when you can steal the hours to get work done and if you'll be in any shape to do the work when those hours happen. If you're under a great deal of stress, as Laura is, cutting back on sleep is a terrible idea. If you're just overwhelmed with carpooling and running errands, you might have to change your work habits by figuring out what parts of your job you can do on the run.

In Laura's e-mail, she adds this, "I'm tapping this out on my phone while sitting in a waiting room with my mother-in-law (she has a doctor's appointment). After I send this, I'll fire up my laptop and try to get something done while I sit around."

Laura is one of the hardest workers I know. She gets a lot done while caring for her family. She's organized and driven, and unwilling to give up her dreams, even though she's in a tough spot right now. She routinely writes five hundred words per day, which is a great deal given her situation.

Yet, as her question says, she feels like she's not doing enough.

So let's take the question bit by bit: how do you know what's slacking?

I think we all know deep down when we're not working hard enough. If we're spending most of our time watching television or playing video games, we're not working hard enough. Some people compare themselves to other freelancers, and think, *I should be working as hard as they are*. That's not the answer either, because everyone is in a different circumstance.

Know your circumstance, know what you're capable of, and then make a realistic assessment of your life. Try to achieve your new daily goal for a week. If you never reach the goal, figure out if the problem is that you weren't putting in enough time, that you didn't have enough time to give (as in Laura's case), or if the goal is just too hard to achieve in a single day *for you*.

Then set a new goal and try that for a week. Work until you find one you have to stretch just a little to achieve, but make sure it is one you can achieve. When you're ill or taking care of something in your life that takes precedence (like sickly elderly parents), then you might have to cut back on your daily goals. When you're in excellent physical shape with no distractions in your life, raise your goals. Don't set anything in concrete. Be flexible, but realistic.

If you can achieve your daily goal in fifteen minutes and spend the rest of the day goofing off, you're slacking. In this case, you need to measure how much leisure time you have. If you're spending too much time recreating, and not enough creating, you're slacking.

The next part of her question: What's too much?

If you have no leisure time, if you're getting repetitive stress injuries, if the people around you whom you trust start telling you forcefully that you need time off, then you are working too much.

In the last two years of our publishing company, our friends started handing Dean articles on stress management. He was putting in 20 hours per day, seven days per week, and it showed. Eventually he collapsed, and no one was surprised—except him.

He's learned how to moderate, although he doesn't like it much. I've learned that he still works harder than anyone else I know. But now he's working a more sensible schedule (10-12 hours per day, with one weekday evening and one full day per week off), and getting 8 hours of sleep per night. He occasionally thinks he's slacking, but no one gives him articles on stress management any more.

And the final part of Laura's question: What's appropriate?

Appropriate is an interesting word, because it implies that there are Standards To Be Met.

The cool thing about being a freelancer is that you set your own standards. What's appropriate for me, a person with few responsibilities and a long-term career with several obligations, isn't appropriate for Laura, or for anyone else reading this.

So let's rephrase the question in a way that Goldilocks and the Three Bears would understand: what's just right?

"Just right" changes. "Just right" may be 500 words per day because you're taking five minutes here and five minutes there. "Just right" might be 5,000 words per day because you have no other obligations, or 8,000 words per day because you waited too long to start that book under deadline.

For a therapist friend of mine, four days of client meetings per week was just right. It kept her fresh for her patients. She was able to maintain her emotional balance at four days, with three-day weekends to recharge. She figured out how many patients she could reasonably handle, how many she could help, and how many would drain her. And she picked the answer that allowed her to remain healthy and to do the work that helped the clients that she had.

Once you've figured out what's just right for you, then make a note of it. Set it up as a goal to be reassessed when the current situation changes. Then strive to meet that goal every single day.

And reward yourself for doing so.

Early on in your freelance career, the only good things will be subtle ones—meeting your daily goal and enjoying the work that you quit your day job to do.

The best way to remain positive is to remind yourself that you're now doing the work you love, day in and day out. Most people aren't that lucky. Most people never get the chance to do what they love.

You have taken that opportunity.

Enjoy it, and value it for what it is—something special. Something worthwhile.

An achievement, in and of itself.

Chapter Fifty-two
Reaching for Your Dreams

Sometimes I have to wonder if I was a history major and am a science fiction writer because I see patterns in what Thomas Jefferson called "the course of human events," or if I see patterns because I had training in both history and science fiction. I suppose that's one of those unanswerable questions. But the one thing that is clear is that my mind doesn't work like other people's.

Let us pause for the expected chorus of "well, duh."

Now that the chorus has passed, let me explain why I started with that blanket statement.

I am a news junkie. I consider the news—however it gets consumed—an essential part of freelancing. Most people who pay attention to the news and stay informed get a sense of what's going on, what to expect, and why to expect it.

But they simply don't get a "course of human events" overview. Not everyone thinks that way.

So...here are the factors that have gone into my thinking when I wrote this chapter. An article in the *Washington Post* on November 11, 2009 about a college graduate whose "bright future" was torn away from her by the recession. The housing statistics that came out this week, which revealed that one in four American homeowners with a mortgage are underwater (meaning they owe more—much more—than the house is worth). For many who choose to (or can) stay in their homes, the houses will not regain their lost worth for another 15 years. (CBS News econwatch blog, November 24, 2009.)

That same week, the Federal Reserve predicted that the high unemployment rate will continue through 2010. Estimates vary, but the rate hovers around 10.2 percent. That 10.2 percent does not include the underemployed—people who want to work full time but can only find part-time work. If those people get included, then the rate of un- and underemployed goes to more than 17 percent. (Turns out the Fed prediction, which I found on Marketwatch.com on November 24, 2009, was right.)

Those statistics—the 25% of all Americans with a mortgage, combined with the more than 17% un- and underemployment—created a perfect storm to make things worse. Because people who received job offers out of state could not afford to sell their houses in order to move.

Think about it. They would sell their home at a loss, then be on the hook for the difference between their mortgage and the sale price. In other words, they might sell their home and be in debt for $100,000 or more.

This led one analyst to claim that people in that situation would be better off walking away from their underwater mortgages. Better to damage your credit rating, Christopher Thornberg of Beacon Enterprises told CBS News, than it would be to continue to throw money down a black hole.

All of this came on the heels of a study that showed the herd mentality is hardwired into human beings. (PBS.org, November 11, 2009.) We feel better if we do what other people are doing—*even if we know it's wrong or does not benefit us at all.*

It takes more than chutzpah to go against conventional wisdom. It takes courage, and perhaps a slightly screwed up internal wiring. Which explains even more about me.

(And there it is again: the "well, duh," chorus. We wait for the sound to pass and now continue...)

So what does this all mean to the historian/science-fiction writer in me? A lot, actually. We are in the middle of more than the Great Recession. We're in the middle of a generational shift. And even more than that, we're in one of those sweeping moments of cultural change.

Dean and I discussed it a bit before I wrote this chapter. The credit rating—which only matters if you're going to borrow money—will lose (and perhaps already has lost) its godlike status in the American mind. So many people did things to preserve their credit ratings. For a long time, Dean and I watched in confusion because, as freelancer writers, we realized that credit ratings had no meaning for us. Then employers started using credit ratings as they hired people (!), and insurance companies started basing rates on credit ratings (!), and businesses stopped taking cash, requiring plastic (!) preferring credit to debit cards and…and…and…we acquiesced to the culture and actually did some work to make sure we had a credit rating, too.

Now most people have no credit rating. Wealthy people are cutting loose second and third homes, homes that have devalued so much as to be worthless to them—thinking, like the analyst said, what's the point of pouring money into a black hole when the money could (and probably should) go elsewhere. Formerly-middle-class people without work are trying very hard to put food on the table, credit rating be damned. And landlords no longer use credit ratings to judge the applications for rentals because they have to keep the units filled to pay the mortgage on their (probably underwater) commercial property.

And on, and on, and on.

The credit rating is but one shift. There is also the shift in attitude toward housing. The conventional wisdom will shift from turning houses over to this: If you're going to be in an area for only a few years, you'll rent rather than buy. If you expect to stay somewhere permanently, you'll buy, but your house won't be an ATM. Your house may increase in value or it may decrease in value, but it will be the place where you live. And, (oh my!) paying off the house will probably become a lot more important than getting your mortgage interest deduction.

How does all of this relate to freelancing? And how does it relate to the girl interviewed in the *Washington Post*, the girl who lost her "bright future"? And the herd mentality?

I've bemoaned an attitude that I saw in generations who were born or came of age after 1980. I knew this was a generational thing; I also realized that they would eventually understand How The World Really Works. (She writes, sounding like the old fart that she is.) But it wasn't me, hoping they'll get their comeuppance, although I did worry what would happen when they finally did realize that the world is an uncertain place. It was me, trying to understand where the attitude came from, and what exactly was going on.

I didn't realize that I had part of the attitude myself until I read the article in the *Washington Post*. I didn't add the link because the article is unremarkable. But this story put things in perspective for me because it spoke to my upbringing. Like me, this girl was raised in a family that believed in higher education. And like my family, hers believed that the better the school, the better the opportunities.

Where our families diverged was only in generational experience. My father, the first person in the American branch of his family to go to college, graduated in the Depression. (That his parents could afford college in the Depression has recently helped me understand why my mother thought them wealthy. By the standards of the day—with my grandfather's regular job as a rural mail carrier which brought in a good salary—my grandparents were well off. It wasn't just because my mother had survived on radish sandwiches and lived in the attic of a boarding house; it was because my paternal grandparents could provide my father [and later, my aunt] with opportunities most families couldn't fathom at the time.) Graduating in the Depression with a college degree opened some doors, but not others. Jobs weren't guaranteed.

Nor were they guaranteed when I graduated from college. Not that I graduated with honors from an Ivy League school. I graduated from a very good state school with an A- GPS in an area (history) that realistically held *no* opportunity for employment for someone with a bachelor's degree.

So when I read in the *Washington Post* article that the guaranteed $200,000 jobs for college graduates with business degrees had dried up in the last few years, I just about choked on my breakfast. Excuse me? Guaranteed *$200,000* jobs? Granted, the article was talking about guaranteed jobs for the A-list graduates of a top school, but still. *Guaranteed*?

Later in the week, I heard another choking statistic: that recent college graduates would have to settle for jobs that paid an average of $50,000. Where the heck would they find those jobs? And wouldn't they be crowded out of the positions by unemployed people my age?

The news has been filled lately with the plight of recent college graduates. Business has finally come to its senses. With a proliferation of candidates—one company that needed 100 workers recently saw 2,000 applicants show up *in one day*—businesses are hiring the people with experience, people with families and a commitment to the community. They're not hiring a hotshot straight out of the Ivy League who needs to learn how the business world works.

And they're not hiring every experienced person either—as many of you well know. It takes hundreds of submitted resumes just to get an interview, and it might take hundreds of interviews to get a job.

Like so many recent college grads, the girl in the article has stopped submitting resumes in her chosen field. Instead, she's thinking of working odd jobs, traveling, and doing what my husband's generation called "finding herself." She has been walking down a path carved out for her from childhood and has finally realized that she needs to look at other paths to see which one suits her.

All well and good. Everyone experiences that at one point or another. As I read the article, I saw opportunity. Her parents saw disaster and a "wasted" education, one they had spent hundreds of thousands of dollars on with the certainty that it would bring their child success after graduation. They blame the fact that the education isn't paying off on her, for failing to submit résumés, not on the sea change that is happening around all of us.

And that's what caught me about this article, as opposed to all the other articles about all the other college students for whom the promise of a bright future has not yet been fulfilled. It was the parents' expectation that if they did A, B, and C, and their daughter did as she was told, that it would all pay off in the end.

I am of this girl's parents' generation. And while I have always believed that marching to your own drummer was the best way to go, I've seen that as an aberrant attitude, not as a sensible one. I've been a bit apologetic for my attitude, a bit militant about it, citing my rebellious nature.

What I didn't see is how an attitude that had come from a wealthy post-war period had become engrained into all of us growing up after World War II. That period of relative stability led to choices and attitudes—even in the deep recession of the 1970s—that became hardwired into everyone in the Baby Boomer Generation. Those attitudes became expectations for our children—of course we're all going to be richer, more successful, and smarter than our parents! We have better opportunities.

Those of us who turned our backs on those opportunities—on the accepted path—were considered odd. And if we didn't succeed, it was our attitude that caused us to fail, or so the accepted wisdom went. Those of us who did succeed did so because we were "lucky" or "talented" or "special"—not because we took risks that paid off.

Now we're watching an entire generation come of age for whom the rules have failed. Some of these kids will become bitter young, as the promises that they heard when they were growing up didn't get fulfilled. And some will succeed on that path they were hardwired to march along.

But the rest, the rest have an opportunity that previous generations didn't have.

The rest don't have to postpone their dreams.

They can follow their dreams because they have nothing to lose. They've already lost the "expected" "certain" path.

We may be approaching a great period of creativity and innovation in American life, creativity and innovation that wasn't born of solid steady work but of necessary risk to survive.

Because for the first time in at least fifty years, maybe more, we have a generation coming of age that has the opportunity to create their own paths. The adults around them are struggling too hard to survive themselves to put the brakes on the younger generation. And any clear-eyed adult realizes that the opportunities for the inexperienced worker have dried up, no matter what their pedigree.

People born in the 1980s now have a chance to take extreme risks, to fail spectacularly, and, maybe, to succeed spectacularly. Because risk, for them, is different.

The Baby Boomers married in their early 20s, had children, and settled on a career that they thought would sustain them for life. Yes, there were the rebels in the late 1960s and early 1970s, but they were seen as outliers—as outsiders, in many ways—and for many of them their hippy/protest days were just a phase.

By the time Baby Boomers realized they weren't doing what they wanted to do, that they were running out of time to make a real difference in the world, to follow their passion, they had a family, a mortgage, regular bills, and a job they were afraid to sacrifice. All that work, all those promotions. They had guaranteed retirement, and they would write or paint or start a small business after the age of 65.

A lot of those Baby Boomers are coming to our writing classes now. These people are retired and they have the time, and many of them have the beginnings of a career—several story sales, a novel sale, maybe more—but they're embarking on a career that can take ten years to ramp up.

In the ten years since Dean and I did our first workshop, two of our students have died—an older man who waited until retirement to start writing, and a driven, middle-aged man who had a non-fiction career and wanted to make a living at fiction. He never achieved the "make a living" part, although he sure published a lot of fiction in his last few years.

I've watched others who have postponed their dreams struggle with years of learned behavior—deference to authority, an unwillingness to rock the boat, an inability to operate outside of a corporate structure. When you get older, you feel the end of your life looming. That feeling of immortality that you had as a teenager is a long-ago memory. The feeling that "anything is possible" that you had in your twenties is gone. As a middle-aged adult, you know that some things are no longer possible. (As I said to one of my students: I now know I will never play professional basketball, no matter how much I want to. She laughed, but understood. Even if I had Michael Jordan's skills, I'd still be fifty—an age that no one (yet) plays professional basketball.)

Postponing your dreams is a dangerous thing to do. Because time does eventually run out. In order to freelance, you need to learn how to take risks, and if you spent a lifetime on the accepted path, risks become something to avoid. Yet freelancers can't survive without it.

When you postpone your dreams, you take a risk that you won't live long enough to pursue them *and to have success*. What most people who postpone their dreams fail to realize is that when they retire, they might have the time to work on their dreams full time, but they might not have the time to achieve them.

There's more to freelancing than the skill that brought you to the table. You must learn how to manage money, how to run your own business, how to survive failure, and how to turn that failure into a success. All of that takes time. And time is the one commodity that we have that we can't count on. We really don't know if we'll get hit by a bus tomorrow. And we shouldn't bank on surviving that bus accident if it happens.

Right now, the economy is providing millions of people with the opportunity to take their destinies into their own hands. So many people postponed their dreams because they felt they had something to lose. If they quit their jobs, they could lose their houses, their credit ratings, the respect of their neighbors. They could force their families into poverty, lose their health insurance, and risk the fortunes of everyone they love, not just their own fortunes.

All of those things are excellent considerations. So many people had to postpone their dreams. One friend of mine got pregnant in high school and spent twenty years raising children, barely eking out a living as a single mom. She postponed her dreams out of necessity, and as soon as the kids moved out of the house, she pursued those dreams with great purpose—and is having great success.

Like her, many of you had no choice. You had to postpone.

But the world has changed. Attitudes have changed *and will remain changed for decades to come*. The credit rating will no longer be so important. No one cares who pays their bills because everyone is struggling right now.

And if you've lost your job, you've already lost your steady income. You're probably juggling bills, trying to survive. Continue to send out resumes, but as you do, consider following your dreams. Because all those things you would have jeopardized ten years ago, when the economy seemed stable, are already in jeopardy.

In other words, you may have very little to lose by trying. And that's an *opportunity* just waiting to happen.

This chapter, though, is also aimed at newly minted college grads who have just realized that they were walking a path that now has a giant roadblock running across it. The easy road is gone. Those $200,000 jobs for you business graduates from Ivy League schools evaporated with the Wall Street meltdown.

Time to look around, to see if the road you're walking is really the one you want to be on. Even if the roadblock goes away, do you want to be a corporate executive? Do you want to work for someone else for the rest of your life? Do you dream of being a musician or a bookstore owner?

Now is the time to start. The economic collapse has instituted a sea change. People who've just graduated from college are in the same boat I was in when I graduated. I never expected to own a home. (And I figured that if by some odd chance I bought one, I'd live in it for the rest of my life, so I had best be certain that was the house I wanted.) I figured I would move from job to job because careers were hard to come by, especially for college grads. I started writing because I liked it—and I had nothing to lose by trying.

Whenever I use that phrase "nothing to lose," I hear the voice of my husband. Dean and I met at a writers' workshop in Taos, New Mexico, in 1986. After the workshop, we both went home—me to Wisconsin, and Dean to Idaho. Within the week, he was driving to Wisconsin to be with me.

I asked him why. We loved each other and had planned to get together in August, after we had settled everything in our lives. We weren't sure where we would be, but we figured we'd work it out by then.

But he went back to Idaho, to the small apartment he had moved into after he had separated from his wife, to the bartending job he had put on hold to go to the writers' workshop, and realized that nothing held him in that small town.

He said to me on the phone from some rest stop somewhere between Idaho and Wisconsin, "I'm coming to you because I have nothing to lose—"

As he said that phrase, I remember thinking, *That's worrisome. He's not coming toward something; he's coming because he has nothing else.* I heard that phrase through the filter of my upbringing: that a person with nothing to lose has failed somehow.

Then he added the important part of the sentence. It wasn't an afterthought for him. It was the central part of his message.

"—and," he said, "I have everything to gain."

He had weighed the risks against the rewards, and realized he was taking no risk at all. He had no risk except the drive itself and a possible rejection by me. (Yeah, right. Like that would have happened. Not.) He had—we had—everything to gain from his willingness to start our relationship immediately.

And twenty-four years later, it's clear he was right. We have gained a great deal because he was savvy enough to realize that he was in the position to do something he wouldn't normally have been able to do.

So many of you are in that position now. Sometimes life forces us to postpone our dreams. Sometimes we postpone them out of fear.

Right now life—and the economy—are giving millions of us nothing to lose, and everything to gain.

If we only try.

Try.

Your life will be richer if you do.

Section Nine:
The Future

Chapter Fifty-three
How to Keep Your Business Alive
After Your Death

I initially wrote this chapter on my new blog, The Business Rusch, *which I have geared toward publishing professionals. I will be doing a long series in 2013 on estate planning for freelancers (mainly writers), but I wanted to do a short introductory piece. I also knew I had left this material out of the Freelancer's Guide, and wanted to at least make a passing mention, without making this book too long to publish.*

After some thought, I decided to keep the chapter with its publishing focus. The general advice here is the same for all business owners. Technically, your business should survive you. So when you see what little specificity I have added for writers, just substitute your business for it. Most of the advice remains the same.

Here's the blog, more or less as it appeared in November of 2012.

So, you want to be an artist. You want to be one of those writers everyone has read, even though you're long dead. You want your work in libraries, on bookstore shelves, and in digital format. You want professors to assign your work, or kids to sneak that "crap" that everyone decries but everyone has read.

There are two very simple ways to do this:

1. *Write a lot of good stories.* Not beautiful words. Good *stories*. Remember, fiction gets translated into a variety of languages, and in those languages, your original words get lost. Only *stories* get translated, stories with great characters, great plots, and unforgettable moments.

2. *Establish Your Estate Long Before You Die.* Your copyrights will outlive you. That's how they're designed. If you don't know what I mean by this, then get yourself a copy of *The Copyright Handbook*, and start reading it now. You don't sell fiction; you license copyright.

Learn what that means, and learn how it will impact your estate, your heirs, and your legacy.

You'd be surprised how much of the entertainment news you consume is about estates. You'd be surprised how much of the books, movies, games, and television you consume exists because someone handled an estate well or someone handled it poorly.

Or didn't have one at all.

Don't be like our friend Bill who, long before he died, would say about his (considerable) estate, "I don't care what you do with it. I'll be dead."

My husband fought Bill for years to get a will, because Bill had some very collectible books and extremely rare pulp magazines, things that had only one or two copies left in existence. Dean thought it a crime for those copies to die with Bill, and badgered Bill into getting a will.

Bill finally executed one, an annoyingly inadequate one, that caused us a lot of legal problems just to get validated. Dean blogged about this entire saga (including the legal issues) in March of 2012. If you want a scare story about estates and what you might leave your heirs with, read the post titled "Personal Post: Estate Done" at deanwesleysmith.com.

Think about this: Bill's collectibles were property, which he disposed of in his will. He left that property to Dean and a few others.

Your copyrights are property. They must go to someone. It will be up to that someone to manage those copyrights—or not.

Dean could have let Bill's books rot in some warehouse somewhere or he could have sold the entire shebang for pennies on the dollar. He chose not to, for a variety of reasons, not the least of which was to honor Bill's life work, which was collecting.

Imagine what happens if you leave your copyrights—your life's work—to your second cousin Edna who has never read a book in her life. Or if you dump those copyrights on your great-grandchild whom you haven't met, or who has no idea how to balance his own checkbook, let alone handle the large business you're about to leave him.

Because here's the truth, folks. As writers (and this applies to any artist), your estate will be infinitely more complicated than our friend Bill's. If you have heirs, particularly children and grandchildren, then your estate becomes even more complicated. If you want your life's work to be well managed, your estate becomes infinitely more complicated.

If you want to be read (or remembered as a writer, artist, musician, etc) one hundred years from now, if you want your business to live beyond you, well, you better have every "i" dotted and "t" crossed, and then you'd better pray a little, because the remembrance doesn't rely as much on those really good stories as you think it will.

It relies on whoever inherits your estate *and how they manage it*.

Here's the place where I have to remind you that I am not a lawyer. I barely know this stuff.

This chapter is a short version of a business book I am writing, a very generic starting point, designed to scare you into at least getting a will completed and signed.

At minimum, you need a valid will.

What composes a valid will? Here's where things get tricky.

In the United States, a valid will gets defined by each *state*, not by the federal government. Wills are governed by state law, not federal law. I have absolutely no idea what happens in other countries. I know what happens if you die in Wisconsin, Idaho, Nevada, or Oregon, and what some (not all) of the requirements are for wills in those states. I know this because of Bill, because of the lawyers we talked to, the judge friends who chimed in on what happens in their states, and what we went through in 2011.

The estate laws between those four states vary so greatly that it's as if those four states were different nations, not part of the same nation.

I'm sure estate law in all fifty of the United States is as varied.

But you *must* have a valid will if you have copyrights (or any other real property). If you have children and you don't have a valid will, shame on you. You need to plan for those kids' future because for all you know, you could get hit by a bus tomorrow, and it will take weeks, sometimes months, to settle what happens to your living, breathing children, let alone what happens to your metaphorical children (your books).

Best case: hire a local attorney who specializes in wills, estates, and trusts, and ask for a minimal will. Promise that you'll be back for full estate planning sometime in the future. But in the short term, hire this person to design a will to cover your ass while you do the research you will need to do in order to plan for the future of your estate and how it will run without you.

Most attorneys won't charge much for this service. You'll probably end up spending a hundred dollars, maybe two or three hundred for this very basic will.

If you don't want to go to an attorney (and why don't you? What are you afraid of), then use a *reputable* service, like LegalZoom. com. We've used LegalZoom for a few things, and I can tell you this: It gives you documents appropriate to your state. It provides accompanying material written in English so that you know what you've got. It also provides the services of a legal aid on the phone to answer a few questions. (Too many questions, and you get charged.)

However, I've been warned by attorneys that if you try anything complicated through an online legal service, you'll probably end up with a messy document. Use the services for something simple; if your will is complex—and generally, with a business, it will be—hire a local attorney.

Honestly, a will isn't something you should do yourself. If our friend Bill had hired an attorney, then we wouldn't have spent time, heartache, and money trying to figure out if his will was even valid. He would have had all the documentation in order and we would have had the confidence that we were doing exactly what he wanted.

But let me tell you this:

A badly executed *valid* will is better than no will at all.

Here's what happens (generally) in the United States if you have no will.

1. *The state determines who the heirs are*. This is done by state law. Generally, family inherits. The closer the family—spouse, children, parents—the more likely they will get the bulk of the estate. But not *all* of the estate. In Oregon, for example, the spouse does not inherit the entire estate unless a will specifies a full inheritance. In Oregon, the spouse only gets a percentage of the estate.

Generally speaking, if there are no heirs, the estate goes to the state itself. Usually the state will have spent an inordinate amount of money trying to find heirs, so this part will take time. Not that it matters to you, because, to paraphrase our friend Bill, you're dead. What do you care? You didn't care enough in life to make these preparations. You have no right to complain if your spirit is hovering over this mess after death.

2. *The estate goes into probate*. Probate is a byzantine process by which the state identifies what the estate actually is. The state has to know how much property the deceased had—including (but not limited to) real estate, money in accounts, valuables, collectibles, and oh, yeah! copyrights. The state must also find and pay off all of the deceased's debts, if any.

I had an aunt and uncle who were waiting, literally, for a very rich relative to die so they could inherit her estate. That very rich relative died without a will. The estate went into probate. When my uncle died years later, he still hadn't inherited the money he felt he deserved because the rich relative's estate was still in probate. Even though my uncle was elderly, he didn't have a will either (probably because he was waiting to find out what he would inherit). His probate was relatively simple: his estate went to his wife. But his death complicated the wealthy relative's probate dramatically. I never heard how that resolved. But when my aunt died less than a year after her husband she, sensibly, had a will.

Most courts won't realize that copyrights have value. Particularly if you are the Emily Dickinson of your family, and you haven't really tried to get published. (For those of you who don't know, ten of Emily Dickinson's poems were published in her lifetime. She sent her poems to family and friends, but didn't try to publish most of her prodigious output. Her sister worked tirelessly to get Dickinson's poems published after her death. And, yes, there were estate problems. Still, the point is, Dickinson wouldn't be known today if it weren't for her family.)

The court will probably ignore your copyrights if you haven't been published. If you have, then determining value becomes very tricky. Because copyright value depends on everything from who licenses it to royalty payments to current trends.

And here's the biggest complicating factor: Copyrights remain valuable property for 70 years after the death of the writer. So for 70 years after your death, your copyrights can continue earning a sizeable sum—but only if your heirs know how to manage those copyrights.

Most writers don't know how to manage their copyrights or even what those copyrights are. How can those writers expect a non-writer to do what the writer doesn't even know how to do?

So, think of it this way:

If you have indie-published some novels and a few short stories, who is going to maintain those publications after you die? Will that person update to the latest technology? Will that person answer a letter from a game designer who wants to build a game around your world? Will that person even know that game designer should not be allowed to build that game for free, but must pay a licensing fee (or come to some other legal arrangement)?

If you have a long-term traditional publishing career, who does your publisher contact with questions about your about-to-be published book? Who handles the foreign rights for a novel, relatively unsuccessful before your death, that has become hot after you died?

Who handles the unpublished works?

What if you die just before the movie version of your first novel is released? What if that movie becomes a success? Who decides what company publishes your backlist? *Is* your backlist available to be published?

Successful writers all know that managing a career is a full-time job, one that we do because we love our work. Now, imagine handing that job to someone who has no clue what a publisher is, who had never seen a publishing contract, and who has no idea what an e-pub file is.

After the death of the author, most literary estates go dormant. The person who inherits has no idea how to maintain that estate.

If you don't have a will, you will *guarantee* that no one will manage your estate. Whoever eventually inherits—years after your death—will have to be motivated enough to rebuild everything you've done, everything that got neglected after you died. If the estate goes into probate, and you have no heirs, the state will not maintain your copyrights unless the state believes they have value.

So, if John Grisham dies tomorrow without a will or any estate planning, someone in his home state will know that his copyrights have value. But if you die, and you've only published two novels, neither of which earn more than $50 per month, will the state care? Will the novels continue to earn while the estate grinds its way through the long probate process? Who knows?

Honestly, estate problems weren't as big a deal for new writers in the early part of this century as they are now. Back then, most writers' work died with them. It was too hard to maintain a budding writer's career, to try to guarantee that something would live beyond her.

But here, as in everything to do with publishing, times have changed. Now a budding writer can indie-publish ten projects and let those ten projects speak for themselves. A year or two after that writer dies, one of those projects might take off. The readers will want more of the writer's work. A savvy heir will indie publish the entire backlist.

But there are rarely any savvy heirs.

Seriously, who wants to do the work of another person in addition to their own? Maintaining a writer's career can be a time-consuming process.

So far, in my research, I've found that the modern estates which do well have some kind of literary manager who gets paid either a percentage of the yearly proceeds from the estate or a straight salary to manage to estate. Of course, all of this happens *after* the estate gets the courts. This is after the heirs get notified, the will gets adjudicated and gaveled down as final, and procedures get set up to keep the work of the writer (artist) alive.

Even then, things can go awry.

When the playwright Tennessee Williams set up his estate, he put knowledgeable people in place to handle all aspects of it, from the publications to play production. Unfortunately, after he died, one of the executors denied the publication of Williams' work, and tried to control the productions of his plays. For years, it became known that Williams' work was impossible to produce, and we almost lost access to one of our most renown playwrights.

The executor died, and shortly thereafter, acclaimed productions of Williams' most well-known plays went into production. A biography came out, and his work returned to print.

Think this was an unusual case? It isn't. I personally know of another case of a big-name author whose executors refuse to allow his work to be reprinted. They believe they're following his wishes, and the heirs (who are not the executors) are suing to have these executors removed.

Such a lawsuit happened with the Dorothy Parker estate nearly forty years ago. There's currently a lot of litigation involved with Michael Jackson's estate—and that's even uglier, since control of the millions comes only through control of the children.

Good executors exist. Priscilla Presley took her former husband's estate from near bankruptcy to a value of $200 million twenty years later. As of last year, the Presley estate's annual earnings were $55 million dollars. In 2004, a public filing showed that the estate had 100 active licenses, 600,000 annual (paying) visitors to Graceland, and intellectual properties including music and film that had grown in value because, as one blogger noted, "the Elvis Presley 'product' had been kept alive."

You want someone like Priscilla Presley to manage your estate. Will you get someone like her? If you're smart and lucky, and set up your estate properly. What's properly? That will depend on who you are, what your intellectual properties are, what condition your estate is in when you die, and who inherits.

So much depends on who gets paid out of the estate. A friend of mine got the lucky task of managing another friend's copyrights after he died, but got no financial benefit from it. All of the earnings went to the deceased friend's children, whom the deceased friend had not seen in years. My friend did his best to maintain the estate, but eventually his own career took precedence. Our deceased friend's work has not been in print for more than fifteen years.

Dorothy Parker left her estate to Dr. Martin Luther King, Jr. After he died, the Parker estate got folded into the NAACP, who wanted the earnings from that estate. Parker's executor, Lillian Hellman, and the NAACP, went to court over the handling of Parker's estate. Hellman eventually got removed as executor, and the NAACP still benefits from Parker's royalties. You'll notice that her work is still in print.

So, the long and short of it is this:

If you want your work to outlive you, you need to plan for that. At minimum, you need a valid will with instructions as to who will handle your intellectual properties (your copyrights) as well as your other properties. You need someone to manage those properties, someone who will *care* enough to do a good job. If that someone is going to manage your literary works, then that someone will need some kind of compensation, whatever that means.

Your heirs have to care about your literary legacy as well, so leave your estate to someone who will make sure your work stays in print.

Last year, as Dean and I went through all of the estate stuff, the Passive Guy, the lawyer who runs the Passive Voice blog, wrote about what a writer needs to consider as she sets up her estate. You can find the information at this link: http://www. thepassivevoice.com/09/2011/what-happens-when-an-author-dies/. Use it as a guideline.

Do not wait until you know everything you need to know before getting a will. Wills need to be reviewed every few years as your life circumstances change. So, get a valid will *right now,* and make sure your heirs know about it. Make sure your attorney keeps a copy.

Plan for that will to be a short-term will, something you will update as you learn what will be best to ensure that your writing will outlive you.

I can guarantee that your work will *not* outlive you if you fail to have a will. So, get busy. This is important.

You work very hard to make your books and stories the best they can possibly be. You want those books and stories in front of readers. But if you fail to protect your estate for those seventy years after your death (minimum), then you are probably invalidating all of that work and all of that effort.

Get a valid will. Do it before the end of the year if you can.

Your heirs will thank you.

And so will your readers.

Section Ten:
The Benefits of Freelancing

Chapter Fifty-four
The Benefits of Freelancing

Several years ago, my career hit a serious downturn, the kind most careers never recover from. I made a series of bad business decisions, including hiring two terrible employees who did everything they could to gut my business. I compounded the initial mistakes by making more mistakes. On top of that, my health collapsed. I was ill twenty days out of every month, incapacitated for at least ten of those days. In the middle of all of that, I hit my mid-life crisis. Don't let anyone tell you a mid-life crisis only hits men. It hits women too.

During those dark days, I kept threatening to give up the writing. Now, you have to understand what this means. Giving up writing—for me—is like giving up breathing. I sometimes say that I, the daughter of two alcoholics, am an addict too, only I'm addicted to writing. If I don't write, I go through withdrawals. This, by the way, is not a joke. If I am in a particularly bad mood, my husband will tell me to go write something. If I take his advice (and I don't always), I feel much better.

So for me to say that I was going to give up writing—and more importantly, *to mean it*—meant that something was seriously, seriously wrong. I felt like I was at the bottom of a very deep pit, and I couldn't figure out a way to climb out, so I simply decided to give up.

Or I would have, if I'd had an answer to the very reasonable question my brilliant husband would ask me whenever I brought up quitting.

"What else would you do?"

I had a list that I worked my way down. At this time, our local radio station needed a news director. I was overqualified for the position, so before I applied, I investigated.

The job paid one-third of what I earned during those bad years if and only if you added in the costs of the benefit package—two-weeks

583

paid vacation and a measly health insurance policy not as good as the one I had as a freelancer. To earn one-third of what I was doing, I would have to commit 40 hours per week (and occasional weekends, if there was a news story) to the radio station. I would have set hours.

I would work for someone else.

In fact, every job on my list—from waiting tables (yes, waiting tables looked good to me then) to going back to editing—required me to work for someone else. On their schedule. With no hope for an increase in pay, except at the once a year or once every two year performance review, and then the increase would be rather small (by my freelancing standards).

The only job I came up with that even marginally approached my freelance lifestyle (but not my freelance income) was teaching at a university. In order to do that, I would have to go back to school, get a master's degree, and get a Ph.D. Not so bad. Sometimes I miss living in a college town.

But to get my degree(s) would cost money. I would have had to uproot my husband (and my cats), move to a part of the country with infinitely worse weather than the Oregon Coast, and—oh, yeah—be on someone else's schedule.

Worse than that, when I graduated, tens of thousands of hard-earned dollars later, I'd be at the bottom of someone else's totem pole, at the bottom of the pay bracket which was at that point (again) one-third of what I was earning in the bad years, and oh, yeah, I'd be working for someone else. Deeper in debt, no promise of job security (not as a first-year professor), and no real way to earn my way out of it all quickly.

I could have opened another small business (which required a capital outlay—and oh, yeah—it would have to be something else I loved. Since I've only had one job I loved for longer than one year [writing], I doubted the new business route worked for me). My husband even offered me the option of loafing for two or three years while he supported me. (Bless him.) I know that was a serious offer, but I also know he understands me very well. He knows that after two days of vacation or two days of "doing what I want"—basically two days of not writing—I'm absolutely miserable. He made the offer, but he knew the chances of me actually succeeding at lying on the couch, eating bon-bons and reading all day were between slim and none. I get cranky when I have a week's worth of research reading and no time to write. Imagine how I'd feel if I had *years* to do that.

584

Okay, some of this is my personal pathology. I'm really not wired to do anything else. But beneath that was an honest, desperate search for solutions by a woman who had hit bottom. I really saw no way to revive my career. I had given up. But I didn't want to do anything else—or nothing at all.

I didn't have a blinding revelation. I didn't have a life-changing insight. I realized slowly and over time that I was doing what I loved, that things had gotten bleak, and I had to rebuild. I found a doctor who helped me live with the health problems, taking my bad days down from 20 per month to seven or so, and taking my worst days down to a maximum of four per month. (This sounds so easy. It took two years of experimentation and work.)

I fired the last bad employee, dug in and figured out what damage he had done, and started to repair it. Then I slowly rebuilt my career, examining every single part of it, figuring out what I wanted to keep and what I didn't, figuring out where I wanted to go in the future, and designing a path to get there.

Slowly—and I do mean slowly—I climbed out of that horrible, deep dark pit. What kept me on that climb was not the goal, or even the ability to work hard. It was a daily reminder—sometimes by listening to the new news director on the local radio station, sometimes by watching the waiters at the local restaurant, sometimes by simply reviewing the options of other jobs (or plain old slacking) and realizing (again) how unsuited I am to all of those.

"Unsuited" really isn't the right word. If I'd had to, I could have done any one of those things. The real key was, deep down, I didn't *want* to.

I didn't want to give up my freelance lifestyle.

I've been an on-again, off-again freelancer for thirty years. Every time I got a real job, I came screaming back to the freelance life. The longest full-time job I ever held lasted three months. Even the news directorship, which I had for years, was intermittent. I was always *acting* news director, stepping aside when a new, permanent news director came on board. (Of course, they lasted only a few months, so I'd get the position again.)

What do I like about freelancing? Just about everything. The pros, the cons, the ups, the downs, everything that I've mentioned in this *Guide*, I've not only experienced, but I prefer to working a day job. I've tried very hard in this *Guide* to keep a measured tone about day jobs because I intellectually understand their necessity. I know why people have them, why people believe that a day job gives them security, and why they would want such a thing. And if I had had children in my twenties, I would have followed a different life path. I would have gotten a day job, and hated every minute of it, and done it for the security, for my dependents.

But I have no dependents. My husband, Dean Wesley Smith, is an equal partner with me in our various businesses (yes, we have more than two), and he likes the risks as much as I do. As I've said before, we really don't see them as risks. We don't take risks. We make educated choices based on all of the knowledge available to us. That we choose to do so without the "safety" and "security" of a large corporation behind us shows our questioning natures from an early age, not any great wisdom or stupidity. As I said in the day job chapters of this *Guide*, I have never believed, even when I was in my teens, that any job was secure. I'd seen too many people lose theirs, too many people fired for no apparent reason.

When I was seven, I watched my dad lose his tenured college position, in part because he had the courage to speak his mind. (A long story, one someone [not me] wrote a book about, but suffice it to say that you can't have tenure at a college that ceases to exist, and you can't easily get a job at another college when you're known as a whistleblower.)

These things—tragedies, really—helped me become a freelancer. I didn't have to jump over as many mental hurdles as some of my freelancing colleagues when they started.

But risk taker or not, traditionally security-minded or not, all freelancers face the same problems and have the same benefits. I'm sure every single freelancer you talk to will have a different list of benefits for doing the work, but here are mine:

1. I work for myself.

I set my hours. I decide what I'm going to do every day. Through the work I choose to do, I set my income levels. Sometimes I turn down boring, high-paying projects. Sometimes I take a high-paying crappy project because I need the money. I make the decision. I don't get assigned that project by someone else.

2. I do what I love.

Yeah, yeah. If you read the entire *Guide*, you know there are parts of freelancing that I loathe. But I do those things—well, not exactly happily, but not unhappily either. Because I'm doing them in service of the work I love. Without those things, I could not do what I do. They make the rest of what I do worthwhile.

3. I never complain about going to the office.

I'm happy to go to work, even if I'm not enjoying the process. I found it fascinating that when I first opened the *Guide* to questions, the first questions I got were about taking time off. I had to ask other professionals how they take vacations because I don't take one.

Many freelancers don't. Why?

Simple. The work we do now was the thing we did for fun in our free time. Why take time off from something you love? (Yes, yes, I know. Rest and all that. I do rest. But I don't see why I need a vacation from something I would do on vacation if I had a day job. That makes no sense to me at all.)

The idea of time off—and time off as part of a job description—comes from having jobs that you don't like, jobs you only do for the money. And if that's the only reason you're freelancing, friend, then go out and get a day job. Freelancing's too hard to do if you don't love the work.

4. I get to design my own workspace.

I almost wrote that I get to work at home, but I've had businesses where I didn't work at home. Even then, I designed a Kris-style work environment, one suited just to me.

5. I am a creator.

I can't tell you how important that is. The economy survives based on how many creators it has. Those of us who develop our own product and our own businesses don't just create that product. We also create jobs. In addition to the people I hire, like the house cleaner and gardener I mentioned in the employee chapter of the *Guide*, there are also the people I keep employed, people whose businesses I frequent with the money I bring into my local community. From the grocery store to restaurants, from the local bookstore to the clothing stores, the money I spend here doesn't come from here. It comes from all over the world, and it helps to fuel the economy in my small town.

6. I am responsible for my own career.

In other words, if I succeed, I succeed because of what I do. If I fail, I fail because of what I do. I mentioned the two bad employees in my first paragraph above, and if you read only that paragraph, you might think I blame them for the downturn in my business. I could, I suppose. A lot of people would.

But I'm the one who hired them, I'm the one who trusted them to do their jobs with minimal oversight, and I'm the one who didn't fire them soon enough. In other words, they caused a lot of damage that would never have happened if I had acted promptly. Their mistakes are my fault.

7. I control my finances.

I might never make as much money as some writers. I might not make as much as I would have made working for that friend who offered me a job in Hollywood all those years ago. But I am not in this for the money, although money is a factor. I can earn more if I work harder. I have put myself in the position, as a lawyer friend once told me, to hit not one, not two, but multiple home runs financially. I might never do so. But I have the chance, a chance I wouldn't have had if I had taken a day job.

That chance means less than you think it would, especially if you're still putting in your 40 hours for a paycheck. Because you are working for the money, so you'd expect me to as well. But I'm not. I'm working for the enjoyment. And study after study after study shows that people who work for themselves are happier than people who work for someone else.

Other studies show that people who are happier live longer than those who are unhappy. I'd much rather be like Frederik Pohl who, in his nineties, is writing a blog and publishing a book a year, than I would be like a friend of mine who has retired in his sixties, doesn't know what to do with his days, and is now worried (because of the changes in the economy) that his pension will run out.

Retirement falls into that vacation mindset to me. I retired from editing at the age of 37, and I was happy to do so. Relieved, actually. I never, ever, want to do that again.

But retire from writing? Whom are you kidding? When I die, I want to die like Jack Williamson did. He was in his mid-nineties and had just finished a novel. Or like Robert B. Parker, who died at his desk, while working on the current book.

8. I have a continual intellectual challenge.

I'm always learning something and doing something new. Not just related to writing, but also related to business. I follow court cases that apply to my field, financial regulations that deal with publishing, the changes in publishing methods now happening all over the world. I constantly work to improve my craft. I'm always reading something weird and interesting connected to my job. I travel to places I would never have seen otherwise, from places as beautiful as Paris to places as unexpectedly interesting as Salt Lake City. Each trip is an adventure and each adventure comes from my work. But I still work. The last time I was in Paris, I slept very little, not just because of the book tour interviews and signings, but because I stayed up late every night, writing down what I did, and making notes for future stories, doing research, and learning as much as I could about a new city and a new country. I think these things are fun and challenging. And lucky me, they're part of my job.

9. The harder I work, the luckier I am.

That's the real secret to freelancing. We seem to have lost the value of hard work. People want to take things easy, and if you're one of them, don't freelance. But if you like to be busy, then freelance. You'll always have too much to do.

But the real secret to freelancing?

Enjoyment. It's all about the fun. When I teach writers, I give them a writing assignment and then tell them to go play. They often look at me as if I'm nuts. But seriously, that's what I do. I'm playing every day. I make things up for a living. I do something I would do even if no one ever paid me for it.

I'm having fun.

Life is hard enough without slogging through your daily existence. We all get sick. We all lose family and friends. We all have setbacks and failures and unexpected (nasty) surprises. Why add on the burden of a hated job if you can at all avoid it? The biggest benefit to freelancing—for me, anyway—is the fact that it makes life enjoyable.

I even recognized that in the depths of my despair a few years ago. The worst day at my freelance job is better than the best day at any day job I've ever had.

That's what has kept me freelancing for thirty years.

And, if I'm lucky, will keep me freelancing for at least thirty more.

About the Author

Award-winning, bestselling writer Kristine Kathryn Rusch has published books under many names and in many genres. She has owned several businesses, and has worked for herself for more than thirty years. For more information on her work, go to kristinekathrynrusch.com.

Index

motivation to keep working, 96–100, 102

need for. *See* boredom; distractions

organization and tracking, 45–46, 65, 153

and snacking, 29, 99

time management, 27, 31, 32

Disney, Walt, 447

distractions, 32, 37–38, 70, 93, 98–100

diversification. *See also* flexibility

    of income stream, 144, 148, 168–69, 171, 188, 421

    of investments, 161

    of product, 442, 443

    of writing genre, 168, 421, 441, 442

doctors, 95, 201, 205, 374, 375

documentation. *See* record-keeping

Douglas, Carole Nelson, 121

downsizing your lifestyle, 50, 125, 126. *See also* budget, strategies to cut expenses

downtime

    to avoid burnout, 115

    during the day, 70, 106

    due to illness. *See* illness or injuries

    leisure time, 31, 326

    and project scheduling, 84, 98, 326, 409, 425

    rewards for a job well done, 104, 555

    vacations, 84, 98, 117–26, 587

Dozois, Gardner, 125–26

A Dragon's Heart (Yolen), 124

Dragon's Keep, 321, 322

dreams. *See* goals and dreams

dress, appropriate, 198, 306, 377, 550

E

earthquake, 398, 402, 422, 426

eBay. *See* online activities, sales

education, 299–306

    as a business cost, 62, 64, 150

    intellectual challenge, continual, 588–89

    Master Class, 129–30, 134–35, 174, 486, 510

    myth of higher education and success, 562–64, 566

    overview, 299–300

    program selection, 300–306

    scam artists as teachers, 299, 307–8, 309, 316

    survival tips for introverts, 319–20

    workshop junkies, 305, 316

Ellison, Harlan, 314, 398

Elvis Inc.: The Fall and Rise of the Presley Empire (O'Neal), 156

e-mail

    back-up, 426

    role in social networking, 340, 343, 345. *See also* online activities

    separate computer for, 37–38, 70, 99–100

embezzlement, 132, 162, 195, 205, 417, 448

emergencies, 405–13. *See also* illness or injuries; insurance; natural disasters; wars

    conducting business during travel, 405, 406

    contingency plan against, 408–10, 411, 412–13, 425–26

    cost of, 62

    documentation for insurance, 402

    finite, 407–10

    ongoing, 410–12

    returning to your day job, 53, 65, 142, 395, 412, 427, 451–57

    savings fund, 55, 160, 408, 418

emotional considerations. *See* psychological and emotional considerations

employees, 191–208

    agents which provide a service. *See* workers

    benefits for, 197

    in cost-benefit analysis, 74–75, 227

    cost of labor, 174, 175, 180

    definition and use of term, 191–92, 199

    firing, 81–82, 113, 194–95, 196, 433, 588

    hiring, 193–94, 195, 196, 207–8, 227

    lay-offs, 195, 198, 352, 417, 418

    motivations of, 387

    respect for the schedule, 81–82

599

stalkers, 366, 368, 398
Starr, Ringo, 488
Star Trek: A Singular Destiny
(DeCandido), 122
stores
advertising, 213, 214
book. *See* book retailers
disability access, 196
effects of lack of professionalism,
374
expansion of business, 228
expectations, unrealistic, 524–25
immediate payment, 180–81
online sales, 34, 75, 294, 336, 348,
443–44, 554
price-setting process, 175–76
projected costs, 42
schedule provides structure, 81,
82–83, 88, 92
seasonal considerations, 75, 88–89
security monitor system, 34
stress, 114, 370, 412–13, 429, 555. *See
also* burnout; jealousy, surviving
someone else's
success, 471–505
definition, official, 471–72
emotional response to, 435, 475, 501
fall from, 485–86
financial strategies to deal with,
158–60, 161
hard work is the secret to, 484, 488,
505, 535–36, 539, 589
interpretation of your own, 483,
499–505
new "friends" due to, 484, 496
other people's definitions, 483–89,
492–93, 497–99, 541
of others, inspiration from, 361, 362,
363
relationship with failure, 450
stress from, 114, 370, 371, 487, 489
surviving the jealousy of others,
364–70, 484
tax on net profit, 158–59
the world's definition, 478–83
as the worst-case scenario, 269
your personal definition, 472–78,
489–99, 502, 503

supervision. *See* employees, supervision
of; workers, supervision of
support. *See* family, support from; help;
networking
"The Sure Thing: How Entrepreneurs
Really Succeed" (Gladwell), 386,
387, 388

T
Tan, Candy, 338, 339
Tatano, Randy, 36, 63, 119, 278–79,
280, 282
taxes
audit, 36, 153
on business profit as well as personal
income, 160
and employees, 192, 195, 196, 197
and estimation of income/expenses,
56, 72, 152–53
home office deduction, 36
and incorporation, 235
mortgage interest deduction, 561
on net profit and windfalls, 158–59
as overhead, 149
pain-in-the-ass (PITA), 72, 184–85,
497
people hired to do your, 151, 153,
279–80
save ahead for estimated-tax
payment, 159, 161
sole-proprietor business, 233
travel deductions, 125, 150, 152
Tayler, Howard, 321
television. See also *specific television
shows*
advertising, 210, 211, 220
Conan-Leno professional
relationship, 356–57
famous actresses, 485
industry trends, 538
job offers from, 490–91
style of dress and professionalism,
377
temp agency, 192, 194
Terry, Mark, 184
tickler file, 169
The Ties That Bind (Ryder), 121

608

4521562R00356

Made in the USA
San Bernardino, CA
28 September 2013